Italy in Colorado

Family Histories from Denver and Beyond

by Alisa Zahller

Dedication

For my grandmother, Emma Carpenter, and those who came before
For my mother, Frances Sawyer, and those in the present
For my daughter, Emma Lucianna Zahller, and future generations

Front cover image: *Angelina (Cominello) Carpinello baking bread in her dome oven at 1801 West Forty-sixth Avenue, c. 1940. Pictured in the photograph are loaves of bread in film canisters Angelina acquired from a neighborhood movie theater. CIAPA Archive. Courtesy Joe Carpinello. PCCLI0175.v4*

Title page image: *Lou and Nancy Garramone, Denver, Colorado, 1927. CIAPA Archive. Courtesy Ange Volpe. PCCLI0863*

Back cover images: *Rose and Antonio Decino inside their store at 157 Santa Fe, Pueblo, Colorado, c. 1910. In 1921, the Decino store was destroyed by the Pueblo flood of 1921. CIAPA Archive. Courtesy Rosemarie McDermott. PCCLI2031.v1*

John Tricarico (left) and Ernest Tricarico (right), by The Post Studio, Denver, Colorado, c. 1927. CIAPA Archive. Courtesy Angela (Tricarico) DeMott. PCCLI5284

All text by Alisa Zahller except foreword by Nicholas P. Ciotola.
All images are from the Colorado Historical Society Collection unless otherwise indicated.

Copyright © 2008 by Colorado Historical Society

All rights reserved, including the right to reproduce this work in any form whatsoever without permission in writing from the publisher, except for brief passages in connection with a review. For information, please write:

The Donning Company Publishers
184 Business Park Drive, Suite 206
Virginia Beach, VA 23462

Steve Mull, *General Manager*
Barbara Buchanan, *Office Manager*
Heather Floyd, *Editor*
Stephanie Danko, *Graphic Designer*
Derek Eley, *Imaging Artist*
Debby Dowell, *Project Research Coordinator*
Scott Rule, *Director of Marketing*
Tonya Hannink, *Marketing Coordinator*

Carey Southwell, *Project Director*

Library of Congress Cataloging-in-Publication Data

Zahller, Alisa, 1969-
   Italy in Colorado : family histories from Denver and beyond / Alisa Zahller ; [foreword by Nicholas P. Ciotola].
   p. cm.
   A companion piece to The Italians of Denver exhibit and part of a larger documentation project The Italians of Colorado.
   "All images are from the Colorado Historical Society collection unless otherwise indicated"—T.p. verso.
   Includes bibliographical references and index.
   ISBN 978-1-57864-466-7 (softcover : alk. paper)
   1. Italian Americans—Colorado—Denver—History. 2. Immigrants—Colorado—Denver—History. 3. Italian Americans—Colorado—Denver—History—Pictorial works. 4. Italian Americans—Colorado—Denver—Biography. 5. Immigrants—Colorado—Denver—Biography. 6. Italian Americans—Colorado—History. 7. Denver (Colo.)—Biography—Anecdotes. 8. Colorado—Biography—Anecdotes. 9. Denver (Colo.)—Ethnic relations. 10. Colorado—Ethnic relations. I. Colorado Historical Society. II. Title.
   F784.D49I89 2008
   978.8'0045107478883—dc22

2007038481

Printed in the United States of America at Walsworth Publishing Company

Contents

6	Acknowledgments		
8	Foreword		
10	Preface		
12	Introduction		
14	**CHAPTER 1**	Beginnings	1850–1869
24	**CHAPTER 2**	Growth	1870–1879
52	**CHAPTER 3**	Influx	1880–1894
86	**CHAPTER 4**	Colonies	1895–1919
140	**CHAPTER 5**	Perseverance	1920–1939
176	**CHAPTER 6**	Prosperity	1940–1959
214	**CHAPTER 7**	Change	1960–1989
260	**CHAPTER 8**	Renewal	1990 to Today
288	Appendix	Colorado's Italian American Organizations	
289	Notes		
310	Bibliography		
314	Index		
320	About the Author		

Acknowledgments

This publication, a companion piece to the *Italians of Denver* exhibit and part of a larger documentation project, *The Italians of Colorado*, would not have been possible without the help of many.

First and foremost, I would like to thank the Italian American community of Colorado for affording the Colorado Historical Society and the Colorado Italian American Preservation Association (CIAPA) the opportunity to work with them and to learn about their history and culture, both past and present. Over the years, I have been humbled by the community's willingness to share their life stories. The community not only welcomed us into their homes, businesses, and organizations, but trusted us with their family histories, life stories, and family treasures. I thank them as well for their patience, gratitude, financial support, and enthusiasm regarding each new phase of the project.

Thank you to CIAPA for your hard work and efforts to collect what is now one of the largest research archives on Italians and Italian Americans in the West. Your guidance, work within the Italian American community, and support over the last several years has been invaluable. I would especially like to thank the following CIAPA members who

Sferra family, Denver, Colorado, c. 1915. From left to right: Grandma Sferra, Grandpa Steve Sferra, Flora "Mary" Sferra, Frank Sferra (seated), Steve Sferra (child), and Jenny Sferra. CIAPA Archive. Courtesy Frank Sferra. PCCLI1029

have been with the project from the beginning and made major contributions: Joe Aiello for his promotion and support of the project; Bonnie Garramone and Fran (Coloroso) Daly for their expertise as genealogists and the research tools they made available to the project; Dr. Frank Palmeri for the hours he spent reviewing microfilm and researching a variety of topics; Clair Villano for organizing and maintaining the research files and assisting with the compilation of the end notes and bibliography at the end of this book; and Jean Woytek for cataloging the entire CIAPA artifact collection and photography log. I would also like to thank Vince Taglialavore and Dr. Janet Worrall for their research contributions and work done with the American Italian Historical Association, and Dawn DeAno and Barb Fenton for volunteering their time and talents photographing the contemporary Italian American community in Colorado. My sincere thanks to the other CIAPA members who have also assisted with the project in a variety of ways over the last several years: Dolores (Wolf) Albrighton, Maria E. Scordo Allen, Philip Antonelli, Corrine (LaConte) Bush, Claudia Carbone, Ida Casagranda, Donna (Calabrese) Delmonico, Don Eafanti, Frank Francone, Jess Gerardi, Phyllis (Lombardi) Greb, Rosalyn (Mastroianni) Hirsch, Juliet (Nicoletti-Schray) Jiracek, Ralph F. Mancinelli, Rosemarie McDermott, Robin O'Dorisio, Gerry Pergola, Joanna (Mautino) Seward, Dutchess (Iacino) Scheitler, Claire Marie (Mauro) TeBockhorst, Yvonne Tricarico, Tonia Williams, Christie Wright, Dominique Yantorno, and Joann Zamboni.

A number of individuals also contributed research for portions of this book. The author gratefully acknowledges the following individuals for their work: Julie Anderies, Keith Chamberlain, Cynthia Elston, Derek Holmgren, James Jeffery, Cyns Nelson, Mary Ann McNair, Colleen M. O'Dwyer, Amy Pallante, Paul Malkoski, Nicole Makinster, Dr. Tom Noel, Dan Shosky, and Judy Steiner.

At the Colorado Historical Society, many of my colleagues have offered the benefit of their expertise during the process of implementing the *Italians of Colorado* documentation project, developing the *Italians of Denver* exhibit, and in the research, writing, and editing of this book. I would especially like to thank Dr. Modupe Labode for working with me and CIAPA from the start, sharing her knowledge on a variety of subjects, contributing research, and reviewing the text found in this book. I am grateful for Moya Hansen, who has supported and contributed to the project from the beginning and offered suggestions based on her experience with community groups. A very special debt of gratitude is owed to Ben Fogelberg and Steve Grinstead for their editing expertise and review of major portions of the text used in the *Italians of Denver* exhibit and this publication. Many thanks as well to Elisa Phelps for supporting the project and recognizing the uniqueness and contributions of different ethnic groups to Colorado's history. I am also indebted to Melissa Bechhoefer, Jay DiLorenzo, Kristol Kumar, James Peterson, and Michael "Spydr" Wren for their assistance in processing and photographing artifacts and scanning and archiving the images included in this book.

Thanks are due, as well, to my fellow Italian American scholars who have offered their advice and expertise and supported the documentation project, exhibit, and this publication, in particular: Dominic Candeloro, Nicholas P. Ciotola, and Vincenza Scarpaci.

Last but certainly not least, I would like to thank my friends and family, especially my husband Kevin, daughter Emma, and mother Frances for their unending patience, support, and encouragement of my work on the research archive, exhibit, and this book.

Foreword

The year of this writing, 2007, marks the centennial anniversary of a momentous, albeit widely overlooked, year in American immigration history. It was one hundred years ago, in 1907, that the immigrant arrival station at Ellis Island processed more people into the United States than in any other year in its long and storied history. In that bustling, peak year of American immigration, over one million people bid tearful farewells to family and friends, braved the rigors of turn-of-the-century steamship travel, survived the harrowing screening process at Ellis Island, and entered the United States with hopes and dreams of better lives. Some, disillusioned by what they found or planning only to make a quick fortune, ultimately returned to their native lands. Those who chose to stay changed the face of America forever. They transplanted to the United States their Old World cultures and ways of life, added to the country's total population, fueled the new industrial economy, and augmented an already complex American mosaic with yet another robust and multifaceted cultural layer.

Of all immigrant groups who came during the Ellis Island era, few made a more significant numerical impact than the Italians. In the peak year of 1907 alone, more than 285,000 Italian immigrants passed through Ellis Island on their way to American cities such as New York, Pittsburgh, Chicago, and, of course, Denver. More than 200,000 immigrant Italians continued to enter the United States annually until 1919, when World War I and increasing nativist sentiment began to curtail one of the most significant migrations in history. In the 1920 census year, over 1.5 million foreign-born Italians resided in the United States. Their total population in that year was greater than any other foreign-born group besides Germans. Ten years later, in 1930, people born in Italy formed the single largest of all American immigrant groups.

Italy in Colorado is an effort to document the impact of Italian immigrants on a city and state greatly influenced by the immigrant tide but largely overlooked by researchers of immigration history. *Italy in Colorado* as a companion publication to a museum collection and an exhibition titled *The Italians of Denver* narrates the experiences of Italians in the city of Denver and other Colorado communities through in-depth personal profiles of immigrant families and their descendants. We learn, in fascinating detail, about the reasons for leaving Italy, the desperate search for work, the support function of the family and community, the process of assimilating to a new land, and, most importantly, the central role that Italians played in the growth and development of a city, a state, and a region.

Italy in Colorado is a triumph for many reasons. On one level, the book helps dissolve a long-standing East and Midwest bias in the study of Italian immigrant history. The Italian diaspora, indeed, sent thousands of immigrants not only to urban manufacturing centers, but also to cities and small towns in the western United States. Nonetheless, despite Andrew Rolle's classic 1968 publication on Italians in the West titled *The Immigrant Upraised* and the work of numerous later scholars, there still remain disproportionately few book-length historical studies on Italians west of the Mississippi. *Italy in Colorado* is an important step in giving these Italian immigrants the historical recognition that they deserve.

On another level, the sheer scale of the collection arm of the *Italians of Colorado* project serves as a veritable clarion call to enact similar material culture preservation initiatives in other cities. Under the aegis of the American Italian Historical Association, leaders in the field of Italian American Studies have made great strides in securing endowed chairs at universities nationwide through partnerships with Italian community groups. These academic positions have helped to establish Italian American history and literature as valid collegiate pursuits and serve to inspire a new generation of young students committed to researching these topics. However, similar partnerships between Italian American communities and museums have not been widely initiated. In households and communities nationwide, there exists a wealth of artifacts, photographs, oral traditions, and other historical research materials which, when archived following professional museum standards, become the tangible essence of a community's collective past. Partnerships between Italian communities and museums can ensure that these materials are gathered and preserved for posterity. The *Italians of Colorado* project is a testament to how these community/museum partnerships can succeed. Other cities with large Italian communities would do well to follow the Colorado Historical Society's lead.

On still another level, the *Italians of Colorado* illustrates the potential to reinvigorate a community through the collection, preservation, and presentation of material culture and, in this sense, has achieved one of the most important objectives of the field of public history. Although the original Italian neighborhoods have long since disappeared, the spirit of the Italian community in Denver and other parts of Colorado endures. *The Italians of Colorado* has proven to be the perfect vehicle to bring Italian Americans of all generations together to reflect upon the past, present, and future of their collective heritage. Thanks in large measure to this important project, Italian American ethnicity in the state of Colorado is far from its twilight.

To her credit, then, project director Alisa Zahller has done a masterful job in forging community partnerships, in galvanizing renewed interest in heritage and ethnicity, and, perhaps most importantly, in amassing a sizeable museum collection on the subject of Italian immigrants in one of America's most dynamic and multi-ethnic states. Coming to fruition at the time of the important centennial anniversary of Ellis Island's 1907 peak year, the *Italians of Colorado* archive collection, the *Italians of Denver* exhibition, and this publication are a powerful—and timely—tribute to the lasting contribution that Italian immigrants have had on Colorado and to the importance of immigrants from all nations in shaping the growth and development of the United States as a whole. The city of Denver, the state of Colorado, the country of Italy, and the Italian American community-at-large owe her a great debt of gratitude for this seminal and unprecedented body of work.

Nicholas P. Ciotola
Curator and Curator, Italian American Collections
Senator John Heinz History Center
Historical Society of Western Pennsylvania
Pittsburgh, Pennsylvania
August 2007

Preface

The origins of *Italy in Colorado* go back to 1999, when curators at the Colorado Historical Society began revising the Society's Collection Plan. The updated version not only guides the content and development of the museum's collections (which after 128 years of collecting, now number in the millions) but calls for cooperation and collaboration with communities statewide to broaden the institution's holdings. Curators discovered that certain communities, including Italian Americans, were underrepresented. So began a six-year project to address the deficiency.

Italians began to settle in Colorado in the late 1850s. By 1910, approximately 15,000 Italians were documented in the state. By 1920, Italians comprised 22 percent of the state's total population. The history of Italians in Colorado is also Colorado's history with Italians playing a significant role in the development of railroads, mining, agriculture, and other industries. Along with other immigrant groups, they added cultural variety and vitality to the Colorado community. Despite their numbers and influence, there has not been an in-depth look at the Italian community in Colorado since 1922, making research on the topic difficult.

Today, Colorado's Italian Americans number over 200,000 and make up 4.7 percent of the state's total population, a testament to the legacy of the community in Colorado. Their experiences, as well as the experiences of other immigrant groups, are worthy of examination and may offer insights into present-day immigration issues. With these points in mind and the lack of research resources available on Italian American history in the state (and the West in general), I proposed a cooperative documentation project focusing on Italian Americans in Colorado. The project, *The Italians of Colorado*, was approved and the results of this collaborative work are featured in this publication, the *Italians of Denver* exhibit at the Colorado History Museum, and the Colorado Italian American Preservation Association (CIAPA) research archive, now housed at the Colorado Historical Society.

Community involvement and support was vital to the project's success. In 2002, the Society founded CIAPA, a volunteer organization with a mission to work collaboratively with the Society and other organizations to develop, support, and coordinate projects that preserve, promote, and celebrate Italian American culture and heritage. The organization has carried out its mission by meeting with people from the Colorado Italian American community, recording their stories, and creating an archive of research materials that includes: family history files, oral histories, photographs, moving images, sound recordings, and artifacts. To date, CIAPA has helped the Society acquire over 200 oral histories, 600 artifacts, nearly 6,000 photographs, and developed over 4,000 research files, all of which document the history, culture, and traditions of Italian American families in Colorado. These materials are the foundation of this publication and the *Italians of Denver* exhibit.

I am often asked why a documentation project on Colorado's Italian American community resulted in an exhibit titled *The Italians of Denver*. Readers of this publication may also wonder why a majority of the material featured in this book pertains to Denver. It should be pointed out that early on, CIAPA members traveled to Italian American communities, big and small, around the state to collect stories. They soon realized how great the interest was, the tremendous support they had from the Italian American community, and the limitations of the project including a finite budget, travel restrictions, and time limitations. A year into the project, the group decided that although they would continue to accept research materials from around the state, they needed to narrow their focus. Given that the majority of CIAPA members live in the Denver-metro area and the process involved in doing such research, they would focus on the Denver enclave within the greater Colorado Italian American community. Many may not be aware that collecting such materials requires meeting with families several times to explain the project; work with participants to complete the project forms; interview individuals; pick up and return items copied (including photographs); identify people and places in photographs and the significance of documents copied; and then organize the vast material gathered so that information remains intact, making future research efficient.

The reality is that Italian Americans in Colorado have an immense amount of material to share and CIAPA's work could continue for years. The CIAPA Archive not only includes information on Denver not utilized in the book and exhibit, but wonderful material on Trinidad, Pueblo, Sterling, Louisville, Silver Plume, and many other communities. An important point to keep in mind is that families continue to participate in the documentation project and the research archive continues to grow, which in the future will certainly result in new projects. The work done so far is only a beginning.

The Society's collaboration with the Italian American community of Colorado has been a tremendous success and the response to the project has been overwhelmingly positive. Because so little has been done on Italians in the West, word about the project and the research archive has spread. I have been asked to contribute materials from the archive to local and national publications that focus on Italian American history and immigration, and have given several presentations on the project, including at the Archives in Rome, Italy, and the American Italian Historical Association's annual conference in Los Angeles. In November 2007, the association's annual conference was held in Denver. CIAPA and the exhibit were featured at the conference, and attendees had the opportunity to see the exhibit, learn about the ambitious documentation project, and consider how similar projects could be done in other parts of the country.

This publication as part of the Colorado Historical Society's comprehensive documentation project on Italians in Colorado is an example of how communities can have a strong voice in the telling and preservation of their own history. This book is also a testament to the importance of personal and community history as a research resource. Readers should consider their own stories, common and different, and the value of documenting and preserving them.

Introduction

Immigrant groups, including Italians, had little time to spend on documenting their personal history and experiences. Instead, they focused on surviving, adjusting to their new lives in America, earning a living, and caring for their family and community. As a result, community history has traditionally been recorded in historical documents such as census records and birth certificates, and secondary source materials such as newspapers and magazines. Often, researchers use these materials as the basis for their study of a community, giving a general overview of the community's history that may list key dates and events and include a few names and general photographs. A diary or other firsthand account that gives details about an individual or family's life and connection to a larger community is a rare find, and thus generally lacking from a historical study of a group.

As a new way of looking at history, the Colorado Historical Society collaborated with Colorado's Italian American community to collect new information, artifacts, and images; much of which is included in this book. In actively collecting personal stories detailing daily life and immigration experiences, genealogical data, and family and community traditions, a complex community history emerged. Individual experiences, when examined together, revealed important information about the Italian community's social customs, religious beliefs, migration and settlement patterns, interaction with one another, their major contributions to the development of Colorado, and the impact of the early Italian community on Colorado's contemporary Italian American community.

Italian immigrants in the mid- to late nineteenth century were drawn to each other and found safety together in America as Italians. For early immigrants, the concept of being "Italian" was, in many ways, something they developed while living in America. It is important to note that early Italian immigrants in Colorado came from different provinces and regions in Italy, a country not completely unified as a nation until 1870. Prior to 1880, many Italians from northern regions including Piedmont, Ligury, Lombardy, and Trento settled in the East and made their way west to Colorado. Italian immigrants between 1880 and 1920 in Colorado came mostly from the southern Italian regions of Abruzzi, Molise, Apulia, Basilicata, Calabria, Campania, and Sicily. As a result, these early Italians held allegiance to their families first, followed by the town, province, and region of Italy they came from. Although they found safety together in America as Italians, they remained Calabrese and Sicilian, speaking their own dialect, eating their own cuisine, celebrating the holidays of their hometown, forming their own lodges, and trusting and helping those from the same region first. Today, these differences, albeit transformed by time, remain within the contemporary Italian American community.

Despite their differences, these early Italian immigrants helped and supported each other and in doing so gave rise to a truly unique ethnic group in America. Today, Italian Americans continue to honor aspects of their ancestors' way of life, preserving the traditions and customs of Italian life in the mid- to late nineteenth century, handed down to them through the generations.

Italy in Colorado, like other community history studies, gives an overview of the Italian community in Colorado, found in the introductions to each chapter. Organized chronologically, introductions for chapters one through four give an overview of early Italian immigration to Colorado. The introductions for chapters five through eight focus on Denver's Italian enclave but also offer insight into what was and is happening in Italian American communities across Colorado. Unlike many other community histories, *Italy in Colorado* includes personal stories in each chapter with details on immigration, daily life, and work and community involvement that serve as evidence to the broader themes outlined in the chapter introduction. Personal stories included in the book also serve to tell the history of Italians in Colorado and their contributions to the development of the state overall. Each chapter also includes additional information on topics covered in the introductions and personal stories under the heading, "A Closer Look." For example, in chapter one, the reader learns about Louis Garbarino, who owned an oyster saloon in Colorado; "A Closer Look" on oyster saloons follows, giving the reader more information on the topic.

The use of *Italy in Colorado* as the title of this book should also be explained. In recording family histories and doing research for this book, it became clear that Italian immigrants in Colorado not only made their own Italy in the state but also saw Italy in Colorado. Many immigrants, including those that came early in the mid–nineteenth century and those who came in the wake of World War II, found in the state—along with employment opportunities and the prospect of owning land—a climate and geography much like those they'd left behind. Like Italy, Colorado is a land of foothills, high mountains, and plains, with distinct seasons that bring dry, sunny weather, cool rains, and cold, wet snow.

Once here, the immigrants built their own "Little Italy" communities. In Denver, Trinidad, Pueblo, and elsewhere, they lived in enclaves that resembled Old World villages. Family members built houses near one another, and neighbors knew and relied on each other. Their communities were for the most part closed to outsiders and self-sufficient; each had its own churches, businesses, and schools.

The communities protected residents from a sometimes hostile world. In these enclaves, immigrants nourished rituals transplanted from Italy; they honored the family with Sunday dinners, home altars, and Saints' feast days. Church traditions marked the passage of life—baptisms, first communions, weddings, and funerals—and brought the community together. In fraternal lodges, social organizations, and everyday life in Little Italy, generations learned the importance of family; the value of helping each other; traditional music, dances, and games; regional cuisine; and time-honored celebrations that survive in Colorado's Italian American communities today.

Like the exhibit *The Italians of Denver*, this publication will certainly not completely satisfy all readers. For those wanting more history, more family stories, and more photographs, the CIAPA Archive now contains a substantial quantity of additional material. Like the exhibit, it would have been impossible to include everything we collected on Colorado's Italian community in this book. Certainly, more research and projects will result from the work already done to build the CIAPA Archive, open *The Italians of Denver* exhibit, and publish *Italy in Colorado*.

L'ILLUSTRAZIONE ITALIANA

Per l'Italia, Cent. 50. - Per la Francia, Cent. 60 il numero.   Anno XI. - N. 23. - 8 Giugno 1884.   Fratelli Treves, Editori, Milano

Per il XXV anniversario della guerra dell'Indipendenza.

VITTORIO EMANUELE II
(dal ritratto ad olio eseguito da G. Bertini nel 1859).

CHAPTER 1

Beginnings
1850–1869

A string of seemingly unrelated events in Italy and the United States brought the first Italian immigrants to Colorado.

With the beginning of Italian unification in 1861 under King Victor Emmanuel II (a process that culminated when Rome joined the unified nation in 1870), those who had the resources could more easily leave the country in search of work, adventure, or opportunity. Italians—many escaping political unrest in the new nation—traveled to Europe, South America, and the United States. Some planned to return; others left Italy forever.

In the midst of America's Civil War, Abraham Lincoln signed the Pacific Railroad Bill in 1862. Italians and other immigrants worked for the Union Pacific and Central Pacific as the railroads raced to complete a transcontinental line. That same year, the Homestead Act gave settlers the chance to own land they had developed and worked. The 1864 Immigration Act encouraged immigrants to fill jobs vacated by soldiers, although it also allowed employers to lock newcomers into restrictive contracts.

Other events inspired people to try their luck in the West. The discovery of gold flakes in 1858 launched the Pikes Peak Gold Rush. Thousands streamed into the area, building settlements like Denver City, Georgetown, and Auraria.

The vast majority of Italians who made their way to Colorado during these years came from northern Italy and lived in other parts of the United States before moving west. Many had not seen Italy in years, but they transplanted much of their homeland to Colorado's cities, mining camps, and farms.

Opposite: Cover of L'Illustrazione Italiana *with an image of Vittorio Emanuele II (English: Victor Emmanuel II) by Riergbis, June 8, 1884, after an 1859 painting by G. Bertini. Vittorio Emanuele II, the first king of united Italy, assumed the title of king on February 18, 1861. Loan Alisa Zahller. IL.2006.32.1*

A Closer Look
The Unification of Italy

The unified nation of Italy as we know it today did not exist until 1870. After the collapse of the Roman Empire in 476 A.D., the region was fought over and sometimes ruled by a succession of foreign peoples, including the French, Lombards, Normans, Arabs, Spanish, and Austrians. Italy remained divided until Napoleon Bonaparte's 1796 invasion.

Napoleon established a centralized government with unified fiscal, judicial, and administrative systems. The policies fostered national identity, but Italians still resented the French emperor's rule. Nationalism, a concept born during the French Revolution, had taken hold. But self-governance continued to be a dream.

In 1814, Austria-Hungary, England, Prussia, and Russia combined forces and invaded Italy, overthrowing the French. The following year, Austria took full control and removed the self-proclaimed King of Italy from power.

Italians revolted against Austrian domination in one city after another. The resistance—known as the *Risorgimento* (or reorganization)—lasted forty-six years. The nation of Italy was born under the rule of Victor Emmanuel II in 1861, though unification wasn't officially complete until Rome joined the republic in 1870.

A Closer Look
Colorado in the 1850s and 1860s

In the 1850s, the American Indians who called Colorado home—including the Ute, Cheyenne, and Arapaho—shared the land with a handful of traders and trappers. There were settlements in the San Luis Valley, and the Santa Fe Trail connected the United States with Mexico.

With the discovery of gold in 1858, as many as 100,000 new settlers surged into Colorado. Italian immigrants were among them. Miners and merchants made their way to present-day Colorado in search of opportunity and riches. The surge resulted in an increase in population, the displacement of American Indians, and the establishment of the Colorado Territory in 1861.

The same guidebooks that promoted mining described rich soil and wide-open ranges, ideal for farming and ranching. The availability of land, at little or no cost under the Homestead Act of 1862, enabled individuals—including

View of Denver, Fourteenth Street between Arapahoe and Lawrence, c. 1865. 2000.129.52

immigrants—to own the land they worked. By the late 1860s, agriculture, mining, railroading, and retail businesses—from restaurants to outfitters—were the mainstays of Colorado's economy.

A Closer Look
Early Denver

Organized on November 22, 1858, Denver, named for Kansas Territorial governor James W. Denver, was home to a few hundred people within a year, but the town grew quickly. By 1860, Denver had a population of nearly 2,600, and many people heading into the mountains made a stop in Denver for supplies.

Denver's growth stalled with slowing output from the gold fields and the Union Pacific Railroad's decision in 1866 to bypass the town in favor of building the nation's first transcontinental line through southern Wyoming. Realizing that Denver would not prosper without a railroad connection, town builders and city leaders formed the Denver Pacific Railway for the sole purpose of connecting Denver to the transcontinental rail line. By 1870, the Denver Pacific and Kansas Pacific railroads linked Denver to the rest of the country. These and other railroads were soon attracting immigrants, transforming Denver and the region.

Beginnings 1850–1869

> **A CLOSER LOOK**
> *Italy Discovers America*

Long before the mass emigration of the late 1800s, Italians had heard about life in the United States. Italian sailors, adventurers, merchants, and missionaries spent time in North and South America, starting in the 1700s. Merchant and surgeon Philip Mazzei arrived in Virginia from Florence in November 1773. He bought land next to Thomas Jefferson's Monticello, forging friendships with Jefferson, George Washington, John Adams, James Madison, and James Monroe.[1]

In the early 1800s, a trip or winter season in Italy became fashionable for American artists and well-heeled tourists. Artists flocked to Italy to learn ancient history and copy the paintings of the masters. When the travelers returned to the United States, they helped promote an idealized vision of Italy.

At the same time, skilled Italian artists, craftsmen, and merchants chanced starting a new life in the Americas. In 1852, Constantino Brumidi was commissioned to paint the frescos in the United States Capitol. In the late 1880s, as more and more Italians considered leaving their country, they relied on stories (and oftentimes money) from friends and family already in America, to help them decide where to go. Sometimes entire villages learned of America from those already settled in the new land. Correspondence, travel guidebooks, advertisements, and publications such as the popular *Frank Leslie's Illustrated Newspaper* all aided the exchange of information and the inspiration to set sail.

GARBARINO

The Garbarino Brothers

In 1858, four brothers—Joseph, Charles, Louis, and Tony Garbarino—left political unrest behind in their hometown of Montebruno, Italy, and sailed to America. According to Rosa Garbarino, the daughter of James Garbarino (who joined his brothers in Colorado in 1870 after a short stay in St. Louis):

> My uncles, four of them (Joe, Charles, Tony and Louis), having heard that the mountains of Colorado were blazing furnaces of gold metal, made up their minds to come to these regions, load up and return to good old Missouri. One bright morning in 1859, a caravan of ox-trains left St. Louis

Union Depot Exchange Building (lower right, with C. Garbareno & Phil M. Luxich sign), near Union Depot at Seventeenth and Wazee Streets, Denver, c. 1885. 89.451.2762

for Denver and my uncles joined as drivers; after a few days they were met by a bunch of Indians who were willing traders. That night, little suspecting any treachery, the Indians stampeded nearly all the animals, including four fine saddle horses belonging to my uncles. The convoy, being left short of work and animals, had no alternative but to send back for other teams, and my uncles were of the party that returned. This unfriendly encounter, however, did not deter them from trying again their luck. They went back with the "boys" and reached Colorado with but a few other mishaps.[2]

Charles Garbarino

In 1866, Charles and Louis Garbarino built the Garbarino Building on Washington Avenue in Golden, Colorado, which housed the brothers' restaurant and hotel. In June of 1866, Charles married Rose Dailey of Peoria, Illinois. As the *Rocky Mountain News* wrote, he came back to Denver with his new bride and "courage to stand before the universal public at Cheney's Billiard Hall and dispense cool comfort to the thirsty million." In 1881, Charles opened the Union Depot Exchange at Seventeenth and Wazee Streets. On September 7, the *News* proclaimed:

> Although the weather is rather disagreeable and the mud deep, business on the corner of Seventeen and Wazee streets will be lively all the same. Messers, Garbareno [Garbarino] & Luxich having fitted up the rooms 198 and 200 Seventeenth

Street, in fine style will today open the "Union Depot Exchange." This firm are importers of fine wines and liquors and the choicest brands will be found at their bar. The finest imported cigars will also be kept. There is also a billiard room attached.[3]

Joseph and Tony Garbarino

Joseph and Tony, after trying their luck at other mining camps, settled in Georgetown as merchants and saloon-keepers. Among their properties were the Garbarino House on Sixth Street, a saloon on Taos Street, and a business on Rose Street.

Louis Garbarino, c. 1865. CIAPA Archive. Courtesy John Louis Garbarino. PCCLI4738

Louis Garbarino

Around 1870, after living a few years in Golden, Colorado, Louis Garbarino moved to the town of Mount Vernon, west of Denver. By 1874, Louis moved to Boulder, Colorado, where he owned and operated a restaurant and oyster saloon at 1100–1102 Pearl Street until 1903.[4] He died the next year. Louis and his wife Elizabeth (Belshe) had six children: Lucinda Marie, Talitha Josephine, Belshe Charles, Christopher Ghio, and Elizabeth Adelina and Louis Francis, who both died in infancy.

Elizabeth Garbarino, c. 1865. CIAPA Archive. Courtesy John Louis Garbarino. PCCLI4742

Garbarino House, Restaurant & Oyster Saloon, owned by Louis Garbarino, Boulder, Colorado, c. 1875. Courtesy Denver Public Library, Western History Collection. X-10081

CLOSER LOOK
Oyster Saloons

When East Coast fortune-seekers came to Colorado during the gold rush, they brought their taste for seafood with them. And they didn't go hungry.

Oysters, plentiful and cheap back east, were consumed in all types of eateries, including pricey restaurants and red-light district "oyster cellars." East Coast companies packed fresh oysters in flour barrels and shipped them as far as Europe, California, and Colorado.

Newspapers published notices when oyster-laden freighters pulled into Denver. On May 10, 1868, the *Daily Colorado Tribune* reported the arrival of fifteen cases of oysters hauled into town on mule-drawn wagons.

Oyster parlor, Trinidad, Colorado, c. 1900. 84.193.275

Most oysters ended up on plates at modest "oyster saloons." On November 13, 1861, George Billings advertised that he had an "eating Stall and Rooms" on Larimer Street, where he served oysters, pigs' feet, tripe, and hot coffee. By 1874, Louis Garbarino opened a restaurant and oyster saloon in Boulder.

Denver's upscale restaurants also served oysters. In 1861, Henry Feuerstein advertised a "spacious Beer Hall and Eating House," where he served oysters and "warm meals," as well as champagne, beer, ale, and cigars.[5] Entrepreneur Barney Ford owned the People's Restaurant and Saloon. In 1863, he ran an ad saying that he got "fresh oysters every day direct from salt water."[6] In 1872, Nick Camelleri opened the Star Restaurant, which specialized in "oysters and game" on F Street (today's Fifteenth Street) between Larimer and Holladay (now Market).[7]

By the early 1900s, fresh oysters were less popular, largely due to the amount of pollution in the harbors of New York, Maryland, and Delaware.

Lucinda Marie Garbarino

The oldest child of Louis and Elizabeth Garbarino, Lucinda Marie was born in 1878. She attended Central School and State Preparatory School in Boulder. In 1901, she graduated from the University of Colorado as a Greek major; she earned a master's a year later. Lucinda went on to teach there in the Classics department, specializing in Latin and Greek. A member of the Daughters of the American Revolution, she owned and contracted for the construction of a building at Eleventh and Pearl; the building still bears the name "L. Garbarino." Lucinda Marie Garbarino died in 1944 in Boulder, Colorado.[8]

Belshe Charles Garbarino

Born in 1881, Belshe Charles was the third child of Louis and Elizabeth Garbarino. He owned an automobile dealership and garage in Boulder at 1100 Pearl Street—the former site of his father's restaurant and saloon. A skilled mechanic, he was regarded as one of the leading automobile men in Boulder. In 1911, he married Freda Marie Gassert of St. Louis, Missouri, and together the couple had three children: Belshe Jr., Freda, and John. He died in Boulder in 1937.[9]

Wedding portrait, Belshe Charles and Freda Marie Garbarino, by Nast Studio, 1911. CIAPA Archive. Courtesy John Louis Garbarino. PCCLI4746

Christopher Ghio Garbarino

Christopher Garbarino was born in Boulder in 1886. The fifth child born to Louis and Elizabeth Garbarino, he attended Central School and State Preparatory School. After graduating from the University of Colorado Law School, he opened his own law office in 1913.[10]

A CLOSER LOOK
Early Italian Settlers in Colorado

In addition to the Garbarino family, many other Italians settled in Colorado during the 1850s and 1860s. These immigrants (mostly single males) made their way to Colorado in search of gold and wealth. Others came to fill jobs as miners, artists, business owners, laborers in construction and agriculture, employees in shops, and musicians. Although many of the early Italian settlers' personal stories remain untold, historical documents serve as evidence to their living in Colorado.

According to the U.S. Federal Census for 1860, Italians living in the present-day area of Colorado included: H. Ottanto, a 28-year-old artist living in Denver, in the Arapahoe County of the Kansas Territory; W. Grozer, a 31-year-old miner living in California Gulch (near present-day Leadville, Colorado), in the Arapahoe County of the Kansas Territory; John Arris, age 28, and his brother L. Arris, age 26, saloon operators living in the Enterprise District (now north of Central City in Gilpin County, Colorado), in the Arapahoe County of the Kansas Territory; and Peter Carle, age 28, and A. F. Florence, age 29, musicians living in Denver in the Arapahoe County of the Kansas Territory.

Concert Hall, Central City, Colorado, c. 1865. PH.PROP.2263

A Closer Look
Musicians in Colorado

Italian *musicanti* took the stage in Denver and Colorado's mountain mining towns in the 1860s and 1870s. Entertaining audiences at the Denver Theater, Central City's Montana Theater, Georgetown's Cushman Opera, Leadville's Tabor Opera House, and other venues, they brought a little Old World culture to the raw and raucous West.

The phenomenon wasn't new—Italian opera made its way to colonial America in the mid-1700s. In 1803, Thomas Jefferson recruited Italians to play in the first United States Marine Corps band.[11] By 1843, Americans had fully embraced opera and welcomed Italian singers and musicians with hearty applause.

In Colorado, performances by Italians were not limited to operas or the new opera houses. They played in saloons, restaurants, and at private functions where their voices and skills compensated for a language barrier that challenged immigrants in other lines of work. Their instruments—mostly violins, concertinas, accordions, and guitars—traveled easily, making their businesses portable and inexpensive compared to shops and saloons that required considerable investment and a good working knowledge of English.

Ne Plus Ultra accordion, c. 1878. H.6200.660

CHAPTER 2

Growth

1870–1879

After years of war, debate, and threats from outsiders who wanted to rule the area, Italy was officially unified in 1870. But the country could not call itself truly "unified." The dominant Catholic Church did not recognize the new state, and regional differences in culture, language, and economy threatened its stability. The government made new demands on its citizens, such as an unpopular draft law requiring healthy young men to serve two or three years in the military. With poverty growing to desperate levels in the rural south, more Italians sought work abroad.

Before 1870, Italian immigrants had found work in Europe, North Africa, and South America. But faced with political unrest in Argentina and yellow fever in Brazil, immigrants increasingly looked north. Efficient steamships and frequent sailings made crossing the North Atlantic—a voyage of about ten days—ever easier.[12]

Colorado's mines, mills, and railroads drew their share of immigrants. The railroads needed laborers to lay tracks, supervise and service cars, and move freight. An 1870s silver boom drew miners, carpenters, and others to the mountains. After arriving in Denver, many Italians followed opportunities to Empire, Fairplay, Georgetown, Leadville, Black Hawk, Central City, and other boom towns. Entrepreneurs, store owners, entertainers, and artisans found a ready market for their talents. Immigrants from both northern and southern Italy formed close-knit communities where they felt safe practicing their Catholic faith and speaking their native language, and where they could eat familiar foods, stay in touch with others from their home region, and share ways to adapt to their new lives in the West.

Opposite: View of the Denver, South Park & Pacific Railroad tracks, Palisade, Colorado, by Otto Westerman, c. 1875. PH.PROP.2989

Barra

Rocco Luigi Barra

Born in 1853 in Anzi, near Naples in southern Italy, Rocco Luigi Barra left home as a young man. A self-described troubadour who played the violin, he first traveled to the Canary Islands and then to New Orleans.[13] After hearing about the silver boom in Leadville, Barra came to Colorado in 1879. In 1881, he went to work as a barkeeper for Joseph Turre at the Turre saloon on Second Street in Leadville.

In 1882, Rocco Luigi married Mary Katherine Brichetto/Brichett, the daughter of Italian immigrants from Genoa, Italy. In 1883, the couple's first child, William Robert Barra, was born, followed by John Louis and Josephine.[14]

Around 1886, the Barra family moved to Denver where Rocco Luigi opened a saloon downtown. In the years that followed, Barra owned several businesses in Denver. According to the Denver City Directories, his businesses included a saloon with Henry Martinazzi (1887), the L. Barra and F. Guerrieri Cigar Company with Frank Guerrieri (1888), and DeCunto and Barra, a wholesale liquor and cigar business, with Frank DeCunto (1890). Rocco Luigi Barra died in Denver in 1936 at the age of eighty-two, followed by Mary, who died in 1959.

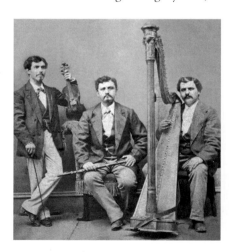

Rocco Luigi Barra (left), Frankie DiStefano (center), Achilie DiStefano (right), Leadville, c. 1880. CIAPA Archive. Courtesy Janet A. Goodwin. PCCLI4965

Rocco Luigi and Mary Katherine (Brichetto) Barra, by Bohm, Denver, 1882. CIAPA Archive. Courtesy Janet A. Goodwin. PCCLI4967

CLOSER LOOK
What's In a Name?

Last Names

Italian and Italian American surnames often have multiple spellings. Typographical and spelling errors made by immigration authorities—or by an illiterate family member—explain many of the differences. For example, an immigration officer might spell DiLuzio as "DeLuzio," not realizing that an "i" in Italian is pronounced "e."

Anti-Italian prejudice compelled some families to make their names sound more American by dropping the end vowel or changing the name entirely. For example, Brichetto became Brichett, Arcieri became Archer, and DiGiacomo became James.

Spelling and pronunciation changes were often permanent, although some families have found the correct spelling through genealogical research and changed their names to the original Italian spelling.

Prefixes—including "di" ("of" or "from") and "la" or "lo" ("the" or "of the family of")—are also a part of Italian naming traditions. Di Napoli refers to someone from Naples, and LaGuardia means "the guardian."

First Names and Nicknames

Historically, Italian families—including those in Colorado—lived near each other and held to traditional naming traditions. In Italy, the first male child is often named after his paternal grandfather, the second after his maternal grandfather, the first female after her paternal grandmother, and the second after her maternal grandmother. Parents named subsequent children after themselves, godparents, favorite aunts or uncles, saints, or deceased relatives.

Community members often ended up with the same names, hence the popularity of nicknames. Some derived from physical traits and habits; others were mispronunciations—in Italian or English—of a first name or initials. Talents and hobbies inspired still others. Nicknames grew so common that friends sometimes forgot each other's birth names!

Dr. Robert Louis "R. L." Barra

Robert Louis and his sister Mary Elvira "Vera" Barra, Denver, 1914. CIAPA Archive. Courtesy Janet A. Goodwin. PCCLI4968

Until the age of eight, R. L. Barra and his sister Vera lived in north Denver on Bell Street (now Osage) with their parents, William R. and Laura M. (Chiolero) Barra. Their father, the son of Rocco Luigi Barra, was a cigar maker. After the death of their mother in 1914, R. L. went to live with his father and grandparents while Vera moved in with Chiolero relatives.

After graduating from Colorado University Medical School in the 1930s, Dr. R. L. Barra opened a private practice in Denver's old Republic Building. An eye, ear, nose, and throat specialist, he often cared for patients who could not afford to pay him, including residents of Denver's Little Sisters of the Poor. R. L. Barra died in 1984.

Capelli

Angelo and Marianna "Mary Anne" Capelli

In 1872, Mary Anne and Angelo Capelli arrived in Denver via St. Louis. Born near Genoa, in northern Italy, they were one of the first Italian families in the Queen City.[15] They opened a fruit stand and diner on Wazee Street near Union Station. By 1873, the family had saved enough money to build the Highland House (today known as My Brother's Bar) at Fifteenth and Platte.

The Highland House saloon and boarding house included a butcher shop, liquor store, and restaurant and fruit business. The Highland House also served German merchants, Irish policemen, and American politicians. The Capellis offered pasta dinners on Columbus Day (for both countrymen and non-Italians), when they draped their business with flags of all nations to celebrate Italian American solidarity.[16]

The Capellis aided many new Italian arrivals, helping them adjust to life in Colorado. They helped fellow countrymen find jobs and housing, and helped with legal matters. In 1880, they helped Gerardo Losasso purchase land. In 1881, they were witnesses to the marriage of Angelo Vignola and Arcangela Losasso, married at Sacred Heart of Mary Catholic Church.[17]

My Brother's Bar (formerly the Highland House) at Fifteenth and Platte Streets, Denver, by Bonnie Garramone, 2002. CIAPA Archive. PCCLI4068

By 1874, their success helped Angelo Capelli's three brothers make their way to Denver. In time, the Capellis owned several taverns, a confectionary shop, a macaroni factory, a meat market, fruit stands, and a real estate business. Angelo's financial success and community involvement led, in 1881, to his appointment as Italian vice consul in Denver, a title given to him by the Italian government.[18]

In 1893, Angelo and Mary Ann moved to Lake View in Jefferson County. They operated the Highland House until 1907, when the Schlitz Brewing Company took over the property.

A CLOSER LOOK
Saloons

In the American West, nineteenth-century saloons were not just drinking establishments. For some people, and especially for immigrants, they served as informal community centers. Newcomers cherished their tap houses and taverns as safe havens where their birthplace was accepted with friendly conversation—often in their native tongue. Like churches and the home, saloons became shelters for a range of social activities. Criticized by some citizens of Denver as dens of moral decay that stirred up political unrest, saloons actually had a positive place in society.

A. Fabrizio Saloon, Louisville, Colorado, c. 1890. Fred Mazzulla Collection. 99.270.1842

In Colorado, Italian-owned saloons were often located within boardinghouses, restaurants, and even dry goods stores. Italian saloonkeepers such as Angelo Capelli, Siro Mangini, Vincenzo Vallero, and Joseph Turre became community leaders. As established immigrants, they were in a position to assist newcomers with the English language, employment, housing, and services such as the translation of American documents.

Peter "Tito" Capoferro

Born in southern Italy in 1852 to Rocco "Richard" and Angelina Capoferro, Tito Capoferro came to America in the late 1870s seeking better business opportunities. He settled first in the East and then made his way west to Denver where he worked for three years in a greenhouse at Thirty-first and California Streets. After saving enough money, he rented land in Adams County where he grew vegetables. Eight years later, he bought ten acres in Welby, Colorado. In 1893, Tito married Rosina "Rose" Arciere at Sacred Heart Catholic Church in Denver. The couple had three children: Jerry Capoferro, Angelina (Capoferro) Albanese, and Jennie Capoferro.[19]

In 1919, the following was written about Tito and Rose Capoferro:

> Their religious faith is that of the Catholic Church. Mr. Capoperro [Capoferro] has prospered since coming to the new world and has never had occasion to regret his determination to seek his fortune on this side of the Atlantic. He found that in America labor is king and that diligence and determination will win success.[20]

John Francis and Rose (Albanese) Gaccetta

John Francis Gaccetta was born in Welby in 1913 to Frank and Theresa (Gato) Gaccetta. His father was born in the southern Italian province of Cantanzaro in the Calabria region and came to America in 1888. After working in Canada and Leadville, Colorado, as a miner, Frank settled in Welby and purchased land to farm. In 1891, he sent for his future bride, Theresa Gato. The couple married in 1892 and had seven children: Joseph, Angelo, Philomena, Mary, Dominic, Elizabeth, and John.

John and Rose Gaccetta on the Gaccetta farm in Welby, c. 1960. CIAPA Archive. Courtesy Gina (Nichol) Jeffries and Alice (Gaccetta) Nichol. PCCLI4901

Like his father, John was a farmer. In 1938, John married Rose Albanese at Assumption Church in Welby. Born in 1919, Rose was the daughter of Vito and Angelina (Capoferro) Albanese. Her father was an Italian immigrant from Bari, Italy, who came to America in 1909, and her mother was the daughter of Tito and Rose Capoferro. John and Rose Gaccetta had two children, Alice Jean and John Francis.[21]

Alice Jean (Gaccetta) Nichol

The daughter of John and Rose Gaccetta, Alice Gaccetta was born in 1939 and grew up in Welby. In 1959, she married Ronald Dale Nichol. In 1960, their first child, Ronda, was born, followed by Renee, Rachelle, and Regina. Alice worked for the Mapleton Public School system. After eighteen years, she retired and ran for Colorado state representative in District 34. She served from 1992 through 1997.

She then served as a Colorado state senator from 1998 to 2004. In 2005, Alice Nichol successfully ran for Adams County commissioner, a position she still holds today.[22]

Cunio/Cuneo

Giovanni "Gian" Battista and Louisa (Rettagliata) Cunio

Gian Battista Cunio (sometimes spelled *Cuneo* in historic documents) was born in 1833 to Andrea and Guilia-Isola Cunio in the town of Zerba, in the Pavia province of northern Italy. In 1855, he married Louisa Rettagliata, also from Pavia. Born to wealthy merchants and land-owning families, Gian and Louisa left Italy for America in 1856.

Cunio family, back row, left to right: Clara (Cunio) Cella and Paul Cella, Joseph J. Cella and Maie (Hefferson) Cella; front row: Louise Cunio, Marie Cella (baby) and G. B. Cunio, c. 1910. CIAPA Archive. Courtesy Paul Cella. PCCLI5942

Gian was twenty-two and Louisa sixteen. After landing in New York, the Cunios made their way to California, where they settled in a mining camp and where Gian successfully pursued mining ventures. In 1872, upon hearing of the state's great mineral and agricultural resources, the family left California for Colorado. After visiting various mining camps in Colorado, the Cunio family settled in Denver, opening a restaurant at Sixteenth Street and Blake called the American House. Gian later went into the fruit business and real estate.[23]

Louisa and Gian had two daughters, Clara and Dora. In 1881, Clara married Paolo "Paul" Cella, a restaurateur and real estate businessman from Milan. After their marriage, the couple lived in a duplex shared with Clara's parents, Louisa and Gian. Clara and Paul had one son, Joseph John Cella. The Cunio's youngest daughter Dora, born in Denver in 1879, was trained as a musician and taught piano in Denver from 1903 to 1905. After Dora married C. Anselmo, the couple moved to Los Angeles, where they had three children.[24] Louisa Cunio died in 1915, followed by Gian, who died in Denver in 1924.

DeCunto

Francesco "Frank" DeCunto

A native of Naples in southern Italy, Frank DeCunto came to Colorado in 1879. He settled first in Leadville, where he initially worked as a musician. He later opened a restaurant and saloon with Rocco Luigi Barra.[25] In 1889, Frank and his wife Mary moved to Denver, where DeCunto and Barra continued their business partnership under the name DeCunto, Barra & Company. That same year, they opened Casa Bianca, a wholesale wine and liquor business with Giuseppe Biancullo.[26] A year later, they opened the wholesale liquor and cigar business, DeCunto & Barra, which remained in business until 1916, when both men retired.

Frank DeCunto died in Denver in 1933 at the age of seventy-three. At the time of his death, the *Rocky Mountain News* published an article on October 29, 1933, titled "Marched Along Together 50 Years: But Only One Came Back This Time." The piece describes their friendship of over fifty years, partnership in business, and the fact that they lived

DeCunto and Barra families, front row, left to right: unidentified woman and man, William R. Barra holding Minnie Louise Barra, and Robert Louis Barra; back row, left to right: unidentified man, Minnie Buck Barra, Kathleen DeCunto, Mary DeCunto, William Buck, Rocco L. Barra, Frank DeCunto, Mary K. Barra, and Frances DeCunto, c. 1925. CIAPA Archive. Courtesy Janet A. Goodwin and Minnie Louise Barra. PCCLI4974

within two blocks of one another and saw each other every day. According to the article, after their retirement in 1916, DeCunto and Barra would meet each other every morning promptly at 9:00 A.M., and their meeting was like this:

"Good morning Mr. DeCunto. And how is your health this day?"

"Excellent, Mr. Barra. And yours?"

"The same. Shall we walk down to the office this morning?"

(They had gone to the office together for more than 30 years before.)

"Certainly, Mr. Barra."

To each, the other was Mister DeCunto or Mister Barra—never Frank or Louie. And so they made their tour downtown together. They smoked the same cigars. They lighted the first one of the day together off the same match.

They knew the history of every building they passed. They loved every landmark for they had helped build the city.

The article goes on to describe how the friends would talk about their business on the way downtown and then check on one of the properties they owned before returning home for lunch, "to meet again on the morrow—promptly at 9 A.M."

At his friend's funeral, Rocco Luigi Barra said: "While he rests I shall walk alone. Men like DeCunto never die. They just rest."[27]

DiBello/DeBell

Gaetano "Clyde" and Concetta "Clara" DiBello/DeBell

In the 1870s, Gaetano DiBello and other men from southern Potenza, Italy, immigrated to America, seeking refuge from harsh and unstable social and economic conditions in their homeland. After a short stay in New York, Gaetano and others from the group traveled to Colorado, where they had acquaintances in Denver.[28]

Once settled, Gaetano sent for his fiancée, Concetta. Upon her arrival with her mother Pauline LaSala in 1878, Gaetano and Concetta were married at Sacred Heart Catholic Church in Denver. Shortly after their marriage, the couple bought a small farm in an area of Denver referred to as "White

City."²⁹ White City was located about one-half mile north of where Regis College is today. The DiBellos remained on their farm with Gaetano working in truck gardening until he fell ill and ultimately died in 1925.

Gaetano and Concetta DiBello had fourteen children born between 1888 and 1908 (many of whom changed their last name to DeBell): Roxie, Pasquale, Mary, Michael, Rose, Angelo, George, Louise, Joseph, John, Carl, Lucia, Vincent, and Gerald.

John and Mary (DiLuzio/DeLuzio) DeBell

In 1928, Mary DiLuzio (sometimes spelled DeLuzio in family records) married John Louis DeBell, the tenth child born to Gaetano and Concetta DiBello, at Assumption Church in Welby. John was twenty-five and Mary was twenty-two. When asked about her wedding day, Mary said:

Gaetano DiBello, Denver, c. 1894. CIAPA Archive. Courtesy Ralph F. Mancinelli. PCCLI1387

> Oh I remember it was such a beautiful day and of course the groom and bride—it wasn't like it is now—the groom was over at the house and we went in different cars to the church and then we went in church together and had the ceremony. There was no Mass, it was just a ceremony and most of the invited guests came to the church. We were planning to have a big wedding, but John's aunt died, just about a month before we had our wedding, so in them days they didn't do things like that, they had to wait a year before they would celebrate a wedding because they were in mourning. They wore black and they wore bands provided by the undertaker on their sleeves and they mourned for a whole year. Also, we used to bring a big wreath to hang on the door and it was either purple—for younger people—or black—for older people. The family would hang the wreath on the door all the while before the funeral for the dead. The undertaker would pick up the corpse at home, embalm it and return the body to the family home where it would stay until the burial.³⁰

Growth 1870–1879

The daughter of Biagio and Columba (DiStefano) DiLuzio, Mary DeBell's parents were married in Torricella, Italy, in the Abruzzi region in southern Italy. In 1902, Biagio, age twenty-four, and his father-in-law Domenico DiStefano came to America. A *contadino*, or peasant farmer, in Italy, Biagio homesteaded a five-acre farm near the Platte River in Welby, Colorado. In 1903, Biagio's wife Columba and other family members joined him, living first in a small shack home until 1913 when the family built a large fourteen-room house. By 1925, the DiLuzio family expanded the farm to twenty-four acres, which produced vegetable crops of all varieties. According to Mary (DiLuzio) DeBell:

> You name it we had it. When I was just a little girl about three years old, I could name every vegetable that we raised. I remember going with my mother when I was four years old and her teaching me the difference between seeds, vegetables and weeds—she taught me how to pull weeds. And then we had of course horses and sleds to carry our vegetables. When we harvested vegetables we used to put everything on sleds and bring them up to the shed where we had to bunch them up for the market or small grocery stores like Archer Brothers down on 15th Street near the loop.[31]

The DiLuzio family also raised hogs, mostly for the family to eat. On special occasions, generally in the summertime, the family would go to the city stores for supplies and specialty groceries, splurging on steak and sometimes even fruit, which the family for the most part ate on holidays. Additionally, the family ate bread, baked in an outdoor brick oven. Mary recalled, "we used to bake 14 or so big loaves of bread to last a week. Bread was our main food with our main meal of soup."[32]

Growing up, Mary went to the Rankin School, a one-room schoolhouse in a private home in Welby. The school had four grades and one teacher—who came by horse and buggy each Monday and stayed all week with one of the

Mary (DiLuzio) DeBell, by Dawn DeAno, Denver, 2004. CIAPA Archive. PCCLICPC0019

farm families in the area—for all the grades. In the school was a potbelly stove, and the children would have to haul water from about a half mile away. The school day started early with exercises, followed by basic studies, and ended in time for the children to return home to help with family chores.

After Mary and John DeBell married in 1928, John worked on the DiLuzio farm and the couple lived in the DiLuzio family house, where Mary was born. The couple lived there for twelve or thirteen years before moving to Arvada, Colorado. John and Mary DeBell had four children: Virginia, Lillian, John L., and Katherine. John died in 1969. Mary turned one hundred in 2006.

Lucia "Lucille" or "Lucy" (DeBell) and Gaetano "Clyde" M. Arcieri/Archer

In 1926, Lucy DeBell, the twelfth child born to Gaetano and Concetta DiBello, married Clyde M. Archer. One of eleven children, Clyde (whose birth name was Gaetano Arcieri) was born in Potenza, Italy, in 1899. In 1901, at the age of two, he immigrated to America (where his family changed their last name to Archer) with his mother, Lucia (Passarelli) Arcieri, brothers Giovanni "John" and Raffaele "Fred," and sister Anna Maria Giuseppa "Josephine." Their destination was Denver, where Clyde's father Rocco and his oldest brother George were already settled. In Denver, six more of Clyde's siblings were born: Gerard, Mary, Anthony, Anna, Concetta "Clara," and John.[33]

In 1929, Clyde and Lucy Archer's first child, a son named Clyde Rocco Archer, was born, followed by a daughter Elizabeth born in 1931. After their marriage, Clyde M. and Lucy Archer operated a family farm in west Denver. The Archer family lived in a four-room farmhouse, heated by a coal stove and with no running water. According to Clyde and Lucy Archer's son, Clyde R. Archer, life was hard but good. Clyde R. Archer recalled that in the winter months the family had no money for groceries so Lombardi's market (on West Thirty-eighth and

Gaetano Arcieri (Clyde M. Archer), Denver, c. 1912. CIAPA Archive. Courtesy Theda and Clyde R. Archer. PCCLI2402

Osage) would carry the bill until summer when the farm crops brought the family money. There was never extra money and therefore holidays, including Christmas, centered on family, not gifts. Clyde and his sister received items including apples, oranges, and little trinkets and celebrated the day by being with family and sharing a meal.

The Archer farm specialty was celery. The Archer family raised the celery seed and sold it to other local farmers. The family also raised their own Pascal Celery and according to Clyde R. Archer, trenching it was very hard work:

> ...you worked in a foot-wide trench eighteen inches deep. You opened up the trench with the horse and blade, removed the dirt by hand. Someone handed you the celery, you put the celery in one bunch at a time kicking it in with the back of your heel. You were on your hands and knees, bent over all day. It was very hard work.[34]

After burying the celery, it was left to bleach out for weeks. The resulting Pascal Celery was then sold to local markets at Thanksgiving and Christmas.

While continuing to farm, the elder Clyde M. Archer went to work for Tivoli Brewing Company in the 1950s. Lucy Archer died in 1971, followed by Clyde M. Archer, who died in 1980.

Clyde M. and Lucy (DeBell) Archer, bride and groom seated with attendants in back, left to right: Mary Archer, Jerry Archer, Carl DeBell, and Ann Archer, Denver, 1926. CIAPA Archive. Courtesy Theda and Clyde R. Archer. PCCLI2404V2

Clyde Rocco Archer

After witnessing a hailstorm on the family farm and seeing the devastating affects both financially and psychologically on his family, Clyde R. Archer decided not to follow in his father Clyde M. Archer's footsteps.[35]

While attending Regis High School in the late 1940s, Clyde R. Archer went to work for the Tennyson Meat Market at Forty-first and Tennyson Streets. On the weekends, he delivered groceries by bicycle in paper bags. Already knowledgeable about making Italian sausage—every January the Archer family would butcher a hog on the farm and make sausage—he also learned how to prepare and cut other meats from the owner of the store, a German man. Clyde's first job prepared him for his job after high school at the Save-A-Nickel grocery store, where he learned more about the meat business.

In 1950, Clyde joined the Navy. After serving in the Korean conflict and being stationed in the Philippines for two years, he returned to Denver in 1953. In 1954, he married Patricia Nowlen and again went to work for Save-A-Nickel until 1959, when he leased the meat market at the Country Gentleman. He started making Italian sausage for a couple of restaurants and eventually the restaurants were buying so much that the city inspectors stopped him from delivering the product to the restaurants. The inspectors informed him that his clients would have to pick up the meat from Clyde's store or pick it up at an inspected meat plant. As a result, Clyde bought "Chick" Belfiore's meat plant in 1964. The building was built in 1961 and located at Thirty-seventh and Inca Streets. With the plant in operation, Clyde could now process and deliver his product anywhere in town.

From 1964 to 1996, Clyde continued to make sausage using his father's family recipe. In 1996, he sold "Clyde's" to Mike Tricarico, the current owner of Clyde's Sausage & Ground Beef Company, Inc., still located on Inca Street in Denver.

Clyde Rocco Archer and his wife Theda (whom he married in 1971) remain active in Colorado's Italian American community. In addition to being members of Denver's Potenza Lodge (an Italian American organization founded in 1899), they also participate in community events including the annual Rocky Mountain Italian American Golf and Bocce tournament.

Clyde R. Archer (right) and Mike Tricarico inside Clyde's Sausage, Denver, by Dawn DeAno, 2006. CIAPA Archive. PCCLICPC001

Gerald Anthony "Tony" DeBell

Tony DeBell, the youngest child of Gaetano and Concetta DiBello, grew up on his family farm north of Regis College.

In addition to his chores, he attended public school—which included Catholic religious education by the Jesuit Fathers at Regis—and also found time to play baseball with his brothers, in his father Gaetano's pasture. Of his grade school graduation, he recalled:

> The graduating class consisted of only eight pupils, four of whom were girls. I particularly remember how each of us held a bouquet consisting of two dozen crimson carnations. Our class colors were crimson and gold. It was quite customary in those days to wear short pants and I must have made quite a picture holding a bouquet of flowers. I was chosen valedictorian of the group, which couldn't have much merit since the group was so small.[36]

Of his high school years, Tony recalled:

Tony and Victoria (Salmonase) DeBell, Denver, 1935. CIAPA Archive. Courtesy Theda and Clyde R. Archer. PCCLI2431

> My high school years were the most eventful for they afforded opportunities in vocational as well as formal pursuits. I was highly interested in manual training and here I had my first opportunity to shape from wood, articles I wanted. Having a love and desire to learn to play some stringed musical instrument, I seized the opportunity to make from a cigar box and a block of wood a fairly suitable ukulele. I could not afford to buy the manufactured product at that time.[37]

Tony's father died in 1925 and his mother became ill while Tony was in high school. As a result, Tony left school to help out at home. During the fall and winter, he:

> ...was able to earn extra money by trapping muskrats within a radius of twenty miles of my home. I arose at four in the morning to cover various sections of swamp land in which I had trap lines. I commuted to these places in an old Model T, getting back in time for a day's work at home. I spent the evenings skinning out the carcasses.[38]

In the late 1920s, Tony continued to work in the produce business, while also growing plants for commercial sale. In 1935, he married his first wife, Victoria Salmonese, who died from complications after giving birth to their daughter Geraldine. In 1941, he married his second wife

Rose Ficco and together the couple had two children: Charles, who tragically died at age three of kidney failure, and Glenn David DeBell.

After serving in World War II, Tony returned to Denver and the truck gardening business, dealing and hauling produce. He also did mechanical work of various types, including fixing appliances. Tony DeBell died on September 18, 1957.

Guerrieri Bros. business card, c. 1890. CIAPA Archive. Courtesy Carol Tucker Andrix. PCCLI5951

Guerrieri

The Guerrieri Brothers

In 1872, the Guerrieri brothers—Vincenzo "Vincent," Francesco "Frank," and Giuseppe "Joseph"—immigrated to America from Calvello, Italy, with their parents Pasquale and Maria Theresa.[39] The family first settled in St. Louis. Four years later, Vincent and Frank moved to Colorado, followed by their parents and their brother Joseph in 1877.[40]

After working as miners and musicians in Leadville, the brothers settled in Denver around 1890 and were playing music together under the names the Guerrieri Brothers String Trio, Guerrieri Bros. Orchestra, and Guerrieri Bros.' Band. Frank and Vincent played the violin while Joseph played the harp.[41] Successful in music, the brothers also pursued other business ventures. After attending Denver University Law School, Vincent became a notary public and real estate dealer, was active in politics, and served as an interpreter for Denver's Italian population. Frank and Joseph started the Colorado Wine and Liquor Company at 2155 Blake Street. The business did well and in 1895, Frank and his wife Maria built a house at 1650 Pennsylvania Street. Certainly influenced by Italian architectural designs—perhaps to recreate a piece of Italy in Denver—the Italianate-style house

Guerrieri Family, front row, left to right: Maria Theresa, Vincent, and Pasquale Guerrieri; back row, left to right: Joseph and Frank, Leadville, Colorado, 1880. CIAPA Archive. Courtesy Carol Tucker Andrix. PCCLI5953

was a reflection of middle-class life in Denver in the early twentieth century. In 1902, the Guerrieri family sold the house to Frank DeCunto, who in 1919 sold it to David Serafini.[42] Frank Guerrieri died in Denver in 1924 at the age of sixty-three, followed by Joseph, who died in 1932 at the age of seventy-one, and Vincent, who died in 1949 at the age of eighty-five.

Mangini

Siro and Josephine (Capelli) Mangini

Siro Mangini was born in the northern Italian province of Pavia in 1839. The descendant of merchants and violin craftsmen, he married Josephine Capelli in Genoa, Italy, in 1865.[43] A year later, the couple set sail for New York, where Josephine's brother Eugene lived. After a short time there, they moved to St. Louis. Around 1872, at the suggestion of Josephine's brother, Angelo Capelli, the couple moved to Denver, where Siro peddled fruit. Around 1880, he opened his first restaurant and hotel. After that business burned, he opened Mangini's Place in 1882 at Twenty-second and Larimer (known by many as El Bronco Bar, which closed in the 1990s).[44]

Siro Mangini's Place (Siro is at left, in vest), the Christopher Columbus Hall at 2219 Larimer, Denver, c. 1900. CIAPA Archive. Courtesy John Edward McEahern. PCCLI1355

Mangini's Place operated as a saloon and also offered a selection of Italian imports for purchase. The family, including the ten Mangini children—Anthony Charles, Louis Angelo, Frank Vincent, Mary Benedicta, Philomena, Frederick Angelo, Clara, George, John Siro, and Adelina Margarita—lived over the saloon.[45] Siro, who spoke excellent French, German, English, and Italian, took care of the day-to-day business while Josephine helped with the bookkeeping. Like other families, the Mangini family had a routine:

> Each Tuesday was washday and the women-folk spent the day in the basement with laundry. On this day the cooking chores were assumed by Siro who delighted the children by preparing his specialty, gnocchi.[46]

In the basement of the saloon, known as Christopher Columbus Hall, the Mangini family hosted dances on Saturday nights with their many friends joining them in food, drink, and song. Additionally, each year, Siro hosted a stag party for his birthday. Guests included Adolph Zang, Adolph Coors, and men from the Neff Brewery and Lammer's Bottling Works.[47] Siro Mangini died in Denver in 1907, followed by Josephine, who died in 1935.

Siro Mangini's Place, the Christopher Columbus Hall with Frank Vincent Mangini (third child born to Siro and Josephine Mangini) behind the bar, c. 1900. CIAPA Archive. Courtesy Tom Noel and Adelina (Mangini) Joy. PCCLI1366

Mazza

Frank Mazza

Frank Mazza was born in Italy in 1850. At the age of twenty, he came to America. After working in New Mexico, he settled in Denver. By 1882, he had opened a saloon, and four years later he bought a macaroni factory that also dealt in imported groceries.[48] At Mazza's business, F. Mazza & Company, Italians also had access to a post office, bank, notary public, and travel agent.[49]

Christopher Columbus Hall business card, Siro Mangini, Proprietor, c. 1900. CIAPA Archive. Gift John Edward McEahern. 2007.3.2

Growth 1870–1879

F. Mazza & Company macaroni factory, Denver, 1900. From Marcello Gandolfo, Gli Italiani nel Colorado, 1899–1900, Denver, 1900. PCCLI1047

Frank and his wife Madeline were married in 1883 and had four children together.[50] Active in the Italian community, Frank founded and promoted Denver's first Italian Society, the Unione e Fratellanza Italiana, organized in 1883. At the time of its establishment, the society had both northern and southern Italians as members. Its leaders included Luigi Mosconi, Joseph Turre, and Siro Mangini.[51] Frank also helped found the San Rocco Society, the Club Italo Americano Politico Indipendente, the Italian Colony Catholic Chapel Association, and the Società Bersaglieri Principe di Napoli.

A Closer Look
The Bersaglieri Society in Denver

Members of the Bersaglieri Society in Denver, left to right: Prospero Frazzini, Salvatore Michele Villano, Frank Mazza, and Michele Taddonio, Denver, c. 1905. CIAPA Archive. Courtesy Michael C. and Clair Villano. PCCLI0027

Founded on August 4, 1889, the Società Bersaglieri Principe di Napoli, or the Bersaglieri Society in Denver, was organized by a group of southern Italian men living in the Denver-metro area. Named after the famous Italian military unit, the Bersaglieri, the organization offered members death and sick benefits, aid in finding work, and help learning English and understanding legal documents. The Society also served to unify Italian immigrants and their descendants through social activities and events, becoming in many ways an extended family for its members.

In 1901, with Frank Mazza as president, the organization had seventy-eight members. Activities of the group included regular meetings and marching with their own band in public parades during which they wore their Society uniforms.[52]

Ruoti/Ruote/Ruota

Rocco and Arcangela (Rivela) Ruote

In 1877, Rocco Felice Pasquale Ruote (spelled Ruoti in his Potenza marriage record and Ruota in other documents), a *contadino*, married Arcangela Rivela in Potenza, Italy. Rocco was twenty-seven and Arcangela twenty-one; both the bride and the groom were illiterate.[53] Shortly after their marriage, they immigrated to America, stopping first in New York before settling in Denver in 1879. Their first child, Mike, was baptized at Sacred Heart Church in Denver in 1882. Six more children were born to the couple: Rosa, Mary, Annie, Jennie, Maggie, and Antonio "Tony."

In 1883, Rocco and Arcangela purchased land in Jefferson County near Forty-first and Harlan Street for $350. The couple lived on the property and Rocco farmed the land. In 1904, Rocco became a United States citizen. He died in 1939, at the age of ninety-four.

In 1926, the Ruotes' son Tony and his wife Elizabeth "Lizzie" Benallo purchased the forty-three-acre Ruote family farm, operating it until 1951, when Tony sold all but three-fourths of an acre, where the family home remains today. That same year, Tony purchased 168 acres of farmland near the town of Platteville, Colorado, which he farmed until his retirement in 1974. According to Tony's 1985 obituary, which appeared in the *Rocky Mountain News*, he "was a pioneer in the state in growing Colorado Pascal Celery." In 2001, Tony's daughter Elizabeth (Ruote) Pelegrin purchased the land in Jefferson County, living in the original family home until her death in January of 2006.

Rocco Ruote, c. 1904. CIAPA Archive. Courtesy Elizabeth (Ruote) Pelegrin. PCCLI4940

Arcangela (Rivela) Ruote, 1904. CIAPA Archive. Courtesy Elizabeth (Ruote) Pelegrin. PCCLI4941

Sbarbaro

Giovanni "John" C. and Louisa M. Sbarbaro

John C. Sbarbaro was born in Ohio in 1849. Louisa M. Sbarbaro was born in Italy in December of 1853 and immigrated to the United States in 1857. In 1871, John C. and Louisa Sbarbaro were married in St. Louis, Missouri, where their first child, Olivia, was born, followed by Theodore and

John L. Sbarbaro. In 1879, the family moved to Denver, where John and Louisa's fourth child, Dalia, was born, followed by Mabel, Louis A., Edward, Louisa, and Hazel Sbarbaro.[54]

In 1880, John opened a fish and oyster house with Louis Mosconi in downtown Denver.[55] The two remained partners until 1890, when John opened the Sbarbaro & Company Oyster House on Larimer Street with John L. Retlia.[56]

In 1889, Louisa Sbarbaro and Clara (Cunio) Cella, as part of the Italian Ladies Committee, spearheaded an Italian Fair in Denver in the Exposition Building at old River Front Park. The fair raised money for a fund that supported charitable causes, such as Our Lady of Mount Carmel Catholic Church. Around 1920, the fund was liquidated and the remaining money used to help build the Queen of Heaven Orphanage.[57]

About 1910, John died, leaving the family business to Louisa and their children. The 1920 Denver census lists Louisa M. Sbarbaro as the proprietor of a fish and oyster house. By 1922, the Sbarbaro children were running the family businesses, including the Blake Street establishment, which was described as "one of the most elegant oyster and fish houses anywhere in the West."[58]

1889 ticket for a fair sponsored by the Italian Ladies Committee, 1889. CIAPA Archive. Courtesy Our Lady of Mount Carmel. PCCLI5315

Turre

Giuseppe "Joseph" Turre

Joseph Turre, the son of Genovese parents, was born in St. Louis in 1851 and served in the American Civil War. In 1876, he came to Colorado and settled in Central City, where he worked as a miner for three years.[59] Later, he moved to Leadville, where he worked in the hotel and saloon industry with business partner Rocco Luigi Barra. After a short stay in Leadville, Joseph returned to Denver and married Beatrice Cuneo of St. Louis. In the 1880s, he opened Turre & Cuneo, a saloon and liquor store at Seventeenth and Wazee Streets with his brother-in-law George Cuneo. The business operated for twenty-one years, closing in 1905.[60]

In addition to his business endeavors, Turre was involved in many Italian societies including the first Italian society in

Joseph Turre, 1900. From Marcello Gandolfo, Gli Italiani nel Colorado, 1899-1900, Denver, 1900. PCCLI5961

J. Turre building at 1316 Twenty-first Street, Denver, by Tom Noel, 1977. Joseph Turre built the J. Turre Building at Twenty-first and Larimer Streets in 1880. Unique because of its unusual corbelled cornice and metal-capped turret with the original owner's name integrated, the building, which originally housed Turre's saloon and store, still stands today. The building is a reminder of the influence of Italians in Colorado as a merchant class.[61] *Courtesy Denver Public Library, Western History Collection. X-24859*

Denver, Fratellanza Italiana, for which he served as vice president. Joseph Turre died in Denver in 1909, followed by his wife Beatrice, who died in 1930.

Vignola

Angelo and Arcangela (Losasso) Vignola

Angelo Vignola—some Vignola families later used the spelling "Vinnola"—came to America in 1873 with Gerardo, Genero, and Gaetano Losasso (in historical and family documents, the name is sometimes spelled LoSasso, Lassaso, or LaSasso). He was the only one from his immediate family to leave his home in Potenza, Italy. He settled first in New York with the Losasso brothers, later following them to Colorado in 1878.[62]

In 1880, Angelo and Gaetano Losasso bought land together in Denver for $1,500 from Gaetano's brothers, Gerardo and Genero Losasso. In 1881, Angelo had a double wedding with Gaetano at Sacred Heart in Denver. Angelo married Arcangela Losasso—born in Potenza in 1861—a cousin of Gaetano. Gaetano Losasso married Josephine Tramutola. According to a September 20, 1881, *Rocky Mountain News* article:

A double marriage ceremony was celebrated in the Church of Sacred Heart, on Sunday morning. Rev. Father Guida officiating. The couples Losasso and Vignola were accompanied by Italian Vice Consul Signor A. Capelli, with his wife, and a large number of countrymen. The bridal party and their friend were driven from the church in four large open carriages to Signor Capelli's residence, where, after partaking of some fine Italian wines and decking themselves with flowers from the vice-council's garden, the happy couples left for their residences, two miles beyond the city.

Messrs. Peck, Crane, Bosson and Johns of Windsor, took part in the enjoyment of the occasion, and by their presence added much to the pleasure of the other guests. Their Italian friends in this city send many congratulations to the newly-wedded pairs.

Angelo and Arcangela Vignola had fourteen children. Daughter Adelina Lena (Vignola) Trollo, born in 1898, was the only child to survive. Angelo Vignola died in Denver in 1923, followed by Arcangela, who died in Denver in 1936.

A Closer Look
Sacred Heart

In 1879, Bishop Machebeuf established Denver's third Catholic parish and purchased a site for a new church on Larimer Street. Sacred Heart, the city's oldest continuously operating church, opened on April 25, 1880.

Its opening coincided with the completion of Denver's first two railroads. Sacred Heart served Irish and Italian immigrants who worked for the Kansas Pacific and Denver Pacific lines. Its first pastor was Father John Baptiste Guida, an Italian Jesuit priest from the southern Italian province of Campania who arrived in Denver in 1879.[63] Shortly after his arrival, he was assigned to Sacred Heart by Bishop Machebeuf.

In addition to serving newcomers—including Hispanics in recent years—the church has been a refuge for well-known citizens of Denver, including Elizabeth "Baby Doe" Tabor.[64]

Sacred Heart and its Jesuit-run school served one of the fastest growing parishes in the city. But over time, the neighborhood and the church deteriorated. Thanks to John Casey—a former Sacred Heart schoolboy who came back as its pastor in 1948—the building was rehabilitated. Casey's successors and generations of parishioners have ensured the continuance of Sacred Heart's proud legacy.[65]

Vitullo/Veto

Pasquale Vitullo

Born in southern Italy, Pasquale Vitullo immigrated to America as a boy. In 1870, he settled in Denver and bought land near Union Station to garden. He is credited with being one of the first truck gardeners in Denver. According to his funeral notice in the *Rocky Mountain News*, published on June 22, 1921, Pasquale Vitullo, "one of the oldest and most prominent Italians in Denver...was a pioneer in raising fruit and vegetables and it is said that he more than any other one man created the vicinity of Denver as a vegetable, berry and fruit district."

In 1880, Pasquale and his family moved to Thirty-second and Navajo Street—where Pagliacci's Restaurant is located today—in north Denver, where he lived until his death in 1921 at the age of eighty-three.[66]

Pasquale and his wife Vincenza had six children: Mary, Sidney, Michael, George, Anthony, and William Vitullo. By 1920, their children had changed their last name to "Veto."

Mary (Vitullo) Fallico Zarlengo and Francesco "Frank" Fallico

Born in Denver in 1881 to Pasquale and Vincenza Vitullo, Mary Vitullo married Francesco "Frank" Fallico in 1895. Frank was born in the southern Italian region of Calabria in 1871 and came to Denver at the age of fifteen with his older brother Salvatore Fallico. Frank and Mary had five children: Chuck, Peter, Eva, Henrietta, and Helen.[67]

In 1904, Frank and Mary Fallico divorced. In 1905, Mary married Daniel Zarlengo and began a new life, without her five children from her previous marriage to Frank. After marrying Daniel, Mary remained in Denver, where their daughter Ruby was born in 1907, followed by a son Henry in 1909. In time, the Fallico children were included in activities at the Zarlengo home.

After his divorce from Mary, Frank Fallico was left to care for five children and was forced to put the girls in the Queen of Heaven Orphanage and the boys in Saint

Mary (Vitullo) Fallico Zarlengo (right) and unidentified women, Denver, c. 1895. CIAPA Archive. Courtesy Irene Fanning. PCCLI5563

Growth 1870–1879

Clara's Orphanage. Eventually, Frank remarried and brought his new wife Isabella and all five children home to 3744 Navajo Street in north Denver. To support his family, Frank worked two jobs. He did well for himself, eventually owning a city block on Thirty-eighth Avenue between Navajo and Mariposa Streets in north Denver. On the property stood the family home, a barn for Frank's horses, the Fallico filling station, a garage in which he stored gasoline for the filling station, the Fallico grocery store, and seven rental properties. Additionally, he received the exclusive contract to haul coke (fuel) for the Denver Gas & Electric Company (later called the Public Service Company of Colorado), which he did with his own fleet of five trucks. Later, he worked for the city of Denver as the market master of the Denargo Market. Mary (Vitullo) Fallico Zarlengo died in Denver in 1936. Frank Fallico died in Denver in 1955.

Fallico family, Denver, c. 1910. Front row, left to right: Helen, Eva, and Henrietta Fallico; seated, left to right: Frank and Isabella Fallico; back row, left to right: Peter and Chuck Fallico. CIAPA Archive. Courtesy Irene Fanning. PCCLI5311

Irene Genevieve (Fallico) Falbo Fanning

Irene Genevieve (Fallico) Falbo Fanning, the granddaughter of Mary (Vitullo) Fallico Zarlengo and Frank Fallico, was born in Denver on July 30, 1920. One of three children born to Peter Paul Fallico Sr. and Mary Ann (Lucci) Fallico, her mother was born in Philadelphia to Peter and

Fallico truck fleet in front of the Public Service Company building, Denver, c. 1925. Left to right: Frank Fallico, Pete Fallico, Harry Wall, unidentified man, Chuck Fallico, unidentified man. CIAPA Archive. Courtesy Irene Fanning. PCCLI5303

Marie (Russano) Lucci. Irene's mother came to Denver after her father died, growing up in the Queen of Heaven Orphanage in Denver where she was privileged to be tutored by Mother Cabrini. Mary began working at Brecht's Candies when she met Eva, Henrietta, and Helen Fallico, and made a match with their brother Peter, the second child born to Mary (Vitullo) and Frank Fallico. In 1918, Peter and Mary Ann Fallico were married at Our Lady of Mount Carmel Church. After their marriage, Peter worked for his father, hauling coke for the Public Service Company of Colorado, and then ran the Fallico Gas Station. Later he was a molder in the foundry of American Manganese Steel Company. In addition to caring for the children, Mary Ann Fallico worked as a power sewing machine operator for the Baily Manufacturing Company for many years.

Wedding portrait, Victor and Irene (Fallico) Falbo, 1945, left to right: Genevieve Rich, Al Rich, Helen (Mancinelli) Eichler, ring bearer Eddie Falbo, Peter Mazza, Irene and Victor Falbo, flower girl Geraldine Falbo, Virginia DiTirro, John Canacari, and Emily Murphy. CIAPA Archive. Courtesy Irene Fanning. PCCLI3147

Growing up in north Denver, Irene attended Bryant-Webster School, Horace Mann Junior High School, and North High School from which she graduated in 1938. In 1942, she graduated Phi Beta Kappa from the University of Denver with a double-major in English and Sociology. That same year, she became engaged to her childhood friend, Victor Falbo, and the couple planned to marry in June of 1942. Their plans were cut short when Victor was drafted in World War II. In 1945, when Victor came home on leave from the service, the couple was finally married at Our Lady of Mount Carmel Church.

After their wedding, Victor returned to the service and Irene returned to work at the Office of Price Administration. After the war, Irene worked for the Home Builders Association and earned her master's degree. She worked as an executive, agency manager, president of the Professional Insurance Agents of Colorado, and national director and regional vice president of the Society of Chartered Property and Casualty Underwriters.

In 1985, Irene's husband Victor died of cancer. In 1991, she married Joseph Fanning. Today, Irene remains active in Denver's Italian American community, including belonging to Our Lady of Mount Carmel Church and the Mount Carmel Altar and Rosary Society.

Chapter 3
Influx
1880–1894

Between 1880 and 1920, the number of Italians immigrating to the United States rose to a level never equaled before or since. Millions of central and southern Europeans crossed the Atlantic in this "Great Migration." In 1888 alone, 205,000 Italians came to the United States.

Migrants from Italy's southern regions—Abruzzi and Molise, Calabria, Apulia, Sicily, Campania, and Basilicata—vastly outnumbered those from northern Italy. The southern immigrants were seeking relief from economic and social strife in their divided homeland. After unifying, Italy had shifted its resources to the industrial North, as southern farmers paid steep taxes and rents. Working in almost feudal conditions, farmers could rarely own land and were often vulnerable to a landlord's demands. Many southern Italians immigrated because they had no choice. Others came west seeking education and employment opportunities for themselves and their families.

Many newcomers found work in Colorado's railroads, mines, mills, and smelters, while some worked as peddlers and day laborers. The influx of southern Italians—often poorer and less educated than the Italians already settled in the West—created tensions within growing communities in towns such as Denver, Pueblo, and Trinidad. Northern and southern Italians often did not speak the same dialect, celebrated different feast days, and scarcely recognized themselves as being from the same country. Churches, clubs, and ethnic neighborhoods helped Italians negotiate their differences and forge an identity in the face of growing hostility to immigrants in Colorado and the rest of the nation.

Opposite: Coal miners coming from work, Trinidad, Colorado, c. 1890. 84.193.3

A Closer Look
Why They Left

According to the U.S. Census, fewer than 4,000 foreign-born Italians lived in the United States in 1850. By 1890, there were over 180,000 foreign-born Italians in America, and by 1920, that number had increased to over 1.5 million.

Before 1880, most Italian immigrants came from northern Italy. They were affluent, educated, and in the United States by choice. Beginning in 1880, immigration patterns shifted. During the Great Migration (1880–1920), most Italian immigrants came from southern Italy. In general, they were uneducated peasant farmers or unskilled laborers who left because they had to.

The unification of Italy caused the shift. While northern Italy prospered under unification, the area south of Rome or *Mezzogiorno* suffered. Railroads, steel mills, and seaports strengthened the North's industries, but the resources that fueled that growth—including labor and materials—were taken from the South.

Family sharing living space with a horse. From Rocco Triani, Potenza e Il Suo Dialetto, *1990. EX.ITAL.83*

In the South, 80 percent of Italians relied on agriculture for food and income. The South's struggling economy worsened as soil erosion caused by deforestation decreased the availability of farmland. Government policies, including the trans-Alpine railroad which opened in 1885, made Italian agriculture vulnerable to foreign competition.

Poor living conditions added to the exodus. In the late 1800s, many southern Italians lived in single-story huts with one room that served as a kitchen, bedroom, and, for many families, a stable. A family of modest means ate meat twice a year: chicken for Christmas and roasted kid (baby goat) for Easter.[68]

Abbiati

Albino Abbiati

The 1848 political upheaval in Italy forced Albino Abbiati's father, Ernesto, to leave his family behind and immigrate to America. In 1855, Ernesto sent for his wife and children, including Albino (born in Venice, Italy, in 1846), to join him in New York. A descendant of artists, including Charles II's court painter Fillippo Abbiati, Albino later returned to Italy to study at the Academy of Fine Arts in Milan.[69]

After completing his education and serving in the Italian military, as required by the 1871 Italian Draft Law, Albino was hired to oversee the decorative work of fifty men on the Palace of Rao Pragmalji in India. Here, Albino learned firsthand the ornamental decorating skills of the Far East, later used in the decoration of theaters, churches, civic buildings, and fine mansions in Denver. In the 1880s, he returned to New York, where he created realistic scenery and props for the Metropolitan Opera before moving to Denver in 1890 to decorate the boxes of the Broadway Theater.[70] He then went to Pueblo, Colorado, where he was commissioned to work on the Mineral Palace. His prior experience served him well. His designs for the Mineral Palace included two huge prop-like plaster statues of the Silver Queen and King Coal, along with a mechanical nymph that picked gold nuggets from a spurting fountain.[71]

Projects at the Tabor Grand Opera, the Brown Palace Hotel, and the South Broadway Christian Church followed. The decorative plaster and woodwork of the church are the only known examples of Albino Abbiati's work remaining in Colorado.

Married for thirty-two years to Mary Hyde, Albino Abbiati had three children—Beatrice, Bianca, and Theodore—all of whom were living in Colorado at the time of Albino's death in 1909.[72]

Albino Abbiati, by Bellsmith Studio, Denver, c. 1890. Gift Jerry Gates. 2006.24.3

Mary (Hyde) Abbiati, c. 1915. Gift Jerry Gates. 2006.24.7

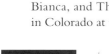

Acierno

Angelo and Antonia (Marino) Acierno

Angelo Raffaele Acierno, the son of Rocco and Rosa (Caggiano) Acierno, was born in Potenza, Italy, in 1857. A twenty-four-year-old *contadino*, Angelo married sixteen-year-old Antonia Marino in 1881.[73] By 1882, he had immigrated alone to America to settle in Kansas City, Missouri. The following year, Angelo and Antonia's first child, a

Influx 1880–1894

Antonia (Marino) Acierno at her produce stand (Acierno Produce Company) on Fifteenth Street between Market and Larimer, Denver, c. 1910. CIAPA Archive. Courtesy George and Ruth Mazzotti. PCCLI2374

son named Rocco, was born in Potenza. Finally, in 1885, Angelo was able to bring Antonia and the baby to Kansas City, where daughter Rosina was born in 1886. Antonia bore twenty more children in the years that followed, only eight of whom survived: Michele, Genri, Annie, Gerardo, Pasquale, Salvatore, Theresa, and Louisa.

Around 1890, Angelo moved the family to Denver, where they found a farm for sale in the Bottoms on Fox Street and bought it for $200—a bargain price considering the crops had already been planted. They also ran a successful produce stand at the City Market on Fifteenth Street, where they sold to local businesses and merchants, including Denver's peddlers who sold produce from horse-drawn wagons in neighborhoods throughout the city.[74] Angelo Acierno died in Denver in 1931, followed by Antonia, who died in 1935.[75]

A CLOSER LOOK
The Bottoms

The Bottoms, an area lying between Union Station and the South Platte River in lower downtown Denver, served as the first neighborhood for many Italians who settled here in the 1880s.

After the Denver Pacific and Kansas Pacific completed rail yards on Wewatta Street and after the construction of Union Station in 1881, the remaining farmland was sold for residential development. The first homes, small and affordable wood-framed houses, were built in 1873. Hotels, banks, grocery stores, and saloons followed.

Immigrants settled in the Bottoms to be near their jobs—many worked at the local rail yards, lumber mills, and stores. Others found work as day laborers, urban farmers, or peddlers. By the 1890s, some saved enough money to move west across the South Platte River to "Little Italy" within the Highland neighborhood.

In 1923, a flood destroyed many of the poorly built homes and forced residents to move away. By then, the area was already becoming more industrial. Flour mills, mining and smelting supply companies, warehouses, and more transportation-related industries crowded out the remaining families. By the 1940s, almost all of the original residents had moved.

Today, the Bottoms is being revitalized as developers fix up existing commercial and industrial buildings and build new high-rise condos and office buildings. Union Station's redevelopment promises to make the area a thriving transportation hub once more.

Postcard showing the North Bottoms after the flood of 1912. Published by H. R. Schmidt & Company, Denver. CIAPA Archive. Courtesy Tom Noel. PCCLI1362

Ralph Acierno

The grandson of Angelo and Antonia Acierno, Ralph Acierno was born in 1925 to Salvatore and Adeline (DeAndrea) Acierno. His father was a farmer, produce peddler, Denver street sweeper, and later a fuel deliveryman. His mother Adeline, born in 1904, was the daughter of Italian immigrants Felicio and Giacinta (DiManna) DeAndrea. His parents were married at Our Lady of Mount Carmel Church in 1927.[76] After their marriage, the couple moved in with Salvatore's parents, who lived at 3507 Mariposa. They raised their children (Ralph, Felix, and Delores) in the house and remained there until the 1980s.

When asked about his grandmother Antonia, Ralph Acierno recalled a woman with an imposing figure—nearly six feet tall—who was hard-working and strict. A businesswoman, she would tell Ralph, "buy ground, buy house."[77]

Ralph Acierno, by Dawn DeAno, Denver, 2004. CIAPA Archive. PCCLICPC005

Wedding portrait, Joseph Victor and Theresa (Acierno) Mazzotti (parents of George Victor Mazzotti Sr.) with attendants (back right), Pasquale "Paskey" Acierno and Lucille Mazzotti, 1919. CIAPA Archive. Courtesy George and Ruth Mazzotti. PCCLI2365

He also fondly recalled his grandmother's statue of Saint Rocco, which she brought to Denver from Potenza, Italy, and kept in her bedroom, a candle always lit next to it. For years, Ralph kept the same statue in his bedroom with a candle burning twenty-four hours a day, in memory of his grandmother.

In 1945, Ralph met his future wife Johnnie Miller while working at the Bowman Biscuit Company. That same year, Johnnie and Ralph were married. Together they had five children: Salvatore "Tony," Ralph, Daniel, Thomas, and Adeline. To support his family, Ralph worked in the bread business for twenty-eight years, including driving a truck for Roxie Carbone's Italian bakery. He also ran a grocery store at Twenty-ninth and Irving and worked in the restaurant business for twenty years, including owning his own restaurant, Cugino's, in Wheat Ridge, which he sold in 1990.

In his later years, Ralph Acierno enjoyed visiting with his family and friends, including talking on the telephone to his sister every day, participating in traditional Italian dinners on Sunday, and hosting the traditional Italian Christmas Eve meal with his children. Ralph Acierno died on January 8, 2008.

George Victor Mazzotti

George Victor Mazzotti, the son of Joseph Victor and Theresa (Acierno) Mazzotti and the grandson of Antonia and Angelo Acierno, was born on September 2, 1922. His mother was born in Denver in 1902 and his father in 1895 in the Consenza province in the Calabria region of southern Italy. His father came to America in 1899 with his parents Francesco "Frank" and Concetta Marie (DiFilippo) Mazzotti.[78]

One of five children, George Victor Mazzotti was raised in the Welby area. In 1936, after completing his education at the North Washington School, he continued working on his family's produce farm in Welby. In 1942, he joined the United States Navy, returning to Colorado in 1945. After the war, he joined other Welby farmers in starting a volunteer fire department. He served as a volunteer until 1964, when the North

Washington Fire Department officially hired him. He retired in 1996 as department chief.

In 1949, George married Ruth Shaball. The couple had two children: George Victor Jr. and Catherine Marie Mazzotti. Today, George and Ruth remain in Welby, Colorado, and are still very active in their community.

A Closer Look
Welby and Assumption Church

In 1908, construction began on the short-lived Denver, Laramie & Northwestern Railroad.[79] Projected to run from Denver to Seattle via Laramie and Yellowstone National Park, the line spawned little communities along the route. One of them was Welby, a farm town nine miles north of Denver that attracted Italian families. Eventually engulfed by its larger neighbor, Welby outlasted the railroad and is still home to a small Italian American community.

In 1909, the Denver-Laramie Realty Company—a subsidiary of the railroad—laid out the twenty-block town.[80] New homes filled up as Italians who once worked in mining

Ruth and George Mazzotti Sr., by Dawn DeAno, Welby, 2006. CIAPA Archive. PCCLICPC0040

Group in front of the Welby Merchandise Company (the first store in Welby, originally owned by Dominic Rotolo and later the Cosimi Family), c.1920. CIAPA Archive. Courtesy Mary (DiLuzio) DeBell. PCCLI0459

and railroading ventured into vegetable farming. Their farms were initially small (about five acres) and produced green onions, carrots, and Pascal Celery—a blanched variety of celery popular at Thanksgiving and Christmas. By the 1920s, more than 300 Italian families were doing small-scale "truck farming" in the Welby area.[81]

Welby's tight-knit Italian community gathered for religious services at Assumption Church, which opened in 1912 and still serves current and former Welby residents.[82] Their unity had economic benefits as well. Truck farmers came together to form the Vegetable Growers Association, an organization that set vegetable prices to ensure reasonably equal profits. Until the late 1940s, the Welby truck farms produced much of the produce sold at Denver's City Market and Denargo Market.

By the 1950s, grocery store chains, the trucking industry, and the development of Adams County land had pushed the truck-farm era around Welby into decline. Although Assumption's high school closed in 1952, the church still brings the community together through religious services, an annual bazaar, and spaghetti dinners.

Violet (Acierno) Astuno

Angelo and Antonia Acierno's granddaughter Violet was born in 1938 to Pasquale and Helen (Mazzotti) Acierno. Her father, who worked for the city of Denver, was born in Denver in 1899 and her mother was born in Scranton, Pennsylvania, in 1902. Helen's parents Francesco "Frank" and Concetta Marie (DiFilippo) Mazzotti came to America in 1899.[83]

Violet grew up in north Denver, where she lived with her parents and four siblings at 3515 Mariposa, in a house next door to her Acierno grandparents. Many aunts and uncles also

Rocco and Violet (Acierno) Astuno on their wedding day, 1956. CIAPA Archive. Courtesy Rocco and Violet Astuno. PCCLI5135

lived on the same street. According to Violet, the house was small and like a "shotgun," with one room following another, first the living room, then a bedroom, another bedroom, and the kitchen.[84]

At a young age, Violet went to work for the Sally Ann Creamery on Navajo Street. There she learned how to make milkshakes, count money, and deal with customers, a majority of whom lived in the north Denver neighborhood. She then went to work for her brother at the Country

Gentlemen Market at Thirty-eighth and Sheridan, where a cousin introduced her to her future husband, Rocco Astuno. They married in 1956 and have three daughters: Roxanne, Patricia, and Denise.

Aiello

Camillo Aiello

John Aiello brought all four of his brothers to southern Colorado from Calabria, Italy, by working as a water boy for the Mexican International Railroad Company. John, Charles, Frank, and Camillo lived in Berwind and Emilio lived in nearby Valdez. John owned a saloon and store managed by his brother Camillo and also built a dry goods store on Commercial Street in Trinidad.[85] All of the brothers bought land in Las Animas County and invested in two mercantile companies and in the International State Bank. They also participated in community activities.

In 1909, Camillo Aiello married Olga Bortolini, a native of the Treviso region of northern Italy. Olga came to America in 1905 to live with her sister Rosina (Bortolini) Albi and Rosina's husband Dr. Rudolph Albi in Denver.

Aiello Brothers, left to right: Emilio, Frank, Camillo, Charles, and John, Trinidad, Colorado, c. 1915. CIAPA Archive. Courtesy Claudia Carbone. PCCLI4360

Aiello Mercantile in Berwind, c. 1910. Loan Claudia Carbone. IL.2006.5.16

Influx 1880–1894

Aiello Family, left to right: Serge, Ada, Olga, and Gino Aiello, Naples, c. 1929. CIAPA Archive. Courtesy Claudia Carbone. PCCLI2670

Wedding of John and Ada (Aiello) Carbone, 1936, left to right: Vince Pigotti, Rose Janne, John, Ada, Millie Albi (sister of John and wife of Fred Albi), and Serge Aiello (brother of Ada). CIAPA Archive. Courtesy Claudia Carbone. PCCLI2206

After their marriage at Sacred Heart Catholic Church in Denver, Olga and Camillo returned to Berwind.[86]

Misfortune struck the family in April 1920 when Camillo Aiello died from a gunshot wound. No one ever discovered who shot him or why, but the family believes that Colorado Fuel & Iron (CF&I) was responsible for a raid on the saloon.[87] CF&I owned the general stores and markets in their company towns where it held workers hostage to high prices by paying them with company script usable only in company stores. Aiello's saloon provided a safe haven for workers to meet secretly to organize, posing a threat to CF&I and local law enforcement that prohibited assembly as a means of discouraging union building. After national prohibition went into effect on January 1, 1920, the company may have arranged the raid on the saloon.

After Camillo's death, his brothers remained in southern Colorado and prospered. Years later, the town of Trinidad named a street in their honor. Camillo's wife Olga, a widow at thirty-six, returned to Naples, Italy, with their three children: Ada, Serge, and Gino. Around 1931, she and the children returned to Colorado, settling in Denver to be near her sister Rosina Albi. Olga remained in Denver until her death in 1949.

Giovanni "John" Antonio and Ada (Aiello) Carbone

Educated in Italy, Ada Aiello, the daughter of Camillo and Olga Aiello, started teaching French and Italian at North High School in 1931. In 1936, she married John Carbone, president of A. Carbone & Company. John and Ada had three children: John Jr., Claudia, and William.

John and Ada participated in and supported many events in Denver's Italian community. Ada was a founding member of Il Circolo Italiano, a cultural and social Italian organization still active in Colorado today. In addition to teaching Italian to members, she also arranged special events for the group, including bringing a young opera singer named Luciano Pavarotti to Denver. John Carbone died in Denver in 1964, followed by Ada in 1976.

A CLOSER LOOK
Carbone Wines in Colorado

Giuseppe Carbone and his family owned vineyards in the southern Italian province of Avellino. A wine exporter, he came to America around 1886 to market his wine. Tragically, he was killed in a train wreck. His oldest son Antonio "Anthony" was eleven years old at the time. Under Italian law, he could not inherit his father's estate because his father left no will and because Anthony was under the age of twenty-one. The estate, including Giuseppe Carbone's vineyards, became the property of the Avellino province.[88]

In 1888, Anthony came to America and settled in Boston with relatives, working as a barber and later in real estate.[89] In 1912, he, his wife Rose, and their five children made their way to Denver, where Anthony took over the Western Union Macaroni Factory on Osage Street in north Denver. After selling his pasta factory to American Beauty, he opened a wholesale wine and liquor business in downtown Denver.[90] With the advent of prohibition in Colorado, Anthony moved the business to Cheyenne. Four years later when national prohibition started, he returned to Denver and started A. Carbone & Company, an importer of olive oil and cheese. Anthony continued to run the business until his death in 1930. After their father's death, Giovanni "John," Arturo, and Americo Carbone took over the operations of A. Carbone & Company. As the oldest son, John assumed the primary responsibilities for the company as president.

Antonio "Anthony" Carbone, 1930. From Attività Italiane nella Intermountain Region, 1930. PCCLI5591

In 1933, following the repeal of prohibition, A. Carbone & Company returned to the wine business and became a bonded winery in Colorado under the label "Carbone Wines."[91] As a government-recognized winery, A. Carbone & Company had the full authority to make, fortify, and distribute wine. After purchasing wine in bulk from California, the company then transported it via sterilized railway tank cars to the plant in Denver, where it

A. Carbone & Company, Inc., 1100 Wazee Street (Wazee Market), 1942. CIAPA Archive. Courtesy Claudia Carbone. PCCLI4308f

was stored in large redwood tanks until bottling and packing for distribution.

In 1942, after a fire destroyed the original A. Carbone & Company warehouse, the Carbone family built a new facility with modern equipment at 1100 Wazee Street. A. Carbone & Company remained in business until 1953, when it was sold to the drug and liquor company McKesson & Robbins.[92]

Pietro "Peter" Albi

Peter Albi was born in 1852 in Grimaldi, a small city in the region of Calabria in the Cosenza Province in southern Italy. An educated man, he left Italy at the age of twenty-four.[93] After a few years in New York, he settled in Denver in 1882 where he opened a saloon at 547 Delgany Street.[94] He later went into business with Pasquale Vitullo, C. Zito, and J. Sacco, operating a number of businesses including the P. Albi & Company grocery and the P. Albi & Company bank, both located in downtown Denver. He also worked as the general manager for the Italian Publishing Company and served as the director and proprietor of *Il Roma*, an Italian newspaper.

In 1894, Peter Albi married Adelina Mosciaro. Peter and Adeline had eight children: Michael, Louis, Fred, Jack, Edward, Josephine, Francis, and Ferruccio. In a 1975 interview with Tom Noel, Louis Albi recalled fondly how his father would take the family to the theater and out for dinners:

My dad had a box at the Broadway Theater and he would help sponsor Italian operas at least once a year. In the Broadway was a real fine restaurant called the Metropole with huge plank steaks served on wooden planks.

Louis also recalled going to Luigi Mosconi's restaurant:

My dad used to take us to dinner there all the time. It didn't cater to just Italians but to everyone. A nice place. A place to take people. Served good imported wines. Not garish but in good taste, with tuxedoed waiters.

Peter Albi was also very active in the Italian community of Denver and the greater Rocky Mountain region. Considered by many the first unofficial Italian consul in Colorado, he helped many Italian immigrants by sponsoring their arrival to America, helping them find jobs and housing, and aiding those unable to read and write by filling out legal documents, reading letters from Italy, and writing letters to be sent back home.[95] So great was his involvement in the Italian community that in 1908 he was honored by King Victor Emmanuel III of Italy with the title of *Cavaliere* (knight) for his devotion and service to the Italian community.[96]

In 1910, while president of the Albi Mercantile Company, Peter Albi suffered a great financial loss when, according to his son Louis, a flood in Denver ruined over $40,000 worth of Havana cigars. Although he remained in business until 1921, he never fully recovered from the loss. Peter Albi died in 1936 at the age of eighty-three.

Dr. Rodolfo "Rudolph" and Rosina (Bortolini) Albi

Dr. Rudolph Albi was born 1874 in Grimaldi, Italy. Educated at the University of Torino, he graduated in 1898 with a degree in medicine and surgery.[97] While in medical school, he met his future wife, a fellow student, Rosina Bortolini. After graduation, Rudolph served as assistant professor of medicine at the University of Torino. In 1902, sponsored by his uncle Peter Albi, Rudolph arrived in Denver and on January 12, 1902, married Rosina Bortolini at Sacred Heart Church.

Rudolph and Rosina Albi, upon arrival in Colorado, had hoped to establish a medical practice to serve Denver's Italian population. Although both had their medical degrees from the same university in Italy, only Rudolph was granted a license in Colorado. Rosina, although unable to practice as a doctor, obtained her midwife license, becoming the first Italian woman in Colorado to do so.⁹⁸

Rudolph Albi set up his medical offices in 1902 at Sixteenth and Larimer Streets. According to an article that appeared in *The Denver Post* in December of 1902, Rosina also worked in the office:

> Dr. Albi is blessed in having a helper who is equally well fitted for her position. His wife, a charming woman, is a graduate of the same college as Dr. Albi and delights in helping her husband in all of his pursuits. She delights in studying with him, looking up each case with him, and in treatment she is willing and glad to devote her time and knowledge to their advancements. Truly, Dr. Albi is blessed in his abundant practice and his able assistant.

For almost fifty years, Dr. Albi served the Colorado community, combining his private practice with public service. He attended to patients in Denver and across Colorado and was part of the staff at Denver General and Saint Anthony Hospitals. He also served as the Denver City commissioner of health, on the Colorado State Board of Health, the State Board of Medical Examiners, and worked with organizations including the Italian Royal Commission of Immigration, the American National Medical Association, the Red Cross, and the Italian-American Cultural Club.⁹⁹

Dr. Rudolph Albi, c. 1935. CIAPA Archive. Courtesy Dr. Rudy deLuise. PCCLI2269

Rudolph and Rosina had four children: Dr. Piero Albi, Dr. Roger Albi, Maria (Albi) deLuise, and Wanda (Albi) Cirese. All of the Albi children studied in Italy. Piero Albi graduated from the University of Torino, Maria Albi studied literature and language in Rome and Florence, Roger studied medicine at the University of Naples, and Wanda attended the college of S.S. Annunziata, where she studied modern languages. As evidenced by the following, which appeared in the book *Attività Italiane nella Intermountain Region*, printed in 1930, Dr. Albi wanted his family to remain connected to his homeland:

In the Albi family the cult for Italy lives with all its lights. Comm. Albi taught his children that the love for one's Homeland is not measured by what one receives from it but by what one gives to it. He taught them that Italy can give nothing or little to the exiled but that their Homeland gave also to them their blood, their word, beauty which makes us so cheerful, faith which raises us, pride which consoles us. Italy needs love: those who do not love her do not know her.

Between 1920 and 1949, Dr. Rudolph Albi received several awards for his service to Italians in both medical and social matters. In addition to the title Commander, the Italian government also awarded him the Star of Solidarity, the Grand Official of the Order of the Crown of Italy medal, and granted him an honorary degree from the Consentina Academy.[100] Rosina Albi died in 1935, followed by Rudolph, who died in 1952.[101]

Pasquale "Charles" Albi

Pasquale "Charles" Albi, the eldest son of Giuseppe (Rudolph Albi's brother) and Assunta Albi, was born in Grimaldi, Italy, in 1893.[102] His parents owned an olive farm and lived in a stone house that had no central heat and no running water. In 1903, at the age of nine, Charles immigrated to the United States. He traveled alone by steamship, in a third-class cabin with three other passengers. Upon arrival in New York, he met his uncle Dr. Rudolph Albi, who brought him to Colorado, where he lived with his uncle Rudolph and aunt Rosina at 1650 Vine Street.

Charles attended the Wyman Elementary School and learned English with the help of his aunt and uncle. Eventually, he went to work delivering papers for the *Rocky Mountain News*. Before school, he would travel to the downtown office (over two miles from the house) to pick up the papers and then deliver them on his route. The money he earned helped pay the way for his brothers Ralph, Frank, Salvatore, and Michael to come to Colorado.

After graduating from East High School in 1914, Charles (who in 1913 became a United States citizen and officially changed his name from Pasquale to Charles) was admitted to the Colorado School of Mines, from which he graduated in 1918 with a degree in mining engineering. Shortly after graduating, he was drafted into the United States Navy, serving as an ensign (the naval equivalent of a second lieutenant) in World War I. After twelve weeks of training in New Jersey, he was assigned to work as an engine room officer on a ship that transported ammunition from Chile (where there were nitrate mines) through the Panama Canal and across the Atlantic to a French port on the Bay of Biscay. After two voyages, the war was over and he was transferred to duty at the New York Naval station until September 1919, when he returned to Denver.

After returning to Colorado, Charles continued his work as a mining engineer. During the 1920s, he was employed by several mining companies, including the Victor-American Fuel Company in Trinidad. He also worked on various projects in Boulder and Weld County and on the Climax Molybdenum Mine project in Kokomo, Colorado, near Leadville.

In 1928, along with his brother Salvatore "Sam," he formed Albi Brothers Coal Company, which had a yard and office at 2143 Nineteenth Street in Denver. The firm supplied heating fuel for residential use and to commercial customers including hospitals, schools, office buildings, and even Lowry Air Force Base.

Charles Albi, U.S. Navy, 1918. CIAPA Archive. Courtesy Charles H. Albi. PCCLI5618

In 1938, Charles Albi married Helen Harker, the daughter of an early Colorado mining businessman in Central City and Leadville. He was one of only two members in his family to marry outside the Italian community. Charles and Helen Albi had one child, Charles H. Albi, born in 1941.

Pasquale "Charles" Albi died in 1957 at the age of sixty-three. Upon remembering his father, Charles H. Albi remarked:

> Today, it is fashionable to celebrate diverse ethnic cultures and customs. Many people are intrigued by their "roots." A century ago, it was different. The Italian immigrants, among others, were looked down upon by those who had come earlier. They were even considered by some to be an inferior species. I recall reading a 1905 newspaper account of a train wreck that states: "there were no casualties except for two Italians." My father strove to be more American than those who were born here. On the day I graduated from high school, he said to me, "Charles, this is America. You can do anything you want."[103]

Ralph Albi

Ralph Albi was born in Grimaldi, Italy, in 1895. Around 1909, he came to Colorado, sponsored by his uncle Dr. Rudolph Albi. After a few months in Denver, he moved to the Delagua mining camp near Trinidad, where he went to work for the Victor-American Fuel Company as a "nipper." Similar to his job in Italy on his family-owned olive farm, where he transported olives to market by burro (donkey), his job in the coal mines was to oversee the transportation of mined coal in cars on rails pulled by burros from deep inside the mine to a coal dumping area located outside of the mine's entrance.[104]

Mining accidents and increasing labor-management issues resulted in Ralph Albi leaving Delagua. In 1912, he returned to Denver and found work as a paper carrier, delivering the *Rocky Mountain News* in the morning and the *Denver Times* in the afternoon. During the day, he made deliveries for the Columbine Laundry and the Chicago Dairy, delivering milk from a horse-drawn wagon.

In 1913, Ralph was seriously injured during a Denver snowstorm. Referred to as the "Denver Snowstorm of the Century," the bad weather forced Ralph to leave his bicycle in the snow and take alternate transportation (the streetcar) to get to his delivery job. As he was exiting a Denver Tramway streetcar, the conductor started to depart before Ralph had fully left the last platform step. As the streetcar started up, he fell under the wheels, and half of his left foot was severed. At a time when there was no workman's compensation or unemployment compensation insurance, Ralph was forced to seek employment at the Home Dairy Restaurant in downtown Denver, where he washed dishes while standing with the aid of crutches for a twelve-hour workday. Six months later, he returned to his job at the *Rocky Mountain News* and *Denver Times*.

In 1925, Ralph Albi married Theresa C. Palese of Denver. Ralph and Theresa Albi had two children: Theresa C. Albi and Joseph R. Albi.

Ralph Albi, by the Denver Art Studio, Denver, c.1920. CIAPA Archive. Courtesy Joseph Albi. PCCLI5133

In 1927, Ralph left the *Rocky Mountain News*—where he had elevated himself from paper carrier to the position of circulation manager—and started the Cascade Laundry and Dry Cleaning Company, a commercial laundry and drycleaner. The firm grew to be one of the largest in the Denver area, employing over 150 workers, and consisting of two plant facilities, seventeen truck routes, and twenty-one outlets. In 1957, Ralph Albi turned the company over to his son Joseph, assuming the duties of vice president.

In 1968, the Cascade Laundry and Dry Cleaning Company was sold and Ralph and Joseph started the Cascade Investment Company. The company was both a real estate holding company and securities stock and bond brokerage firm. In 1971, the firm was sold to another large broker-dealer. Four years later, Ralph Albi died.

Of his father and uncles, Joseph Albi reflected:

> All the Albi Brothers were extremely patriotic individuals who loved their adopted country. Charles proudly served as an officer in the United States Navy after his graduation from the Colorado School of Mines with a BS in Mining Engineering. Dad; Frank (who then was a dentist); Michael (who was a registered pharmacist); and Salvatore (a co-owner with Charles of a large coal distributing company that was vital to the war effort) were not of draftable age during WWII and thus could not serve their adopted country in this manner.
>
> I vividly recall in October 1949 on my eighteenth birthday my father drove me to the downtown U.S. Post Office and instructed me to get out of the laundry truck, go into the building and register for the draft. He said, "Joe, this is the greatest free country in the world, everyone has to pay their dues—go in and register for the draft, it's your duty to serve this great Nation." It should be noted that at the time the U.S. was involved in the Korean War. He was extremely proud of me when in January 1951 I enlisted in the U.S. Air Force (even though I was only a Private).
>
> All the brothers deeply loved this Nation and had a true appreciation of the privilege of living in a free country. I recall that every time Dad went back to Italy to visit his remaining family, he couldn't wait to get back to the good old USA as quickly as possible.
>
> The Albi brothers were successful in their own professional endeavors and possessed high moral and

ethical values. They were never afraid of work and believed that if one labored hard enough in their pursuits, anything was attainable in this country. I remember my Dad would often tell me, "Joe, the man that sits on his ass will always stay there." They all worked tirelessly and truly earned the successes they achieved. They were deeply devoted to the great "American Free Enterprise System."

I am proud to be a member of the Albi family and pay high tribute to five Italian immigrant boys who looked far beyond their humble upbringing and initial early years of very limited education to achieve "The American Dream."[105]

Frank Samuel Albi

Born in 1899, Frank Albi left Italy for America at the age of sixteen, arriving in Denver in 1915. Frank first attended Franklin School in Denver, where he was placed in kindergarten because he was unable to speak English. Although an unacceptable solution today, Frank and other immigrants of his time had few options. Unlike today, there were no programs in the public school system to help immigrants learn English. After Franklin School, Frank attended Manual Training High School and then the University of Denver, where in 1925 he earned his Doctor of Dental Surgery degree from Denver University's College of Dentistry.[106]

Like his brothers, Frank worked to pay his own way through school, delivering milk from a horse-drawn wagon. Each morning, after studying late into the night, he would rise well before dawn so that he could complete his delivery before going to class at D.U. Long hours at work, school, and time spent studying left little time for sleep, and one morning Frank overslept. To make up time, Frank ran his horse from stop to stop in order to finish the deliveries on time. Upon returning to the dairy, Frank's supervisor noticed the horse was overheated and angrily asked him why he worked the horse so hard. Sleep-deprived and frustrated, Frank snapped back, telling his supervisor he should be as concerned about how hard he was working. The next morning, the supervisor sent another man to wait for Frank so that he could train the new man who would be taking his job.

In addition to the often unforgiving working conditions of the 1920s, Frank Albi also experienced discrimination at the hands of the Ku Klux Klan, who persecuted Catholics and Italian immigrants equally. Active in Colorado in the 1920s, Klansmen confronted Frank prior to his graduation from dental school and threatened to harm him if he did not withdraw from school. Frank refused and graduated from dental school, just ten years after settling in Colorado.

In 1929, the stock market crash, followed by the Great Depression, forced Frank to return to one of his former jobs, delivering newspapers for the *Rocky Mountain News* and the *Denver Times*. According to his children, Frank would recall how after resuming his paper route in the 1930s, subscribers from time to time would remark to Frank that they remembered when his "brother" the dentist used to deliver their newspapers. Frank said they would ask how he was doing. A proud man, Frank would assure the subscribers "his brother the dentist" was doing fine.

After recovering from the devastation of the Depression years, Frank Albi returned to dentistry, from which he retired in 1981. Frank Albi died in California in 1992.

Salvatore "Sam" Natale Albi

Born in 1902, Sam Albi immigrated to the United States in 1920 at the age of nineteen. Alone and unable to speak English, the trip was a frightening experience that began in France where he boarded the ship. He saw a dead horse hanging in a butcher shop near the port. Afraid he would be served horse meat on the ship, Sam ate very little, living on canned sardines which he brought with him. As a result, he was ill and weak upon arrival in America.[107]

Unlike his brothers, who were met by Dr. Rudolph Albi on arrival, no one was waiting for Sam in New York. Instead, he had a series of notes in English that he gave to railroad ticket agents along the way, saying he wanted to go to Chicago and then to Denver. When he arrived in Chicago, he experienced another frightening situation as he tried to find his way to the train headed for Denver. When he asked a Union Station clerk for help, he thought the clerk said there was no train to Denver. Finally, a police officer intervened and found an Italian-speaking shoeshine boy, who was able to help Sam get on the right train.

After making his way to Colorado, Sam lived with his brothers Frank, Ralph, and Charles at 1219 East Twenty-second Avenue in Denver. To learn English and a trade (meat-cutting) he attended the Emily Griffith Opportunity School. While in school, he worked as a carrier for the

Rocky Mountain News in the Capitol Hill area. According to his family, he liked selling newspapers because it didn't require him to know much English. He also liked the fact that the more newspapers he sold or delivered, the more money he made.

While working as a news carrier, Sam experienced discrimination at the hands of the Ku Klux Klan. He was harassed and robbed of his collection money many times until one day he stood up to them and fought them off with a baseball bat. Additionally, he often felt discriminated against because of his Italian accent and lack of formal education. He was called a "wop" and saw signs in Denver restaurant windows and at the amusement parks that said, "NO ITALIANS."

After completing his training at the Opportunity School, he went to work as a butcher and then for Swift & Company packinghouse. Work in the packinghouse was difficult and competitive as speed in cutting meat determined how much you earned and the degree of respect by which you were regarded. Here, too, he experienced discrimination, often referred to as a "wop" or other derogatory terms for Italians. In spite of the challenges he faced, he became one of the fastest and most respected workers at Swift & Company.

In 1928, Sam went into the coal business with his brothers Charles and Michael, founding the Albi Brothers Coal Company. A successful business for over forty years, it struggled through the Depression years.[108] According to his family, Sam talked vividly of the Depression and trying to survive as a small business owner especially when he would deliver coal on credit, knowing some customers and friends would never pay the bill. He felt especially fortunate because he had been able to build and pay for the family home, which in his opinion enabled him to survive such hard times. Like many others of his time, the Depression resulted in a conservative attitude toward spending money, as evidenced by the fact that Sam kept the same car—a straight-eight Hudson—from 1938 to 1958 and would rarely go out to eat, let alone go on a vacation.

In 1941, Sam Albi married Rose Mary Veltri. The couple lived their entire married life at 3381 West Thirty-fourth Avenue in Denver with their three children: Eugene, Lynn, and Michael. In the early 1970s, Sam Albi retired from the coal trucking business. He died in Denver in 1983.

Michelangelo "Michael" Bruno Albi

Michael Bruno Albi was born in Grimaldi, Italy, in 1904 and came to America in 1920.[109] Upon arrival in the United States, he was almost sent back to Italy when during questioning by immigration officials, he told them he had tuberculosis and rheumatic fever as a child. Finally, after joining his brothers in Colorado, he attended first grade for one year to learn English. He was sixteen at the time. After graduating from Manual High School, Michael attended the University of Colorado and later became a registered pharmacist. He owned a pharmacy at Seventeenth and Park Avenue and later at Thirty-sixth and Tejon. In the late 1960s, he worked for Walgreens and was employed as a pharmacist at King Soopers at the time of his death in 1971. He was survived by his wife Margery and their two children: Joyce Albi, M.D., and Roberta Albi, Ph.D.

Albi Brothers, left to right: Michael, Pasquale "Charles," Salvatore "Sam," Ralph, and Frank, c. 1941. CIAPA Archive. Courtesy Charles H. Albi. PCCLI2338

Chiolero

Giovanni Battista Pietro "Peter" Chiolero

Peter Chiolero was born in Ceres, Italy—in the Piedmont region in northern Italy—in 1851. In 1865, he left Italy for new opportunities and adventures in South America. Peter

Chiolero Family, back row, left to right: W. R. Barra, Joseph Chiolero, Peter Chiolero, Stephen Chiolero, and Carlo Grosso; middle row, left to right: Mary Clara (Chiolero) Grosso, Laura (Chiolero) Barra, Catherine Chiolero (Peter's wife), and Catherine Chiolero; front row: Marguerita Chiolero holding Rocco Louis Barra, c. 1906. CIAPA Archive. Courtesy Ann L. Chiolero. PCCLI4934

was the only member of his family to leave Italy. The third son born to Giuseppe and Maddalena (Torreno) Chiolero, he left home knowing his oldest brother would inherit his entire family estate and that unstable economic and political conditions in Italy would make it hard for him to find work.[110]

After contracting and recovering from yellow fever while working in South America as a miner, Peter returned home in 1868, to fulfill his required service in the Italian military. Three years later, Peter traveled to Belgium, France, and Mexico, finally settling in Braidwood, Illinois, around 1878, where he worked as a coal miner. A year later, he married Italian-born Catherine Trione, and in 1880, their first child, a son named Joseph, was born. That same year, the silver boom brought the Chiolero family to Georgetown, Colorado, where Peter worked as a miner. In 1881, Peter and his partner Joseph Kerschenbaumer of Austria opened the Little Casino saloon and boardinghouse. In Georgetown, Peter and Catherine's children Stephen and Laura were born. Two years later, Georgetown's harsh living conditions and a physical attack on Peter resulted in the Chiolero family moving to Denver, where four more children were born to Peter and Catherine: Mary Clara, Catherine, Horace, and Marguerita.

In Denver, Peter opened Chiolero & Cunio, a cigar and importing business with partner Gian Battista Cunio. Other partnerships followed, including Cajal & Chiolero, Vola & Chiolero, and P. Chiolero & DeSilvestro. In 1905, Peter and the Chiolero family opened their own cigar factory, and in 1906, established the Chiolero Importing Mercantile & Investment Company, which Peter continued to run until his death in 1917.

Frank Damascio, c. 1900. Fred Mazzulla Collection. 99.270.4756

Damascio

Frank Damascio

In 1878, Frank Damascio of Abruzzi, Italy, settled in Trinidad, Colorado. A contractor, builder, and sculptor, he is credited with the construction of many Trinidad buildings, including the old courthouse.[111] Frank moved to Denver in 1890 and established himself as one of the city's leading contractors and builders, working on the Brown Palace Hotel (1892), the Mining Exchange Building (demolished), and the Cathedral

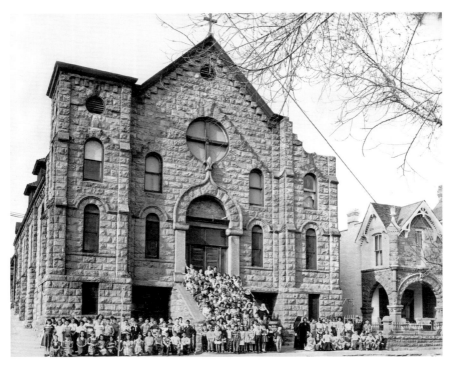

Mount Carmel Parish School (formerly the San Rocco Chapel) with Damascio house at right, by Van's Studio, c. 1945. CIAPA Archive. Courtesy Our Lady of Mount Carmel. PCCLI0720

of the Immaculate Conception (started in 1902).[112] Other Damascio buildings include the North Denver Mercantile on Osage, the San Rocco Chapel/Mount Carmel Parish School (demolished), and the Damascio home at 3611 Osage Street. A testament to his success and wealth, the home includes an elaborate stone exterior with beautifully carved details, bay windows, marble floors, and fourteen rooms, many with Damascio's hand-carved fireplaces.[113]

Frank Damascio's activities in the Italian American community included belonging to Il Circolo Filodrammatico Italo-Americano, a dramatic and literary society that supported the arts and continued use of the Italian language in the community.[114]

Frank and his wife, Veronica (Capaldi) Damascio, had three children: Joe, John, and Elisa. Frank Damascio died in 1922 at the age of seventy-two.[115]

Elisa "Lizzie" (Damascio) Palladino

Like her father, Elisa Damascio worked for the betterment of Italian American people. One of the first Italians in Denver to graduate with a nursing degree, by 1922 she had opened a private hospital in the Damascio home that offered Italians affordable medical services.[116] She had also hoped to build a new hospital for the Italian community in Denver but the idea was never realized. Active in the Italian community, Elisa served as an officer for the Italy America Society of Colorado, the Dante Alighieri Club, and Il Circolo Filodrammatico Italo-Americano. Also active in politics, she became the first woman to serve on the Denver City Council after Mayor George Begole appointed her to fill the term vacated by Eugene Veraldi. Elisa chose not to run for a second term, and instead supported Michael A. Marranzino, a lifelong friend who served on the council for many years.[117]

Elisa Damascio married Horace Palladino and had three children: Frank, Veronica, and Guiliette.[118]

Francone

Carlo and Caterina (Aliberti) Francone

Carlo Francone was born in the Piedmont region in northern Italy in 1857.[119] In 1888, he married Caterina Aliberti, born in 1867 to Francesco and Margarita (Garrone) Aliberti.[120] In 1890, after seventeen days aboard ship (traveling third class steerage), Carlo arrived in the United States, landing at Castle Garden in New York.[121] He did not speak English, but he managed to make his way through immigration, followed by a train ride from New York to Colorado where he met his brother-in-law Feliciano Aliberti in Silver Plume. Feliciano, who came to America in 1887, owned a saloon in Silver Plume, Colorado.[122]

After working as a miner for a year, Carlo sent for his wife Caterina and their oldest son, also named Feliciano. The family settled in Brownville, a small community just west of Silver Plume where five more of their children were born: Mary, Maggie, Frank, Della, and John.[123]

In 1901, the Francone family left Brownville after Carlo Francone followed up on an advertisement in a newspaper that sought a family to lease a one-hundred-acre farm in the town of Orchard in Morgan County, some ninety miles northeast of Denver. Carlo's decision to move the family was likely based on a declining silver mining industry in Brownville, the opportunity to work in agriculture and own land (the family eventually purchased land in Orchard), and the fact that Carlo's brother Joe Francone lived in nearby Weldona, Colorado.

Life in Orchard was good for the family, but not easy. The new family homestead lacked a place to live, water, and a protected area for livestock. After digging a well for water, the family built a house out of sod bricks from soil, straw, and water. In addition to the homestead, Carlo needed to develop the farm, so Carlo and his sons Phil and Frank worked as sheepherders. Frank, who was seven years old at the time, was earning $7.00 a month. Carlo also leased some land near the homestead and the family planted sugar beets. The Francone children helped on the farm by hoeing, thinning, and harvesting the beets.

In addition to hard work, the Francone family also had to deal with discrimination in Orchard. As the first Italian family to move into the area, they were not welcomed. Among other things, the Francone children were taunted and abused by other children who played a game called "whip the wops" after school.

Around 1905, the Francone family moved to Goodrich, Colorado, where they leased land and where Carlo and Caterina's youngest children, Armond and Annette, were born. In 1911, the Francone family moved to Montrose, where Carlo died. Caterina and her sons continued to run the family farm until around 1924, when Caterina moved to Denver. Caterina remained in Denver until 1950 when she moved to Sterling, where she died in 1954.

A Closer Look
Italians in Silver Plume

Silver Plume, Colorado, named for the Silver Plume Mine, was founded as a mining camp in 1870 and incorporated as a city in 1880. In 1884, Silver Plume and Georgetown, Colorado, were connected by a railroad, which transported freight, ore, and passengers between the two settlements. By 1898, Silver Plume had grown to support twenty-five mines in the Silver Plume district.[124]

Once silver was discovered around Silver Plume, there was a need for cheap labor to work the mines. The first to fill this need were the Cornish immigrants, who lived mostly in Brownville (a suburb west of Silver Plume).

View of Silver Plume, by Barkalow Brothers of Denver, c. 1890. 2000.129.207

The Italian influx began soon after 1880 with Italians displacing many of the Cornish immigrants in Brownville. Around 1890, approximately three hundred Italians were living in the Silver Plume area.[125]

A majority of Italians in Silver Plume worked in the silver mines which supported the Silver Plume economy. Although no Italians owned any of the twenty-five mines in the Silver Plume District, a few Italians operated and owned businesses in the town including saloons, bakeries, or stores, which supported the miners and their families. In 1898, Italians owned five of the seven saloons in Silver Plume.

The repeal of the Sherman Silver Purchase Act in 1893 helped cause a nationwide depression. The act had subsidized silver production by requiring the U.S. government to buy silver. Some mines continued to operate, but with smaller crews earning lower wages. Others shut down completely.

In reaction to the changes occurring in Silver Plume, many Italians chose to utilize their newfound power as citizens and formed political groups such as the Italian Independent Political Club, in the hopes of increasing the influence of silver in the U.S. economic system. In March of 1896, the *Silver Standard* newspaper in Silver Plume reported:

> Early in last December a political club was formed by the Italians in this place which now numbers 80 members, and it is expected that the membership will be largely increased in a short time. The name of the organization is the Italian Independent Political Club, and we are informed that the object of the organization is to disseminate a knowledge of the system of voting in use in this state; to support the best men for office regardless of politics, and also vote for none but silver men, as the members are what the name indicates—independent in politics, and no goldbut [one who does not support the silver mining industry] candidate will get their votes.

Over time, most Italian immigrant families left Silver Plume to join other Italian communities or start new settlements in Colorado including in Trinidad, Pueblo, Weldona,

Montrose, Sterling, Denver, and Louisville. On April 27, 1907, the *Silver Standard* newspaper of Silver Plume reported that:
> ...having disposed of his mining interests here, Gabriel Martolomea [Bartolomeo] departed on Thursday for Sterling, where he will give his attention to raising sugar beets and other farm produce.

A Closer Look
The Bersaglieri Society in Silver Plume

The Società Bersaglieri di Savoia, or the Bersaglieri Society of Savoy, was one of many mutual aid and benevolent societies in Silver Plume. Over the seventeen years that the Society was active, more than three hundred men were members, forty-six of which were recorded as dying during that time. The benefits offered by the Bersaglieri Society included helping the members' families in times of illness, death, financial need, language, and cultural difficulties.

Named for the military Bersaglieri of Italy, the organization was founded on February 2, 1899, by Italian immigrants living in Silver Plume and the surrounding area.[126] The Bersaglieri of Italy was an infantry troop formed in the mid-1800s by the House of Savoy, before the unification of Italy in the Kingdom of Sardinia. The troop was trained to travel long distances as fast as possible on foot. Their uniform included a hat with a long plume of rooster feathers on the side, symbolic of bravery and fighting ability. This hat was also worn by the members of the Bersaglieri Society in Silver Plume as part of their uniform.

Regulations of the Society included that each member pay for the uniform issued to them. The uniform was modeled after the Italian military troop and included epaulets, the hat and plume, encased sword, jacket, pants, ribbon, pin, and sash. Each member was required to wear the uniform at every meeting of the Society and on special occasions.[127]

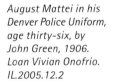

August Mattei in his Denver Police Uniform, age thirty-six, by John Green, 1906. Loan Vivian Onofrio. IL.2005.12.2

Mattei

Augusto "August" L. Mattei

August Mattei, son of Filippo "Philip" Mattei, arrived in Denver with his family in 1874 at the age of three.[128] In 1888, at age eighteen, he married Giusti Elisabetta "Betta" Locono, also a native of Italy.

August Mattei's Metropolitan Restaurant, Denver, 1911. CIAPA Archive. Courtesy Vivian Onofrio. PCCLI2088

Sometime before 1900, August became the first Italian police officer in the Denver Police Department, where he worked for eighteen years.[129] In 1904, he opened the Metropolitan Restaurant at Seventeenth and Market Streets. He later started the Home Dairy Restaurant at Sixteenth and Welton Streets in Denver. August operated the Home Dairy until 1948, when he retired. He died at his home on Shoshone Street in north Denver in 1960, leaving behind his widow and six children: Mary, Fred, Charles, Marcus, Rose, and Agnes.[130]

Morrato

Frank Morrato, 1923. CIAPA Archive. Courtesy Aldo Notarianni. PCCLI0404

Frank Morrato

The son of Louis and Elizabeth (DeSciose) Morrato, Frank Morrato was born in southern Italy in 1874.[131] In 1884, at the age of eleven, Frank, his parents, and sister Rosina (Morrato) Notary left their homeland and immigrated to America, where they settled in Denver. In time, Frank found work shining shoes and selling newspapers and tobacco.

In 1888, at the age of sixteen, Frank returned to Italy, where he married Enrichetta Morrato. A year later, the couple returned to Colorado, where their daughter Elisabetta was born, the first of ten children.[132] By 1900, Frank and his family lived at 528 Bell Street (now Osage) along with his mother,

Influx 1880–1894

> **TELEFONO 1652.**
> CAMPIONI GRATIS DIETRO RICHIESTA.
> **NOTARY E MORRATO,**
> **North Denver Liquor House e Palmer Avenue Liquor House.**
> NEGOZIANTI IN VINI E LIQUORI.
> Proprietarii della più grande ditta di vini e liquori nell'Ovest.
> Diretti importatori, Banchieri Italiani, ecc., ecc.
> **528 BELL STREET**
> E
> **3352-54-56-58 PALMER AVENUE,**
> DENVER. COLO.
> Le mercanzie sono portate gratuitamente in ogni parte della città.

Advertisement for Notary E Morrato. From Marcello Gandolfo, Gli Italiani nel Colorado 1899–1900, *1900*. PCCLI5632

brother Nicolas (born in Colorado in 1885), and his nephews Vincenzo and Nicolo DiSciose, whom Frank sponsored to come to Denver.[133] Later he would sponsor their brother, Louis, in 1906. Both Nicolo and Louis DiSciose became successful musicians in Denver.[134]

In addition to owning a business, Frank also worked as a banker, real estate dealer, advertising manager (for the weekly Italian newspaper *La Nazione*), and publisher. He owned a popular saloon, successful wholesale liquor business (with his brother-in-law Michele Notary), and several properties in Denver including the Morrato Block at 2900 Blake Street.[135] Frank Morrato died in Denver on March 17, 1937.[136]

Notary/NotarFrancesco

Michele "Michael" and Rosina "Rosie" (Morrato) Notary/NotarFrancesco

Michele Notary left Potenza, Italy, for Denver in 1880.[137] The son of peasant farmers Antonio and Antonia (Brienza) NotarFrancesco, Michele married Rosina Morrato in 1885 at Sacred Heart Catholic Church.[138] Together the couple raised eight children: Tony, Luigi, Rocco, Frank, Josephine, Millie, Enrichetta, and Elizabeth.[139]

In 1901, the couple built a home at 3357 Palmer Street (later Navajo). Devoted to helping others in the Italian community, the Notarys opened their home to Mother Cabrini in 1902. Mother Cabrini established a convent, school, and orphanage in the house, and although the orphanage relocated to Fourty-eighth and Federal in 1905 and the school moved to Osage Street in 1908, the Cabrini Sisters' convent remained in the Notarys' house until 1926.[140]

Michele Notary and Frank Morrato co-owned the North Denver Liquor House, a wholesale liquor business.[141] Michele also acted as a notary public and travel agent for other Italian immigrants making their way to Colorado. Michele helped found Denver's first and oldest Italian Catholic society in Denver in

Michele Notary, c. 1930. Gift Lou and Bonnie Garramone. 2005.84.2

1891, the Mount Carmel Society, and the Società Nativi di Potenza Basilicata in 1892. Rosina Notary died in 1911, followed by Michele, who died in Denver in 1935 at the age of seventy-six.[142]

Check, 1917. Drawn on the First National Bank of Denver, made out to Peter McDonnell by agent Michele Notary for Antonetta Garramone's railroad ticket in the amount of $40. Gift Lou and Bonnie Garramone. 2007.20.2

A CLOSER LOOK
The Mount Carmel Society

In 1891, Michele Notary and Giacomo DiGiacomo organized the Our Lady of Mount Carmel Society, the forerunner of the Our Lady of Mount Carmel Church.[143] The first Italian Catholic organization in Denver, this group helped Mount Carmel's first priest, Rev. Felice "Felix" Mariano Lepore, buy land for the first church. Before the church was built, the society met in a building that had a dry goods store and shoe repair shop with rented apartments on the second floor. Over time, as membership in the organization increased, the society converted the first floor into one large hall and later acquired the entire building. In 1967, Our Lady of Mount Carmel Church purchased it from the society.[144] The church still uses the hall for parish activities such as the Mount Carmel Altar and Rosary Society's craft

View of the procession of the statue of Our Lady of Mount Carmel in honor of her feast day celebration with the Mount Carmel Society Hall in the background at right, by Rocky Mountain Photo Co., 1920. CIAPA Archive. Courtesy Mary Pomarico. PCCLI5602

Influx 1880–1894

The Italian Colonial Band gathered in front of the Mount Carmel Society Hall (originally owned by the Mount Carmel Society, the building is now the Mount Carmel parish hall) and New York Market Grocery for the Our Lady of Mount Carmel Feast Day celebration, 1922. CIAPA Archive. Courtesy Our Lady of Mount Carmel Church. PCCLI0149.v2

and bake sale, the cultural reception for La Prima Domenica (Mass in Italian on the first Sunday of the month), and the Saint Joseph's Day Table—a Sicilian feast day celebration.

Pavoni

Antonio Pavoni

Antonio and Luisa Pavoni, by F. E. Post Photography, 1890. Gift Harold Benoit and Betty Pierce. 2006.47.2

Antonio Pavoni was born in Venice, Italy, in 1866 to Antonia Depauli. According to his descendants, he was the illegitimate son of an important and wealthy Venetian count whose last name was taken by his mother.[145] He was raised by his mother and stepfather, Davi Pavoni, in Forni-di-Sopra in the Udine Province with his half-brothers Umberto and Leone. In 1887, Antonio came to the United States, settling first in Pennsylvania before moving to Denver a year later, where he established himself as a stonecutter.[146] His projects in Colorado include the Colorado State Capitol, the Cheesman Dam, the Cathedral of the Immaculate Conception, and a monument in Silver Plume dedicated to ten Italian miners who died in an avalanche in 1899. Antonio, his mother, and two brothers also owned Douglas County quarries including the Stars and Stripes, Alva Adams, Teddy Roosevelt, and Martha Washington located in the West Creek Mining District. Later, he formed the South Platte Granite Company.[147]

In 1890, Antonio married Luisa Barbogalata in Denver and together they had eight children: David, Louis, Emil, Mary, Alvena, Paul, Emma, and Harold.[148] Antonio Pavoni died in Denver in 1939 at the age of seventy-three.

Stonemasons at Milne Granite Yard at Sixth and Curtis, Antonio Pavoni (second row, fourth from left under checkmark), c. 1925. Gift Harold Benoit and Betty Pierce. 2006.47.5

A CLOSER LOOK
The Cheesman Dam

Antonio Pavoni was one of many men who worked on the construction of the Cheesman Dam. Located on the South Platte River, about six miles southwest of Deckers (a town about sixty miles southwest of Denver), the Cheesman Dam was completed in 1905. Considered an architectural wonder, the dam was the first major gravity-arch masonry dam built in the world. The dam was the solution to Denver's water supply problem. Beginning in the early 1890s, it became apparent that if Denver was to continue to grow in population and industry, more water was needed. The answer was the Cheesman Dam. At 221 feet in height, the dam supports the Cheesman reservoir that when filled to capacity, holds nearly 80,000 acre feet of water, enough to provide water to nearly half a million people for one year.

Cheesman Dam Construction, c. 1905. Gift Harold Benoit and Betty Pierce. 2006.47.6

Chapter 4
Colonies
1895–1919

As Italians migrated to Colorado, the men often settled first, drawn by the promise of work. They sponsored family members to join them. At the same time, large industries recruited workers. Italians soon made up more than 20 percent of Colorado's population. In 1900, nearly half of the state's Italians lived in the counties where coal mining and heavy industries dominated: Las Animas, Pueblo, Huerfano, and Fremont.

But this was a time of hostility toward immigrants. In the 1890s, the Colorado branch of the American Protective Association flourished, along with its message of "nativism": an intolerance of those who were not Protestant, white, or born in the United States. Italian immigrants endured taunts and discrimination—and worse. Angry crowds lynched an Italian man in Denver and three in Walsenburg.

Many politicians and reformers urged immigrants to "Americanize," to shed their distinctive food, culture, and languages. The image of the Italian as exotic, superstitious, violent, and clannish seeped into popular media, prompting native-born Coloradans to assume that Italians were at best quaint, and at worse a menace.

Threats to immigrants persisted for decades. Yet, Italians could find comfort in their colonies. In Colorado, Italian colonies developed in several cities, the three largest in Denver, Trinidad, and Pueblo, with many others in rural and urban neighborhoods and company-owned mining camps around the state. The colonies were big enough to support stores, churches, and even some factories. And while not all Italian immigrants lived in colonies, the settlements provided a safety net for those who did.

Opposite: Main Street, Pueblo, Colorado, c. 1900. PH.PROP.2745

A Closer Look
The Denver Colony

The growth of Denver's Italian colony kept pace with the surging numbers of Italian immigrants settling in the United States after 1880. Arriving with few resources, many of these newcomers settled among other poor people in the "Bottoms" of the South Platte River valley, while others found homes throughout the city.

Later, Italians moved out of the Bottoms area and resettled across the river in north Denver. The area became known as "Little Italy," though non-Italians lived there too. Residents disagreed about the colony's exact boundaries, but there was consensus that it lay between Broadway and Zuni, from east to west, and between Forty-sixth and Thirty-second Avenues, from north to south. In 1894, the community financed and built Our Lady of Mount Carmel Catholic Church on Navajo Street—its domes became Little Italy's defining landmark. Schools, grocery stores, taverns, community bread ovens, and gardens also distinguished the neighborhood and made it a haven for Italians.

Denver's non-Italians felt ambivalent about the immigrant population. A 1901 *Rocky Mountain News* article commented that the Italians worked hard, were patriotic, and were an asset to the city. The paper boasted that Denver's colony was second only to San Francisco's Italians in terms of "intelligence, conduct, and morality." But its description of the average Italian man as "simple, industrious, affectionate...with a quick temper" shows that stereotypes were alive and well.

Buccino

Michael "Mike" Clyde and Angelina "Angie" Carmella (Villano) Buccino

Angelina "Angie" Buccino was born in 1910 to Gerardo "Jerry" and Gerarda "Geraldine" (Lutito) Villano. Her parents were married in Denver at Sacred Heart Church in 1900. Her father came to the United States from Potenza, Italy, around 1892. After working menial jobs including pulling weeds for twenty-five cents a day, he went to work for the railroad, laying tracks through Colorado and Utah, eventually settling in Denver, where he worked as a vegetable peddler. Angie's mother Geraldine was born in Potenza in 1881. After the death of her mother, Geraldine came to America in 1887, where her father was already living.[149]

One of ten children, Angie Villano attended Webster School to the sixth grade and Skinner Junior High to the ninth grade.[150] As a young girl, she attended Our Lady of Mount Carmel Church services faithfully and for a time even considered becoming a nun. While attending the Emily Griffith Opportunity School, she also worked for Montgomery Ward & Company to help support her family. In 1939, Angie married Mike Buccino at Our Lady of Mount Carmel, where the couple first met. One of six children, Mike was born in Denver in 1913 to Luigi and Rosa (Labriola) Buccino. His father came to the United States in 1876 from Potenza, Italy. He worked as a cook on the railroad and for many years with the Denver Water department before marrying Rosa, also born in Potenza.

Mike Buccino, like his wife, grew up in Denver's Little Italy. Early in his teens, he entered the Denver Art Institute Academy, where he mastered the skills of illustrated art and figure drawing. During the Depression, he worked at Bailey-Underhill Company, a maker of overalls. He then landed a job at J.C. Penney's painting background scenes for window displays. After marrying Angie, Mike went to work for the tramway driving streetcars, a job he kept until the end of World War II, when he returned to the Denver Art Institute Academy to take a teaching position. When the school closed, he went to work for Samsonite Corporation, from which he retired in 1975.

In addition to caring for his family and working to provide for them, he continued to produce art; in particular, religious art. In the early 1950s, he started the Catholic Art Services Bureau, which provided religious illustrations to various Catholic publications such as the *National Catholic Register* and the *Denver Catholic Register*. He published and illustrated two books: *The Rosary Album* and *Seven Sorrows*.

Cover, Rosary of the Seven Sorrows, illustrations by Michael Clyde Buccino, 1975. Gift Angie Buccino. 2006.14.9

During his retirement, he helped his parish, Our Lady of Mount Carmel, by supplying them with many drawings for various projects.[151]

Mike and Angie Buccino had five children: Jeannine, Michael, Loretta, Louie, and Mary Ann. Mike Buccino died in Denver in 2000. Angie Buccino still lives in the Denver-metro area.

Capolungo/Long

Gerardo "Jerry" and Amelia Capolungo/Long

Gerardo Capolungo was born in the southern Italian province of Potenza in 1866. In his early twenties, he immigrated to America with his father, Gaetano, and his fifteen-year-old brother, Pasquale. The men worked for the railroad, saved their money, and returned to Italy for their families.[152]

In 1894, Gerardo Capolungo, his wife Amelia, and their son Thomas returned to America (along with Gaetano and Pasquale and other relatives) and settled in the Denver Bottoms, near the South Platte River in an area now occupied by Auraria Campus. Gerardo worked as a produce peddler and was involved in the local Italian community including belonging to the Bersaglieri Society in Denver while Amelia stayed home to care for their family. In all, the couple had ten children: Thomas, Clara, Josephine, Lucy, Mary, Ralph, Julia, Tony, Rocco, and Edith.[153]

In 1898, Gerardo and Amelia decided to move to north Denver. They moved to have more room for their growing family, to live near relatives and other Italians in the Little Italy neighborhood, and to be close to the new Catholic Church, Our Lady of Mount Carmel, which was under construction. Gerardo bought a house at Thirty-sixth and Mariposa from his brother Pasquale for $600. Pasquale bought the house next door and moved in with their parents, Gaetano and Mary.

Around 1905, the family decided to change its name from Capolungo to Long. Although living in Denver's Italian

Gerardo and Amelia Capolungo/Long, Denver, c. 1940. CIAPA Archive. Courtesy Ralph and Kay Long. PCCLI4978

enclave, the family was not sheltered from discrimination. When Lucy, Gerardo and Amelia's fourth child, started first grade in the Denver Public Schools, there were few Italian teachers. On her first day she was sent home because the school staff, including her teacher, could not pronounce her name. She was sent home every day for several days until Gerardo "got the message" and changed the family name to Long. Gerardo and Amelia Capolungo/Long both died in Denver in 1952.

A Closer Look
Denver Peddlers

In 1879, Denver issued its first peddler's license to Louis Ferrari, an Italian immigrant.[154] City code defined a peddler as any individual who went from place to place selling, delivering, or bartering goods, wares, or merchandise from a pack, pushcart, or other vehicle.

Requiring little investment, the job attracted newly arrived Italians—especially southern Italians who lacked marketable skills but were willing to work long hours. Peddling was an occupation they were familiar with—some had worked as *merciaiuoli ambulanti* back home. It was also potentially profitable. In 1922, author Giovanni Perilli observed that some Denver peddlers had been in the business for a long time and "by their frugality have accumulated nice homes and are well to do."[155]

Colorado peddler's license issued to Dominic Figliolino, April 6, 1911. CIAPA Archive. Courtesy Rosalyn (Mastroianni) Hirsch. PCCLI4003A.

Peddlers often started out on foot, selling bread, produce, and other items from a basket. As they acquired more capital, they upgraded to a cart or even a horse-drawn wagon. Early peddlers provided rural areas and ethnic neighborhoods with everyday necessities: dry goods, glassware, plates, notions, and secondhand clothes. Some sold flowers, vegetables, and fruit they grew themselves in gardens or five- or ten-acre farms.

Nicola "Nick" Cavarra

Portrait of Nicola "Nick" Cavarra, 1930. From Attività Italiane nella Intermountain Region, *1930. PCCLI2545*

Nick Cavarra was born in Taranta, a town in Peligna, Italy, in 1887.[156] In 1906, he came to the United States with his parents Rose and Rocco Cavarra.[157] By 1908, his family was living in Denver, where his father worked as a decorator and Nick as a retoucher of photographs for H. V. Rothberger. A few years later, Nick opened his own photography studio in partnership with Umberto Morganti. The partnership was short-lived, and in 1912 he went to work as a photo printer for Frederic E. Post at The Post Studio in downtown Denver. Around 1922, Nick Cavarra took over the operations of The Post Studio and opened his own studio, which operated out of his home at 3556 Osage, the former residence of Frank Damascio.[158] Nick Cavarra remained in business in Denver as a photographer from 1921 until 1961.[159]

In 1930, the following concerning Nick Cavarra appeared in the book *Attività Italiane nella Intermountain Region*:

He is the owner and the director of the renowned Cavarra Studio...and is a true artist of photography as demonstrated by his large and fine pool of clients surrounding him. His windows are always admired and they recall the continuous attention of the most refined public. In Cavarra's studio the richest aristocracy of Colorado goes by daily and they do not know where to find a better place to satisfy their desires and to have the most delicate and exquisite works done.

In 1925, Nick Cavarra married Amalia DeSimone in Naples, Italy. Shortly after their marriage, the couple returned to Denver where their five children were born: Ada, Lillian, Josephine, Rocco, and Henrietta. Nick Cavarra died in Denver in 1964, followed by his wife Amalia who died in 1973.

Colacito

Domenico "Domenic" and Maria Angelina (DiManna) Colacito

Domenico "Domenic" Colacito was born in Abbruzzi, Italy, in 1876 to Giacinto and Raffaela (Sylvestri) Colacito. In 1895, he traveled alone to the United States at the age of nineteen. After living in New York, Connecticut, and Utah, he settled in Colorado around 1900, where he met and married Maria Angelina DiManna in 1902. Domenic and Angelina, the daughter of Vincenzo and Filomena (Vecchiarelli) DiManna, were the first couple married in the present-day Our Lady of Mount Carmel Church, after a fire destroyed the original church.[160] Angelina came to the United States, where her father was already living, in 1892 from Agnone, Italy.[161]

After their marriage, Angelina and Domenic moved into a home at 3614 Kalamath Street in north Denver's Little Italy. A short time later, they sent for Domenic's parents to join them in Denver. Later they purchased a home for Angelina's parents across the street from their own house. Together, Domenic and Angelina had fifteen children, eleven who survived infancy: Jerry, James, Edith, Assunta, Mary, Michael, Julia, Lucille, Anthony, Viola, and Esther.[162]

A homemaker, Angelina, who finished three years of formal schooling, spoke fluent English. Domenic had no formal education, but learned to read and write English fluently. In addition to working for the Denver Water Company until his retirement at the age of seventy, he also owned Clyde's Pub at Thirty-sixth and Jason Street for a time. Domenic was very active in the Mount Carmel Church where he served as an usher and as a president of the Saint Anthony's Society in the 1920s. Angelina Colicito died in 1940, followed by Domenic, who died in 1956.

Domenic and Angelina (DiManna) Colacito, by The Post Studio, Denver, 1902. CIAPA Archive. Courtesy Esther (Colacito) Head. PCCLI4679

Mick "Buck" and Lucille "Lou" (Appugliese/Appuglise) Colacito

Lucille Colacito (photo c. 1944), Fritsh AAGPBL baseball card, 1995. CIAPA Archive. Courtesy Esther (Colacito) Head. PCCLI4687

One of four children born to Joseph and Katherine Appugliese, Lucille "Lou" (Appugliese) Colacito was born in Florence, Colorado, in 1921. Her father Joseph was born in Italy around 1898 and came to America around 1915.[163] In 1919, he married Katherine, born in Colorado in 1905 to an Italian father and American mother. Joseph Appugliese worked for a number of years in the Colorado coal mines. In 1924, he moved his family to Denver, and by 1930 he was working as a mold maker for a steel works company.[164]

Around 1939, Lou started playing softball for local teams. One of her coaches was Mike "Buck" Colacito, son of Domenic and Angelina; they married in 1941. With Buck overseas in World War II, Lou signed a contract with the Kenosha (Wisconsin) Comets, a pro baseball team. Playing two seasons in 1944 and 1945, she was the first Denver woman to reach baseball's big leagues.[165] Her pay was $55 a week, plus $6.50 meal money a day when the team was on the road.[166] She went on to teach bowling to handicapped children and junior bowlers. In 1984, Lou Colacito was inducted into the Denver Softball Hall of Fame. Lou Colacito died on January 30, 1998.[167]

Domenico "Dominic" and Angelina "Angela" (Lorenzano) DeRose

Born in Caserta, near Naples, in southern Italy around 1862, Dominic DeRose came to America in 1883.[168] After living in Leadville, Colorado, where he worked as a railroad laborer, he moved to Denver and took a job with the Losasso family, who owned a farm near present-day Union Station. While working for the Losasso family, he met Angelo Covillo who showed him a picture of his sister-in-law in Italy, Angelina.[169] Dominic eventually returned to Italy where he proposed to her, and in 1888, the couple returned to Denver and were married at Sacred Heart Church. In 1890, their first son Frank was born, followed by: Joseph, James, Rose, John, Antoinette "Nettie," Elizabeth, Louie, Della, Albert, and George.[170]

By 1910, Dominic DeRose was peddling vegetables and the DeRose family was living off Thirty-third Avenue in north Denver's Little Italy. Dominic and Angelina's oldest sons, Frank and Joseph, were operating a grocery store, while James worked as a fruit-handler, John as a musician (he played the coronet), and the younger children attended school. Dominic DeRose died in Denver in 1930, followed by Angelina who died in 1950.

Fante

DeRose family, front row, left to right: Albert, Angelina, Dominic, George; middle row, left to right: Della, Nettie, Rose, Elizabeth, Louie; back row: John, Frank, Joseph, and Jimmy DeRose, c. 1914. CIAPA Archive. Courtesy Dick DeRose. PCCLI4363

John Thomas Fante

John Fante was born in Denver, Colorado, in 1909, and baptized at Our Lady of Mount Carmel Church. His father Nicola "Nick" Fante was a native of Torricella Peligna, Italy, who immigrated to America by way of Argentina. His mother Mary (Capolungo) Fante was born in Chicago to Italian immigrants from Potenza, Italy.[171] The son of a stonemason, he grew up poor. He attended parochial school in Boulder and Regis High School in Denver before attending college at the University of Colorado in Boulder.[172]

In 1929, John Fante dropped out of college to write. Around 1930, he moved to California, where in 1932 his first short story was published in *The American Mercury* magazine. He went on to publish several stories and books, and became interested in screenwriting. His most acclaimed work is *Ask the Dust*. Major themes in his works include poverty, Catholicism, family life, Italian American identity, and sports.

In 1937, John married Joyce Smart and together the couple had four children: Nick, Dan, Victoria, and James. In 1938, John's first novel, *Wait Until Spring, Bandini*, was published. The book, which was later made into a movie, was the first in a four-part saga about Arturo Bandini—the hero and Fante's alter-ego.[173] In the book, Fante returns to his working-class origins, showing the constant struggle with a person's class and ethnic affiliations as evidenced by the following quote, taken from *Wait Until Spring, Bandini*:

> His name was Arturo, but he hated it and wanted to be called John. His last name was Bandini, and he

Mary (Capolungo) Fante (left), Nick Fante (center), and Rose (Capolungo) Masselli (right), c. 1915. This photograph was likely taken at Lakeside Amusement Park, just west of Denver. CIAPA Archive. Courtesy Dan Fante. PCCLI5320

Wedding portrait of John and Mary (Varello) Ferrero, by Geo. Dalgleish, Georgetown, Colorado, 1897. CIAPA Archive. Courtesy Marie (Ferrero) Cosimi. PCCLI0691

wanted it to be Jones. His mother and father were Italians, but he wanted to be American. His father was a bricklayer, but he wanted to be a pitcher for the Chicago Cubs.

The other novels in the Arturo Bandini saga are *The Road to Los Angeles, Ask the Dusk,* and *Dreams from Bunker Hill,* his last novel.

In 1978, John Fante lost his eyesight and the use of his legs due to diabetes, forcing him to dictate his last novel to his wife. He died in California in 1983.[174]

Ferrero

John and Mary (Varello) Ferrero

John Ferrero was born in Torino (Turin) in the northern Piedmont Region in 1867 to Gaspare and Andrea (Poletto) Ferrero.[175] After serving in the Italian Army, he decided to make his way to America. In 1891, the twenty-four-year-old came to the United States and settled in Silver Plume, Colorado, with relatives, including a sister who ran a boardinghouse. He helped out in the boardinghouse saloon, found work as a miner, and served as an assistant to the undertaker, preparing the dead for burial.[176]

Mary Varello arrived in the United States around 1893 with her sister and uncle. Her mother had died in childbirth, and Mary and her sister, Lucy, were living in an orphanage when her father Carlo sent for them.

In May 1897, Mary Varello wed John Ferrero in Silver Plume. Two years later, the couple's first child, a daughter named Andriena, was born. The couple had five more children over the next fourteen years: Louise, Gosper, Charles, Marie, and Joseph.[177]

In 1905—having seen area miners come down with miner's consumption, a lung disease—John decided to leave Silver Plume. He bought a ten-acre farm in Welby. With his wife and children, he ran the farm until his death in 1925 from complications related to the harsh conditions of mining. His sons managed the farm for the next fifty years. Mary Ferrero died in Welby in 1953.

Anthony and Marie (Ferrero) Cosimi

John and Mary Ferrero's fifth child, Marie, was born in Welby in 1910. In 1929, Marie left Welby to attend the Colorado Teachers College (now the University of Northern Colorado) in Greeley, at a time when few women attended college. After graduating, she traveled with her mother to Europe; the two made a pilgrimage to the Ferrero family home in Torino (Turin).

After returning from Europe, Marie took a teaching job in Edgewater, Colorado, in 1931. Three years later in Denver, she married Anthony Cosimi, the brother of a childhood friend. Marie and Anthony had two sons: Ronald and Anthony Benedict.

Benedict Cosimi, at left, and Mike Cosimi, Firestone, Colorado, 1913. CIAPA Archive. Courtesy Marie (Ferrero) Cosimi. PCCLI0673

Anthony Cosimi was born in Rome in 1904. His parents came to America in 1907; uncertain of living conditions in the United States, they left him with his grandmother in Italy. Anthony's father, Benedict, worked in the Pennsylvania coal mines for four years, and after a brief return to Italy with his wife, Emma, he came to Colorado to mine coal in Firestone. After saving enough money, he sent for his family to join him. Benedict left mining for farming, and settled his family near Welby in 1920.

After their marriage, Anthony and Marie moved into the Cosimi family home in Welby, next to Assumption parish. Anthony helped manage the farm while Marie cared for their children and soon went back to teaching. She went on to serve as principal in the Adams County Elementary School System for more than forty years. Anthony was an active member of the Knights of Columbus, and Marie avidly pursued documentation of Welby history. Anthony Cosimi died in 2001, followed by Marie, who died in 2005.

Marie (Ferrero) Cosimi on the Cosimi Farm, Welby, by Dawn DeAno, 2004. CIAPA Archive. PCCLICPC0041

Lotito

Vincenzo Gaetano Antonio Lotito

Vincenzo Lotito was born in the southern region of Potenza, Italy, in 1848. In June 1872, he married twenty-year-old Maria Gerarda Cominiello, also from Potenza. Two years later, their first child, a daughter named Gerarda, was born, followed by Antonia, Rosa, and Rocco. In Italy, Vincenzo worked as a *guardiano* or foreman on a large farm near the city of Potenza. Around 1887, a man tried to extort money from Vincenzo's boss, the owner of the farm. After an altercation, the extortionist was killed, forcing Vincenzo to leave his homeland.[178]

Vincenzo left his family behind and arrived in America in 1888. He found work with the Union Pacific on a section gang, laying track in Utah and Idaho for a dollar a day. After a year, he had saved enough money to send for his family. By the time his wife and children arrived, the forty-one-year-old Vincenzo was physically unable to work on the section gang, and the family relocated to Denver. Soon, Vincenzo was in the peddling business. Every morning, he bought fresh fruit and vegetables wholesale from the Denver produce markets and sold them from his horse-drawn wagon along a route in south Denver.

In 1891, Vincenzo and Maria's last child, a daughter named Anna, was born in Denver. Sadly, Maria Lotito died three years later. Vincenzo married Louisa Sileo around 1895. Vincenzo Lotito died in Denver in 1909.

The Lotito family, back row, left to right: Vincenzo, Louisa (Sileo) Lotito (second wife of Vincenzo), and Sileo Lotito (Louisa's son from her first marriage). Front row, left to right: Rocco, Anna, Rosa, and Antonia Lotito, c. 1900. CIAPA Archive. Courtesy Michael and Lucille (Lotito) Pesce. PCCLI5616

Rocco Lotito Sr.

Born in Italy to Vincenzo and Maria Lotito, Rocco Lotito grew up in north Denver and attended Our Lady of Mount Carmel Catholic Church, where Mother Cabrini taught him catechism. After the sixth grade, he apprenticed with a leather-working company, the Colorado Saddlery Company, making harnesses and saddles. When his father died in 1909, the twenty-two-year-old took over his father's peddling route. That same year, while visiting a neighbor, Rocco saw a photograph of his neighbor's half-sister, the sixteen-year-old Concetta Maria Francesca Ruoti. He began writing to her in Potenza, and in 1910 she left Italy for America, arriving in Colorado that same year.[179] They were married at Our Lady of Mount Carmel, and in 1911, their first child, a son named Rocco Jr. was born, followed by Vincent "Jim," Lawrence, and Lucille.[180]

With the peddling business facing competition from new supermarkets, Rocco went into truck farming. In 1929, the family moved to Wheat Ridge, where Rocco rented an eight-acre farm. When he couldn't make a decent living on eight acres, Rocco bought thirty acres in Arvada. The Lotito Farm prospered, raising spinach, radishes, asparagus, rhubarb, strawberries, lettuce, corn, cabbage, carrots, Pascal Celery, pansies, and daisies. Rocco was soon known as the "Pansy King" for his four-inch-diameter flowers.

After World War II, Rocco and his son Jim built a greenhouse, where they grew chrysanthemums and other flowers year-round. The Lotito Farm became the Lotito Greenhouses, eventually expanding and moving to a bigger facility.

In 1919, Concetta had contracted the Spanish flu in the worldwide epidemic, leaving her heart weakened. She never fully recovered. In 1933, she died at age thirty-eight. Rocco Lotito died in Denver in 1967, leaving the business to his son Jim Lotito. Today, part of the original farm remains in the Lotito family, and Rocco and Concetta's daughter Lucille lives on the property.

Concetta Ruoti, Italy, 1909. CIAPA Archive. Courtesy Michael and Lucille (Lotito) Pesce. PCCLI1506

Colonies 1895–1919

Rocco Lotito Sr. (left), and Rocco Lotito Jr., planting raspberries on their farm in Arvada, c. 1935. CIAPA Archive. Courtesy Michael and Lucille (Lotito) Pesce. PCCLI1524

Mancinelli

Pasquale and Angelina (Palese) Mancinelli

Pasquale Mancinelli was born in 1877 in the southern Italian province of Potenza. Around 1906, he left his family to find work in America. After working as a laborer in construction and with the Denver & Rio Grande Western Railroad, he saved enough money to send for his family in 1909.[181] After eighteen days spent crossing the Atlantic, Pasquale's wife, Angelina, and their young children arrived in New York. They traveled by train to Denver. Pasquale met them and took them in a buckboard wagon to the town of Silt, where he was working on a reservoir near Harvey Gap. For two and a half years, the family lived in a tent with dirt floors. When the reservoir was completed, the Mancinelli family moved to New Castle, Colorado, where Pasquale took up farming.[182]

The Mancinelli family stayed in western Colorado until around 1920, when they moved to Denver.[183] A short time later, Pasquale and Angelina opened a neighborhood grocery at Thirty-fifth and Navajo Streets, in the lower level of the present-day parish hall of Our Lady of Mount Carmel.[184] The Mancinelli family, including Angelina and Pasquale's eleven children: Rocco, Lucia, Jenny, Vera, Angelo, Edith, Tony, Josephine, Helen, Albert, and Marie, lived in an apartment above the store. One of many family-owned Italian stores in north Denver, P. Mancinelli & Sons Grocery and Market was reminiscent of old country stores, with hanging gourds of provolone cheese and slabs of meat cut by handsaws and knives. The cheese was handmade (a skill Pasquale had learned as a boy and as a sheepherder in Italy), as was the sausage they made every day.[185] Images of the Mancinelli family and Italy hung above the shelves.

P. Mancinelli & Sons, 3300 Osage Street, Denver, with Tony Mancinelli behind the counter and Pasquale Mancinelli near the column, c. 1930. After a number of years at Thirty-fifth and Navajo Street in the present-day Our Lady of Mount Carmel Parish Hall, P. Mancinelli & Sons moved to its second location at 3300 Osage Street. After fifty years at Thirty-third and Osage, it moved to 3245 Osage Street in 1974, its last location. CIAPA Archive. Courtesy Albert "Ice" and Marie Mancinelli. PCCLI5566.

Pasquale and Angelina Mancinelli, Denver, 1944. CIAPA Archive. Courtesy Albert "Ice" and Marie Mancinelli. PCCLI0308

The store sold fresh vegetables, meats, cheeses, pasta, imported olive oil and canned goods, peppers, pasta-making equipment, and even bocce balls, used for the Italian lawn-bowling game.

One of the oldest continuously owned family stores in north Denver, P. Mancinelli & Sons closed in 1993 after seventy-two years in business. According to Tony Mancinelli (Pasquale and Angelina's son, who ran the store with his father and later his wife Virginia, daughter Angela, son Tony Jr., and sister-in-law Marie), the longevity and success of P. Mancinelli & Sons was due to specialization and reputation. The store specialized in Italian goods, including the family's homemade products, did not try to compete with supermarket chains, and relied heavily on the family's reputation.[186] Angelina Mancinelli died in Denver in 1947, followed by her husband Pasquale, who died in 1962.

Albert "Ice" and Maria "Marie" Rose (Inglese/English) Mancinelli

Born on Christmas Day, 1922, Albert "Ice" Mancinelli was named after Prince Albert of Italy. His siblings were a little upset at the disruption of the Christmas festivities that his birth caused. The son of Pasquale and Angelina Mancinelli, Albert was "Ice" from early on. He was the only child with blond hair in his family; when his siblings asked their mother if the ice delivery man was blond, the name stuck, even after his hair darkened.[187]

Albert "Ice" and Marie (English) Mancinelli, by Dawn DeAno, Denver, 2004. CIAPA Archive. PCCLICPC0024

Growing up in the Depression, Ice Mancinelli experienced hard times and good times in Denver's Little Italy. At age ten, he started boxing at Checkers Night Club, located at West Thirty-third and Pecos Streets, and at thirteen he was fighting in Golden Gloves amateur tournaments; he won his first of five titles when he was fourteen. He

Marie and Albert Mancinelli Jr., in Mancinelli Sporting Goods truck, 1955. CIAPA Archive. Courtesy Albert "Ice" and Marie Mancinelli. PCCLI0312

is the only Denver fighter to win division titles in five weight classes. In 1940, Ice won his first professional fight against Kid Corbett in three rounds. He was destined for a career in boxing until he joined the Navy in 1941. He served in World War II in Alaska and Japan and aboard the USS *Saratoga*. In February 1945, the *Saratoga* was fired upon and bombed by nearly twenty Japanese planes, including five Kamikaze pilots who crashed into the carrier. Radiation from the attack cost Ice two fingers and half of his left foot. His right leg was later amputated below the knee.[188]

After his discharge, Ice returned to Denver's Little Italy. He worked as a buyer at Denargo Market and owned Mancinelli Sporting Goods at 4036 Tejon Street. In 1949, he married Maria "Marie" Rose Inglese/English. Born in Denver, Marie met Ice when she took a job at the Mancinelli family grocery store. Marie and Ice moved into the home originally owned by Marie's mother, and the couple has remained there for over forty years. Ice and Marie had four children, all born in Denver: Albert Jr., Maria, Helen, and Daniel.[189]

Frank and Mary Mancini, Denver, c. 1964. Frank Mancini married Denver-born Mary Concetta Libonati in 1901. Together they had three children: Philomena, Francis, and Rosalyn. CIAPA Archive. Courtesy Aldo Notarianni. PCCLI0811

Mancini

Francesco "Frank" Mancini

Born in Italy in 1887, Frank Mancini left for America in 1901.[190] He came to Denver at the urging of his uncle,

La Nazione, *November 28, 1903. CIAPA Archive. Courtesy Our Lady of Mount Carmel. PCCLI5317*

Father Felice Mariano Lepore, the pastor of Our Lady of Mount Carmel Catholic Church. Father Lepore hoped his nephew would become a priest, but Frank had other ideas. After briefly working for the railroad, he took a job as a writer with the Denver newspaper *La Nazione*, an Italian-language weekly founded by Father Lepore (*La Nazione* was published from 1896 to 1920).[191]

In 1905, Frank founded his own Italian-language newspaper, *Il Risveglio*, or "The Awakening." The independent newspaper featured articles about Italians and news from around Colorado and Italy. Over time, Frank bought four other Italian-language newspapers and incorporated them into his own. In 1923, he started a weekly newspaper in English, *Colorado*. The paper survives as *The Colorado Leader*, a law publication.

Active with the unions and forever standing up for the rights of working people, Frank Mancini gave speeches to striking workers during the Ludlow coal-mining strike

Mancini Press *(where the newspaper* Il Risveglio *was published and printed), left to right: Lindo Perucca, the bookkeeper; Frank Mancini, the editor; and Gregorio Notarianni, a writer, c. 1922. CIAPA Archive. Courtesy Aldo Notarianni. PCCLI0812*

of 1914. Throughout the Depression, he helped his fellow Italian immigrants find employment. He belonged to nearly every Italian organization and served on many boards, including the State Department of Labor. The honors bestowed on him included the Star of Solidarity (awarded by the president of Italy to prominent American citizens of Italian heritage) and the dedication of the Frank A. Mancini Senior Center in north Denver in 1979.[192] Frank Mancini died in Denver in 1977 at the age of ninety.

Mastroianni

John Battista Mastroianni

John Battista Mastroianni, the son of Liberato and Rosina (Villano) Mastroianni, was born in Denver in 1902. His parents were married in Denver in 1901. John's father was from Boiana, Italy, and immigrated to America in the 1880s. A widower with two children, Liberato worked as a miner and laborer for the railroad, setting ties and rail throughout the western part of Colorado. John's mother Rosina was from Potenza and came to Colorado in 1891 with her husband Pasquale Vignola. Rosina's sister, Gaetana Villano, was already living in Colorado at the time. Sadly, Rosina's husband Pasquale died in 1900, leaving Rosina a widow with five children: Joseph, Paul, Anthony, Michael, and George. After Rosina and Liberato married, Liberato went into farming to support his family including his children with Rosina: John, Angelina, and Louise.[193]

Wedding portrait, Theresa Figliolino and John Mastroianni (left) with attendants James Labriola and Julia Longo, by Cavarra Studio, Denver, 1924. CIAPA Archive. Courtesy Rosalyn (Mastroianni) Hirsch. PCCLI0229

In 1924, John Mastroianni married Theresa Figliolino in Denver. Theresa, the daughter of Italian immigrants Dominic and Feliciana (Pierro) Figliolino, was born in Denver in 1904. Her father worked as a fruit and vegetable peddler while her mother worked at the Baily-Underhill Manufacturing Company.[194]

Tritch Hardware Company with John Mastroianni, front row, second man from left, wearing a white shirt, tie, and cap, Denver, 1922. CIAPA Archive. Courtesy Rosalyn (Mastroianni) Hirsch. PCCLI1100

In 1926, Theresa and John had one daughter, Rosalyn (Mastroianni) Hirsch. John worked as a hardware salesman at the Tritch Hardware Company until he contracted tuberculosis in the late 1920s. After recovering from the disease, he worked at the Goldberg Brothers Hardware Company in the late 1930s and 1940s. A graduate of the Barnes Business School, he eventually acquired the Johnson & Loud Hardware store around 1955. John Mastroianni died in Denver in 1981.

Morganti

Umberto Morganti

Umberto Morganti was born in the southern Italian city of Castel di Sangro in the Abruzzi region in 1878.[195] Educated in Florence, he chose publishing as his profession. He worked as a newspaperman and photographer in Livorno, where he met Noemi Rossetti, whom he married in 1901.[196] Both were from prominent Italian families: Umberto's brother Victor was a professor of philosophy, languages, and mathematics at the University of Tunis; Noemi's brother, Manlio, was one of the largest stamp and coin vendors in Paris; and her sister, Velia (Rossetti) Sgarbazzini, owned a tailor shop with her husband in England.[197]

Active in politics and critical of the Italian government, Umberto Morganti was fined for reporting a scandal involving the mayor of his town. Discouraged by the incident, and at the urging of a friend, he left Italy, arriving at Ellis Island in May 1907.[198] In a 1956 *Rocky Mountain News* article, Umberto recalled his experience arriving in America:

Attilia Becuzzi (left), Ugo Castagnoli (center), and Umberto Morganti (right) in front of the Instituto Tecnico di Livorno, c. 1896. CIAPA Archive. Courtesy Debbie (Spaulding) Fugate and Sandra (Morganti) Spaulding. PCCLI3626

> On Ellis Island, I sit down in this large room with a bunch of people. I clutch my valise [suitcase] and slide along the bench as names are called. Once called for inspection we moved to a hall where a man examines our eyes and tongues. He paints two letters on my shoulder. Then he sends me to his dark little room like a jail cell. I

ask myself, "What is this?" as only I and two other men go to this room. Soon a doctor comes and examines me some more. He pounds on my chest and listens. "This man doesn't have TB," he said and rubbed the letters off my shoulder.

After passing the inspection at Ellis Island, Umberto arrived at Battery Park in New York, where he asked a taxi driver:

> ...to take me to this hotel written on this note where I know other Italians stay. He drives me around for 20 minutes and I end up across the street from where I was. The man wants $3 and all the money I have is a 500-lira note. Some Italians help me and I get my change.[199]

Umberto finally made his way to the hotel and after a short stay in New York, arrived in Denver. Once he was settled, he sent for Noemi, who arrived after twenty-one days on board a crowded ship, caring for their two-year-old son, Emilio.

In Denver, Umberto went to work for the Italian newspaper *La Capitale*, a weekly independent newspaper published in Italian. Umberto wrote editorials on issues such as the killing of an Italian man named Jerry Carabetta in 1919. The paper enjoyed a twelve-year run between 1907 and 1919, during which time Umberto worked closely with fellow Italians Giuseppe Cuneo and friend Giuseppe "Joseph" Mapelli. Umberto worked as its manager, editor, staff writer, and eventually, director. In addition to his work for *La Capitale,* he wrote the Italian column for the *Denver Times* (1914 to 1919) and for the *Rocky Mountain News* (1913 to 1922). In 1920, he published the first issue of *La Frusta,* or "The Whip," an Italian-language paper

Umberto and Noemi Morganti in front of their home at 741 Kearney Street, Denver, c. 1925. CIAPA Archive. Courtesy Debbie (Spaulding) Fugate and Sandra (Morganti) Spaulding. PCCLI3620

that featured local, national, and international news as well as fiction.[200] The paper was a strong anti–Ku Klux Klan voice in 1920s Denver.[201] Umberto also taught Italian at the Emily Griffith Opportunity School and was a playwright, publishing three plays in 1945.[202]

Of his many accomplishments, Umberto Morganti is most remembered as a portrait photographer. Countless Colorado families have among their prized possessions photographs bearing the mark "Morganti Studio." Morganti opened the Denver studio in 1909 and worked as a photographer for over fifty years.[203]

In 1908, Noemi and Umberto's son Cesare was born, the second of six children who lived past infancy.[204] The Morganti family lived in north Denver on Navajo Street for a number of years before moving to south Denver, where they lived at 741 Kearney Street for over forty-five years. In 1916, Emilio died of heart disease. Umberto died in Denver in 1965, followed by Noemi who died in 1968.[205]

Cesarino "Cesare" Emilio Morganti

Cesare Morganti was born in Denver in 1908, the son of Umberto and Noemi Morganti. In 1931, he graduated from the University of Denver, where he majored in romance languages.[206] Like his father, Cesare worked as a photographer and journalist and had a passion for theater. At a young age, he helped out at his father's photography studio, processing orders and photographing clients. He also helped with his father's newspaper assignments and edited the youth page of *The Trumpet* (he became the newspaper's managing editor in the 1940s). While in college, Cesare was hired to do dialect roles in plays at Elitch's Summer Theater. In the mid-1930s, he traveled to California, where he found work with the Call Board Theater, earning $18.50 a week—a fair salary during the Depression.

Although Cesare remained passionate about acting, photography became his career. He opened his own studio and later took over his father's. Over the years, he noticed that many of the young women he photographed were uncomfortable in front of the camera and often

Wedding of Cesare and Carolina (Odisio) Morganti (Cesare's first wife), 1933. CIAPA Archive. Courtesy Debbie (Spaulding) Fugate and Sandra (Morganti) Spaulding. PCCLI3708

Morganti children, Mario (left), Cesarino "Rino" (center), and Sandra Morganti (right), c. 1950. Cesare and Carolina (Odisio) Morganti had two children together: Sandra and Mario Morganti. Rino Morganti was Cesare's son with his second wife Gladys. CIAPA Archive. Courtesy Debbie (Spaulding) Fugate and Sandra (Morganti) Spaulding. PCCLI3669

unfamiliar with makeup, so in the 1940s he and his second wife, Gladys Nickerson, opened a charm and modeling school.[207]

Cesare retired in 1968 and moved to Greeley with Gladys. They bought and remodeled the old La Grange School outside of town, and Cesare took advantage of his surroundings to pursue an interest in color landscape photography.[208] A photographer for over forty years, Cesare Morganti was also active in the Italian American community. He served for many years as president of the Italian-American Civic League, which promoted the advancement of Italian Americans and helped families in need.[209] Cesare Morganti died in Greeley in 1983.

A Closer Look
The Morganti Studio

The Morganti Studio was opened by Umberto Morganti in 1909. At a young age, Umberto's son Cesare started working with his father in the photography studio. According to

Morganti Studio, by Umberto Morganti, 1918. CIAPA Archive. Courtesy Debbie (Spaulding) Fugate and Sandra (Morganti) Spaulding. PCCLI3700

Morganti Studio with Cesare (left) and Emilio Morganti, by Umberto Morganti, c. 1914. CIAPA Archive. Courtesy Debbie (Spaulding) Fugate and Sandra (Morganti) Spaulding. PCCLI3707

Cesare Morganti, "I was born with 'hypo' [a chemical used to fix photographic images] in my veins."[210] Together, Umberto and Cesare Morganti photographed countless families, events, and places in Denver, Central City, and other parts of Colorado. Umberto Morganti worked at the Morganti Studio from 1909 to 1961.[211] Cesare Morganti worked at the studio on and off from around 1938 to 1968.

Noce

Angelo Noce

Born in Genoa in 1847, Angelo Noce came to America at age three. His family ended up in California, following news of gold. After college, Angelo found work as a typesetter and was an interpreter for the courts of Sacramento. He worked as a writer and notary public and served as president of the California Typographical Union.[212]

In 1882, Noce and his family came to Denver. Angelo found work in a printing office and was appointed as the city's deputy assessor. In 1885, at his own expense, he founded the first weekly Italian newspaper in Colorado, *La Stella*—the only Italian newspaper between New York and San Francisco at the time. In the first issue of *La Stella*, published on October 3, 1885, Angelo Noce wrote to his readers:

OUR BOW TO THE PUBLIC

To-day, we respectfully place before the public

the first issue of *La Stella*. Believing that the Italian population of this city and surroundings has reached such proportions as to warrant the publication of a weekly journal in the Italian language, we have set ourselves to the task, earnestly hoping that our venture will meet with the success it deserves. *La Stella* will be independent in politics, fearless in its discussion of men and things. No political "boss" will control its columns; no "ring" will dictate the policy it shall pursue. It will be the aim of this journal to give its readers the latest and most important telegraphic news, domestic and foreign, and its local columns will keep the public posted as to doings of Denver and vicinity. It may not be amiss to state here that this is a personal venture. The proprietor and manager will alone be responsible for what appears in the columns of the paper—uninfluenced by the prejudices of race, party or religion.

A competent corps of editors will always be employed and politics discussed from an unbiased standpoint. If the venture fails, we alone will be the losers. If the public respond to what we think an urgent need, we will consider ourselves amply repaid for our trouble and expense.

In order to convince the public that we mean what we say, we will furnish *La Stella* gratis for three weeks. If in that time we become convinced that our nationality is patriotic enough to endorse our enterprise, we will continue. If we be convinced to the contrary, we will give up the venture as impracticable, and no complaints will be made.

With these few words of greeting we launch *La Stella* upon the turbulent waters of journalism.

Respectfully,
   ANGELO NOCE,
    Proprietor and Manager

Angelo Noce, 1922. From Dr. Giovanni Perilli's Colorado and the Italians in Colorado, Denver, 1922. PCCLI2553

La Stella featured articles in Italian about the Denver community, local and national politics, and Italy. Noce printed the paper until 1889, when he was appointed deputy sheriff for Arapahoe County. In 1896, he went to work as a clerk for the state House of Representatives. Two years later, the Labor Party nominated him as its candidate to the House.[213]

Born in the same province as Christopher Columbus, Angelo Noce joined the ranks of Italians who celebrated Columbus as a way to honor their homeland while paying tribute to the contributions of Italians to the development of their new home in America.[214] In addition to proposing a monument and lobbying to rename Mt. Massive in Colorado to "Mt. Columbus," Noce wrote a bill to make October 12 the legal holiday of Columbus Day.[215] After failing in 1905, the bill passed in 1907—making Colorado the first state in the Union to officially celebrate Columbus Day.[216] Noce also researched and documented the history and contributions of Italians in Colorado, which he shared with Dr. Giovanni Perilli, who included the information in his book *Colorado and the Italians in Colorado* published in 1922.[217] Angelo Noce died in California on January 5, 1922, at the age of seventy-four.[218]

A Closer Look
Columbus Day in Colorado

Columbus Day Program, Denver, 1934. CIAPA Archive. Courtesy Isabel (Veraldi) Vecchiarelli. PCCLI2305A

On October 12, 1907, Colorado became the first state to celebrate Columbus Day as an official annual holiday. In Denver, Italian societies marched in a parade with seventy-five German American veterans from the Franco-Prussian War. Angelo Noce—the man who initiated the idea in the 1880s and led the drive for its designation—served as grand marshal. Antone Garibino, color bearer for the Garibaldi Society, dressed as Columbus. The parade ended at the Capitol with a speech by Governor Buchtel. Other states followed Colorado's lead, and in 1937 President Franklin D. Roosevelt declared the date a national holiday.

The first celebrations—which took various forms from picnics and parades to fireworks and festivals—happened during a time when Italian Americans faced widespread discrimination. For them, commemorating the Genoese seafarer's arrival in the New World was a way to affirm their heritage while proclaiming pride in their adopted country.

Opposition to Columbus Day in Colorado emerged in the 1990s. American Indians and others questioned the so-called "discovery" of a continent already inhabited by diverse peoples with rich and ancient cultures. When Denver's Italian community planned a parade marking the five hundredth anniversary of Columbus's voyage in 1992, activists threatened to block the route. To avoid a potentially volatile confrontation, the leader of the celebration called off the parade twenty minutes before it was scheduled to begin.

The debate continues to this day. In Colorado, perhaps as in no other place in the country, October 12 annually reignites the struggle over the meaning of Columbus Day.

Pastore

Frank and Mary (LaCivita/Lansville) Pastore

Frank Pastore was born in Caramonica, Italy, in the southern province of Abruzzi in 1887. He came to the United States at sixteen, settling first in Boston. After working for the railroad, he moved to Denver around 1904. He bought a horse and wagon and peddled produce in Denver neighborhoods well into the 1930s. Meanwhile, he also used his horse and wagon to excavate for house foundations. Soon working as a general contractor, Pastore built more than one hundred homes and other buildings in Denver.[219]

At age twenty-one, Frank married the sixteen-year-old Mary LaCivita/Lansville at Our Lady of Mount Carmel Church. Born in Gunnison, Colorado, in 1893, Mary had moved to Denver as a child and attended Our Lady of Mount Carmel School. Frank and Mary's first child, Mildred, was born in 1910, followed by Ernest, Josephine, Ellen, Adeline, Rose, Lillian, Irene, and Frank Jr.[220]

In 1973, *The Denver Post* reported on the reunion of Frank Pastore, age eighty-six, and his brothers, Giacomo (seventy-three) and Joe (eighty-one). The *Post* reported that Frank had intended to leave Italy for only a short while and then return home to his family.

Wedding portrait, Frank and Mary (LaCivita/Lansville) Pastore, Denver, 1908. CIAPA Archive. Courtesy Mildred (Pastore) LaConte and Corrine (LaConte) Bush. PCCLI5083

Colonies 1895–1919

Frank Pastore (right) and customers at his peddler wagon at 3710 Vallejo Street, Denver, c. 1920. CIAPA Archive. Courtesy Mildred (Pastore) LaConte and Corrine (LaConte) Bush. PCCLI0580

When he left, his brother Giacomo was only three. But like countless others, Frank never returned to Italy. It was seventy years before he and Giacomo saw each other again. At the reunion Giacomo, who spoke no English, had his son translate his words into English: "I'm just really glad that God favored me to see my brother again." Frank Pastore died in Denver in 1979, followed by his wife Mary who died in 1994.

Father Felice Mariano Lepore, c.1891. CIAPA Archive. Courtesy Our Lady of Mount Carmel Church. PCCLI5080

A Closer Look
Our Lady of Mount Carmel Catholic Church

When Italians moved out of the Bottoms area along the South Platte River to north Denver, many began to attend St. Patrick's Church. The mostly Irish parish sufficed for a while, but the Italians wanted their own place of worship. They found a champion for their cause in Father Felice "Felix" Mariano Lepore.

Father Lepore, a native of the province of Avellino in southern Italy and the founder of the newspaper *La Nazione*, already had a reputation as an advocate for the Italian community. Assisted by the Mount Carmel Society, Father Lepore bought seven lots on Palmer Avenue (now Navajo Street) in 1894. There, he built a small wood-frame church in honor of Our Lady of

Interior of Our Lady of Mount Carmel Church, Denver, c. 1925. CIAPA Archive. Courtesy Our Lady of Mount Carmel Church. PCCLI2023

Our Lady of Mount Carmel Church, Denver, 1950. CIAPA Archive. Courtesy Ralph F. and Rosemary Mancinelli. PCCLI1321

Mount Carmel. The structure burned down in 1898, but the parish didn't despair. In 1904, they dedicated a new Mount Carmel Church.[221]

Today, Our Lady of Mount Carmel remains a predominantly Italian parish that continues to unite Denver's Italian American community. Former residents of Little Italy return for fellowship and friendship. Even the less active members return for the annual bazaar and the monthly La Prima Domenica (First Sunday) celebration, which includes a cultural reception following an Italian-language Mass.

Pollice

Angelo Michael Pollice

The youngest of nine children and the son of a leading architect, Angelo Michael Pollice was born in 1875 in Montagano, Italy, a commune in the southern province of Campobasso. After eight years of musical study, he earned his certificate to direct a municipal band. He went to Bojano, also in southern Italy, where he directed a forty-five-piece band and taught music theory for ten years.[222]

Pollice's Concert Band of Denver, with bandmaster Angelo Michael Pollice (pictured wearing bow tie at left of child with baton), Denver, c. 1915. CIAPA Archive. Courtesy John Pollice Jr., Mary (Pollice) Metz, and Angela (Pollice) Kelsey. PCCLI0725

In 1905, Angelo married Concetta Maria Anna Mariano, also of Montagano. The couple immigrated to the United States in 1910. Four years later, their family settled in Denver, where they lived on Navajo Street in the heart of Little Italy with their sons, John and Emilio. Angelo worked as a composer, arranger, teacher, and director of various bands, including the Denver Municipal Band, Mount Carmel Church Band, and Assumption Parish Band in Welby, Colorado.

In 1925, Louis S. Spallone built a store building at 3554 and 3558 Navajo for Angelo and Maria. They later opened a drugstore and dry goods store, which the Pollice family ran for many years. In 1940, after Maria Pollice's death, the store at 3558 Navajo was sold to Sam Scaglia, who opened the Sally Ann Creamery there. The creamery remained in business at the location until 1962.

In 1948, the Usaly Club of Denver (a club of Americans of Italian descent) honored Angelo Pollice for over thirty years of contributions to the development of music among Denver youth. The Rocky Mountain Accordion Society paid additional honors to Angelo as the first musician to play and teach accordion in the state.[223] Angelo Pollice died in Denver on March 15, 1962.

Santangelo

Raffaele "Ralph" and Antonia (Lotito) Santangelo

Raffaele Santangelo was born in 1872 in Potenza, Italy. At twenty-eight he left his home and family—including his wife Antonia Maria—and came to America. Five years later, Ralph (his Americanized name) sent for his wife and children to join him in Denver, where others from Potenza had already established themselves.²²⁴

At their home at Thirty-ninth and Pecos Streets in north Denver, Antonia cared for the couple's nine children: Louis, Mary, Jeanette, Sam, John, Ralph, Joe, Tony, and Rosa. To support his family, Ralph peddled fruits and vegetables, selling produce from his horse-drawn wagon.²²⁵ In 1918, the couple bought a fifteen-acre farm at Sixty-second and Pecos.²²⁶ Soon, Santangelo Produce was selling a variety of crops to customers and at the produce market downtown, to which Ralph traveled early every morning.

After the death of her husband in 1927, Antonia ran the farm with her children. She died in 1939, leaving the farm to her sons Tony and John. After struggling to keep the family business going, Tony went to work for Dawson Produce. In the 1950s, he bought the produce company, renamed it Santangelo Produce Company, and brought John on as a partner. The Santangelos distributed produce across Colorado until the 1980s.²²⁷

Ralph Santangelo with his horse and peddler's wagon, Denver, 1912. CIAPA Archive. Courtesy Al and Ralph Santangelo. PCCLI5109

Vallero

Vincenzo Vallero

In 1885, immigrant Vincenzo Vallero came alone to Silver Plume, where he worked as a miner. His wife, Catarina, and two children joined him later. In 1892, the family moved to Central City, where Vincenzo opened the Vienna Saloon, offering customers a selection of wines and cigars.

During the late 1890s, Vincenzo, Catarina, and their five children left Central City to open a store in Denver.²²⁸ After a trip to Italy to secure sources of wine and olive oil, they selected a site at West Thirty-fourth Avenue and Bell Street (now Osage) in north Denver's Little Italy. The new

Vallero Mercantile, West Thirty-fourth Avenue and Osage Street, Charles Vallero (driver), and Frank Maracci (passenger), c. 1910. Gift Terry Zaremba. 90.456.1

store opened in 1901 with family living quarters above the business. The Valleros rented space behind the store to boarders, usually men living alone and working to save money to bring their families to America.

Vincenzo delivered his merchandise to restaurants and individual customers, first by horse and wagon and later by delivery truck. When he died in 1909, his sons Carlo "Charley" and Dominick took over the business. Charley ultimately became the sole proprietor, keeping the business alive through the Depression, Prohibition, and World War II by cutting back on the grocery business, operating as a wholesale house, and moving the company to downtown Denver. After one hundred years in business, the Vallero Mercantile, still managed by the Vallero family, continues to distribute imported and domestic fancy groceries.[229]

Villani/Villano

Salvatore Michele and Giulia "Julia" Palma (Manta) Villano

Salvatore Michele Villano (sometimes spelled Villani in historical documents) was born in Potenza, Italy, in 1870. Around 1890, he immigrated to the United States, following his sisters, Gaetana Villano and Rosina Vignola.

After working in Denver for about ten years, Salvatore Michele returned to Potenza to find a wife. In 1901, at age thirty, he married the sixteen-year-old Giulia "Julia" Palma Manta. Shortly after their wedding, the couple returned to the United States along with Salvatore Michele's older brother, Andrea, and the son of his oldest sister Maria, Michele Taddonio.[230]

Although Julia had a cousin in New York, her husband insisted they go back to Denver, where they settled in the Bottoms north of Union Station. In 1902, their first child, a son named Rocco, died in infancy. Their second child, Caroline, died from the measles at age three. Their next eight children all lived to adulthood: Louise, Paul Joseph, Carolyn, Anthony "Red," Vincent, Paul Clyde, George, and Pearl.

Villano family, left to right: Salvatore Michele, Caroline, Julia, Paul Joseph, and Louise Villano, Denver, 1910. CIAPA Archive. Courtesy Michael C. and Clair Villano. PCCLI0026

While Julia cared for the children at home, Salvatore Michele peddled produce from his wagon in the Capitol Hill area. Around 1910, he and Julia moved the family to north Denver. The home was modest and typical of north Denver housing: it had an outdoor oven in the back, a little garden plot, and a rabbit hutch and chicken coop. By 1927, Salvatore Michele was a laborer for the Union Pacific, and by 1931 the family had saved enough money to expand their home.

Julia Villano was in the process of becoming a naturalized citizen when she died of a heart attack in 1943. At the time of her death, four of her sons were serving in World War II. Salvatore Michele Villano died in Denver in 1951.

Election card, Paul Joseph Villano, Denver, District No. 9, c. 1950s. CIAPA Archive. Courtesy Michael C. and Clair Villano. PCCLI0025

Paul Joseph Villano

The fourth of Salvatore Michele and Julia Villano's ten children, Paul Villano left school in the eighth grade when his father became ill. He sold newspapers and worked in the Globeville meatpacking houses to support his family. While delivering meat for the Iacino brothers at the Diamond A Market, he met his

Colonies 1895–1919

Paul and Margie (Jachetta) Villano, Denver, c. 1925. CIAPA Archive. Courtesy Michael C. and Clair Villano. PCCLI5270

future wife, Margaret "Margie" Rafael Jachetta, who worked in the store as a cashier. Paul and Margie were married in 1928 and had two children together: Paul J. and Michael C. Villano.[231]

In 1943, Paul Villano and Ernie Anselmo opened Ernie and Paul's Market in north Denver. In addition to running the market, Paul was a precinct committeeman for over twenty years and served under Mike Pomponio, captain of District 10, for the Democrats. He oversaw the polling location for the north Denver precinct, located in his mother-in-law's home. Voters cast their ballots in a locked wooden box in the Jachetta kitchen after marking their choices behind one of six canvas voting booths in the dining room.

After twenty years in the meat business, Paul Villano sold the market to focus on politics, working for a time as a bailiff. In 1974, he retired, and in 1983 Paul died in Wheat Ridge, Colorado.

Michael C. Villano

Paul and Margie's son, Michael C. Villano, was born and raised in north Denver. He attended the University of Denver as one of the first Boettcher Scholars, earning his law degree in 1958. Shortly after, he left home for the first time to serve in the U.S. Army's Judge Advocate General's Corps. While in the service, he met Clair Elizabeth Pittman, the daughter of the post commandant at Fort Meade, Maryland. They married in 1960 and had three children together: Stephen, Michael Jr., and David.[232]

Michael C. Villano's law career included government and private practice. In 2005, he retired as a Senior Judge. He holds the longest continuous membership in the Potenza

Michael C. and Clair (Pittman) Villano, Ft. George G. Meade, Maryland, 1960. CIAPA Archive. Courtesy Michael C. and Clair Villano. PCCLI5506

Lodge; his father started paying his dues when he turned sixteen. Clair worked in consumer protection and taught sociology at Regis University for twenty years.

A CLOSER LOOK
The Pueblo Colony

Pueblo's smelters, railroads, mills, and steel works first drew Italian immigrants to the city. Some Italians came from other parts of the country, especially New Orleans, New York, and Philadelphia, while others came straight from Italy—particularly the southern regions of Sicily, Calabria, and Campania.

Many Italians lived and worked in Bessemer, a company town near Pueblo's steel mill. By the 1920s, Pueblo itself had a large Italian colony. Most Italian men worked for Colorado Fuel & Iron, with others working for the railroad, at the coke ovens, or in the area's coal mines, mills, and limestone quarries. Additionally, many Italian families in Pueblo ran small businesses including grocery stores, bars, and restaurants.

Pueblo's Italians formed fraternal organizations such as the Società Protettiva e Beneficenza di Pueblo, Società Cristoforo Columbo, and the Società Fedeltà Italiana. The groups offered financial and emotional support for Italians and sponsored a variety of social functions. Many members joined the societies for the death benefit, which covered a traditional funeral and the sending of a photograph of the deceased to the family back in Italy.

A key to the Italian community's spiritual and social life was the Roman Catholic Church. The first resident priest of Pueblo was Italian Reverend Charles M. Pint, S.J., who arrived in 1872. By 1900, the Italian community had grown big enough to build its own church, Mount Carmel, which opened several years later.

Chiariglione

Ettore "Hector" Chiariglione

Hector Chiariglione was born in northern Italy in 1856 and migrated to the United States in 1880.[233] He settled in New York, where he met and married his wife Mary, the daughter of Italian immigrants. In 1883, Hector and Mary moved to Denver, then to Breckenridge, and finally to Pueblo, where they raised their children: Andrew, Louis, Marie, and John.[234]

In Pueblo, Hector opened a jewelry store, followed by a travel office. In 1897, he started the weekly Italian-language newspaper *L'Unione*. He served as its director until 1921, when a flood destroyed the business's offices and printing shop. After the flood, Hector sold the newspaper to one of his employees, Vincent Massari.[235]

Pueblo newspaper office, left to right: Vincent Massari, Hector Chiariglione, and Joseph Battaglia, c. 1915. CIAPA Archive. Courtesy John Panepinto. PCCLI5949

Hector Chiariglione was deeply involved in the Italian community.[236] In 1894, he founded the Cristoforo Colombo Lodge No. 1309 in Pueblo, and from 1896, he served as the national president of the Colombian Federation of Italian Associations of America, a position he held for eight years.[237] He helped organize Pueblo's Columbus Day Parade (which began in 1900) and erect the Christopher Columbus Monument in Pueblo.

In 1924, Hector moved to southern California. He died on April 22, 1940, at the age of eighty-three.

DiSipio

Angelo and Concetta (D'Orazio) DiSipio

Angelo DiSipio was born in 1879 in the southern Italian province of Chieti. In 1903, he married Concetta D'Orazio, also from Chieti, and in 1905, their daughter Louisa was born.[238] That same year, Angelo left his family and homeland for the United States. In 1909, his wife and daughter joined him and the family settled in Pueblo, where five more children were born: Tony, Anna, Nick, Ermelinda, and Rosie.[239]

Angelo DiSipio worked at Colorado Fuel & Iron's steel mill. Concetta and Angelo returned to Chieti in 1939. Angelo died in Italy on January 5, 1968.

A Closer Look
Colorado Fuel & Iron Company

Angelo DiSipio, c. 1910. CIAPA Archive. Courtesy Pauline Annette DiSipio. PCCLI5642

The Colorado Fuel & Iron Company (CF&I) powered Colorado's economy, politics, and culture from the 1890s to the mid-twentieth century. It started as the Colorado Coal & Iron Company (CC&I), a Pueblo steel mill established in 1881 that made rails for the Denver & Rio Grande Railroad. The company also owned thousands of acres of coal-bearing deposits throughout the region. In 1892,

Colorado Fuel & Iron plant, Pueblo, c. 1930. PH.PROP.216

Colonies 1895–1919

Tony DiSipio announcing the "Music from Italy" radio program on Pueblo's KDZA, c. 1955. CIAPA Archive. Courtesy Pauline Annette DiSipio. PCCLI2920

CC&I merged with the Colorado Fuel Company to form the Colorado Fuel & Iron Company, a company that would become the state's largest employer and landowner.

In its heyday, CF&I was a leading manufacturer of steel rails, spikes, nuts, nails, cast-iron pipe, rebar, and copper wire. Its operations stretched from New Mexico to Wyoming. From 1903, John D. Rockefeller Sr. owned the company, and its size gave Pueblo the nickname "Pittsburgh of the West." Many of CF&I's workers lived in company towns. The company's size and labor practices led to strikes, including the infamous strike that lasted from 1913 to 1914 and culminated with the Ludlow Massacre.

CF&I's fortunes rose and fell with wars and recessions. The Rockefellers sold the company in the 1940s. It struggled with declining production and increased competition thereafter. CF&I declared bankruptcy in 1990.

Anthony "Tony" DiSipio

Born in 1909 to Angelo and Concetta DiSipio, Tony DiSipio married Dorothy Passanante in 1937 at Mount Carmel Church in Pueblo. Tony and Dorothy had two children together: Concetta Constance "Connie" Marie DiSipio and Paolina "Pauline" Annette DiSipio.

Tony and Dorothy DiSipio, Pueblo, 1959. CIAPA Archive. Courtesy Pauline Annette DiSipio. PCCLI2926

The DiSipio family lived on Elm Street in Pueblo where Tony worked at the Colorado Fuel & Iron Company steel mill for thirty years. He worked first in the open hearth section and later in the blast furnace department. Additionally, he worked at KDZA, a radio station in Pueblo, announcing the "Music from Italy" radio program. Tony DiSipio died in Pueblo in 1967, followed by Dorothy, who died in 1998.

Gobatti

Giovanni "John" Gobatti

John Gobatti was born in 1890 in the northern Italian province of Rovigo. A descendant of the musician Stefano Gobatti (who wrote the operas *The Goths, Alice,* and *Cordelia*), John attended the School of Arts and Materials in Milan. He enlisted in the Italian Army in 1910, and fought in the Italian-Turkish War.[240] After completing his military service, he immigrated to the United States and settled in Connecticut, where he worked as a machinist.

In 1916, John married Etelvina "Ethel" Barlanti, and in 1918 their daughter Alvira was born. An only child, Alvira became a musician.[241]

In 1920, the family moved to Pueblo, where John operated the Gobatti Manufacturing Company. The shop built and repaired machines, made models, did tool and die work, and provided other services to Pueblo's industries, such as metal stamping and gear cutting.[242]

John was also active in the Italian American community, serving as president of the Protective and Benevolent Society (known from 1938 as Lodge No. 222 of the Columbian Federation). He died in Pueblo in 1977.

John Gobatti, 1930. From the book Attività Italiane nella Intermountain Region, *1930. PCCLI5645*

Biagio and Vincenza (Tropea) Granato, c. 1930. CIAPA Archive. Courtesy John Panepinto. PCCLI5499

Granata/Granato

Biagio Granato

Biagio Granata was born in Spezzano della Grande in the southern Italian province of Cosenza in 1866. Searching for a better life, he left his homeland and family in 1895 and made his way to America.[243]

After settling in Colorado, Biagio Granato (his last name had changed to "Granato," likely the result of an error made by immigration officials) bought farmland on the St. Charles Mesa in Pueblo County. He saved enough money to return to Italy in 1898 for his wife

Vincenza and their first son, Frank. Six more children were born to Biagio and Vincenza in Colorado: Florence, Julia, Perry, Louis, Catherine, and Mary.²⁴⁴

On his farm, Biagio grew vegetables—including peppers, onions, peas, and cabbage—and occasionally cultivated wheat and alfalfa. He sold the produce and other crops in Pueblo from a horse and wagon, and later from a truck. Biagio also kept goats and a few hogs, butchering the hogs with the help of other community members, to make sausage, prosciutto, and lard.

Vincenza Granato died in Pueblo in 1944. Biagio continued to work on the farm until his death in 1956. The Granato land is still in the family, managed by Bill Williams, the grandson of Frank Granato, who bought the land from his parents, Biagio and Vincenza.

Occhiato

Michael "Mike" Occhiato

Michael "Mike" Occhiato was born in 1878 in Potenza, Italy, to Carl and Frances Occhiato.²⁴⁵ His father went to the United States for work, and the family reunited in New York City around 1885. They eventually settled in Denver. To help the family, Mike sold copies of the *Denver Republican* newspaper on downtown street corners, shined shoes, delivered telegrams, and ran errands. At the age of fourteen, he started working for the Denver & Rio Grande Railroad on a construction crew, and by age twenty, became a foreman.²⁴⁶

In 1900, Mike's parents arranged his marriage to Serafina "Sarah" Giordiano. After paying for her passage to America, Mike married her in Denver. Shortly after, the couple moved to Pueblo, where Mike worked in the steel mill. Together Mike and Sarah had nine children: Carl, Frances, Mary, Anthony, Rose, Jennie, Joseph, Theresa, and Helen.²⁴⁷

In 1905, Mike and Sarah bought a beer distribution business, which they operated out of the basement of their home. Mike delivered beer by horse and wagon, and customers filled pails from a keg or bought bottles, washed and filled at home by Sarah.

Portrait of Mike Occhiato, 1930. From Attività Italiane nella Intermountain Region, *1930. PCCLI2547*

When Prohibition went into effect in 1916, the Occhiatos opened the M. Occhiato Mercantile which sold "near beer," candy, tobacco, and soft drinks. Mike put in twelve-hour shifts at the steelworks while his eldest son Carl ran the business. In time the business and inventory grew, and in 1936, the Occhiato family obtained the Pepsi-Cola franchise followed by the Schlitz beer franchise in 1937.

M. Occhiato Mercantile Company, Pueblo, c.1930. CIAPA Archive. Courtesy Rose M. Occhiato. PCCLI4887

Mike retired from the thriving family business in 1952, but not from community service. He was a Pueblo city councilman from 1951 to 1958, and in 1960 he formed the Mike Occhiato Foundation to support the Colorado State Fair. Over the years, he was also active in several Pueblo Italian organizations including the Società di M.S. Vittorio Emanuele III, Società di Madonna del Monte Carmelo, Società Fedeltà, and the Società Cristoforo Colombo. In 1948, Sarah Occhiato died, followed by Mike, who died in 1979.[248]

Panepinto

Antonio "Tony" and Maria "Mary" Antonia (Cilino) Panepinto

Antonio "Tony" Panepinto was born in Palermo, Sicily, in 1882. After completing his mandatory military service in 1906, he married Maria "Mary" Antonia Cilino, also from Palermo. Their families tried to block the union because Mary was upper-class and Tony's family was working-class.[249]

The couple came to the United States in 1908 and made their way to Pueblo, where Tony found work at a smelter. They moved to Massachusetts a short time later to be near Tony's brother, but returned to Pueblo by 1910. Tony worked in a brickyard and later as a laborer in Colorado Fuel & Iron's steel mill. The Panepintos opened a small grocery store around 1920. Mary operated the store, extending credit to customers during the Great Depression. Her generosity led to the store's eventual closure. Tony retired from the steel mill around 1950.

Tony and Mary raised seven children: Giuseppe "Joe," Jennie, Francesco "Francis," Rosa, Thomas, John, and

Tony and Mary Panepinto, c. 1940. CIAPA Archive. Courtesy John Panepinto. PCCLI5500

Vincent.[250] In addition to caring for her family, Mary Panepinto belonged to the Pueblo Ladies Fidelity Lodge. Mary's grandson, John Panepinto (now a pharmacist in Pueblo), recalled lodge meetings where the older women wore black and spoke Italian.[251]

Tony and Mary never returned to Italy, though Tony kept his Italian citizenship. Mary became a U.S. citizen in 1954. Tony died in 1964, and Mary died two years later.

When asked about his grandparents, John Panepinto remarked:

> I owe a tremendous debt to their courage in coming to America and their strong belief in family and tradition. All the grandchildren and great-grandchildren have worked diligently to become educated and productive Americans while honoring their Italian heritage.[252]

A Closer Look
The Trinidad Colony

Long one of the most important towns in southern Colorado, Trinidad also became one of its most diverse when coal companies developed the area.

Starting in the late 1800s, the companies recruited Italian, Mexican, Jewish, Polish, Slavic, German, Greek, and Irish miners. And though Trinidad did have an Italian Avenue, it was not a colony in the traditional sense. Most Trinidad-area Italians lived in coal camps spread throughout Las Animas County: Cokedale, Starkville, Sopris, Valdez, and many others. In these camps—essentially company towns—Italians lived among people speaking more than twenty languages. Many children grew up learning Spanish as well as English and Italian.

Mount Carmel Church, built in 1907 for Italian- and Spanish-speaking Catholics, became a focal point of the area's Italians. People came from mining camps and farms to attend services, and in 1918 the congregation held its first annual festival to honor the feast day of Our Lady of Mount Carmel. An Italian-born Jesuit priest, Father Felix S. Ziccardi, led the congregation from 1923 to 1949. Ziccardi gave sermons in

Italian, Spanish, and English. The congregation also supported a grade school.

The last major coal mine closed in 1996. Two years later, Mount Carmel Church closed after holding its eightieth and final festival.

Bonacquisti

Ambrogio and Margaret (Polumbi) Bonacquisti

Ambrogio Bonacquisti came to the United States to work in the Pennsylvania coal fields in the late 1800s. Around 1905, he returned to Italy, where he married Margaret Polumbi in 1907. In 1913, Ambrogio heard that miners were needed at the Rockefeller-owned Delagua mines, seventeen miles northwest of Trinidad. He returned to the United States and made his way to Colorado. World War I delayed the arrival of his wife and two sons for seven years.[253]

After Ambrogio began working in Delagua, the miners went on strike. He was at Ludlow on April 20, 1914—the day of the massacre. "I was there," he later told his family, "and I did what I had to do."[254] His descendants still own the Winchester lever-action rifle he used that day.

After the strike, Ambrogio returned to the Delagua mines. In 1920, his wife and sons Joe and Frank joined him in Colorado. The couple had two more children, Yolanda and George. When the Delagua mines closed, Ambrogio went to work at the mines in Valdez, where he stayed until retirement. Margaret died in 1937 of pneumonia. Ambrogio died in Trinidad from black lung disease in 1962.[255]

Margaret and Ambrogio Bonacquisti with their daughter Yolanda, Trinidad, 1922. CIAPA Archive. Courtesy Richard Bonacquista. PCCLI4369

A Closer Look
Italians and the Ludlow Massacre

The early 1900s was an explosive time for Colorado's mining industry. Miners, many of them immigrants from southern and eastern Europe, demanded better working conditions, pay, hours, and paychecks of real money—not

Ludlow tent colony ruins with Red Cross nurses and clergy, Ludlow, 1914. 89.451.4862

scrip that they had to spend in company stores. Mine owners refused to meet with workers and accused them of being radicals or anarchists. The struggles caused frequent strikes.

The United Mine Workers of America called one of these strikes in 1913. The companies evicted workers from their housing, and the union set up tent colonies on private land at Ludlow and other places. Day after day, striking miners confronted mine owners, mine guards, and "scabs" (miners who ignored the strike). Mine owners asked Governor Elias Ammons for help. Ammons responded by sending the Colorado State Militia, a precursor of the Colorado National Guard.

On April 20, 1914, members of the militia opened fire on the colony. Tents caught fire, and when the smoke cleared, two women and eleven children who had taken shelter in a cellar under a tent were found dead; they had suffocated. Thirteen others died in the gunfire. Many of the victims were Italian. Miners fought the militia until the arrival of federal troops. The United Mine Workers ended the strike in December 1914, the miners' demands still unmet.

Martin Marta

Martin Marta, the son of Giovanni and Mary (Bersono) Marta, was born in 1878 in the northern Italian province of Torino (Turin) in the Piedmont region. He came to the United States in 1902 to join his siblings and worked as a carpenter in Illinois coal mines. Martin eventually settled in Lester, a southern Colorado coal camp. In 1908, he wrote home to an acquaintance, Veronica Domenica Pricco, asking her to marry him. Veronica arrived in 1909. They married at Trinidad's Holy Trinity Church and settled in Martin's one-room, company-owned house. Together they had three children: John, Mary, and Katherine "Kate."[256]

Marta family, left to right: Mary, Martin, John, and Veronica, c. 1915. CIAPA Archive. Courtesy Veronica (Marta) Goodrich. PCCLI5087

In 1913, shortly before the Ludlow strike, Colorado Fuel & Iron expelled the Martas from their home with a day's notice because they were union sympathizers. Martin, jobless, and Veronica, pregnant with daughter Mary, moved to Trinidad, where fellow Piedmontese took them in. A friend hired Martin as a partner in his blacksmith shop.

The blacksmith shop struggled, and Martin eventually left the business. His marriage ended in 1924, a time when divorce was rare. In 1928, Martin and his brother Prospero, a master baker, opened the Marta Bakery in Trinidad. The bakery became famous for its bread, breadsticks, and *torchetti* (sugared pastries).[257] In 1947, Martin and Prospero sold the bakery to Louis Bergamo and Charles Cassio.

Left to right: Prospero Marta, Kate Marta, and Martin Marta in front of the Marta Bakery truck, Trinidad, c. 1935. CIAPA Archive. Courtesy Veronica (Marta) Goodrich. PCCLI5089

Martin Marta never married, and after his retirement remained in Trinidad until his death in 1952. Veronica Marta married Charles Bonino in 1924. She died in Trinidad in 1963. Prospero Marta moved to Michigan after the sale of the bakery and died there in 1948.

Bonino

Charles Borromeo Bonino

Born in 1886 to Domenico and Marianna (Panetti) Bonino, Charles Bonino was from the small town of Strambino, Italy, in the northern province of Torino (Turin), in the Piedmont region. News of employment opportunities in Colorado's coal mines from Italian countrymen brought Charles Bonino to America.[258]

In 1910, Charles made his way to Las Animas County where he found work in the mines and later joined the United Mine Workers of America. In 1914, his cousin Charlie Robino was killed during the long Ludlow Massacre strike. As a result, Charles joined fellow union members who fought against federal troops in the weeks after the massacre.[259]

In 1917, Charles enlisted in the United States Army to fight in World War I. After the war, he returned to Colorado, and in 1924, married Veronica Marta. In 1925, the couple had one son, Reginald Bonino.

During the Depression years, Charles was unable to work as a miner. However, he was hired to work on projects for the government under the Works Progress Administration (WPA). By 1939, he was back at work in the Morley Mine in Trinidad. In the 1940s, Charles left mining to work at Walter's Brewery in Trinidad, but returned to the mines in Huerfano County for a few years before his retirement. Charles Borromeo Bonino died in Trinidad on January 30, 1956.

Charles and Veronica Bonino, Trinidad, 1924. CIAPA Archive. Courtesy Veronica (Marta) Goodrich. PCCLI5088

Cesario

Giuseppe "Joseph" and Tomasina (Luchetta) Cesario

One of four children, Joseph Cesario was born in San Fili, Calabria, in southern Italy in 1873. He came to America at the age of twelve with his parents, Domenico and Carolina Cesario. The family eventually settled near Trinidad, where they owned a small farm, growing vegetables Domenico sold from the back of a spring wagon, going from house to house in Trinidad.[260] Like his father, Joseph was a farmer. In 1898, he married Tomasina Luchetta in Las Animas County.[261] Joseph and Tomasina had sixteen children, twelve that lived past childhood: Mary, Jenny, Lucretia, Irma, Caroline, Louise, Frank, Anthony, Samuel, Benjamin, William "Bill," and Albert "Al" Cesario.

After Tomasina's death in 1918, Joseph embraced several different religions, and baptized his children in several Protestant denominations before he became associated with the Italian Presbyterian Church (now the First Church of the Nazarene in Trinidad). Instrumental in helping to build the church, he became an ardent follower of the Italian preacher and first pastor of the Italian Presbyterian Church, Reverend Solomanetti.[262]

Albert "Al" Frank and Maria Carmela "Mary" (Vallone) Cesario

The son of Joseph and Tomasina Cesario, Al Cesario was born in Trinidad in 1910. In 1933, he married Mary Vallone, the daughter of Francesco and Angela (Marretta) Vallone. After working as a butcher for his brother-in-law, Charlie Gagliardi, proprietor of the G and D Grocery in Trinidad, and as a Jewel Tea salesman in La Junta, Al Cesario entered the baking trade with his brother, Bill Cesario, and his brother-in-law, Joe Vallone. After moving to New Jersey to study the profession, he returned to Trinidad and found work as a baker in Kendall's Bakery.

In 1939, Al and Mary Cesario and their daughter Angela Ann moved to Walsenburg, Colorado, where they purchased the Jolly Boy Bakery from Al's brother Bill. They operated it until 1942, when they moved back to Trinidad to run the Cesario's Bakery with Bill. During World War II, the mines surrounding Trinidad increased production and the bakery prospered. Soon their bakery became well known in Trinidad and across Colorado.

In 1945, after Bill moved with his family to California, Al continued operating the business. Soon Mary started helping in the bakery, decorating cakes, and in time she became a master cake decorator. The bakery continued to grow and Al's brother-in-law, Joe Vallone, joined as a partner. In 1955, Al Cesario and his family moved to California, leaving Joe Vallone to operate the bakery. In the late 1950s, the Cesario Bakery closed as a result of the coal mines closing in the Trinidad area.

After the death of Al in 1969, Mary left the bakery business and began a new

Carolina and Domenico Cesario (Joseph Cesario's parents) in front of the Cesario family home on Nickerson Avenue, Trinidad, c. 1900. Gift Angela Ann Cesario. 2006.111.3

Albert Cesario family, left to right: Mary, Angela Ann, and Al, c. 1943. Gift Angela Ann Cesario. 2006.111.20

career as a trilingual (English, Italian, and Spanish) business office administrator with a hospital in California. She retired in 1979 and lived with her daughter Angela Ann in California and Colorado Springs until her death in 2003.

Angela Ann Cesario

Angela Ann Cesario, born in 1936, was the only child of Al and Mary Cesario. Named for her grandmother, Angela (Marretta) Vallone, and her aunt, Ann (Vallone) Cesario, Angela Ann spent her early childhood years in Walsenburg, Colorado. In 1942, she returned to Trinidad, Colorado, with her parents and attended Holy Trinity School, from which she graduated in 1954.

In 1955, she attended the University of Colorado, Boulder. The transition from a small Catholic school in the small town of Trinidad, Colorado, to the large Colorado University was very difficult for Angela Ann. Her life until that point had been very constant, and to a degree, sheltered. Most of the students at Holy Trinity were of either Italian or Hispanic descent, and Catholic; people whose families were known to each other for several generations back. The University of Colorado was a completely different world. After a rocky first year, Angela Ann adjusted to her new environment and new experiences and made new friends. She later transferred to the West Coast to be near her family, graduating from the University of California, Berkeley in 1958. She then attended the Medill School of Journalism at Northwestern University, later working as an administrative manager in several hi-tech companies including IBM and MCI. Angela Ann Cesario is now retired and living in Colorado Springs, Colorado.[263]

Cesario Bakery, Trinidad, c. 1945. Gift Angela Ann Cesario. 2006.111.25

Vallone

Francesco and Angela (Marretta) Vallone

Francesco and Angela Vallone emigrated to America from Prizzi, Sicily, in 1914 with their children Antonia "Ann" and Giuseppe "Joe."[264] Angela was thirty-nine and Francesco was fifty-three. Angela and the children immigrated first, followed by Francesco, because immigration laws at that time discouraged the immigration of handicapped persons. Francesco was considered handicapped as the result of a hunting accident in Sicily in which he lost one eye when his rifle backfired.

After a short stay in New Jersey with Angela's brothers, the couple and their children relocated to Trinidad, where Francesco's brother had purchased land. In April of 1914, just a few months after arriving in America, Angela gave birth to the couple's daughter Maria Carmella, or "Mary." In Trinidad, Francesco tried several enterprises, including operating a macaroni factory and a second-hand store, to support his family before returning to a skill acquired in Sicily—farming. He moved his family to a small, six-acre ranch on the northwest outskirts of Trinidad where he raised horses, cows, and most importantly, goats. He began making and selling cheese from the goats' milk and soon became one of the prominent cheese-makers in southern Colorado. Clients came from Denver and other parts of Colorado for his specialty, goat cheeses. Francesco operated his cheese-making business until around 1936, when he lost his eyesight from glaucoma. He died in 1949.

After Francesco's death, Angela moved with her daughter Mary and son-in-law, Al Cesario, to California. She died there in 1957.

Francesco Vallone, c.1930. Gift Angela Ann Cesario. 2006.111.13

Cimino

Domenico "Domenic" and Mary (Carpita) Cimino

Domenic Cimino was born in 1874 in Cefalú, Sicily. In 1889, he came to the United States when he was only fifteen. After passing through Ellis Island, he went to New Orleans, where he harvested sugar cane.[265] A year later, he left New Orleans and made his way to Las Animas County, Colorado, where he worked as a coal miner and learned English by attending public school with first- and second-graders.[266]

In 1904, Domenic married Mary Carpita at Holy Trinity Catholic Church in Trinidad. Mary, who was born in New Orleans in 1886, moved with her family to Sopris, Colorado, when she was three years old. After her mother Francesca died in childbirth in 1901, Mary was raised by her father Nick, who worked as a night watchman for Colorado Fuel & Iron.

In 1905, Domenic and Mary's first child was born, a son named Vincent, followed by twelve more children: Vince, Faye, Frances, Nick, Rose, Thomas, Frank, Rose, Carl, Sarah, Lena, and Dominic. After sixty-four years of marriage, Domenic Cimino died in 1968. Mary died in 1981.

Gerald "Jay" Domenic Cimino

Gerald "Jay" Cimino was born in Trinidad, Colorado, on April 20, 1936. The grandson of Domenic and Mary Cimino and the son of Vincent and Elvera Marie (Gagliardi) Cimino, Jay grew up in Trinidad along with his four siblings: Mary Ann, Arnold, Agnes, and Sylvia. While his mother Elvera worked as a homemaker and teacher, his father Vincent worked as a funeral director.[267]

After graduating from Holy Trinity High School in 1954, Jay Cimino joined the United States Marines. In 1956, he returned to Colorado, where he attended Trinidad State Junior College and the University of Denver, completing his Bachelor in Business Administration degree in 1960. That same year, Jay Cimino married Emily Jean Roitz and together they had four children: Gina, Vincent, Michael, and Laurie.

Out of college, Jay Cimino went to work for B. F. Goodrich as a territory manager for the Front Range (Colorado, New Mexico, and Kansas). In 1965, he moved to Pueblo, where he took a job at Jess Hunter Ford, and in 1972, moved with family to Santa Fe, New Mexico, where he became the general manager and partner of the Santa Fe Buick, Pontiac, and General Motors Company dealership.

In 1975, Philip Long convinced Jay Cimino to join his well-known Phil Long Ford Dealership, in business since 1945. As the general manager and partner, Jay, along with Philip Long, expanded the business into what it has become today, the fifth largest privately owned company in Colorado with eighteen dealerships in Colorado and Arizona.

Today, Jay Cimino is the majority owner and CEO of Phil Long Ford. His sons Mike and Vincent are also involved in the business, which employs more than 1,300 people in Colorado and gives back several millions of dollars for community initiatives, including scholarships, youth and cultural organizations, and financial support for military families, to name a few. Over the years, Jay Cimino has been honored for his philanthropy, including a street in Colorado Springs named after him—Cimino Drive.

Maio

Giuseppe Garibaldi Maio

Giuseppe Garibaldi Maio was born in 1866 in the small town of Grimaldi in the southern Italian region of Calabria. After graduating from the University of Cosenza, he entered the Italian military.[268] In 1898, he married Maria Antionetta Anselmo, and together the couple had eight children: Victor, Emillio, Armando, Silvio, Franscesco, Giovanni, Derna, and Mario.[269]

Soon after his marriage, Giuseppe entered the Italian Consular Service and received his first assignment in Sao Paulo, Brazil, where he served as the consul and also directed a newspaper called *Reclame*.[270] In 1902, Giuseppe was transferred to Denver, where he took up his post as Italian Consul. Two years later, the Maio family moved to Trinidad's Consular Office, where Giuseppe assisted Italian immigrants in the area with issues related to immigration and citizenship. Shortly after taking up residence in Trinidad, Giuseppe began an Italian newspaper, *Il Corriere di Trinidad*.[271] In 1919, Giuseppe received the title of *Cavaliere* from Italy's King Victor Emmanuel III for his service to the Italian community.

Giuseppe Maio, Italian Consulate Officer, c. 1898. CIAPA Archive. Courtesy Sylvia (Maio) Lackey. PCCLI5433

Il Corriere di Trinidad *printing office, Trinidad, c. 1910. Giuseppe Maio at right (hands on railing) and his son Victor (third from left in bow tie). CIAPA Archive. Courtesy Eugene Maio. PCCLI5292*

After his retirement in 1933, Giuseppe's sons Emillio, Silvio, John, and Mario took over *Il Corrierre*, changing it from an Italian weekly newspaper, into an English-language daily, *The Morning Light*, which was published until 1953. Giuseppe Maio died in 1941, followed by his widow, Maria, who died in 1967.[272]

Maio family, by Aultman Studio, Trinidad, c. 1920. Seated in front, left to right: Maria Antionetta Maio and Giuseppe Maio; standing, left to right: John, Frank, Victor, Emilio, Armand, Silvio, and Mario Maio. CIAPA Archive. Courtesy Sylvia (Maio) Lackey. PCCLI5431

Lattuda/Latuda

Francisco "Frank" Latuda

Francisco Lattuda was born in 1867 in Magnano, Italy, in the northern region of Lombardy. He was raised by his older sister, and in 1887, he came to America.[273] He settled first in Walsenburg, Colorado, where he worked as a miner and was known as Frank Latuda.[274] Around 1890, he traveled to Castle Gate, Utah, to find work and then to Dawson, New Mexico, where mine owner Frank Cameron requested his help in dealing with Italian miners in the area. In 1896, he married Costanza Latuda. The couple's first child, a daughter, was born in 1898 and died in infancy from an infection. Tragically, in 1899, Costanza died after giving birth to the couple's son, who also died soon after. After losing his family, Frank moved to Illinois for a short time, but returned to New Mexico to work again with his good friend, Frank Cameron.

In 1910, Frank Latuda retired from the mining industry and returned to Italy to find a bride. There he met Rose Scompini, an accomplished dressmaker. After returning to Trinidad where he purchased a house, he sent for his future wife. Frank and Rose were married in New York in 1910, at the Italian Mission, a governmental agency that aided Italian immigrants with legal paperwork. In 1911, Frank and Rose's first son, Charles, was born in Trinidad. Charles died in 1918 when he was accidentally shot and killed by a neighborhood boy. Rose and Frank had four more children together: Frank Jr., Robert, Alexander "Bud," and Charles Latuda III.[275]

Frank Latuda, 1930. From Attività Italiane nella Intermountain Region, *1930. PCCLI5646*

In 1913, Frank Latuda came out of retirement when he opened a mine in Utah with Frank Cameron. Although Latuda's primary residence remained in Trinidad, he often traveled between Utah, Colorado, and New Mexico. In 1916, Frank Latuda became president of the Liberty Fuel Company, headquartered in Salt Lake City, Utah, a position he held for over fourteen years.[276] Frank Latuda died in 1931, followed by his wife Rose, who died in 1969.

Scavotto

Mary Bernarda (Alishio) Scavotto

Mary Bernarda Alishio was born in Parish Reserve, Louisiana, in 1886 to Angelo and Concetta Alishio. Her parents came to America in 1880 from Sicily, Italy, and moved to Trinidad in 1889, where her father found work as a miner and bartender.[277]

In 1901, at the age of sixteen, Mary, or "Bernarda" as she was called, married Joseph Scavotto, a barber from St. Louis. That same year, she enrolled at the St. Louis College of Midwifery in Missouri. Upon her graduation in 1905, she returned to Trinidad where she started her medical practice as a midwife.[278]

Until her death, day or night, rain or shine, Bernarda traveled by horse and buggy to care for her patients. Although she delivered most babies in their own homes, Scavotto maintained a maternity room at her own residence. She spoke Italian, Spanish, and English, as evidenced by her business cards, which note her business as Levatrice, Partera and Midwifery.

For a flat fee of $15, Scavotto provided a prenatal examination, counseling about hygiene, rest, and exercise, the delivery, and some postnatal care. For poorer patients, she traded services for chickens, coal, and wool. Not licensed to prescribe medication, she often consulted doctors. But, respecting the customs of her clientele, she also allowed the use of traditional remedies.

Joseph and Bernarda Scavotto had five children: Theresa, Clara, Pauline, Joe, and Paul.[279] Joseph died in 1928, followed by Bernarda who died in Trinidad in 1943.

Scavotto Family, left to right: Joe Jr., Joseph, Clara, Theresa, Paul (in front of Theresa), Bernarda, and Pauline, Fromm Studio, Trinidad, Colorado, c. 1915. Gift Mary Mendine Roberts. 95.128.28

CHAPTER 5

Perseverance

1920–1939

The 1920s brought strict immigration quotas. New laws discriminated against the most recent immigrants—southeastern Europeans—and the number of Italian immigrants dropped dramatically.

But Italians had gained a measure of public acceptance. Children attended parochial and public schools, the church played a growing role in the community at large, and Italians' sense of responsibility for their own people impressed outsiders. More and more Italian businesses served the entire city and beyond. By the late 1920s, many Italian American sons and daughters qualified for skilled and white-collar jobs.

The passage of Prohibition in Colorado in 1916 drew ire toward Italians, for whom wine was a staple and winemaking a ritual. Prohibition played into the hands of the Ku Klux Klan and other anti-immigrant groups, which trumpeted that Little Italy was a center of bootlegging and organized crime. With the end of Prohibition came the Great Depression, but Italians reacted with resourcefulness. They relied on their small gardens for food, and on community ovens for fresh bread. Chickens and goats in backyards supplied eggs and milk and Sunday dinners. Women canned vegetables, jams, and jellies for the winter months.

Despite hard times, Little Italy was home, and it was a time of fond memories. Grocery stores gave credit. The Model T brought new freedom. Young people went to Elitch's Trocadero ballroom, the Rainbow dancehall, or the Casino Theater at Lakeside Amusement Park. Couples played cards and picnicked. Others gathered at the soda fountain, and neighborhood theaters offered movies for a nickel or a dime.

Opposite: Ku Klux Klan parade in Denver, Colorado, 1926. PH.PROP.1734

Perseverance 1920–1939

Aiello

George "Chubby" Aiello

George "Chubby" Aiello was born in 1906 at his family home on Mariposa Street. His parents were Carmen "Mike" and Arcangela "Maggie" (Tolve) Aiello. His mother was born in Brooklyn, New York, in 1883, and came to Denver with her Italian-born parents around 1891. Chubby's father was born in Italy in 1858 and came to America in 1878, where he found work as a railroad foreman in Trinidad. His parents met during a feast day celebration in Denver at Our Lady of Mount Carmel and were married at the same church in 1896.[280] Together they had nine children: Frank, Jerry "Chat," Concetta "Clara," Angelina, George "Chubby," Salvatore "Sam," Pasquale "Pat," James "Jimmie," and Nickolas "Nickie."[281]

Chubby attended Bryant School and by age ten was helping his father in their family restaurant at Thirty-seventh and Navajo Street, opened by Mike in 1911. In 1921, the Aiello family restaurant moved to Thirty-sixth and Navajo and reopened as the Italian Village. In 1941, Mike died and Chubby took over the family business. After Mussolini and Hitler declared war on the United States, the Aiello family decided to change the name of their restaurant from the Italian Village to "Patsy's Inn." This decision reflected the family's fear of

Chubby Aiello inside Patsy's Inn at 3651 Navajo Street, by Roger Whitacre, c. 1985. CIAPA Archive. Courtesy Tom Noel. PCCLI0876

Men outside Patsy's Inn, c. 1950. CIAPA Archive. Courtesy Our Lady of Mount Carmel. PCCLI2009

being labeled anti-American (a phenomenon that also affected German families in the neighborhood). They believed that the new Irish name would make them less of a target.

Chubby Aiello managed Patsy's Inn well into the 1990s. He died in Denver in 2002. Although the Aiello family no longer owns the business, Patsy's Inn remains open at 3651 Navajo Street in north Denver.

Canino

Frank and Mary (Granato) Canino

Frank Canino was born in 1870 in Sorbo San Basile, in the southern Italian province of Catanzaro in the Calabria region. In 1891, he came to the United States, settling first in Illinois, where he worked for the railroad. In 1900, he married Mary Granato at Our Lady of Mount Carmel Church. Mary was born in the same province as Frank in 1881, and came to the United States in 1899 with her family.[282]

Around 1910, Frank took a job as a street cleaner with the City of Denver's White Wings division, named after the early street cleaners who wore white suits. Frank's division was responsible for keeping the streets of Denver clean. In 1939, he earned $5 a day. He arrived at work around 7:15 A.M. to check out his equipment—which included a push-cart, brooms, and a shovel—in a station near Twelfth and Curtis. The work included long hours in snow and cold, chipping away at the ice.[283]

Frank and Mary (Granato) Canino on their fiftieth wedding anniversary, 1950. Gift Rose (Canino) Villano and Michael C. and Clair Villano. 2005.38.15

Frank and Mary Canino had six children: Sam, Tony, Salvatore, Flora, Rose, and Elvira. For many years, the family lived at 3745 Jason Street in north Denver.[284] In 1950, Frank and Mary celebrated their fiftieth wedding anniversary. Five years later, Frank died in Denver, followed by Mary, who died in 1974.[285]

Joseph John and Elena "Lena" Carmella (Pagliano) Canino

Joseph John Canino was born in Calabria in 1890 and came to the United States in 1903 with his parents, Clyde John and Assunta (Ursetta) Canino, and his two brothers,

Rosario and Sam.²⁸⁶ They settled in Pennsylvania, where Joseph completed the fifth grade and worked in the coal mines. He then traveled to Wyoming before coming to Denver, where his relative Thomas Canino lived.²⁸⁷

After serving in World War I, Joseph married Elena "Lena" Pagliano. Born in 1896 to Gustavo Luigi and Rosa Santa (Granato) Pagliano, she settled in Denver with her family when she was a year old. Joseph and Lena had five children: Rosario "Russell," Assunta "Sue," Luigi "Louie," Rose, and Anthony "Tony." To support his family, Joseph worked at the American Beauty Bakery, studied meat-cutting at Mapelli Brothers market, and opened a grocery store.²⁸⁸

Canino family, front left to right: Joseph, Rose, Luigi, and Lena; back row: Anthony (left) and Assunta (right), by Anderson Photo, Denver, 1940. CIAPA Archive. Courtesy Anthony Canino. PCCLI5694

In 1935, Joseph, Lena, and their children moved into an apartment at 3500 Navajo Street in north Denver. The couple paid $3,500 for the apartment complex, which included seven terrace apartments along Thirty-fifth Street and Dr. Daniel Lucy's old office on the corner facing Navajo Street that Joseph expanded to house the Navajo Meat Market. The corner grocery store featured fruit in the storefront window as well as bins for cookies, spaghetti, and a meat counter. The market specialty was sausage, made by Joseph and Lena from a recipe given to them as a wedding present from Joseph's mother Assunta, who brought the family recipe from Calabria, Italy. In 1957, the market became Canino's Italian Sausage Company. In 1969, Joseph died. In 1970, his grandson, Joe Tarantino, bought the company. Lena Canino died in Denver five years later.²⁸⁹

A Closer Look
Canino's Sausage Company

As a homemaker, Diana Payne didn't have much business experience—but she had plenty of courage. And that's all she needed to maintain a family legacy.

Diana's husband, Michael Payne, operated Canino's Italian Sausage Company for almost twenty years. His involvement began in 1970, when his longtime friend

Joe Tarantino bought the business and enlisted his help as a partner. Michael took over in 1988, and changed the name to Canino's Sausage Company. Tragically, Michael died a year later.[290]

Despite her lack of experience, Diana decided to keep the company. Founded several decades earlier by Joseph and Lena Canino, it had become an important part of north Denver history.[291] She went to work the day after her husband's funeral, learning the ins and outs of the business. Her decisiveness and fortitude paid off and by 1997 the company was grossing over $1 million annually. Today, Canino's modernized facility (located just north of the original location on Navajo Street) mixes, grinds, stuffs, and ships 5,000 pounds of sausage daily.[292] Canino's sausage is sold in restaurants and stores throughout Colorado and the surrounding states.

Canino's Italian & German Sausage graphic, c. 1975. Loan Diana Payne. IL.2006.41.8

Canino's Sausage Company remains a family-run business with ties to Denver's Italian American community. Diana's maternal grandfather, Michael Santangelo, was born in Potenza, Italy, in 1886, and came to Colorado around 1900. He married Mary Carmella, another Potenza native, at Our Lady of Mount Carmel Church in 1911. They had nine children: Joseph, John, Theresa, Clyde, Angelina, Alvera (Diana's mother), Louis, George, and Salvatore Santangelo.[293]

Tommaso "Thomas" and Rose (Laurenti) Canino

Tommaso Canino was born in Calabria and immigrated to the United States in 1893. After passing through Ellis Island, he worked in Chicago for the railroad before settling in Alma, Colorado, and then moving to Denver. In time, Thomas encouraged his relatives to join him in Denver, including his cousin Joseph Canino, who founded Canino's Italian Sausage Company. In 1901, Thomas married Rose Laurenti.[294] They settled in north Denver and had seven children: John, Clyde, Joe, Tony, Thomas Jr., and twins Mary and Teddy.[295]

Thomas opened a grocery store and later owned the American Beauty Bakery at Thirty-fifth and Navajo. He ventured into business with the Frazzini brothers,

Canino's Casino, left to right: unidentified woman and man, Joe Canino, Johnny Canino, Angelo Nardillo (behind Johnny), unidentified, Clyde Canino, Tony Canino, unidentified, unidentified, unidentified, Thomas Canino, and Della (DeRose) Canino, Denver, c. 1937. CIAPA Archive. Courtesy Debbie (Spaulding)Fugate and Sandra (Morganti) Spaulding. PCCLI3451

operating the Shane Furnace Company, and later owned the Sunset Billiard Parlor at Thirty-fourth and Navajo. Around 1937, Thomas opened Canino's Casino, a dance hall on Pecos Street. Thomas Canino died in Denver in 1948, followed by Rose, who died in 1966.

Clyde G. Canino

The grandson of Thomas and Rose Canino, Clyde G. Canino grew up in north Denver with his parents Gaetano "Clyde" and Susie (Iannacito/Cito) Canino.[296] In 1951, he married Patricia Courtney and together they had four children. Clyde worked for an auto dealer before opening the Hollywood Auto Polish Company with Don Ciancio. Then, in 1953, he opened Canino's Pizzeria at 2076 South

University. He has since owned successful restaurants including Tico's and Bambino's, which he opened with his brother Roland. Clyde helped his sons, Vince and Marty, with their restaurant, Piccolo's, and Clyde III, who owns Canino's Restaurant in Fort Collins.

In 2003, Clyde Canino was interviewed by *The Denver Post*. When asked about his Italian heritage, he said, "I truly think that my heritage is love. When I see my old friends, I realize that when you belong to the fraternity of Italians, it's a real fraternity."[297] He fondly remembers watching his aunts cooking and walking in north Denver and smelling the bread baking in people's backyard ovens. He recalled his father telling him that "bread was the staff of life, that if you had bread, everything else would be okay."

Clyde G. Canino inside Northglenn plant, by Dawn DeAno, 2007. CIAPA Archive. PCCLICPC0042

Today, Clyde Canino enjoys time spent with his second wife, Jan, whom he married in 1999, his family and friends, raising and breaking polo horses, and baking bread in his own outdoor oven, which he built to keep the memory of his family, heritage, and the neighborhood he grew up in, alive.[298]

Cerrone

Ludivicio Atillio "Ottey" and Mildred (Pedotto) Cerrone

In 1893, Horace Palladino, Carmine D'Donato, and Frank Damascio opened the North Denver Mercantile Company in the heart of Denver's Little Italy.[299] Damascio—famous for building the Brown Palace and the Cathedral of the Immaculate Conception—built the market adjacent to his own house. In 1928, Carmine D'Donato sold the company to Antonio Cerrone and his son Ottey.[300]

Born in Pescara, Italy, Antonio Cerrone landed in Boston in 1901. He made his way to Utah, where he worked for the railroads and in a copper mill. He and his wife, Mary, hid their Italian identity, changing their last name to Carson, praying

Mildred Cerrone cleaning butcher blocks at Cerrone's Market, by Tom Denger, 1986. CIAPA Archive. Courtesy Tom Noel. PCCLI0875

the rosary at home, and refraining from speaking Italian in public. In 1913, their first child, Ludivicio Atillio Carson, or "Ottey," was born.³⁰¹ By 1926, the family had grown to nine, including seven children between the ages of fourteen and two. The family moved to Denver in 1928.³⁰²

After acquiring the mercantile, Antonio and Ottey changed its name to "Cerrone's." Father and son ran the store together until 1934, when Ottey took over. That same year, Ottey married Mildred Pedotto and together they had two children: Mary Ann and Donald. The family lived in the house next to the market, which offered customers imported Italian goods, homemade sausage, fruits, breads, olives, and pasta.³⁰³ For decades, Ottey and Mildred worked twelve hours a day, seven days a week, without a break or vacation.³⁰⁴ Cerrone's—a centerpiece of Little Italy for many years—closed in 1995.

Ottey Cerrone, Cerrone's Market, by Roger Whitacre, 1980. CIAPA Archive. Courtesy Tom Noel. PCCLI0873

A CLOSER LOOK
Discrimination

In the early 1920s, the Ku Klux Klan (KKK) had more than 35,000 members in Colorado, and countless more supporters. The governor, Denver's mayor, and a majority of state representatives were among them. Portraying itself as a law-and-order group, the KKK built its political platform on a framework of hatred toward Jews, blacks, Catholics, and what Governor Clarence Morley called "undesirable aliens." Italians throughout the state viewed the rise of the Klan with fear.³⁰⁵

The KKK's burning crosses—seen atop South Table Mountain and Pikes Peak—illuminated a bigger problem: anti-Italian prejudice existed both before and after the Klan's heyday. Stereotypes portraying Italians as violent and criminal wound up in official policy. In 1911, the U.S. Senate validated these stereotypes by reporting that Italians were clannish and slow to assimilate. Its conclusions eventually led to the 1924 Immigration Act, which severely restricted immigration from southern and eastern Europe.

In Denver, some Italians tried to escape discrimination by Anglicizing their name before applying for a job. But they still had a hard time getting into white-collar professions.

Social reformers who saw little merit in ethnic ways of life tried to "Americanize" immigrant groups. In north Denver, the Neighborhood House offered sewing, reading, and cooking classes to Italian immigrant children in the 1930s and 1940s.[306] The Public School Cottage—supported by Denver Public Schools, Daughters of the American Revolution, and the Visiting Nurses Association—offered English lessons and courses in sewing, cooking, citizenship, and childcare to Italian women.[307]

Carabetta / Corbetta

Antonio and Antonia (Guida) Carabetta

Antonio Carabetta was born in Potenza, Italy, in 1860 to Gerardo and Eufemia (Abroila) Carabetta.[308] The son of peasant farmers, he left Italy in 1880. Seven years later, he married Antonia Guida at Sacred Heart Church in Denver. Also from Potenza, Antonia and her mother Paola (Tolve) Guida came to America in 1881 to join her father Gerardo, already living in Denver.

In 1888, Antonio and Antonia Carabetta's first child, a son named Fiore, was born, followed by: Michael, Jerry, Santina "Sadie," and James. The Carabetta family lived in the Bottoms along the South Platte River, where Antonio

Antonio Carabetta with his peddler's wagon, Denver, c. 1915. CIAPA Archive. Courtesy Mike Martelli. PCCLI5865

worked as a fruit and vegetable peddler. Later the family moved to north Denver, where Antonio ran a small grocery store in the back of the family home at 1757 West Thirty-fourth Avenue. Antonio Carabetta died in Denver in 1945, followed by Antonia, who died in 1958.

Santina "Sadie" (Carabetta) Martelli

The daughter of Antonio and Antonia Carabetta, Sadie Carabetta attended Webster School through the fifth grade when she left to help her mother at home. Growing up, she loved dancing, baking, and baseball, often watching her brothers, all of whom played on a team.[309]

In 1917, Sadie married Frank Martelli, a native of Torando Palegina, a town in the southern Italian province of Chieti in the Abruzzi region. The son of peasant farmers Maria Madonna and Pietro Martello, Frank grew up in a house with two levels in which his family occupied the top floor, with their animals living below. In 1910, Frank, age fifteen, left Italy to join his father Pietro in America (who had changed the family name to Martelli). With few belongings and a tag attached to his coat lapel listing his name and destination, Frank traveled alone to Denver.

Frank and Sadie had nine children together, six that survived infancy: Salvador, Virginia, Frank, Lorraine, James, and Antoinette. To support his family, Frank worked for the Union Pacific Railroad, a job he held for over thirty years. A farmer at heart, Frank enjoyed tending to his vegetable garden and fruit trees, which provided Sadie with produce for canning and pie-baking. Frank Martelli died in Denver in 1956, followed by Sadie, who died in 1984.

Wedding portrait, Frank and Sadie (Carabetta) Martelli with attendants Michael Carabetta and Frances Mauro (at right), 1917. CIAPA Archive. Courtesy Antoinette (Martelli) Massimino. PCCLI1473

Jerry Carabetta/Corbetta

The son of Antonio and Antonia Carabetta, Jerry Corbetta (he changed his name around 1917), a veteran of World War I and a member of Denver's Italian community, was shot on June 9, 1919, by George Klein, the head of the Denver Police Bootleg Squad.[310] The shooting occurred during a bootleg raid on Corbetta Brothers and Guida soft-drink parlor in north Denver.[311] The next day, Corbetta died from his injuries.[312]

Funeral procession for Jerry Corbetta showing mourners carrying oval photograph of Corbetta, June 15, 1919. CIAPA Archive. Courtesy Antoinette (Martelli) Massimino. PCCLI1476

The shooting outraged the Italian community, who believed that the police were unfairly targeting them, that excessive force was used during the raid, and that the police were trying to cover up Corbetta's killing, as evidenced by the very different statements given by the victim and police officer. According to Klein, he entered the business after hearing that they might be running illegal liquor and found a number of men inside intoxicated. He then noticed Corbetta running out of the building holding a bottle and while chasing him, fell and accidentally shot Corbetta.[313] According to Corbetta, who gave a statement at the hospital:

> I, J. Corbetta, believing I am about to die, make this statement. George Klein shot me at Fortieth and Pecos Streets. He shot me for nothing. He never told me to stop or gave me any warning of any kind. He fired twice. He was right on top of me when he fired, about ten feet.[314]

Three days after Corbetta's death, over 4,000 Italians marched across the Twentieth Street Viaduct to City Hall where they demanded Klein be punished.[315] Their demands were not met. On June 13, 1919, a jury exonerated Klein after concluding that he shot Corbetta in the line of duty.[316]

A Closer Look
Prohibition

Colorado banned alcohol on January 1, 1916, four years before national Prohibition took effect. Supporters of the legislation—the Women's Christian Temperance Union (WCTU) and the Anti-Saloon League (ASL) in particular—blamed alcohol consumption for crime, violence, and immoral behavior. Saloons, associated with these vices, became prime targets.

The WCTU and the ASL branded saloons as gathering places that isolated immigrants and impeded their "Americanization." The ban hit Italians especially hard. Their taverns had served as safe havens and social centers.

Although Prohibition outlawed liquor sales, it allowed the use of liquor for sacramental, medicinal, and industrial purposes. It also permitted personal use of fermented fruit or grape drinks made at home. Most Italian immigrant families were used to drinking wine with their meals, both in their homeland and in their adopted country. During Prohibition, they bought imported grapes and made their own wines.

Though legal, the practice attracted attention from the police and the Ku Klux Klan. And when a few community members broke the law and made large amounts of wine for sale, the entire community felt the effects. Bootlegging increased suspicion of Italian Americans in general and fed anti-Italian stereotypes and sentiments.

Corbetta family, back row, left to right: Rosa (Pomponio) Corbetta, Tony Corbetta, Michael Corbetta; front row, left to right: Richard Corbetta (Tony's brother) and Raymond Corbetta (Tony's brother), c. 1943. CIAPA Archive. Courtesy Tony Corbetta. PCCLI4807

Anthony "Tony" Felice Corbetta

Anthony "Tony" Felice Corbetta, a third-generation Italian American, was born in 1923 to Michael and Rosa (Pomponio) Corbetta. Rosa, the daughter of Felice and Michelina (Meolfese) Pomponio, was born in Denver in 1899.[317] Michael Carabetta, the son of Antonio and Antonia Carabetta, became Michael Corbetta when he started school in Denver. He later changed his name to Corbet when he applied for a job with the railroad, which he believed preferred Irish workers over Italian laborers. In the early 1920s, Michael lost his job with the railroad when he went on strike with the union. After being blacklisted for a number of years, he was rehired in 1938.[318]

Growing up in north Denver, Tony Corbetta recalled the safety of Denver's Little Italy, never having to lock a door, sleeping on the lawn in the hot summer months, his grandmother making bread, visiting with friends, family, and neighbors—not by telephone but in person—making wine with his grandfather, canning produce, going to movies at the Navajo Theater followed by ice cream at Se Cheverell-Moore drugstore, and his grandfather's Pascal Celery patch.[319]

While attending North High School, Tony went to work for the Iowa Dairy on West Forty-fourth Avenue, where he cleaned milk bottles and served ice cream to customers in the creamery shop. Later, while attending the Colorado School of Mines, he was drafted into the Navy, where he served as a naval aviation bombardier and navigator. The experience was overwhelming for a boy who had never been outside of Colorado before entering the service. After the Navy, Tony completed his degree in engineering at the Colorado School of Mines and went on to work as a sales engineer for the Colorado Fuel & Iron Company in Denver and Grand Junction.

In 1947, Tony Corbetta married Lucille Yacovetta. Together they had three children: Diane, Paul, and Patricia.

Carpanzano/Carpenter

Samuel "Sam" Aiello Carpanzano/Carpenter

The oldest of five children, Samuel "Sam" Aiello Carpanzano was born in Chicago in 1902. Around 1910, his family, including his Italian-born parents Francesco and Maria Annunziata (Guido) Carpanzano, came to Colorado.[320] They settled first in Pueblo, where his father worked on a railroad as a laborer. By 1920, the Carpanzano family had returned to Chicago, where Sam, age eighteen, was working as a packer in a furniture factory.[321] A few years later, Sam returned to Colorado to work in the Las Animas County coal mines. He met and married Almadora "Emma" Iannacito in 1923. Together the couple had six children: Frank, Rosella, Delphine "Del," Edward, Thomas, and Frances "Fran."[322]

After their marriage (and Sam's involvement in bootlegging), Sam and Emma moved to Chicago for a few years. In 1929, they returned to Colorado and settled in Louisville near Emma's relatives. Sam returned to working in the coal mines. In a 1960s interview, Sam recalled his days in the mines:

Perseverance 1920–1939

Working conditions in the mines were terrible. The companies didn't give the men the proper equipment and sometimes we had to shovel for 30 feet without ties, timber, spikes, or rail. We mined coal for 52 cents a ton in 1930. We would load a two-ton car and get credit for only one ton. Things finally got so bad that the State Industrial Commission held a hearing in Lafayette Union Hall. I testified at the hearing along with Johnny Gross, Jack Green, Joe Symanski, and O. F. Nigro.[323]

After testifying, Sam was promised he would not get fired for his actions, and he was not; however, he was reassigned to a shoveling job in water-filled mines. Ultimately, he quit and joined the United Mine Workers Union and soon found out that he was blacklisted from all non-union mines. Sam eventually found work with the Rocky Mountain Fuel & Iron Company, kept his membership with the Union, and worked with others to improve mining conditions in the state. During the 1930s, he also served as a Democratic committeeman in Boulder County, secretary to the Federal Labor Union No. 20114, and secretary of the Boulder County Labor Central Committee.[324]

In 1938, Sam Carpenter (he had changed his name around 1930) was hired as an electrician with the Pullman Company. During World War II, he worked as an assistant foreman, supervising the reconditioning of the Pullman railroad cars used to transport troops. He worked for Pullman until 1957, when he was forced to retire due to a serious illness.[325]

In 1959, Sam Carpenter was appointed bailiff of the Superior Court of Colorado. From 1962 to 1966, he served under Judge Sherman G. Finesilver.[326] In 1967, he was appointed Sergeant of Arms of the Colorado Senate. Sam Carpenter died in Denver in 1969.

Sam Carpanzano, Louisville, Colorado, 1930. CIAPA Archive. Courtesy Edward Carpenter. PCCLI5624

Almadora "Emma" (Iannacito/Cito) Carpanzano/Carpenter

Almadora "Emma" Iannacito was born in Louisville, Colorado, in 1905, above the Track Inn tavern. The daughter of Amadore and Antonia "Anna" (DiGiacomo/James) Iannacito, her father was a native of Pagliarone, a village in the southern Italian province of Campobasso. Emma's mother Anna was born in Como, Colorado, in 1883, the daughter of Italian immigrants Mariano and Rosaria DiGiacomo.[327]

Married at eighteen, Emma and her husband separated in 1943. Her husband Sam Carpenter was an ambitious man who focused on success in his public affairs, and gave little attention to his family life. After their separation, Emma settled into a house at 4614 Bryant Street in north Denver, where she remained a homemaker, supporting her family by washing and ironing clothes and renting out one of the two bedrooms in her home to boarders.

Emma Carpenter's industriousness and ability to adapt was certainly handed down to her from her mother, Anna, who lived a very non-traditional life. Anna, a widow (her husband Amadore died the year Emma was born) and single parent of three daughters (Mary, Lucy, and Emma) at a very young age, became an astute businesswoman, running boardinghouses in several mining camps and towns in Colorado. Needing to both work and care for her children, Anna was faced with many hard decisions including sending her daughters to live with their grandparents, Rosaria and Mariano DiGiacomo, on their farm in Wellington, Colorado. In her later years, Emma Carpenter recalled fondly the time spent there and told stories of riding buckboard wagons, trading eggs for candy at the general store, walking miles on dirt roads to visit neighbors and attend school, fearlessly killing rattlesnakes, and simple days of hard work and little playtime. Even after Anna remarried and had three more children (Vernon, Virgil, and Beverly Phillips), she continued to work.

Emma Carpenter's home at 4614 Bryant Street, Denver, c. 1940. CIAPA Archive. Courtesy Frances (Carpenter) Sawyer. PCCLI5441

Although a "simple woman" at heart, who struggled in her youth and marriage, Emma was the Carpenter family matriarch. According to her daughter Frances:

> She never learned to drive a car, never drank alcohol, smoked cigarettes, or dated another man before or after her marriage to Sam. She rarely left her home for more than a few hours, always preferring guests to visit her. Forever a caregiver, anyone who

Perseverance 1920–1939

Emma Carpenter working in her garden at 4614 Bryant Street, Denver, c. 1960. CIAPA Archive. Courtesy Frances (Carpenter) Sawyer. PCCLI5462

entered her home was soon asked "what can I give you to eat or drink?" and always sent away with a plate of food for the road. Often that plate included her homemade bread and a jar of her grape jelly. Emma Carpenter's world was filled with the joy of everyday work and familiar events. She took pride in her neat and tidy house, prepared food that was an expression of love for those who ate it, and felt great joy in keeping a wonderful flower and vegetable garden as well as tending aged grape vines.[328]

Few knew it, but Emma, with only a sixth grade education, wrote poetry. These poems, which she wrote and kept for herself, were often written at her kitchen table. In 1965, Emma Carpenter wrote the following poem:

LITTLE DREAM ISLAND

My days will all be pleasant
I'll draw pictures in the sand
My problems all forgotten
In this oh so beautiful land

I'll talk to the birds and flowers
I'll sing with the gentle breeze
Just wondering around a hilltop
Among mother natures trees

The stars will be my friends at night
Oh Gosh it's a wonderful thrill
To live on my little dream island
Right next to my make believe hill[329]

Emma Carpenter died in Denver in 1999.

The Italian American Bank, left to right: Cesare Frazzini, unidentified man, Felix Frazzini, and Prospero Frazzini, c. 1920. CIAPA Archive. Courtesy Debbie (Spaulding) Fugate and Sandra (Morganti) Spaulding. PCCLI4188

The Frazzini Brothers

Prospero Pio Frazzini was born in southern Italy to Nicolangelo and Francesca (Carlino) Frazzini. He arrived in New York in 1883, and by 1890 had sent for brothers Cesare, Felicito "Felix," and Antonio to join him. By 1902, the brothers had settled in Colorado, where they owned and operated a number of saloons in Denver, as well as a grocery store.[330]

In 1909, the Frazzini Brothers opened the Italian American Bank; Prospero was the bank president and cashier, Cesare and Felix were vice presidents, and Antonio was an assistant cashier until his death from appendicitis in 1912.[331] The brothers—with several other Frazzini family members—expanded their ventures to include a merchandising business, importing company, printing office, appliance store, saddle-making store, bakery, and coal mines at Frederick and Firestone, Colorado.[332]

Italian American Bank and Frazzini & Brothers Mercantile, Fifteenth Street, Denver, c. 1920. CIAPA Archive. Courtesy Debbie (Spaulding) Fugate and Sandra (Morganti) Spaulding. PCCLI4088

The brothers received many honors for their success, including one of Italy's highest honors, the title of *Cavaliere Officiale* to the Italian Crown for Prospero (awarded to him in 1915) and Cesare (awarded to him in 1922).[333] Prospero and Cesare were also knighted by King Victor Emmanuel III for their service to the Italian Red Cross.[334] Prospero also served as president of the Saint Anthony of Padua Society and won election to the Colorado Legislature.

In 1925, the Frazzini brothers' success story ended when Denver newspapers reported that the Italian American Bank had closed its doors due to insufficient cash as a result of Prospero's loans and investments totaling $237,000 (including the $87,000 he invested in the International Fuel Corporation, which subsequently went bankrupt) and that Prospero, the bank's president, had disappeared. When he finally surrendered, he pled guilty to charges of embezzlement and grand larceny and was sentenced to five to seven years in prison. Many people lost their savings.[335]

With the closing of the bank, Cesare Frazzini operated a candy store for four years prior to his death in 1929. Prospero died in prison in 1926. Felix went into the tailoring business and died in Denver in 1937. All were buried in a family plot at Crown Hill Cemetery.

A CLOSER LOOK
The Saint Anthony's Society

Founded in Denver on January 17, 1901, membership in the Saint Anthony of Padua Society, or the Saint Anthony's Society, was originally limited to natives of the southern Italian province of Campobasso. The Society helped members find work and housing and provided death benefits to a member's family.[336]

Today, the Saint Anthony's Society is still active in Denver.

Members of the Saint Anthony's Society (wearing sashes) and other Saint Anthony Feast Day celebrants, on the steps of Our Lady of Mount Carmel Church, during the bidding for the honor of carrying the statue in the saint's feast day procession, Denver, 1918. The statue of Saint Anthony pictured in the photograph was donated to Mount Carmel Church by the Saint Anthony's Society in 1901 during the first year of the Society's existence. CIAPA Archive. Courtesy Rosalyn (Mastroianni) Hirsch. PCCLI0218A

Nicoletti

Tommaso "Thomas" and Giulia "Julia" (Mazzei) Nicoletti

Tommaso "Thomas" Nicoletti was born in the southern region of Calabria in 1865. The son of Rosaria (Mauro) and Giuseppe Nicoletti, a blacksmith, Thomas came to the United States as a young man and settled in Denver in 1891.[337] In 1893, he applied to become a United States citizen. Citizenship was granted to him ten years later.

In 1897, Thomas opened the Nicoletti Bros. saloon in downtown Denver at Thirteenth and Larimer Streets. That same year, he married Giulia "Julia" Mazzei, a native of Rogliano. The couple had two sons, Joseph and Ernest Nicoletti. Julia died in Denver in 1923, followed by Thomas, who died in Denver in 1929.[338]

Thomas Nicoletti, by Nast Studio, Denver, c. 1920. CIAPA Archive. Courtesy Juliet Nicoletti-Schray Jiracek. PCCLI0191

Joseph Nicoletti

The son of Thomas and Julia (Mazzei) Nicoletti, Joseph Nicoletti was born in Denver in 1898. In 1918, he enlisted in the United States Army and served in France as a typist in World War I.

Nicoletti Bros. saloon (with Thomas Nicoletti behind bar), Thirteenth and Larimer, Denver, c. 1900. CIAPA Archive. Courtesy Juliet Nicoletti-Schray Jiracek. PCCLI0195

Perseverance 1920–1939

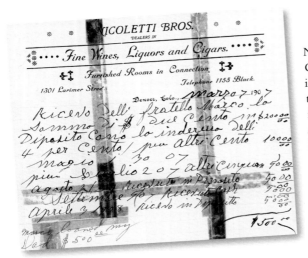

Receipt from the Nicoletti Bros. saloon, 1301 Larimer, Denver, 1907. CIAPA Archive. Courtesy Juliet Nicoletti-Schray Jiracek. PCCLI0189

After the war, Joseph Nicoletti returned home to Colorado. Like many others in the Italian community in the 1920s and 1930s, he got involved in bootlegging. A small-time bootlegger, he was arrested several times for violating the state prohibition law, including an arrest in 1920 when State Prohibition Officers entered his home at 1238 Tenth Street with a search warrant and found over twenty-five gallons of bootleg whiskey and a fair amount of wine. The whiskey and wine were hidden in a secret compartment under the clothes closet and in the basement in apple boxes, and hundreds of new pint bottles were found in sacks and boxes in the house. After paying a fine and serving a short sentence, he was released.[339]

Joseph's bootlegging days were short-lived. When he married Adeline Margherita Mauro in 1924, he gave up his illegal activities. Adeline was born in Denver in 1907, to Raffaele Riley and Marietta (Guida) Mauro. Together Joseph and Adeline had four children: Juliet, Thomas, Marie, and Jo Ann Rose.

Sunshine Laundry with employees, by Hebard and Hargrave, Denver, 1930. CIAPA Archive. Courtesy Juliet Nicoletti-Schray Jiracek. PCCLI0222

Interior view of the Sunshine Laundry with employees at work, 2900 Zuni Street, Denver, c. 1930. CIAPA Archive. Courtesy Juliet Nicoletti-Schray Jiracek. PCCLI0198

In 1926, Joseph's father lent him money to start the Sunshine Laundry and Dry Cleaners with his brother Ernest and cousin Joseph Mauro. The business offered its services to individuals and industries. As the business grew, the Nicoletti brothers opened four more locations. At its peak, the laundry employed sixty people—most of them women—from the north Denver community.[340]

In 1954, Joseph's brother Ernest died, and in 1956 Joseph closed the Sunshine Laundry. He died in 1966, followed by Adeline, who died in 1998.

Joseph Nicoletti in his World War I uniform, September 2, 1918. CIAPA Archive. Courtesy Juliet Nicoletti-Schray Jiracek. PCCLI0199

A Closer Look
Italians and Crime

Italian immigrants were no more likely to be involved in crimes than any other group. But many Americans, bombarded with stereotypes created by the media and perpetuated by the government, thought otherwise.

Stereotypes linking Italians with crime emerged long before Hollywood films like *The Godfather*. Most Italian immigrants settled in overcrowded areas of eastern cities with high crime rates. When they did break the law, newspapers sensationalized the incidents. A 1911 U.S. Senate report legitimized public misconceptions by quoting an Italian official who said that the decline in crime in southern Italy was due to criminals coming to the United States. No statistical evidence supported the claim.

The situation worsened under Prohibition. Criminals saw the ban on alcohol sales as an opportunity to shift their activities to liquor trafficking and organized crime. A few high-profile cases involving Italians led to the stereotype that Italians dominated illegal liquor traffic.

In Denver, newspaper editorials falsely named Little Italy as the source of bootlegging and lawlessness. In reality, most Italians distanced themselves from criminal activities. The individuals from the Italian community involved in illegal activities became favorite subjects of the papers.

After Prohibition ended in 1933 and as second-generation Italians entered skilled professions, public perception slowly changed. Italian Americans began to be judged on their own merits, rather than the stereotypes of their nationality.

Raffaele Riley and Marietta (Guida) Mauro

Raffaele Riley Mauro—the father of Adeline Margherita (Mauro) Nicoletti—was born in Grimaldi, Italy, in 1878 to Rosario and Francesca (Colistro) Mauro. His father, after serving in the Italian Army under General Giuseppe Garibaldi, came to the United States in 1881 with Raffaele's brother John. Rosario settled in Denver where he found work with the Denver & Rio Grande Railroad. In 1890, Rosario's wife Francesca, son Raffaele, and daughters Maria and Luisa joined him in Denver.

In 1900, Raffaele Mauro married Marietta Guida at Saint Patrick's Church in Denver. Raffaele and Marietta had eleven children: Frances Marie, Rose Ann, Adeline Margherita, Josephine Pauline, John, Louis, Fredrick, Charles, Ralph, Marie, and Roger.

In Denver, Raffaele worked as an attendant at the Windsor Turkish Baths at 2901 Stout Street. In 1904, he went to work as a driver for Peter Chiolero Wines and Liquor, and by 1908 he owned the Guida & Mauro Saloon at 2397 Nineteenth Street in downtown Denver. In 1913, Raffaele established and became president of the Denver Coal & Timber Company, located at 2210 Nineteenth Street (near present-day Coors

Wedding portrait, Raffaele Mauro (second from right, standing) and Marietta Guida (right), with attendants John Mauro, brother of Raffaele (seated), and John's wife Mary Mauro (left), 1900. CIAPA Archive. Courtesy Juliet Nicoletti-Schray Jiracek. PCCLI0208

Field). By 1930, the coal company sold eighteen to twenty million tons of coal per year in addition to wood to keep Denver homes warm.[341] Raffaele Mauro died in Denver in 1944, followed by his wife Marietta in 1984.

Notarianni

Gregorio "Gregory" Notarianni

Born in Falerna, Italy, in 1895, Gregory Notarianni served in the Italian Cavalry. After contracting the flu in 1918, he returned home. Interested in travel and wanting to see the world, he immigrated to America in 1920 and settled in Denver. In 1922, he married Adele Libonati and worked for his brother-in-law, Frank Mancini, at the Mancini Press, writing for the Italian-language newspaper *Il Risveglio*. Gregory and Adele had one son, Aldo, born in 1925.[342]

In 1923, Gregory started his own publication, *America*. A year later, he left the publishing business and acquired the

Francesca and Rosario Mauro, c. 1895. CIAPA Archive. Courtesy Juliet Nicoletti-Schray Jiracek. PCCLI0201

Gregory Notarianni wearing Italian Cavalry uniform, c. 1913. CIAPA Archive. Courtesy Aldo Notarianni. PCCLI0610V2

Third-class travel ticket for Gregory Notarianni, from Italy to America, 1920. CIAPA Archive. Courtesy Aldo Notarianni. PCCLI0621

Perseverance 1920–1939

Procession in front of the Navajo Theater (at right) and Se Cheverell-Moore Drug Store, c. 1930. CIAPA Archive. Courtesy Our Lady of Mount Carmel Church. PCCLI2011

Gregory and Adele Notarianni in their yard at 3626 Clay Street, Denver, 1938. CIAPA Archive. Courtesy Aldo Notarianni. PCCLI0655

Star Movie Theater. In 1926, he purchased the Navajo Theater in the heart of Little Italy. A popular place, the Navajo showed movies for ten cents for children and fifteen cents for adults. After purchasing tickets, patrons could buy candy from the Se Cheverell-Moore drugstore, which was connected to the theater by a door in the lobby.[343]

Gregory sold the theater in 1938. Adele Notarianni died in 1968, followed by Gregory in 1983.

A Closer Look
Non-Italians in Denver's Little Italy

In the 1880s, the number of Italians living in Denver increased significantly. By the 1890s, more and more Italians were moving into north Denver and opening businesses that catered to Italians, giving rise to Denver's Little Italy. This trend continued into the 1960s. Although predominantly an Italian community, there were non-Italian residents and businesses in Little Italy. The four most popular were: Daniel Lucy's doctor's office, Louis Zimmerman's mercantile, K. Levine's general store, and Se Cheverell-Moore, a drugstore owned by Eddie Moore.

Dr. Daniel Lucy

The son of Irish farmers, Dr. Daniel Lucy (originally "Lucey" but changed to Lucy before Daniel left Ireland) came to the United States in 1880 at the age of twenty.[344] He left Ireland when under English rule he refused to give up his native language, Gaelic, and because he either could not, or would not, pay taxes on his sheep.[345] After working as a miner and stable hand in Boston, he came to Denver in 1893 and enrolled in the Gross Medical School (later part of the University of Denver). In 1898, he completed his medical training and started treating fellow Irish immigrants in north Denver. Like those he served, Dr. Lucy had few financial means and settled first in an apartment at Thirty-fifth and Navajo (later owned by Lena and Joseph Canino), where he lived and operated his practice. Dr. Lucy also made house calls to visit sick patients or deliver a baby. In lieu of money, Dr. Lucy readily accepted payment in homemade products such as sausage, pasta, garden vegetables, and wine. After his marriage to Margaret Lucy in 1901, Daniel Lucy purchased a building site at the corner of Thirty-sixth and Navajo (across the street from his old residence and practice), where he built a combination residence for his family and medical facility for his patients.

Remembered by many as a quiet kind-hearted man who made his rounds in a Model T coupe, Daniel Lucy was also active in Denver city government in the north Denver district, serving as city councilman from 1919 to 1925 and 1927 to 1929. He also invested in real estate and was a landlord to businesses and residents in north Denver.[346]

Louis Zimmerman and Sons

Louis Zimmerman came to the United States from Germany in 1884.[347] After settling in north Denver, he built a building on the corner of Thirty-seventh Avenue and Navajo Street. There he lived with his wife Dina and their four sons, Louie, Frederick, Carl, and Otto.[348] The building also housed the family business, the Zimmerman Mercantile. In time, Louis' sons ran the original Zimmerman Mercantile and a second store located at Thirty-eighth Avenue and Irving Street. The two stores operated cooperatively, offering customers a variety of goods and home delivery services. Both stores hired Italians as clerks and delivery boys. The stores offered credit to all and never demanded payment, even through the Depression.[349]

Perseverance 1920–1939

Zimmerman's Mercantile, Thirty-seventh Avenue and Navajo Street, Denver, 1920. Pictured in the photograph, from left to right: C. Larson, Fred Zimmerman, Louis Zimmerman, Louie Zimmerman, Mrs. Yacovetta, Mrs. Gunnau and child, Mrs. Louis Hattler and child, and Karl Zimmerman. CIAPA Archive. Courtesy Elaine (Zimmerman) Ciccone. PCCLI1372

Kadish Levine

Kadish Levine, a Russian immigrant, came to the United States around 1904. His wife Minnie was born in Palestine, and immigrated to America in 1893.[350] After landing in New York, she made her way to north Denver's Jewish neighborhood, where her sisters lived and owned grocery stores. After their marriage, Kadish and Minnie opened K. Levine Dry Goods at 3659 Navajo Street. The couple lived above the store with their three children: Bonnie, Helen, and Guscile "Gus."[351]

The K. Levine Dry Goods store dealt in goods of every kind, including a small selection of clothing, shoes, undergarments, stockings, bedding, kitchenware, and hardware, as well as plumbing and electrical supplies.

After the death of Kadish, Minnie and the children ran the business. During World War II, the Levine boys served in the Army while Minnie and daughter Helen ran the store. After the death of Minnie in 1967, the K. Levine Dry Goods store closed.

Edward "Eddie" K. Moore

Edward K. Moore was born in Ohio in 1872 and came to Denver in 1897. In 1922, he and Hugh B. Se Cheverell joined as partners, operating four Se Cheverell-Moore Drug Stores in Denver. A registered pharmacist, Edward filled doctors' prescriptions for his customers, mixing his own recipes for colds, coughs, muscle pains, and body aches. Moore employed many youths in the neighborhood and mentored those interested in becoming pharmacists.[352]

After World War II, Se Cheverell-Moore, like other small drug stores, had a hard time competing with larger franchised stores. Se Cheverell-Moore, despite changes in the business, remained open until Edward was murdered in his store at 3658 Navajo Street during a robbery attempt in 1956.[353]

Eddie Moore (at left) inside Se Cheverell-Moore Drugstore, with Josephine Long and unidentified man at right, c. 1940. CIAPA Archive. Courtesy Marilyn (Natale) Vecchiarelli. PCCLI4316

Maria Grazia "Mary Grace" (Lloullo) Rose Tolve

Maria Grazia "Mary Grace" Lloullo was born in Naples, in southern Italy, in 1865. At age fifteen, she came to the United States.[354] According to her descendants, she and her husband, Angelo Rose, had twenty-one children, many of whom died in infancy.[355] One son—Richie Rose, whom she was said to have favored—died tragically in November 1922 while on patrol as a Denver police officer.[356]

After the death of her husband, Mary Grace moved to north Denver. There, in 1931, she married Rocco Tolve, and she became known as *La Strega*, "The Witch." Called a witch because of her unconventional healing methods, Mary Grace was often asked to help those who did not trust or believe in "modern" medicine—and by those who couldn't afford a conventional doctor.

Mary Grace's methods were a mix of magic and herbal remedies. When a baby was born, she said a prayer at the baptism and put a mixture of oil on the baby for protection from bad omens. If a baby had croup, she placed a candle in a cup to warm it and then put the cup on the baby's chest and covered it to create a medicinal heat. If the baby was congested, she wrapped the child in bread dough. Mary reportedly put curses on people who displeased her by placing pins or knives in oranges; if they were in her presence, she put crossed needles or knives in their chair.[357] Mary Grace died in Denver in 1935.

A Closer Look
The World of Magic and Healing in Italy

A mixture of wheat and olives can ward off the evil eye. Blackberry leaves can heal minor cuts. For some members of Denver's Italian community, these practices weren't just Old Country superstitions; they were real and effective ways to manage some of life's troubles.

In the early 1930s, many north Denver Italians sought aid from Mary Grace (Lloullo) Rose Tolve, a traditional healer also known as *La Strega*, or "The Witch." In Mary Grace's native southern Italy, magic permeated everyday life and involved people within a tight-knit community who shared the same basic beliefs.

Traditional healers, especially in southern Italy, cured people through ritual sayings or through the use of amulets (protective medals or charms), plants, herbs, and formulas believed to have magical powers. But these practices weren't mere herbal remedies. They were expressions of a logic based on finding similarities between two normally separate things.[358] People like Mary Grace used these similarities to do something in one dimension (the magical gesture or formula) to affect the problem in another dimension.

Today, members of Denver's Italian American community practice their own version of magic—though many do not recognize it as such. For example, Italian Americans often wear necklaces with medals and amulets, including the *corno*, or "horn," which tradition says protects the wearer from the evil eye and negative forces.

Smaldone

Gaetano and Caterina "Catherine" (Aquino) Smaldone

Gaetano Smaldone was born in Potenza, Italy, in 1834. He worked as a *contadino* and married Catherine Aquino, also from Potenza, around 1856.[359] They had three boys: Angelo, born in 1858; Luigi, born in 1860; and Raffaele

"Ralph," born in 1882.[360] In 1884, Catherine, Gaetano, and Ralph left Potenza and made their way to America. They settled in New York, where Luigi was already established (Angelo most likely remained in Italy). The Smaldone family stayed there until 1889, when they made their way to Denver.

In Denver, Gaetano worked as a day laborer while Luigi worked for F. Mazza & Company.[361] When Luigi died tragically in 1893, Gaetano was so distraught that he stabbed himself on the day of the funeral. Gaetano survived the incident, and by 1900 he and his family were living at 3319 Bell Street (later Osage).[362] According to the 1900 census, neither Gaetano, Catherine, nor their son Ralph could read or write; only Ralph could speak English. Gaetano Smaldone died in 1917 at the age of eighty-three.[363] Catherine Smaldone remained in the family home on Osage Street until she died in 1931 at the age of ninety.[364]

Fiore Smaldone

Fiore Smaldone, the son of Luigi and Rose (Rosa) Smaldone, was born in Colorado in 1891. His father died when he was just three.[365] Later, his mother Rose married Gerardo Benallo and the family moved to a farm in Henderson, just north of Denver.[366] Fiore grew up there with ten brothers and sisters. He never attended school and never learned to read or write. Fiore's education came from working on the family farm. He also worked for the Burlington railroad and later became a produce peddler and broker at the Denver City Market and Denargo Market. As a produce broker, he provided local farmers with laborers. Needing to communicate directly with the farm workers, Fiore—who was already fluent in Italian and English—learned to speak some Russian, German, Japanese, and Spanish. He also brokered the sale of produce to corner grocery stores, restaurants, and, eventually, supermarket chains.[367]

Around 1912, Fiore's parents met Raffaele and Gerarda Muro at a wedding. During their conversation,

Fiore Smaldone selling produce at the Denver City Market, c. 1925. CIAPA Archive. Courtesy Luigi Smaldone. PCCLI2645

the Benallos and Muros decided that their children would be a good match and arranged a wedding. On February 2, 1913, Fiore Smaldone married Lucia "Lucy" Muro. They had one child, Luigi, born in 1926.[368] Lucy Smaldone died in Denver in 1957, followed by Fiore who died in Denver in 1976. Luigi Smaldone now lives in California.

Raffaele "Ralph" and Mamie (Figliolino) Smaldone

Raffaele "Ralph" Smaldone was born in Potenza, Italy, in 1882. He settled in Denver with his parents, Caterina and Gaetano, in 1889. By 1900, Ralph was working as a laborer and living with his parents on Bell Street (now Osage).[369] In 1901, he married Missouri native Mamie Figliolino.[370] Ralph and Mamie had nine children: Corrine, Clyde, Angelina, Eugene, Anthony, Andrew, Genevieve, Ralph, and Clarence "Chauncey." From 1920, the family lived at 3427 Osage Street.[371]

Ralph worked as a foreman on the railroad and later as a vegetable peddler while Mamie cared for the children.[372] In the 1920s and 1930s, they operated several businesses, including the Checkers Nightclub, the Tejon Street Café, and the Tejon Bar & Café.[373]

In 1947, twelve years after her husband Ralph's death, Mamie and her sons Clyde, Eugene, and Anthony moved the Tejon Street Café to Thirty-eighth and Tejon Street and renamed the restaurant "Gaetano's." Initially, Mamie and her son Ralph lived in one of the apartments above the restaurant. Mamie continued to help run the family business and made the spaghetti sauce, ravioli, and lasagna. Even after Mamie died in 1962, Gaetano's remained at the center of the Smaldone family's social and business life. It stayed in the family until 2004.

Ralph and Mamie Smaldone, c. 1900. Gift Gene Smaldone. 2007.28.2

Clyde George Smaldone

Clyde George Smaldone was born in Denver in 1906 and was Ralph and Mamie Smaldone's second-oldest child. He grew up in north Denver's Little Italy. After a short time at North High, Clyde left school to help support his family. He worked various jobs and eventually started delivering liquor for local bootleggers. Like a number of other families, Clyde's family also bootlegged. In the early 1920s, the police raided his family home and charged Mamie and Ralph Smaldone with manufacturing and selling alcoholic beverages. Clyde and his brother Eugene made a deal with the authorities and served the jail terms on behalf of their parents.[374]

By most accounts, Clyde Smaldone's involvement with illegal activities began in the 1920s with bootlegging. However, there was more to his life. In the mid-1920s, Clyde caught sight of Mildred Wackenreuter, a model, coming out of the Golden Eagle Department Store. He was too nervous to approach her, but a mutual friend introduced them a few months later. Mildred was the daughter of German and Irish immigrants. She was born in New York, but by 1920 her family had relocated to Denver, not far from the Smaldone family home.[375]

After their marriage in 1928, the couple moved to a home at 3042 West Forty-first Avenue, next to Clyde's older sister, Corrine. Clyde and Mildred had two boys, Eugene "Gene" and Charles "Chuck," both of whom graduated from the University of Denver. Gene enjoyed a thirty-five-year teaching career and co-founded the Summer Fun Day Camp. Chuck operated a men's clothing store in Arvada.[376] Both Gene and Chuck remember their parents as loving and their youth as stable, despite their father's involvement in illegal gambling-related activities.

Clyde Smaldone's descendants, relatives, and friends do not deny his involvement in illegal activities. However, they remember the man behind the legend as a father, grandfather, uncle, friend, and community member.

Gene and Chuck Smaldone recall that their father made many charitable (sometimes anonymous) gifts to people in need and donated money for the construction of

Clyde Smaldone, c. 1935. CIAPA Archive. Courtesy Gene Smaldone. PCCLI5424

Our Lady of Mount Carmel High School in the 1950s. The sons also noted that Clyde used his time productively while he was in prison in Leavenworth, Kansas. He finished his high school education, earned college degrees, and learned to cook and paint. Clyde Smaldone died in Denver in 1998 at the age of ninety-one.

Clarence "Chauncey" Michael Smaldone

The youngest child of Ralph and Mamie Smaldone, Clarence "Chauncey" Smaldone was born in Denver in 1924 and grew up in the family home on Osage. He joined the Army in 1943 and married Pauline Blasi while stationed in San Antonio. A Colorado native, Pauline also grew up in north Denver.[377]

Pauline returned to Denver when Chauncey left for the South Pacific, where he worked with the chemical warfare division. After Chauncey returned from the service, he worked as a bartender at Gaetano's, the family-owned restaurant and bar. Pauline also worked at the restaurant as a waitress. Pauline and Chauncey had two children: Paul, born in 1944, and Claudia "CJ," born in 1949. For several years, the family lived in the apartment above Gaetano's with Chauncey's mother and his brother Ralph.[378]

When asked about their father, Paul and CJ recalled his soft-spoken and loving ways, family outings, and traditional Sunday meals. Like their cousins, Paul and CJ endured media and police surveillance and the stigma associated with their family's name. Their father was away from the family for ten years while he was in prison. Acknowledging their father's involvement in gambling-related activities, they believe in the importance of revealing his lesser-known aspects, including his role as a good father and his generosity to his community.[379] Chauncey Smaldone died in Denver in 2006 at the age of eighty-two with his children by his side.

Chauncey Smaldone and Pauline Blasi on their wedding day, 1943. CIAPA Archive. Courtesy CJ (Smaldone) Foxx. PCCLI5875

A CLOSER LOOK
The Smaldone Brothers

When the general public and press talk about organized crime in Denver, they almost always mention the Smaldone brothers: Clyde, Eugene, and Clarence (or Chauncey). During Prohibition, Clyde and his father, Ralph, ran a small-time bootlegging operation.[380] In the 1930s, Clyde and his brother Eugene went on to other illegal activities, mostly related to gambling. In the 1940s, the Smaldone family opened Gaetano's restaurant at 3760 Tejon Street, which served as the center of the Smaldone family's business and social life for more than fifty-five years.[381] In the 1950s, Clyde and Eugene's brother Chauncey, some twenty years their junior, joined the Smaldone gambling operations, which they continued into the 1990s. The brothers all served time in prison.[382]

Although they were not the only Colorado family involved in illegal activities, newspapers and the Denver Police Department appear to have focused on the Smaldones. Denver's Organized Crime Unit followed the brothers and recorded their activities.[383] The unit used this intelligence to raid Clyde, Eugene, and Chauncey's businesses and homes. The police monitored the brothers' families, friends, and even patrons of Gaetano's. Many of these people were labeled "Smaldone Associates," a designation given only to the Smaldone family and those connected to them.

The brothers played a complex role in Denver's Italian community. Clyde, Eugene, and Chauncey were sons, brothers, uncles, and childhood friends to many and were active participants in their north Denver community. They were also businessmen who offered the community financial services, protection, and avenues for gambling. The Smaldone Brothers in many ways filled a need, created by a complicated relationship some Italian Americans had to activities such as payoffs, payment for financial services, and alcohol. This "need" was deeply rooted and traces back to many places in Italy in which paying for monetary services, buying protection from the police, as well as playing dice games or betting on a variety of activities were either legal or common. Although many immigrants hoped to escape such situations, these activities—illegal in the United States—persisted and often led outsiders to view Italians as uniquely criminal.

The appearance of Italian immigrants ignoring or breaking American laws was often tied to the fact that many immigrants did not fully understand American laws because they did not speak, read, or write English. Instead, they relied on others to interpret the law. For example, some could not comprehend that wine—a staple in Italy—could be prohibited. Other immigrants, not trusting the police or banks, turned to powerful insiders such as the Smaldones for protection from outsiders or for loans.

Today, the popularity of television shows such as *The Sopranos* and a continued interest in organized crime are leading scholars to re-examine the relationship between Italians, the media, Prohibition, crime, and anti-Italian movements to better understand the power behind the gangster image and the continued fascination with individuals such as the Smaldone Brothers.

Eugenio "Gene" Veraldi

The son of Rosario and Caterina Veraldi, Gene Veraldi was born in Denver in 1893. His parents had come to the United States from Italy in 1890.

In 1919, Gene married Mildred Rende at Our Lady of Mount Carmel Church. Mildred was born in Welby,

---

Banquet

GIVEN IN HONOR OF COUNCILMAN

Eugene J. Veraldi

SPONSORED BY

THE ITALIAN-AMERICAN PROFESSIONAL & BUSINESS MEN'S CLUB

Argonaut Hotel, 233 E. Colfax Avenue

JUNE 28, 1933

7:30 P. M.

N⁰ 277

Ticket for banquet in honor of Gene Veraldi, 1933. CIAPA Archive. Isabel (Veraldi) Vecchiarelli. PCCLI2302

Colorado. The couple lived with Gene's parents who owned a grocery store and meat market in Little Italy. Gene and Mildred had four children: Isabel, Catherine, Hebert, and James.[384]

Interested in neighborhood and community issues, Gene got involved in politics. In 1929, he was the first Italian elected to the Denver City Council.[385] A politician of the people, he controlled the Italian vote in north Denver. He was instrumental in creating Columbus Park and was active in the community, taking part in such events as the Columbus Day parade. Gene also served on the Colorado State Industrial Commission and several business-affiliated boards. In 1933, Gene was honored for his achievements by the Italian-American Professional & Businessmen's Club, which held two banquets in his honor. The first was held in June at the Argonaut Hotel. The second was held in December at the New Edelweiss Café with those in attendance including Italian community members Frank Ciancio, Marion Iacino, and Joseph Morrato, along with political leaders Governor Johnson, Justice E. V. Holland of the state supreme court, and Earl Wettengal, district attorney.[386]

Gene Veraldi served as a Denver councilman from 1929 until 1935, when he resigned to accept an appointment on the Colorado Public Utilities Commission. Elisa (Damascio) Palladino replaced him on City Council. Michael A. Marranzino filled the seat from 1935 to 1946.[387] Eugene Veraldi died suddenly in 1936 at the age of forty-two.

Wedding portrait, Gene Veraldi (back row, second from right) and Mildred Rende (back row, third from right), Denver, 1919. CIAPA Archive. Isabel (Veraldi) Vecchiarelli. PCCLI2307V1

CHAPTER 6

Prosperity
1940–1959

The rise of Italy's fascist dictator, Benito Mussolini, divided Colorado's Italian Americans. Some were staunch anti-fascists; others supported Il Duce. On December 7, 1941, Italy joined Japan in declaring war on the United States. That day, government officials started arresting suspected "enemy aliens" of Japanese, German, and Italian descent. The United States interned hundreds of Italian nationals and Italian Americans and arrested thousands more.

Men and women from Denver joined more than 500,000 of their fellow Italian Americans to serve in World War II—in Little Italy, fourteen first-generation men from one block of Osage Avenue alone. Other Italian Americans worked for the war effort, and truck farmers kept local military bases and industries stocked with produce.

With the war's end, returning soldiers took advantage of the G.I. Bill to go to college. Using Veterans' Administration loans, they bought houses and land and opened businesses. More than ever, the grandchildren of immigrants were finding opportunities and marriage outside of Little Italy. And although they were fiercely proud of their culture, many no longer even spoke Italian, the result of older generations of Italian immigrants working to be "American." Between 1948 and 1958, the construction of the Valley Highway—today's Interstate 25—plowed through several ethnic enclaves. Little Italy was one of them.

Italian American politicians, sports heroes, and entertainers—such as Fiorello LaGuardia, Joe DiMaggio, and Frank Sinatra—were now in the mainstream. Americans looked to Italian fashion and loved Italian art and movies. Denver hosted the "Festival of Italy" in 1955.

And men and women explored new ways to be Italian and American.

Opposite: Members of the North High School baseball team, left to right: Amadeo Ligrani, Alex Risoli, George Hanel, Joe Pontarelli, and Pete Fallico, Denver, 1940. CIAPA Archive. Courtesy Alex Risoli. PCCLI2300

Prosperity 1940–1959

Busnardo

Frank Mario Busnardo

Valentino Busnardo was born in the northern Italian province of Vicenza in the Venetian region. One of ten children, he left his homeland in 1909 with his brothers Basilio, Bortolo, and Pietro. After traveling through Illinois and Montana, the brothers settled in Sterling, Colorado. In 1916, Valentino met and married Annie Ferrero, born in 1900 in Montezuma, Colorado, to Italian-born parents. Annie's parents had left Valperga, a town outside Torino (Turin) in the Piedmont region, in the late 1890s; they had settled first in Silver Plume, moving to Montezuma a few years later.[388]

In 1922, with their three children, Edith, Frank, and Florence, Valentino and Annie returned to Casoni, Italy (just northeast of Vicenza), to invest in a villa. In Italy, four more children were born to them: Inez, Josephine, Luciano, and Juliana. Sensing that war was looming, in 1938 Valentino sent his eighteen-year-old son, Frank, and daughter Florence back to America. It was the last time father and son would see each other.[389]

Frank attended the Emily Griffith Opportunity School to learn English and find work. He washed dishes

Valentino and Annie (Ferrero) Busnardo in front of their villa in Bassano, Italy, 1946. CIAPA Archive. Courtesy Luciano Busnardo. PCCLI2905

Busnardo children, left to right: Inez, Frank, Luciano (baby in walker), Edith, Florence, and Josephine, Bassano, Italy, 1932. CIAPA Archive. Courtesy Luciano Busnardo. PCCLI2906

and unloaded trucks before going to work for Longaro Boilermakers. In 1948, his mother and three of his siblings joined him in the United States. Later, his two other sisters joined the family as well. Retired since 1983, Frank has owned a grocery store and several saloons: the Hinkydink, Academy, and Venice.[390] He remains active, spending time with family including his wife and five children and participating in religious, civic, fraternal, charitable, and cultural organizations.

Luciano Albino Busnardo

Luciano Busnardo was born in Casoni di Mussolente, Italy, in 1931. He worked in his family's grocery store, attended school, and played soccer. During World War II, the Germans took over his family's home, forcing them to move to Casoni. He saw his home bombed and his cousin hung by the Germans from a tree in town. He had to keep silent about what was happening and was forced to attend fascist classes on Saturdays.[391]

At seventeen, after the death of his father Valentino, Luciano left for America with his mother, Annie, and siblings. After fifteen days aboard a ship, they arrived in New York and then traveled by train to Denver, settling near his brother Frank and sister Florence "Flora." Like his brother, he attended the Opportunity School to learn English. He worked as a presser at the Sunshine Laundry until 1951, when he was drafted into the Korean War, serving in the Italian Intelligence Division of the U.S. Army.

Luciano Busnardo in his garden, by Dawn DeAno, Lakewood, 2006. CIAPA Archive. PCCLICPC0043

After the service, Luciano learned the terrazzo trade (laying tile) from a cousin. In 1959, he met and married Beverly Kenfield, and together they had five children. He went to work for Martino's Terrazzo Company and was soon appointed business manager of the local union. He was later elected vice president of the international union. He has since excelled at amateur soccer and represented the United States in international bocce tournaments. Luciano has kept active in several Italian American organizations, including the Sons of Italy Denver Lodge No. 2075, for which he has served as trustee, vice president, and president since joining in 1959.[392]

Calabrese

Joseph "Joe" Vincent Calabrese

Joe Calabrese, c. 1925. CIAPA Archive. Courtesy Vince Taglialavore. PCCLI3183

Vincenzo "Vincent" Taglialavore in his baker's uniform, c. 1925. CIAPA Archive. Courtesy Vince Taglialavore. PCCLI2249A

Joseph "Joe" Vincent Calabrese was born in Denver in 1911 to Giuseppe "Joseph" and Josephine (Mortellaro) Calabrese. His father, the son of Italian immigrants, settled in Denver in 1888, where he worked for the Union Pacific Railroad for many years. His mother, born in 1893, was a native of Sicily, Italy, and came to America with her parents in 1905.

In 1922, when Joe was eleven, his father died of pneumonia. His mother provided for the family by working as a seamstress while Joe helped out by selling copies of *The Denver Post* in downtown Denver, working as a junk peddler, and selling ice cream and refreshments from a horse-drawn wagon.[393]

In 1927, Joe earned his high school diploma from the Emily Griffith Opportunity School and went on to attend Parks Business School, taking courses in shorthand, typing, and bookkeeping. After working various jobs, including operating the Sunshine Bakery at Thirty-second Avenue and Tejon Street with his brother-in-law Vincent Taglialavore, Joe entered politics. In 1932, he was elected committeeman in his Democratic precinct. A year later, he served in the Colorado Legislature, and in 1933 he took a municipal job with the city of Denver, working outdoors on a variety of tasks, including helping John Malpiede install the Civic Center Christmas decorations.

In 1935, Joe married Elizabeth McAuliffe. The couple settled into a home at 3909 Wyandot Street. In 1936, their son Donald was born, followed by their son Larry, born in 1941. Both Donald and Larry were born with special needs, leading Joe and Elizabeth to found Laradon Hall in 1948, a school for the mentally challenged, which is still open today.[394] Joe Calabrese died in Denver in 1986.

Vincenzo "Vincent" and Margaret (Calabrese) Taglialavore

Margaret Calabrese was born in Denver in 1913 to Giuseppe "Joseph" and Josephine (Mortellaro) Calabrese. After her father's death in 1922, Margaret, like her older brother Joe, left school to help support the family. She took a job with the telephone company and also worked at Dieter Bookbinding Company.[395]

In 1932, Margaret married Vincenzo "Vincent" Taglialavore at Our Lady of Mount Carmel Church. Vincent, born in 1905, was the son of Italian immigrants Gaspare and Francesca (Mortellaro) Taglialavore. At the age of seventeen, he went to Chicago to learn the baking trade, after which he opened a bakery in Cheyenne, Wyoming, with his family. A few years later, he decided to move to Denver, where he found work at the Mother's Home Bakery, followed by the Cefalú Bakery.[396]

After their marriage, Margaret and Vincent lived on Mariposa Street with their only son, Vincent "Vince" J. Taglialavore. Vincent continued to work in the baking industry, and in 1948 he opened his own bakery at Thirty-eighth and Quivas called the "Ideal Bakery."

Margaret Taglialavore died in Denver in 1980, followed by her husband Vincent, who died in 1989. Their son Vince lives in Denver with his wife Gay. Before he retired, Vince taught music and special education in the Denver Public Schools system from 1957 to 1990. Active in the Italian American community, Vince belongs to a number of organizations, including the Dante Alighieri Society and the Amici of the University of Denver.

Calabrese family, back row, left to right: Helen, Joseph, Frank, and Hazel Calabrese; front row, left to right: Josephine (Mortellaro) Calabrese and Margaret (Calabrese) Taglialavore with son Vince, Denver, 1934. CIAPA Archive. Courtesy Vince Taglialavore. PCCLI2945

Mariano Michele "Mike" Calabrese

Mike Calabrese was born in 1887 in the southern Italian province of Avellino in the Campania region.[397] The son of Giovanni "John" and Rosina (Marra) Calabrese, he left Italy for America in 1896.[398] After a short stay in New York, Mike made his way to Kansas City, Missouri, where other relatives, including his father John, were already established. There he opened the Central Fruit House with his cousin Nick Marra. The business sold fruit, candies, cigars, and tobacco.[399]

Prosperity 1940–1959

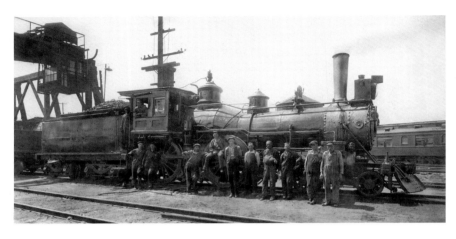

Railroad crew with John Calabrese, father of Mike Calabrese, at far right, c. 1915. CIAPA Archive. Courtesy Michael and Betty Calabrese, Lorraine and Harry McIntosh, and Fran (Coloroso) Daly. PCCLI5390

Mike Calabrese (left) and Nick Marra in front of the Central Fruit House, Kansas City, 1908. CIAPA Archive. Courtesy Michael and Betty Calabrese, Lorraine and Harry McIntosh, and Fran (Coloroso) Daly. PCCLI5398

Around 1910, Mike and his father moved to Denver, where both men worked for the Chicago, Burlington and Quincy Railroad; Mike worked as a machine helper in the roundhouse and John as a laborer in the sand house, responsible for maintaining the railroad track beds.[400] Father and son lived at 1413 West Thirty-fourth Avenue in north Denver, in a home owned by Michele and Filomena Distefano, the parents of Mike's future bride, Angelina. Mike and Angelina were married in 1911 at Our Lady of Mount Carmel Church.

In 1913, while still working for the railroad, Mike and his brother-in-law Joseph Distefano opened a saloon on 3132 Osage Street. Mike worked hard to provide for his family including his children: John, Marion, Oliver, Michael, and Lorraine.[401] In the mid-1930s, Mike left railroading and opened the Alpine Inn at 3551 Tejon Street with his brother-in-law, Angelo Distefano. Named after a village near Avellino, Italy, the neighborhood tavern was formerly an automobile paint and body shop owned by Angelo. Mike

Mike Calabrese in front of the Alpine Inn at 3551 Tejon Street, Denver, c. 1945. CIAPA Archive. Courtesy Michael and Betty Calabrese, Lorraine and Harry McIntosh, and Fran (Coloroso) Daly. PCCLI2142

and Angelo ran the business, a favorite place for men in the Italian community to play cards, socialize, and share a drink and a bite to eat, until the late 1950s, when they sold it to Mike Musso.

Mike and Angelina enjoyed time spent with family and friends. Parties held at their home treated guests to a homemade meal, Italian cookies, wine, and a glass of Mike's homemade anisette. After dinner, the group gathered around the dining room table to play cards. Mike and Angelina also enjoyed picnics in the mountains and day-trips to such places as Boulder Canyon and Colorado Springs. Mike was also active in a number of organizations including the Fraternal Order of Railroad Workers, the Ancient Order of Foresters No. 8908, and the Saint Michael's Society, which he helped found in 1912 and served as president of in 1927. Mike Calabrese died in Denver in 1967, followed by Angelina, who died in 1975.

Tony Mancinelli's San Michele Arcangelo Società Badge, c. 1935. Gift Ralph F. and Rosemary Mancinelli. 2004.112.1

A Closer Look
The Saint Michael's Society

The San Michele Arcangelo Società, or the Saint Michael's Society, was founded in Denver on May 14, 1912, as a nonprofit mutual benefit society to help its members in need during their lifetime and in case of death. Originally associated with Our Lady of Mount Carmel Church, the group held dinner-dances at the parish hall and an annual high Mass honoring Saint Michael in September.[402]

Prosperity 1940–1959

Charter Members of the Saint Michael's Society in front of Coors Hall at Thirty-fourth and Navajo, May 8, 1912. Back row, left to right: unidentified, Emanuel Gargaro, Emanual Gargaro's brother, John Piccardi, Mr. Jackson (uncertain), Nicola Pizzichino, unidentified, Mr. Mangone (uncertain), Mr. Lombardi (uncertain), Mr. Carbone (uncertain); middle row, left to right: unidentified, Alex Marranzino, Mr. Riccardi (uncertain), Fred Pizzichino, Andrew Nardillo, M. Muro (uncertain), Pasquale Ficco (uncertain), unidentified, Pasquale Marranzino; front row, left to right: Michele Distefano, Salvatore Lombardi, Rocco Tolve, Frank Fallico, J. Gargaro, Michael Marranzino, Mike Calabrese, Mr. Brunetti (uncertain), Antonio Vitullo (Tony Veto), Frank Russomano, unidentified. Proposed gift George Andrew. R.90.2004.1

Still active in Denver today, the organization meets monthly and sponsors appreciation dinners, breakfasts, and an annual golf tournament to benefit its scholarship program, which since 1994 has given several monetary awards to aid students at accredited universities.[403]

Carpinello

Joseph Gerald and Giuseppina "Josephine" (Santarelli) Carpinello

Joseph Carpinello was born in Denver in 1923 at his family home at 3446 Navajo Street.[404] The son of Joseph and Angelina (Cominello) Carpinello, his father came to the America from Potenza, Italy, in 1912.[405] A produce peddler in the Denver Bottoms, his father also worked on the Chatfield Dam under the Works Progress Administration (WPA).[406]

Joseph's mother, also born in Denver, was the daughter of Rocco and Maria Arcangela (Laguardia) Cominello, immigrants from Potenza, Italy.

After graduating from North High School, Joseph served in World War II and then attended the Colorado State College of Education in Greeley (now known as the University of Northern Colorado) under the G.I. Bill. An educator from 1949 to 1984, Joseph also worked part-time as a recreation teacher, football official, and mutual clerk at race tracks in Colorado.[407]

In 1949, Joseph married Giuseppina "Josephine" Santarelli. The daughter of Italian immigrants Joseph Cesidio and Luigia Ginetta "Jennie" (Piroddi) Santarelli, Josephine grew up in north Denver. In 1950, Joseph and Josephine's first child, Barbara, was born, followed by Jody, Donald, and Kenny.[408]

Angelina (Cominello) Carpinello (Joseph Carpinello's mother) baking bread in her dome oven at 1801 West Forty-sixth Avenue, c. 1940. Pictured in the photograph are loaves of bread in film canisters Angelina acquired from a neighborhood movie theater. CIAPA Archive. Courtesy Joseph Carpinello. PCCLI0175.v4

A Closer Look
Outdoor Bread Ovens

Angelina (Cominello) Carpinello's photograph near her bread oven documents an important part of daily life for Italians in Colorado. Built by hand, these brick dome ovens, taller than a person, dotted the landscape of Italian communities across Colorado, including Denver's Little Italy. The all-day process of baking bread started early in the morning with bread dough set to rise while a fire in the oven burned for hours until the oven bricks were red hot. Once the logs in the fire had burned to ash, a special mop was used to clean the oven. Once clean, the oven was ready for the oversized bread loaves. Pushed swiftly into the back of the oven using a bread oven paddle, the loaf of dough cooked for about an hour with the door sealed tight. Once removed, the smell of homemade bread permeated the neighborhood.[409]

Prosperity 1940–1959

Ciacco

Albert "Al" Ciacco

One of seven children, Albert "Al" Ciacco was born in 1910 to Italian immigrants Francesco and Carmella (Mazza) Ciacco. His father came to America in 1899 from Calabria, Italy.[410] Around 1905, Francesco moved to Denver, where he worked as a laborer for the Rio Grande Railroad.[411] Al's mother Carmella, a native of Bucita in Cosenza, Italy, was born in 1890 and immigrated to America with her family in 1907.[412] In 1908, she married Francesco at Our Lady of Mount Carmel Church.

After completing two years of high school at North High, Al Ciacco left school at the age of fifteen to help support his family. A few years later, he went to work for a jeweler, and in 1939 was hired by Hershon and Fiorella Company in Denver, where he made jewelry by hand and did ring casting. In 1942, Al served in World War II as an electrical instrument mechanic responsible for disassembling, repairing, and calibrating electrical instruments on aircrafts. After the war, Al returned to work at Fiorella Jewelers, and in 1946 he married Julia Colacito at Our Lady of Mount Carmel. Al and Julia had two children: Marilyn and Rosalyn.[413] Julia Ciacco died in 1988, followed by Al, who died in Denver in 2001.

*Al Ciacco, c. 1935.
CIAPA Archive.
Courtesy Marilyn
(Ciacco) Actor.
PCCLI4684*

Colarosa/Coloroso

Dominic Anthony Colarosa/Coloroso

Dominic Anthony Coloroso was the youngest of five children born to immigrant parents Perigio and Maria Fedela (Vecchiarelli) Colarosa. Growing up in north Denver, he worked as a caretaker at Elitch Gardens and helped care for his parents and his aging grandparents. He attended Bryant School and was one of fourteen students to graduate in 1917. He went on to earn a high school education by attending night classes. In 1919, he became an office boy for Denver Gas & Electric Company (renamed Public Service Company of Colorado). Over time he served as a clerk, cashier, and investigator and worked in public relations for the company. His career with Public Service lasted twenty-six years.[414]

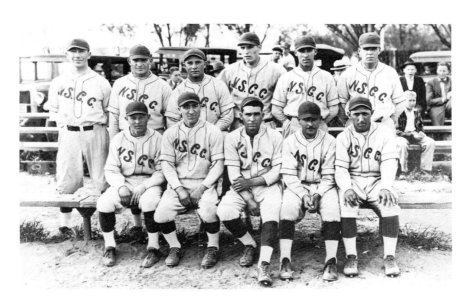

Northside Community Center baseball team, front row, left to right: Red Luchetta, Frank Baldi, Ernie DiCroce, Roxie Long, Frank Curcio; back row, left to right: Dominic Coloroso, Sandy Comito, Anthony Vecchiarelli, Fred Sabon, Tony Longo, Coach Weber, by Colorado Photo Company, Denver, c. 1920. CIAPA Archive. Courtesy family of Dominic and Helen Coloroso. PCCLI0786

In 1930, Dominic married Helen Distefano of Denver at Our Lady of Mount Carmel Catholic Church. The couple had three children: William, Frances, and Donald. Like his father, Dominic spent much of his life offering support to those in need, especially those in his Italian community. He spoke fluent Italian and served as an interpreter, sponsor, and benefactor for many of Denver's Italians. He was elected to Colorado's House of Representatives in 1934, the only Italian American among the sixty-five representatives. He went on to serve five additional two-year terms between 1938 and 1970.

After leaving the Public Service Company in the 1940s, Dominic opened and operated the Micky Manor Restaurant and Tavern on Federal Boulevard in north Denver. He retired in 1986. He died in 1991 at the age of eighty-eight.

Dominic and Helen (Distefano) Coloroso, 1930. CIAPA Archive. Courtesy family of Dominic and Helen Coloroso. PCCLI0755

Distefano

Paul Albert Distefano

The oldest of three children, Paul Distefano was born in Denver in 1923 to Angelo and Katherine

(Spero) Distefano. His father was born in Denver to Italian immigrants from the southern Avellino province. His mother was born in Wyoming to immigrants from Scanno, in the southern Italian region of Abruzzi.[415] For many years, Paul's father Angelo, with Mike Calabrese, owned and operated the Alpine Inn, a neighborhood tavern in north Denver.

Growing up, Paul dreamed of being a baseball player. He idolized Joe DiMaggio, the "Yankee Clipper," and listened to radio broadcasts of Yankee games. He played on neighborhood teams and on championship squads including the 1938 Denver League team and the 1941 North High Denver High School League team. At college in Greeley, Paul played for the Colorado State College of Education (today's University of Northern Colorado) team, the Bears. He and his teammates were later inducted into UNC's Athletic Hall of Fame.[416]

A year into his schooling at Greeley, Paul Distefano joined the Army to serve in World War II. He was training in the Philippines when the war ended. After his honorable discharge, he took advantage of the G.I. Bill and returned to his studies in Greeley, where again he played baseball for the Bears during his remaining four years at school. Even after graduating, he played semi-professional baseball for teams in Colorado, Kansas, Nebraska, and South Dakota. In 1947, Paul married Roberta "Rach" Plunkett, and together the couple raised four children. A teacher for thirty-seven years in the Denver Public Schools system, Paul is now retired.

Joseph Carpinello (left) and Paul Distefano after baseball practice, 1940. CIAPA Archive. Courtesy Paul Distefano. PCCLI5715

Ferretti

Henrietta "Kate" (Malnati) Ferretti

Henrietta "Kate" Malnati was born in Denver in 1891 to Henrico "Henry" and Louisa "Louise" Malnati, natives of Lombardy, Italy.[417] Her father came to the United States in 1886 to work on the Colorado State Capitol, later working on projects at the Denver Mint and City Park in Denver.[418] Four years later, Kate's mother arrived in Denver. One of six children, Kate grew up in a house built by her father at 3509 West Sixth Avenue. As the only Italian family in the neighborhood, Kate and her siblings were teased unmercifully by other neighborhood children.[419]

Kate inherited her father's artistic skill, and applied her creativity to fashion. When she was thirteen, she went to work in the millinery department of the Golden Eagle Dry Goods Company.[420] A short time later, Kate took a position as a hat maker at Denver Dry Goods, followed by a job with Mrs. Molly Mulroy's Villa de Paris, a leading millinery shop in Denver. Employed at the store for ten years, Kate earned a reputation for her creative style, designing hats for a number of affluent women, including Molly Brown, May Bonfils, and Genevieve Chandler Phipps. When asked about the design of her hats, Kate Ferretti recalled two she made for Molly Brown:

> One was a big, broad-brimmed sailor with a crown five inches high. It was covered in real leopard and it had a black ostrich plume sticking up high on one side. Mrs. Brown loved that hat, and she went next door to a furrier and had a leopard skirt made to match it. The other hat I remember was a large brown felt, and across the front, I had a big white bird with wide-spread wings. It was gorgeous.[421]

While working at Villa de Paris, Kate met Jacob "Jack" Ferretti, an Italian American food broker sixteen years her senior. The couple married in 1917 and settled in north Denver, where Kate continued to make hats while raising five children: Anne Louise, Virginia (who died young), and triplets: Joan (who died at the age of five), Joseph, and Jack Jr.

In 1939, Kate opened the Kate Ferretti Showroom and Studio at 4240 Tejon Street. At the height of her business, Kate employed her daughter Anne and five full-time assistants. After World War II, she expanded her business to include haute couture, and made buying trips to Europe with her sons Joseph and Jack Jr.

In 1954, Kate Ferretti, along with her family, now all involved in the business, celebrated fifty years in the millinery design business. Local members of the Denver Fashion Group planned a dinner in Kate's honor but, as the fashion editor Gretchen for *The Denver Post* noted, "...typical of the generous Italian spirit, Kate Ferretti and her charming clan, 'turned the tables' and hosted the whole group Thursday night at a real Italian supper party at the Ferretti home."[422]

In 1959, Jack Ferretti died. Kate Ferretti continued in the fashion business until her retirement in

*Kate Ferretti, c. 1920.
CIAPA Archive.
Courtesy Don Eafanti.
PCCLI5018*

1971. In an article that appeared in the *Rocky Mountain News* in 1977, Kate Ferretti commented about her life and business:
> I've loved my business and loved my life. As a young girl, I wanted to be a painter, and I did a number of paintings during my life. But millinery satisfied my creative urge. And the hats I made, made people happy. Women came to my place and said it gave them a lift. It gave me great satisfaction.[423]

Kate Ferretti died in Denver in 1987.

Gaccetta

Angelo and Rose (LoSasso) Gaccetta

One of seven children, Angelo Gaccetta was born in Welby in 1896 to Frank and Theresa (Gato) Gaccetta. His father came from Italy in 1888 by way of Canada and worked as a miner in Leadville before settling in Welby in 1890 and sending for Angelo's mother to join him a year later.[424] The son of a farmer, Angelo grew up in a house built by his father at 7150 North Washington. He attended Rankin School through the eighth grade, leaving school to help his father and brothers on the family's twenty-acre farm. Angelo later served in World War I, returning to Welby in 1919, where he married Rose LoSasso in 1920. Together the couple had two children: Theresa and Laura.[425]

During the Depression years, Angelo continued to farm and worked as a foreman for WPA projects, setting fence posts and cleaning ditches for sixty dollars a month. In 1939, Angelo, along with other local farmers, organized the Vegetable Producers Cooperative Association (also known as the Garden Association) to ensure fair prices for their crops.[426] The center of commerce for the organization was the Denargo Market, Colorado's largest farmers' market from 1939 through the 1960s. Angelo retired from farming in 1955.

Active in the community, Angelo served on the Adams County School Board and as an election judge for twenty years, attended Assumption Church, and was a member of the Foresters and the Knights of Columbus. Angelo died in Welby in 1992 at the age of ninety-six.[427]

Joe Gaccetta (left) and Angelo Gaccetta, 1916. CIAPA Archive. Courtesy Robin O'Dorisio. PCCLI5381

Constantino "Con" and Laura (Gaccetta) Molinaro

Constantino "Con" Molinaro was born in Rende, Italy, in 1922 to Saverio "Sam" and Rose Molinaro. As a boy, he worked on his family farm, recalling:

> My grandfather used to get up first thing in the morning and tie bags to his feet so the dirt from the field wouldn't get everywhere when he came home. He would work until 8:00 in the morning. Then he would come home for breakfast and go back to the fields. They had to do everything by hand. They didn't have any plows or anything. I was just starting to do that when we left. Good thing we came [to the United States].[428]

In 1925, Con's father left Italy for America, settling first in New York, where he found work in a barbershop. He later lived in Racine, Wisconsin, where he worked in a piano factory, before moving to Welby, Colorado, to farm. In 1932, Sam sent for his wife and children, including Con, to join him. Growing up, Con and his siblings worked

Wedding portrait, Con and Laura (Gaccetta) Molinaro, from left to right: Frank Losasso, Marie (Adducci) DiAnnie (seated), Con Molinaro, Laura Molinaro, Theresa Mazzotti, Loretta (Gaccetta) Kunith, Joe Palermo, Delina (Langrani) Saccamano (seated), and Jerry LaRusso, 1946. CIAPA Archive. Courtesy Robin O'Dorisio. PCCLI5377

on his family's farm doing everything from plowing to irrigating the fields and planting seed. Increasingly, his father needed his help, and after falling behind in his studies, he left school at age fourteen to work on the family farm full-time.[429]

In 1946, Con married Laura Gaccetta at Our Lady of Assumption Church in Welby. The daughter of Angelo and Rose Gaccetta, Laura was born in Welby in 1927. After their marriage, Con and Laura remained on the Molinaro Farm until moving to 6500 North Washington where they raised their four children: Norma, Sam, Kenny, and Randy.[430]

Now retired, Laura and Con Molinaro continue to value the same family traditions they enjoyed growing up, including hosting weekly spaghetti dinners on Sunday and helping with the Our Lady of the Assumption Church annual bazaar and spaghetti dinner.

Gioso

Rocco and Shirley (Losasso) Gioso

Rocco Gioso was born in Denver in 1927 in his family home on Navajo Street.[431] His father, Michael Gioso (originally Gioioso), came to America from Potenza, Italy, around 1915. After working in Pittsburgh as a machinist and for several railroads, he settled in Denver, where he worked as a butcher, construction worker, and organizer of a labor union. Rocco's mother, Rose, was born in Denver to Italian immigrants Frank and Serafina (Mannerbino) Biamonte; she raised the children and worked at the Sunshine Laundry.[432]

After graduating from Holy Family High School, Rocco went on to attend the Colorado State College of Education (today's University of Northern Colorado) where he excelled at baseball, playing for the NCAA Western Division Championship team in California in 1949. After graduating with a B.A. in education and playing semi-professional baseball, Rocco took a job in

Rocco and Angelina (San Pietro) Gioso with son Michael (Rocco's father), c. 1900. CIAPA Archive. Courtesy Rocco and Shirley Gioso. PCCLI5572

Trinidad teaching and coaching. In the 1950s, he returned to Denver, where he taught in the Mapleton Public Schools for thirty-one years. He also served as principal and director in the school district.

In 1951, Rocco married Shirley Losasso, born in 1929 to Rocco and Gerarda (Laguardia) Losasso, immigrants from Potenza. Shirley's father came to America in 1885 and worked as a produce peddler before opening the R. L. Losasso & Sons Greenhouse in Denver. She grew up on Navajo Street in the heart of Denver's Little Italy.[433]

Rocco and Shirley Gioso raised three children and are now retired, and remain active with the Wheat Ridge Democratic Party, Potenza Lodge, Our Lady of Mount Carmel, the Colorado Veterans Board, and the American Association of Retired Persons, for which Rocco has served as director. A World War II Navy veteran, Rocco remains active with the Veterans of Foreign Wars Post No. 6616 in north Denver, for which he served as post commander, state commander (the first Italian American to do so), and district commander.[434]

Rocco Gioso, age seventeen. CIAPA Archive. Courtesy Rocco and Shirley Gioso. PCCLI5574

Iannacito

Edward "Eddie" Pasquale Iannacito

Eddie Iannacito was born in Denver in 1920 to Domenic Antonio and Maria Lucia Iannacito, immigrants from the southern Italian province of Campobasso. Eddie was an only child, and his parents worked at Elitch Gardens.[435]

In 1940, after graduating from North High, Eddie joined the United States Navy. His first assignment was on a seaplane field, at Ford Island, just off the harbor in Hawaii. He was there the day Pearl Harbor was bombed on Sunday, December 7, 1941. Off-duty that day, he witnessed the attack:

> We were close to the tarmac, where our seaplanes landed at Luke Field. The Japanese were strafing our planes on the ground. Pieces of

Eddie Iannacito, U.S. Navy, c. 1942. CIAPA Archive. Courtesy Eddie Iannacito. PCCLI2173

those seaplanes went flying in the air. We saw a couple of the planes peel off....They bombed the hell out of the battleships, and they were sinking....The fire burned for two weeks. The oil on the water lasted days and days. That day, a lot of boys grew up to be men. I was one of them.[436]

After the attack on Pearl Harbor, Eddie was transferred to a fueling station in Kanton Island and later to Espiritu Santo in the South Pacific. His final mission was in Olathe, Kansas, and while home on leave in 1944, Eddie married his high school sweetheart Theresa Lorraine Allegretto at Saint Dominic's Church in Denver. Eddie and Theresa had two sons together: Daniel and Steven.

After returning from the service in 1947, Eddie went to work in the Elitch Gardens greenhouse and later for Coors Porcelain, from which he retired after twenty-five years. Today, Theresa and Eddie still live in Denver.[437]

Losasso

John Losasso

John Losasso, one of eleven children born to Paschal J. and Elizabeth (Figliolino) Losasso, was born in Denver in 1912. His father was born in New York (his mother went into labor as the ship entered U.S. waters) in 1875 to Gerardo and Filomena Losasso, who settled in Denver in 1878.[438] John's mother was born in Naples, Italy, in 1879 and came to the United States with her parents Andrew and Mary (Romellino) Figliolino in the 1890s.[439]

The son of a produce grower and peddler, John helped his father deliver orders from Paschal's horse-drawn wagon. He would ride behind his father, hop down at a stop, collect the order, and then carry it into the house for the customer. Produce sold from the wagon was grown by John's parents on a one-acre plot next to their home at Thirty-fifth and Pecos. Recalling his mother and the garden, John said, "I thought her day would never end. She cooked all day and helped dad in the garden. She'd pick stuff and help him wash it."[440]

At the age of thirteen, John left school to work in the produce business full-time.

Wedding portrait, Paschal J. and Elizabeth (Figliolino) Losasso, by Nast Studio, Denver, 1898. CIAPA Archive. Courtesy Rosalyn (Mastroianni) Hirsch. PCCLI0238

He worked for his brothers at State Fruit and Vegetable Company and for other produce sellers, loading trucks and delivering the produce to grocery stores. In the late 1930s, he started his own business, and in 1939 opened American Fruit and Produce at the Denargo Market. The business, referred to as a "jobber store," primarily sold produce to local grocery stores in Denver.

At the Denargo, sellers specialized in different kinds of produce. One of John's specialties was watermelons. Known as the "Watermelon King," he dealt in large shipments of the fruit that others avoided because of the difficulty in packing, shipping, and unloading the item, especially in large quantities. John and his crew would unload the watermelons one by one, shipped in bulk by the boxcar, sort them, and then wheel them into his Denargo store.

While serving in World War II, John married Mildred Haas in 1945 and together the couple had two children: LaVel and Linda. After the war, John returned to the produce business, which during the 1950s began to change as neighborhood grocery stores were being replaced by supermarket chains that relied less and less on wholesale produce brokers, opting instead to purchase produce in other states, then ship it by truck and air to their store. Ultimately, these changes led to John's retirement, when in 1978, after nearly seventy years in the produce business, he sold American Fruit and Produce.

John Losasso, Denver, c. 1920. CIAPA Archive. Courtesy John and Margaret Losasso. PCCLI4942

A Closer Look
The Denargo Market

In the early 1880s, three curb markets and small produce stands supplied residents and Denver businesses with fruits and vegetables locally grown on small plots of land.[441] In 1899, the City Market at West Colfax and Curtis Street near the Cherry Creek was established. An open-air market with covered sheds for farmers and their horses and wagons, the market supplied everyday citizens, local produce peddlers, corner grocery stores, and restaurants with fresh produce.

By the early 1930s, the City Market was cramped as a result of the growth and expansion of the produce business in Denver. The Market had also suffered a series of

Prosperity 1940–1959

Bird's-eye view of Denver's City Market, c. 1900. 89.296.7682

floods from the Cherry Creek, damaging the site, and it was inconveniently located some distance from the rail yards, "resulting in produce that was shipped by rail having to be handled twice and carried by truck to the market from the yards."[442] Denver City officials and local farmers and businesses agreed that a new produce market was needed, but ultimately, they could not agree on a location. As a result, local farmers formed the Growers Public Market Association in 1938 and entered into a partnership with the Union Pacific Railroad.[443] A heavy transporter of fruits and vegetables, the railroad offered the farmers a sixty-acre tract of land near their rail yards at Broadway, Brighton Boulevard, and Twenty-ninth Street.[444] They also offered farmers the opportunity to own and operate the new market.[445]

In February of 1939, the Union Pacific began building Denver's new produce market, without financial help from the city of Denver.[446] Named after the old Denver and Argo neighborhoods, the Denargo Market officially opened for business on May 22, 1939, with thousands in attendance. The new Denargo Market allowed for convenient access to Union Pacific railcars and included 304 open, steel-covered stalls; 15 small stores; 12 produce building stores; 30 large produce warehouses with state-of-the-art ripening rooms; a city retail trade area for local vendors; an administration building; and a restaurant.[447]

According to researcher Daniel Shosky:

During the first year of operation, there were twenty-seven thriving businesses at the Denargo, most family owned and operated. Businesses leased stalls and buildings at an average price of $12.00 for the season, which ran from early May to October. In later years, the market master would determine the price for each stall. The price would depend on location and the type of produce that the farmer was trying to sell. By the late 1940s, rental fees for stalls reached $80.00 a season.

Unlike the earlier City Market, the Denargo Market was a distribution market for produce where farmers from around the state and region could set-up shop and sell their produce in bulk. Distributors and buying agents would contract with farmers from the surrounding areas, including Arvada, Welby, and Wheat Ridge, to grow specific crops such as lettuce or delicacies like Pascal Celery on a seasonal basis. Once these contracts were satisfied, farmers would display what produce remained for local merchants to buy.

Buying agents at the Denargo Market, c. 1940. Buying agents from around the country were common at Denargo Market. Even before the springtime planting, these agents would try to secure the best price and produce for their clients. 86.296.7678

Between the war years of 1941 and 1945, the Armed Services became the largest buyer of produce at the Denargo. In 1948, there were over sixty-two merchants open for business at the Denargo. Centrally located within the United States, with state-of-the-art refrigeration systems and ripening rooms, the Denargo Market became a central distribution point for produce from Latin America and the United States in the 1950s. Denargo merchants received 8,000 railroad carloads of produce a year and supplied the surrounding twelve-state area with items such as Guatemalan bananas, Mexican pineapples, California oranges, Florida avocados, Massachusetts cranberries, and other tantalizing items from around the globe.

The opening of chain supermarkets including King Soopers and Millers Super Market in the late

1950s and early 1960s resulted in a decrease in business for the Denargo. With grocery stores relying more on air transportation for shipping produce, there was a decreasing need for a produce market located near a railroad yard. Additionally, farmers could contract with large food-selling organizations and ship their goods directly to airports and area distribution centers owned and managed by giant food conglomerates.[448]

After a number of years as a home for various distributors dealing with specialty items, the Denargo has been sold and is now being developed as a multi-family community.

Malpiede

John Malpiede

Born in 1891, John Malpiede grew up in north Denver with his parents Giuseppi "Joseph" and Gerarda "Geraldine" Malpiede.[449] An altar boy at Our Lady of Mount Carmel and the son of a stonemason-turned-vegetable-gardener, he married Mary Palmasano in 1911 and went to work as an electrician for the city of Denver.[450] In 1919, John decorated

John Malpiede (at far right) with workers in front of the Denver City and County Building with Christmas decorations, c. 1945. Gift Beverly (DeFrange) Christine. 2007.5.5

Denver's Civic Center for the first time in the city's history. At first, only the evergreen trees were decorated—at a cost of about $200.[451] The public response was overwhelming, and from there the project grew. Evergreen boughs were added to lampposts, then a lit Christmas tree was placed in front of the State Capitol, and in 1926, John persuaded Mayor Stapleton to let him decorate the exterior of City Hall (today's City and County Building) with a $400 budget. In 1938, the Christmas lights became an official project of the City and County of Denver.[452]

For twenty-nine years, John improved his exhibit by adding more garlands one year, new bulbs another, and additional figures, flowers, and even paintings the next. When he retired in 1956, the display included an eighty-five-foot artificial tree, hand-made reindeer, candles, giant poinsettias, 25,000 bulbs, seventeen miles of electrical wiring, and twelve tons of evergreen boughs at a cost of $30,000.[453]

Since 1985, the Keep the Lights Foundation has raised the roughly $100,000 needed to display, maintain, and dismantle the lights each year. Since 1996, about half a million people every year see the elaborate display of lights begun by John Malpiede.[454]

John and Mary Malpiede had one child, a daughter named Geraldine. John died in Denver in 1976.

Malpiede family; front row, left to right: Lena, Joseph, Anthony, Geraldine, Josephine; second row, left to right: Rose, Christine, Anna, and Mary; back row, left to right: Michael, John, and Clyde, c. 1910. CIAPA Collection. Courtesy Beverly (DeFrange) Christine. PCCLI5709

Denver City and County Building with holiday lights, c. 1950. CIAPA Archive. Courtesy Beverly (DeFrange) Christine. PCCLI5615

Mapelli

The Mapelli Brothers

In 1899, Giuseppe "Joseph" and Guido Mapelli, two of thirteen children born to Marco and Ezilda (Iacobucci) Mapelli, left their home in the Abruzzi region of Italy and came to America.[455] They settled in Denver in 1900, later sponsoring their younger siblings, Ambrogio "George," Armando "Herman," Rudolfo "Rudolph," Assunta, and Mario, who made their way to the United States in the early 1900s. Five of the Mapelli siblings stayed behind.

Prosperity 1940–1959

Mapelli Brothers Grocery Company with Mario Mapelli (wearing tie, behind white truck at left), Herman Mapelli (in hat), Nunzio Frazzini (driver of white truck), Sonny Mapelli (truck behind white truck), Tom Simones (third truck), Jay Lombardi (fourth truck), and M. Jacovetta (fifth truck), 1937. Fred Mazzulla Collection. PH.PROP.4031

Mapelli brothers; left to right: Joseph, Guido, George, Herman, Rudolph, and Mario, 1924. CIAPA Archive. Courtesy Pat Lauterback. PCCLI5517

Joseph, the head of the family, found work as a laborer on the Moffat Tunnel. His brothers worked as miners, barkeeps, and butchers.[456] In 1906, Joseph, Herman, and George opened the Mapelli Brothers Grocery Company at Fifteenth and Court in Denver.[457] Joseph headed the administrative office and credit department; Herman was president of wholesaling and of the purchase and sale of meats (he also made the sausage and cooked for the meat counter); and George oversaw retail sales at the meat counter. Mario—the last brother to immigrate to the United States—joined his brothers in the store, overseeing the grocery department and imported goods.[458] By 1930, the store had thirty clerks, seven butchers, and six trucks for the distribution of the groceries to people's homes and businesses.[459] In 1935, Joseph Mapelli died after a brief illness.[460] His brothers continued to operate the store until 1962, when it closed after the death of Herman and Mario.[461]

After joining his brothers in Denver, Guido Mapelli established himself as a shoemaker and then found success as a beer distributor, founding the Western Distributing Company in 1933 with his brother Rudolph. After the partnership dissolved, Guido became the sole owner of the company. His business expanded to encompass other liquors, and in the late 1940s, Guido's son Herman joined the company. After Guido's death in 1975, his family continued to run the business, which remains in operation today under the leadership of Guido's grandsons, Vieri and Carlo Gaines.[462]

In 1902, Rudolph joined his brothers in Denver, where he worked as a delivery boy at his brothers' market, delivered telegrams for the Western Union, and owned the Western Distributing Company with his brother Guido. In 1919, Rudolph established the R. Mapelli Music Company, followed by the Western Music and Radio shop, which offered customers a large selection of Italian music. Later, he owned a ranch near Bailey and orchards in Texas, where he died in 1989.[463]

Palmeri

Frank James Palmeri

Frank Palmeri was born in Denver in 1926 to Antonio "Tony" and Elena "Helen" (Di Iorio) Palmeri. His father, a native of Calabria, Italy, came to the United States in 1909, settling first in Chicago and then moving to Sheridan, Wyoming, where he worked in the coal mines. In 1917, Tony Palmeri enlisted in World War I, settling in Denver a few years later where he took a job with the Chicago, Burlington & Quincy Railroad.[464] Frank's mother, Helen, was a native of the southern Italian region of Abruzzi and came to America in 1921. Tony and Helen were married in 1923 at Our Lady of Mount Carmel and settled in Little Italy, where they raised their four children: Mary, Alice, Frank, and John.[465]

After graduating from North High in 1944, Frank Palmeri enlisted in the Navy. Discharged after World War II, he returned to Denver. During his career in education, Frank was a teacher, coach, media specialist, and administrator of audiovisual programs. In 1951, he married Rosemary LaBriola, a Denver neighbor born to Salvatore and Lucia (Rossi) LaBriola. After their marriage, Frank and Rosemary remained in north Denver, where they raised four children. They later moved to

Frank Palmeri's first communion, May 1932. Gift Frank and Rosemary Palmeri. 2005.26.6

Wheat Ridge, where they live today and remain active in the Italian American community, belonging to Our Lady of Mount Carmel and other organizations including the Sons of Italy Lodge No. 2075.[466]

Interested in radio broadcasting from a young age, Frank Palmeri began working as a sports public address announcer for the Denver Parochial High School League in 1948.[467] For over fifty years, he has announced high school sports, state high school championship tournaments, league games, and even a few professional baseball games and dog racing.[468]

Perito

Nick Perito

Nick Perito was born in Denver in 1924 to Rocco and Gerarda "Jennie" (Cominello) Perito. His father left Potenza, Italy, in 1898 at the age of fifteen, and after twenty-nine days on a ship in steerage, he reached New York City. Rocco then traveled for another three weeks by train to Denver, where in 1903, he married Jennie Cominello, also a native of Potenza, Italy. The couple settled in north Denver at 3321 Osage Street, where they raised four children, including Nick.[469]

At the age of five, Nick Perito started music lessons with Ernest Bonvicini, a friend of his father. Soon, he was

Rocco Perito (Nick Perito's father) inside his store, Perry's Fruit Store, Denver, c. 1910. CIAPA Archive. Courtesy Nick Perito. PCCLI2278

playing the accordion for family and friends at social occasions. In 1939, he took a job with KLZ, a radio station in Denver, playing accordion and piano in a trio known as the Yawn Patrolman. After graduating from North High School in 1942, Nick attended the Lamont School of Music at the University of Denver. An Army medic in World War II, he also played music with the United States Army Band. After the war, Nick attended the Juilliard School of Music in New York City and went on to work as an arranger, composer, conductor, and pianist.[470] Over the years, he worked with artists such as Judy Garland, Dorothy Dandridge, Peter Nero, Ferrante and Teicher, the Ray Charles Singers, and Perry Como. Nick was also the musical director for Perry Como, and in 1979, he joined the Kennedy Center in Washington, D.C., as the musical conductor of the "Kennedy Center Honors" annual television specials.

Nick Perito, c. 1935.
CIAPA Archive.
Courtesy Nick Perito.
PCCLI2290

In addition to his many and varied accomplishments, Nick garnered eleven Emmy nominations for his work as a musical director in television, released several albums, wrote a score for a movie, and wrote a book about his life in 2005, titled *I Just Happened to Be There...Making Music with the Stars*.

In 1949, Nick Perito married Judy Stone and together they had three children: Jennie, Danny, and Terry. Residents of California for many years, Nick and Judy often returned to north Denver to visit family and friends, and Nick performed at local functions.[471] Nick Perito died on August 3, 2005.

Schiola

Frances Pauline (Schiola) and Angelo George Pastore

Frances Pauline Schiola was born in Denver in 1935 to Anthony "Tony" and Maria Carmella "Mildred" (Blasi) Schiola.[472] Her father was born in Chicago to immigrants from Laurenzana, Italy. Her mother, Mildred, was also from Laurenzana. While visiting Chicago, Mildred

Prosperity 1940–1959

Frances (Schiola) Pastore, in the backyard of her family home at 3947 Pecos (attached to Schiola's Market), 1955. CIAPA Archive. Courtesy Angelo and Frances (Schiola) Pastore. PCCLI2592

Mildred (Blasi) Schiola inside Schiola's Market, c. 1950. CIAPA Archive. Courtesy Angelo and Frances (Schiola) Pastore. PCCLI2602

Men outside Schiola's Market; left to right: Salvatore Blasi, Frank Schiola, Joe Benedetto, and Anthony Schiola, father of Frances (Schiola) Pastore, c. 1950. CIAPA Archive. Courtesy Angelo and Frances (Schiola) Pastore. PCCLI2495

met her future husband, Tony, whom she married in 1931 in Denver. The couple bought a store from Mildred's brother for $7,000 and opened Schiola's Grocery & Market on Pecos Street in north Denver.[473] Schiola's sold homemade sausage, fresh Italian bread, olives, cheese, bulk cookies, frozen bananas, household products, canned goods, and, at Christmastime, fish for the traditional Italian Christmas Eve dinner.

In 1956, after her father died, her mother continued to manage the store with Frances doing the paperwork and her brother Frank helping with the store operations. The store, despite the changes in the neighborhood and the popularity of bigger store chains, stayed open until 1986.

In 1959, Frances Schiola married Angelo Pastore. One of ten children, Angelo was born in Denver in 1933 to Angelo and Marietta (Garramone) Pastore. His father, a native of Potenza, Italy, came to the United States around 1901. In Denver, he owned a farm and sold produce at the local city market and as a peddler in Five Points and north Denver. Angelo's mother, also from Potenza, came to Colorado in 1904 with her family. In addition to caring for Angelo and his siblings, she also helped in the fields, looked after the house, and cooked, both in her home as well as in her summer kitchen—a separate room above the wine cellar in the backyard, equipped with a stove that burned coal as well as oil and was used for canning and cooking during the summer to help keep the main house clean and cool.[474] Angelo worked at Lowry Air Force Base in the printing department until 1988, when he retired as branch chief of the printing division.

Sabelli/Sabell

Fred Leo Sabell

Fred Leo Sabell was born in 1928 to Sabatino and Sarafina (Masciotra) Sabelli/Sabell. In 1903, his father left Agnone, Italy, for America.[475] After landing in New York, he was processed by immigration officials at Ellis Island, who dropped the "i" at the end of his name; from then on, he was known as Sabatino Sabell. He then traveled west, where he settled with relatives in Pueblo and found work in a smelter. After a year, he sent for his wife and the couple's oldest son, Mike.[476]

Around 1910, the Sabells relocated to Denver, where Sabatino worked in a Globeville smelter and later for the Union Pacific Railroad. By 1930, the family had eleven children and Sabatino was working a second job digging graves at Crown Hill Cemetery for a dollar a day. Sarafina helped by cooking meals for laborers out of the family's two-bedroom home on Kalamath Street in north Denver. She also worked in nearby fields, picking crops in exchange for a bushel of produce. As the youngest child, Fred helped his mother make sausage, bread, and wine to sell to the neighbors. Fred sold loaves of bread baked daily in Sarafina's outdoor dome oven for twenty-five cents apiece. She also had a summer kitchen, where she canned fruit and vegetables.[477]

Fred Sabell and his Ford Fairlane, 1953. CIAPA Archive. Courtesy Fred Sabell. PCCLI1211

The only Sabell child to finish school, Fred graduated from Holy Family High School in 1948. He went on to Fort Lewis Junior College and the Colorado State College of Education on an athletic scholarship. While in school, he was drafted as a medic in the Korean War. He sent money home to his mother to help pay the bills. Sarafina saved it in a coffee can and gave the money back to Fred when he returned home. Fred used the money to buy a 1951 Ford Fairlane for $1,700.[478]

In 1954, Fred finished his education. After teaching physical education and coaching for a few years, he earned his master's at the University of Denver. A devoted teacher and coach, Fred Sabell worked in the Denver Public School system for over thirty years. He taught American history, driver's education, and health while working as a counselor and coach for teams including the Northside Community Center's Rough Riders teams.

Spano

Giuseppe "Joseph" and Anna (Calabrese) Spano

At the urging of his cousin Giovanni Calabrese, already in Denver, Giuseppe Spano and his son Giuseppe "Joseph" left their home in Palermo, Sicily, arriving in New York via Naples in 1899. Giuseppe's wife Maria Rosalia (Petrucci) Spano remained in Italy with their other five children.[479]

In Denver, Giuseppe and Joseph stayed with Giovanni at 258 Bell Street (now Osage Street). A short time later, father and son took a job near Leadville with the Rio Grande Railroad. Giuseppe worked as a muleskinner (in charge of the mule-drawn cart that hauled supplies and men to railroad construction crews) and Joseph as a water boy. After the death of his father, Joseph returned to Denver, where he worked in Welby for the DeRose family on their farm. By 1902, he had saved enough money to send for his brother Serafino "Sam" Spano. Joseph and Sam continued working in the Welby vegetable fields, and a year later, the brothers sent for the rest of their family. All but Giovanna, who had an eye infection, were allowed to enter the United States; she finally joined the family in 1908.

In 1905, Joseph married Anna Calabrese at Our Lady of Mount Carmel Church in Denver. Anna, the daughter of Agostino and Provvidenza (D'Alfeo) Calabrese, was

Joseph and Anna (Calabrese) Spano, 1935. CIAPA Archive. Courtesy Ahnna Rose (Spano) Klug. PCCLI5358

born in Denver in 1888. As a child, Anna attended Saint Patrick's School but left to take care of her siblings after her mother became blind from cataracts; she also helped her family financially by working in the strawberry fields in Wheat Ridge and hand dipping chocolates at the Nevins Candy Company in downtown Denver.

After their marriage, Joseph and Anna lived in a rented shack at Seventieth and York Streets in Welby, near property Joseph rented to farm. Together they had eleven children: Maryann, Florence, Jennie, Samuel Joseph, Clara, Rose, August John, Anthony, Elizabeth, Jack, and Pauline. In 1931, the Spano family moved to Arvada, where they purchased land to farm, growing—among other things—Pascal Celery, a labor-intensive specialty item sold mostly at Thanksgiving and Christmastime. Over the years, Joseph expanded his business to include lettuce sheds in Granby and Parshall, Colorado, where Joseph and his partners purchased lettuce from farmers in the area who brought it to the lettuce sheds for packing, sale, and distribution.

Over the years, Joseph Spano made five return trips to his native homeland. Although he still felt a strong sense of connection to Italy, he became an American citizen in 1927. Joseph Spano died in 1938, followed by Anna, who died in 1977.

A Closer Look
Pascal Celery

In Colorado, truck farming became increasingly popular with Italians in the first decades of the twentieth century. In order to have cash flow throughout the year, farmers needed a variety of crops to rotate, cultivate, and bring to market. Radishes, spinach, rhubarb, and asparagus were the spring crops. In July, the crops included strawberries, raspberries, beets, and turnips. From August until the first frost, usually mid-September, farmers harvested sweet corn, tomatoes, bell peppers, eggplant, cabbage, broccoli, and cauliflower.

Harvesting celery on the DiLuzio family farm, Welby, Colorado, c. 1920. CIAPA Archive. Courtesy Mary (DiLuzio) DeBell. PCCLI0493

Prosperity 1940–1959

"Bleaching celery" or wrapping celery in newspaper while still in the ground and bleaching it (or making it tender and white) before sending it to market, Tony Persichetti Farm, Clear Creek Gardens, 6100 Pecos, 1942. CIAPA Archive. Courtesy Theresa (Persichetti) Judish. PCCLI4556

Pascal Celery wrapper from the Spano Farm in Arvada, c. 1935. Gift Ahnna Rose (Spano) Klug. 2007.4.1

With the advent of frost, the focus was on root crops such as carrots, parsnips, turnips, and rutabagas.[480]

In addition, some farmers grew Pascal Celery, a nationally known holiday crop and a specialty of Italian truck farmers. The height of its popularity was in the 1930s and much of it was grown in Arvada, Wheat Ridge, and Clear Creek Gardens (in unincorporated Adams County).

Referred to as "the prince of crops," Pascal Celery's attraction to growers was the promise, not always fulfilled, of high cash returns.[481] Its drawback was the labor-intensive twelve months needed to cultivate and bring the product to market. Sold from Thanksgiving until Christmas, Pascal Celery was considered a delicacy, and growers took great pride in providing it for holiday tables. Production of the specialty celery began to decline during World War II, the result of labor shortages and the resulting increase in wages. Pascal Celery had simply become too expensive to grow and was replaced by more cost-effective crops.

Samuel "Sam" Joseph Spano

Samuel "Sam" Joseph Spano, son of Giuseppe "Joseph" and Anna (Calabrese) Spano, was born in Wheat Ridge in 1912. As the oldest son, he helped with the family farm from the time he was a young boy. In 1939, he married Rose Orlando, the daughter of Domenico and Agata (Battaglia) Orlando. After their marriage, the couple built a house near Sam's parents. Together they had two children: Ahnna Rose and Orlan.[482]

After the death of his father, Sam took over the operations of the Spano farm, still plowing the fields using a draft horse. In the 1940s, Sam started buying modern farming equipment, including tractors, to help plant and harvest a variety of vegetables he then sold at the Denargo Market. In the mid–1950s, he started growing bedding plants. Pansies became his specialty. Sam's bedding plants did so well that between 1961 and 1965, Sam built greenhouses west of his house that enabled him to grow plants during the cold weather.

When Sam went into semi-retirement around 1978, he grew a variety of garden vegetables in a field east of his house along Fifty-second Avenue. He also ventured into the sweet corn business, planting several small patches of corn seeded at intervals so that fresh corn was available throughout the summer. The first patch was planted in rocky soil that held a lot of warmth, which in turn enabled him to harvest the crop often by July fourth if it survived the frost and/or hail.

Spano farm, bunching broccoli, left to right: Joe Gonzales, Rose Spano, Sam Spano, and Ahnna Rose (Spano) Klug, c. 1950. CIAPA Archive. Courtesy Ahnna Rose (Spano) Klug. PCCLI5361

Prosperity 1940–1959

The corn and other vegetables were sold at a vegetable stand in the Spano backyard under the trees. Most vegetables were picked early in the morning. Sam picked corn several times a day so that it would be fresh. A big wooden sign was placed on Fifty-second Avenue against the mailbox advertising "CORN." People would drive in and buy their corn and vegetables from their cars. Sam also sold vegetables to Bernard's Restaurant in Arvada. Many people ordered several dozen ears of corn for freezing.

In 1986, Arvada Urban Renewal purchased the Spano Farm and all of the houses on the south side of Fifty-second Avenue from Wadsworth to Marshall Street. Sam and Rose Spano moved to Sixty-eighth and Allison in Arvada. Sam Spano died in Arvada in 1995. Rose Spano still lives in Arvada.

Vecchiarelli

John Louis Vecchiarelli

The son of Anthony and Josephine (Pagliano) Vecchiarelli, John (or Muzzy to his friends) Vecchiarelli was born in Denver in 1930.[483] His father, the son of Italian-born parents Liberatore "John" and Amelia (Antonelli) Vecchiarelli, worked in the Denver foundries and as a welder. His mother Josephine, born in Denver to Italian parents Gustavo and Rosa Pagliano, worked at the Denver Dry Goods Company while caring for John and his two brothers.[484]

After graduating from Holy Family High School, John attended the University of Denver, where he earned a degree in education. He went on to teach physical education in the public school system, as well as coach a number of teams, including the Rough Riders, a team he played for in his youth that was sponsored by the Northside Community Center at Thirty-sixth Avenue and Lipan Street. In his twenty-one years coaching the team, he mentored several well-known players including Freddie Steinmark and Jim Liley.[485]

Vecchiarelli family, from left to right: Lou, Anthony Jr., Josephine, Anthony Sr., and John Vecchiarelli, c. 1950. CIAPA Archive. Courtesy John and Bonnie Vecchiarelli. PCCLI1878

In 1952, while serving in the military, John Vecchiarelli met and married Jacqueline Jean Morrison, a native of Broadwater, Nebraska. Together, John and Jacqueline raised four children, all born in Denver. Today, John Vecchiarelli and his second wife Bonnie (his first wife died in 1976) live in Aurora.

O'Dorisio

Olga Ester (Zarlengo) O'Dorisio

Born in 1917, Olga Ester Zarlengo was the seventh child of Italian immigrants Charles and Linda Zarlengo.[486] After graduating from North High in 1936, she went to work as a secretary for her brother in his medical practice. In 1940, Olga married Angelo O'Dorisio at Saint Catherine's Catholic Church in Denver. Angelo's father Fred had come from Italy and worked as a boilermaker at a Pueblo steel mill. His mother Lucy was born in Colorado to Italian-born parents.[487] Angelo was an art teacher and later worked as the editorial art director for *The Denver Post*.[488] He and Olga had five children together: Charles (who died in infancy), Thomas, Joseph, Michael, and Richard.

Angelo and Olga (Zarlengo) O'Dorisio on their wedding day with Linda Zarlengo (left) and Lucy O'Dorisio (right), 1940. Loan Robin and Steve O'Dorisio IL.2006.40.18.7

Tragedy again struck Olga's family on Mother's Day in 1970, when Olga's youngest son, Richard, died in a rafting accident. He was just eighteen years old. Not until Father's Day was his body found. So devastating was the event that it contributed to the death of Olga's husband Angelo in 1971. Refusing to let the loss of her husband and another child take over her life, Olga vowed to keep her mind and body active. At age fifty-four, she went to work as a paraprofessional at Columbian Elementary—a job that turned into a thirty-three-year career.[489]

Olga O'Dorisio loved her family, her job, and the children she worked with. She also loved cooking, caring for others, and contributing to her community. She died in 2004 at the age of eighty-seven.

A Closer Look
The Zarlengo Brothers

Zarlengo brothers; standing, left to right: Gaetano "Charles," Giochino "Jack," Giovanni "John"; seated: Ottavio and Adorino "Dan," c. 1900. Charles and Jack Zarlengo were two of six brothers who immigrated to the United States from Campobasso, Italy. Only Charles and Jack have direct ties with Denver. CIAPA Archive. Courtesy Vincent Zarlengo. PCCLI4642

Gaetano "Charles" Zarlengo arrived in America in 1890 with his father Francesco. At thirteen, Charles worked as a water boy alongside his father on railroad section gangs laying track through Idaho. The dangerous working conditions led father and son to Silver Plume, where they found contract work cutting cordwood and hauling ore by burro for use as fuel in the area mines. Charles's fourteen-year-old brother, Giochino, or "Jack," joined them in 1895.[490]

In 1910, with the decline of the mining industry in Silver Plume, Charles and Jack moved to Denver, where they formed the Zarlengo Brothers Contracting Company. They cleaned and maintained Denver streetcars, loaded coal cars for smelters in Golden and Globeville, and operated coal chutes for railroads, shoveling coal out of railcars into chutes leading into coal bins. Later, the brothers established a lumber camp near Tolland, Colorado, that supplied timber braces for nearby mines; by the 1920s, the lumber camp was one of the biggest producers of timber props in northern Colorado, supplying timber for projects including the Moffat Tunnel.[491]

While Jack oversaw the coal business in Denver, Charles supervised the lumber camp. They also ran their own coal mines at Mount Harris in Routt County and in Louisville and Frederick, Colorado. The company employed Italians in all of its operations and often paid the fares for Italian immigrants to come to Colorado.

In addition to their strong work ethic, the Zarlengo brothers were also devoted to their families. In 1900, Jack married Elizabeth Fabrizio in Denver and together they had nine children: Ida, Ruby, Anthony, Albert, Loretta, Ersilia, Eleanor, Roland, and

Arthur.[492] In 1905, Charles returned to Italy and married his childhood sweetheart Linda Moauro. Together they raised nine children in Denver: Henry, Mary, Ernest, Dominic, Frank, Louis, Olga, Charles, and Vincent. Elizabeth Zarlengo died in Denver in 1936, followed by Jack, who died in 1953. Charles Zarlengo died in 1947, followed by his wife Linda, who died in 1965 at the age of seventy-six.[493]

Both Jack and Charles believed in the value of honest work, good citizenship, and education. In 2001, their descendants honored that legacy by founding the Zarlengo Foundation, which supports schools, scientific research, and religious programs throughout the Denver area.

CHAPTER 7

Change
1960–1989

In the 1960s and '70s, much of Denver's growing population left the city for new suburban developments. Third- and fourth-generation Italian Americans moved from north Denver to the suburbs, buying homes that were newer and bigger than their parents'.

At a time of civil rights movements for African Americans, Hispanics, American Indians, and women, Italians in many ways had "made it" into mainstream culture. And by the 1960s, Little Italy was changing again as Italians moved out and Hispanics moved in. Once childhood friends, neighbors had to take sides in controversies over the ownership of shared spaces like Columbus Park. Those controversies sometimes led to violence.

Many former residents of Little Italy drifted from their local parish, Our Lady of Mount Carmel. The drop in parishioners led to the closing of Mount Carmel's grade school and high school in 1968. The junior high closed in 1971. Districts 9 and 10—Little Italy and its environs—had stalwartly favored Italian American politicians since the 1930s. By the 1980s, that too had changed.

Many truck farmers sold their land in the 1960s as they struggled to break even. Italian American grocery stores, markets, and delis closed as bigger chain stores opened. By the end of the '80s, only a handful of Italian American businesses remained in north Denver—products of an earlier time and proof that former residents still came back to Little Italy. The 1990s would see Italian Americans revisit their traditions, culture, and family histories.

Opposite: Our Lady of Mount Carmel High School at Thirty-sixth and Zuni Streets, Denver, c. 1955. CIAPA Archive. Courtesy Our Lady of Mount Carmel. PCCLI2002

Brunetti

Anthony "Tony" Gerald Brunetti

Tony Brunetti was born in Denver in 1938 to John and Josephine (LaGuardia) Brunetti. His mother was from Denver and his father was born in Naples, Italy. His parents divorced when Tony was five. As a result, Tony, his mother, and three siblings moved in with his grandfather Gerardo LaGuardia.[494] Gerardo, a native of Potenza, Italy, came to the United States around 1890, later sending for his wife Rosina (Laurita) LaGuardia, who died in Denver in 1937.[495] Tony's mother, Josephine, was the family's sole supporter for years and continued working after marrying Joseph Luchetta in 1946.

In the eighth grade, Tony met fellow student Marcia Olguin Trujillo. The two dropped out in their junior year and married in 1956. They lived with Marcia's parents, and Tony worked in construction. Soon, he followed his uncle into the sheet-metal trade. Later, the family bought Tony's childhood home on Osage Street from his mother. While Marcia cared for their two daughters, Tony worked and went to night school.

Their happiness was marred by tragedy in 1961. Visiting a nearby pharmacy, Tony found himself in the midst of a robbery. A wounded police officer shot him in the abdomen, mistaking him for one of the thieves.[496] Tony was unconscious for a week and spent two months in the hospital. Insurance covered only part of his $6,000 medical expenses, and he was unable to return to work for months.[497]

The community pitched in: Marcia's parents stayed with the family while friends, police officers, and parishioners at Our Lady of Mount Carmel raised money. Tony returned to work in 1962, and that year the couple's third daughter was born, followed by another in 1964. The Brunettis stayed in north Denver until 1968, when a robbery occurred at their home and they decided that the neighborhood was no longer safe for their family.

Tony Brunetti, 1961. CIAPA Archive. Courtesy Tony and Marcia Brunetti. PCCLI5653

Today, Tony and Marcia Brunetti live in Northglenn and are enjoying their retirement. They stay connected to the north Denver community, where they remain parishioners at Our Lady of Mount Carmel. Additionally, Tony enjoys playing the game of morra with fellow members of the Morra Society of Denver.[498]

A Closer Look
The Morra Society of Denver

Romans, Greeks, and Egyptians all played the game of *morra*. Called *micare digitis* in Latin, or "twinkling fingers," the game survived the fall of empires and remains an important tradition among Italian Americans.[499]

Usually a men's game, morra requires no equipment. All you need is your hand, a steady voice, a little luck, and a lot of attitude. It can be played informally with two players or with teams of multiple players in competitive tournaments. Either way, the object of the game is to score points. Players raise one hand, extending or "throwing" one to five fingers or a closed fist (indicating the number one), while shouting a number between two and ten. If the number called by one player corresponds to the total number of fingers shown by both players, the correct caller gets a point. If the numbers thrown do not match the shouted numbers, no one scores. In competitive games a "pit boss" confirms the points. The loser steps aside and the winner stays to challenge the next opposing player. The first team to score fifteen points wins.

In Denver, the non-gambling Morra Society has been in existence since 1946. Members started gathering at DeJones restaurant on Thirty-third and Navajo for competitions.[500] In the early days, there were several morra teams in north Denver sponsored by businesses such as the Columbus Park Inn, Coors Tavern, Patsy's, and the Pinecone Inn. Over the years, the organization has met at various locations including the Veterans of Foreign Wars Post, the Disabled American Veterans, Lombardi's Roman Gardens, and the Hyland Hills Golf Course. Currently, the president of the Morra Society of Denver is Dave Falbo. Membership includes on average sixty players, who play every Friday night, October through April.

Capillupo

Ernest "Ernie" Capillupo

Ernest "Ernie" Capillupo was born in 1914 in the southern Italian region of Calabria. His parents, naturalized American citizens, had returned to Italy for a visit and were set to return to the United States when World War I broke out.[501]

At the age of six, Ernie and his parents, Carmine and Rose (Canino) Capillupo, retuned to the United States and settled in Sheridan, Wyoming, where his father worked as a coal miner. In 1927, when the coal mines shut down, the family moved to north Denver, where Ernie graduated from Regis High School.[502] He went on to attend the University of Denver, and in 1938, married Louise G. Jinacio with whom he had one son, Vincent Paul Capillupo.[503]

During World War II, Ernie worked as a personnel manager and safety engineer at American Manganese Steel in Denver. He later worked as a finance officer for Continental Airlines and as an insurance agent before opening his restaurant and lounge in 1943 called Ernie's (also known as Ernie's Supper Club). Ernie operated the restaurant, located on West Forty-fourth Avenue and Federal Boulevard, until 1986, when he retired after forty-five years in business.[504]

Interested in politics, Ernie believed in "good government," which, according to him, was the Democratic Party—a sentiment surely influenced by his father, who often told him as a young man, "Number one, you're an American! Number two, you're a Democrat!"[505] In 1960, he was a Democratic candidate for the Colorado House. Although he did not win the election, he became a leader in promoting the Democratic Party in north Denver, because he could help bring in around 40,000 votes for the candidate of his choice in a district that was predominantly Italian American with 90 percent of the voters registered Democrat. Ernie also served as a member of the plumbing examiner's board and was appointed to the Board of Adjustment-Zoning in 1973 by Mayor Bill McNichols. He was reappointed to the position by Mayors Federico Peña and Wellington Webb and served as chairman of the board in 1976, 1981, and 1986.[506]

Ernie Capillupo had deep ties to Denver's Italian American community and traditions that extended beyond just politics. In addition to serving as president of the Order Sons of Italy Denver Lodge No. 2075 from 1965 to 1968,

Ernie and his wife were also active parishioners of Our Lady of Mount Carmel Church. Ernie also worked to preserve the traditions of his heritage, including making traditional Italian sopresatta sausage with his family and friends, most of which he gave away as a gift. Concerned that the labor-intensive process was quickly becoming a "lost art" in the community, he offered to teach the art to younger generations.[507] Ernie Capillupo died in Denver in 1994 at the age of seventy-nine.

Carbone

Father Joseph Carbone

Joseph Carbone was born in 1926 in his family's Navajo Street home, across from Our Lady of Mount Carmel Church.[508] Anthony, as he was then known (he took the name Joseph when he became a priest), was the youngest of seven children born to Vincenzo and Louisa Carbone. His parents were from Vaglia, Italy, in the Tuscany region. In 1907, his father Vincenzo came to the United States and

Left to right: Vincenzo and Louisa with children Viola "Helen" and Rocco "Roxie" Carbone, Denver, 1911. CIAPA Archive. Courtesy Louise (Carbone) Ackman. PCCLI5546

Father Carbone at the altar of Our Lady of Mount Carmel, by James Baca, 1984. CIAPA Archive. Courtesy Our Lady of Mount Carmel Church. PCCLI2018

settled in Illinois, where he found work with a railroad. In 1911, after settling in Denver and working for the Union Pacific Railroad, Vincenzo sent for his wife Louisa and children: Rocco "Roxie" and Viola "Helen."[509] In Denver, five more children were born to Vincenzo and Louisa: Dominic, Giorgio "George," Carmella, Daniel, and Anthony.[510]

In 1945, Anthony entered the Servite seminary in Welby. He continued his religious education in Illinois but came back to Denver when his father died in 1949. He took a job with Samsonite Luggage for three years and served two years in the military as a chaplain's assistant before returning to his religious studies. He studied in California and Italy, and in 1959, was ordained in Rome.[511]

After a trip to Italy (where he said Mass in the church where his parents were married), Father Carbone took assignments in Chicago and Colorado, including Welby and Denver. In 1977, he was appointed associate pastor of his childhood parish, Our Lady of Mount Carmel. In 1980, he became pastor of the parish. Regarding his return to Mount Carmel, Father Carbone said "I never thought I'd wind up back at my own parish... it was like coming home."[512] The neighborhood of his youth had changed into a predominantly Hispanic community.[513] Father Carbone welcomed all at Our Lady of Mount Carmel and worked tirelessly to make positive changes in the parish, including remodeling the church and parish hall. When asked about being a priest, Father Carbone said:

> I am proud of being a priest. My parents gave me this culture and faith and most of all my vocation....I approach my work with great joy and great expectations to do something for my people and service to anyone who needs my help. I enjoy my Masses and other services I do.[514]

Now retired, Father Carbone is still active with Our Lady of Mount Carmel.[515]

Ad for Carbone's Italian Bakery (owned by Father Carbone's uncle Dan Carbone and brothers Roxie and Dominic) from Mount Carmel Parish and School Bazaar booklet, 1952. CIAPA Archive. Courtesy Our Lady of Mount Carmel Church. PCCLI5617

A CLOSER LOOK
Mother Cabrini's Legacy in Denver

Mother Frances Xavier Cabrini, born in 1850 in the northern Italian province of Lombardy, came to the United States in

1889. The first American canonized a saint by the Catholic Church, she served Italian immigrants around the country, but did some of her most important work in Denver.[516]

In June of 1902, the Missionary Sisters of the Sacred Heart in Denver—co-founded by Cabrini—opened a convent and school in the Notary family home on Navajo Street. When it opened, the school welcomed more than two hundred daughters, sons, and grandchildren of Italian immigrants. The formal dedication of the school was reported on by the *Denver Times*, which noted:

> Two hundred little tots in gala array assembled in the new school building of Our Lady of Mt. Carmel this morning to be presented to Bishop Matz and to do honor to Father Lepore and the Missionary Sisters of the Sacred Heart. The new mission school is Father Lepore's pride, and not even the parents of the dark-eyed babes in white dresses and satin slippers with Sunday ribbons a flying or the sturdy little chaps in velvet knickerbockers or blue overalls were filled with greater delight than he at the fine showing made by the roomful of foreign looking little faces.
>
> Bishop Matz, in the part of his address to the parents, dwelt on the fact that previous to the opening of this mission the two hundred little ones had been scattered from one end of Denver to the other, many of them attending no school at all. He besought them to remember that while the children were to become true American citizens, speaking English intelligently and fluently, that they were not to forget the music, the sentiment, and the pathos of the mother county and the mother tongue. The Missionary Sisters, some of whom speak only Italian while others are equally at ease in English, were counseled to keep before them the finest traits of the two races and combine them for the children's best good.
>
> Father Lepore is confident that from a beginning of two hundred, the Italian mission school will grow to a thousand or more and that the building that is still fresh with new paint will someday, and that before very long, be replaced with a much more commodious and convenient structure.
>
> Father Pantanella and Father Gubitosi shared in the general rejoicing though half hidden behind the rose offerings piled up on the table during the ceremony.[517]

Change 1960–1989

In October of 1904, the sisters founded an orphanage when they took in two orphans, setting up living quarters for them on the third floor of the Notary home.[518] The orphanage for girls quickly outgrew the Notary property, and in 1905, Cabrini's order bought a new facility for the orphanage. Regina Coeli, or "Queen of Heaven," accommodated 160 children, whereas the Notary house served only eighteen. Located at Forty-eighth and Federal in a renovated farmhouse, the original building was replaced in 1921 by a new, much larger facility. Many of the orphans at Queen of Heaven were there because one parent had died, forcing the other to work long hours, leaving the children alone during the day.[519] Some orphans lived there full-time while others stayed at the orphanage during the week, returning to their family on the weekend. The girls both lived and attended school at the orphanage. Educated according to Cabrinian pedagogy, which was designed to teach them a love of religion and the practice of virtue, the orphans also attended Mass, prayed, played outside, and were responsible for household chores.[520] To supplement the orphanage's income, the girls embroidered towels and tablecloths, sold by the sisters through a Denver ladies guild.[521]

In 1908, the Missionary Sisters of the Sacred Heart moved the Mount Carmel School to the unused Saint Rocco Chapel on Osage Street. Built in 1901 by Frank

Postcard showing the new Queen of Heaven Orphanage, 4825 Federal Blvd., Denver, c. 1926. 95.128.149

Damascio, Damascio remodeled and adapted it for a school by dividing the intended sanctuary into two floors, with seven classrooms on the lower floor and a gymnasium/auditorium on the upper level. The Mount Carmel School's continued growth ultimately led to the construction of a high school in 1951 and a new grade school in 1954.[522]

In 1910, Cabrini founded a summer camp for the orphans in Mount Vernon Canyon west of Denver. Lacking water, the site was thought to be useless until Cabrini located an underground spring. The faithful consider her feat miraculous.[523]

Mother Cabrini died in 1917, but her Colorado legacy remains strong. Though the Mount Carmel schools closed in the 1960s—due to the neighborhood's declining Italian population and because fewer families chose to send their children to the parochial schools—and the Queen of Heaven Orphanage was torn down in 1973, the summer camp, now known as the Mother Cabrini Shrine, still houses the Missionary Sisters and attracts thousands of visitors yearly.

Mutual Benefit Society of St. Frances Xavier Cabrini

Founded on the 6th day of May, 1923 in Denver, Colorado.

43

Title page from membership booklet with image of Mother Cabrini, Mutual Benefit Society of St. Frances Xavier Cabrini, 1923. Gift Rose (Canino) Villano and Michael C. and Clair Villano. 2005.38.11

A CLOSER LOOK
The Mother Cabrini Lodge

In the early twentieth century, the popularity of Mother Frances Xavier Cabrini was so great that a number of lodges were organized in her honor, including the Mother Cabrini Lodge in Colorado. Founded in 1923 with fifty-eight members, the lodge was originally called the Mutual Benefit Society of St. Frances Xavier Cabrini. Membership was open to women of Italian descent and benefits included payment of medical expenses and a death benefit of $100 for the member or the member's spouse. During the mid-1920s and 1930s, the lodge grew, and in 1947 was renamed the Mother Cabrini Lodge No. 18.[524] Today, the Mother Cabrini Lodge still exists in Denver with forty-eight members eligible for a $1,200 death benefit; membership is now open to women of all nationalities.

Ciancio

Francisco "Frank" Amerigo Ciancio

Frank Ciancio was born in Welby in 1902 to Carmine and Louisa (Bruno) Ciancio. In 1900, Frank's father, at age forty-eight, had left his home in Bucita, a town in the southern Italian province of Cosenza, and came to the United States.[525] Carmine brought his son, Giuseppe "Joseph," age fourteen.[526] Carmine worked as a coal miner in Pennsylvania. In 1901, he sent for his wife, Louisa, and their seven other children in Italy.[527] The Ciancio family settled in the town of Elyria in Adams County, Colorado, where Louisa's sister Carmella and her husband Benimeno Perri/Perry lived. Carmine worked as a produce peddler and Louisa cared for the children, including four more born in America. Soon, the family had its own farm in Welby.[528]

Mary and Frank Ciancio, c. 1945.
CIAPA Archive.
Courtesy Don C. Ciancio.
PCCLI4833

The first child born in America, Frank Ciancio was given a middle name, Amerigo, that celebrated his Italian family's new homeland. After graduating from Manual High School, the only one in his immediate family to do so, his older brother Joseph helped Frank get a job in the Denver Treasurer's office.[529] While working as a clerk, he met Mary Yashvin, the daughter of Lithuanian Jewish immigrants and secretary to Mayor Ben Stapleton. In 1925, both Frank and Mary lost their jobs as a result of the religious and ethnic discrimination of the time.[530] In 1926, Frank and Mary were married and moved to Welby, Colorado, where they opened the Welby Mercantile Company with Frank's older brother Joseph and his brother-in-law Frank Reale. Frank and Mary's home sat between Assumption Church and the mercantile. Mary initially had a difficult time in the Welby community due to her national and religious background, but in time, she won over her critics.

The Welby Mercantile carried a variety of products and also had three gas pumps in front of the store. After the repeal

Ciancio's Famous Dinners, Welby, Colorado, c. 1945. CIAPA Archive. Courtesy Don C. Ciancio. PCCLI4832

of Prohibition in 1934, Mary and Frank added a restaurant and bar—Ciancio's Famous Dinners.[531] Their four children, Don, Carol, Frank Jr., and Geno, later washed dishes and delivered groceries for the establishment.[532] The "unofficial Mayor of Welby," Frank was also a Democratic Party leader in Adams County.[533] Although he never held a public office, he became an important power broker in state politics.[534] Some of his major accomplishments included aiding in the development of the Denargo Market through negotiations with the Union Pacific Railroad; serving as the chairman of the Adams County Works Progress Administration; and working as campaign manager for Senator Edward C. Johnson and Colorado presidential candidates Averill Harriman and Adlai Stevenson.[535] Frank Ciancio died on May 1, 1988.

Joseph "Joe" Ciancio Jr.

Joe Ciancio Jr., the grandson of Louise and Carmine Ciancio, was born in 1922 to Giuseppe "Joseph" and Frances (Rende) Ciancio. Among other jobs, his father worked as a railroad worker for the Civilian Conservation Corps, as a politician, and as assistant market master at the City Market, a produce market in Denver. Joe's family owned the Ciancio Brothers grocery store in Elyria, Colorado.[536]

In 1940, Joe Ciancio Jr. joined the Army Signal Corps. He served four years on active duty, including fourteen

Change 1960–1989

Wedding of Rose and Joe Ciancio Jr., back row, left to right: Madeline (Antonucci) Rose, Bernice (DiLorenzo) Perry, Anne (Elio) Ciancio, Marie (Sottlie) Schberth, Joe Ciancio Jr., Rose (Sutley) Ciancio, George "Dutch" Hanel, Larry Perry, and Leonard Muzzelo; seated, left to right: Lena "Mickie" Cimaglia–Stuley, Norma Lee Florida, and Peter Ciancio, 1942. CIAPA Archive. Courtesy Joe Ciancio Jr. family. PCCLI5625

Ciancio Brothers grocery store with Carl Ciancio (left) and Joe Ciancio Sr. (right), Elyria, Colorado, c. 1920. CIAPA Archive. Courtesy Joe Ciancio Jr. family. PCCLI5754

months in Asia during World War II. In 1942, Joe married Rose Sutley, whom he met at a dance at the Northside Community Center. Rose and Joe had two daughters: Barbara and Pam. In 1946, Rose and Joe opened a package liquor store in Elyria at 2223 East Forty-seventh Avenue. In 1955, Joe entered the Ninth District city council race and won.[537] He represented the district for a decade and twice served as council president. In 1965, he left the council for an appointment as manager of Parks and Recreation. Twelve years later, Joe was in charge of 169 parks, 77.7 miles of parkway, 7 city golf courses, 33 recreation centers, 19 swimming pools, 137 tennis courts, 13 lighted playing fields, and 88 playgrounds.[538]

One of the city parks Joe oversaw was Columbus Park, located at Thirty-eighth Avenue and Navajo Street. Established by Italians in north Denver, the park had been a popular destination for Little Italy residents well into the 1950s. When the demographics in north Denver shifted and the neighborhood's new Hispanic residents sought to change the park's name to "La Raza Park," Joe Ciancio Jr. became a voice of opposition.[539] In a controversial decision, he fired popular Columbus Park manager Arturo Rodriguez in 1972.[540] He defended his decision, and today the park is still named Columbus Park.

Joe Ciancio Jr. retired from Denver's parks department in 1983 as the longest-running park manager in Colorado history. In addition to family and work, Joe believes in the importance of preserving and promoting Italian heritage and culture. In 1959, he served as a founding member of the Order Sons of Italy in America Denver Lodge No. 2075, and served two terms as its president. In the 1990s, he founded the Grand Lodge of Colorado, and later, the Grand Lodge of Colorado Foundation, dedicated to helping Italian Americans through programs including a scholarship fund.[541]

Ciancio Brothers grocery store with family behind counter, left to right: Joseph Ciancio Sr., Peter Ciancio (in front of Joe), Frances Ciancio, Louis Ciancio (in front of Frances), Della Lotito, and Carl Ciancio (in front of Della), c. 1920. CIAPA Archive. Courtesy Joe Ciancio Jr. family. PCCLI5760

A Closer Look
The Order Sons of Italy in America

In 1905, six Italian Americans in New York established the Order Sons of Italy in America (OSIA) as a mutual aid society for fellow immigrants in times of need, illness, or a death in the family. Originally called *L'Ordine Figli d'Italia* ("The Order Children of Italy" or "The Order Sons of Italy"), this national organization remains active. Today it serves an estimated twenty-six million Italian Americans. In Colorado, the OSIA maintains lodges in Denver, Pueblo, and Salida.

The OSIA encourages the study of the Italian language and culture in American schools and universities, helps preserve Italian American history and heritage, and promotes cultural relations between the United States and Italy. It also debunks stereotypes by fighting oversimplified and negative portrayals of Italian Americans in movies, television, ads, and the news. Initially, men dominated the OSIA's membership. Today, about half of its members are women.

Covillo

Lillian R. Covillo

Lillian R. Covillo was born in Denver in 1921 to Italian American parents, John and Philomena (Piscitella) Covillo. Her father worked in vegetable gardening on the Covillo family farm in Welby. Around 1930, Lillian's parents decided to move the family to east Denver, where Lillian attended Saint Philomena's Grade School and Cathedral High.[542]

Discovering ballet as a girl, Lillian went on to perform in Denver operas. As a student at the University of Denver, she started teaching in the physical education department at the Cathedral Catholic schools. She taught dance (including ballet, modern, and folk), basketball, and softball to students in second grade through high school. Around 1940, she served as ballet mistress and choreographer for the Denver Grand Opera Company. In the late 1940s, she and fellow dancer Freidann Parker founded the Covillo-Parker School of Dance, which in turn led to the Covillo-Parker Theater Ballet.[543]

The first Covillo-Parker Theater Ballet production, *The Betrothal*, debuted in 1951. The ballet, written by Freidann, was based on a true murder mystery of the Old West and set to a score composed by Denver Symphony Orchestra cellist Robert Tweedy. Lillian and Freidann danced the leads, made the costumes, took care of the staging, and even engineered the lighting in their first production. To supplement their company, both Lillian and Freidann worked as freelance choreographers. At the suggestion of fellow dancer George Zoritch, Lillian and Freidann created a not-for-profit company so they could receive tax-deductible donations. They named their new company the Colorado Concert Ballet.[544]

During the Colorado Concert Ballet's first season in 1961, Covillo and Parker produced Denver's first full-length production of *The Nutcracker*. In 1968, Lillian Covillo and Freidann Parker received the Governor's Award for Excellence in the Arts. Ten years later, they changed the name of the company to the Colorado Ballet—today a mainstay of the Denver cultural scene. Parker died in 2002. Covillo, now in her eighties, still lives in Colorado.

Lillian Covillo, c. 1958. CIAPA Archive. Courtesy Lillian Covillo. PCCLI5447

DeFrange

John Joseph and Gloria (Briola) DeFrange

One of fifteen children, John DeFrange was born in Oklahoma to Italian immigrant parents Joseph and Sabathena "Maggie" (Carano) DeFrange.[545] John's father came to America in 1878 and worked as a miner and laborer.[546] His mother left Italy after her mother died, joining her siblings in Oklahoma in 1888. In 1940, at age twenty, John joined the 13th Air Force serving in the Philippines. During his tour of duty, he fell ill and was sent to Fort Logan in Denver for medical treatment. Invited to a friend's house for dinner, John met Gloria Briola; the two married four months later and together had two children: Gary and Beverly.[547]

Gloria was born in north Denver to Italian American parents John and Rose (Malpiede) Briola. She learned to

Change 1960–1989

John and Gloria (Briola) DeFrange, 1945. CIAPA Archive. Courtesy Beverly (DeFrange) Christine. PCCLI5147

play music as a child, and in her teens, organized an all-women's dance band: Gloria Briola and Her Sweethearts of Rhythm. They were wartime regulars at the Knights of Columbus hall downtown, playing the Catholic USO dances on Saturday nights. Gloria also taught accordion, an instrument John played as well.[548]

After John's honorable discharge, the couple settled in north Denver. While Gloria cared for their children, John taught accordion at the Monarch Accordion Studio. He was a member of the Denver Musicians Union and played accordion in dance bands, including the Ultimates and the Eddie Santangelo Combo. In time, he opened the DeFrange Accordion Studio on Federal Boulevard. Active in the Rocky Mountain Accordion Society, John arranged for many of his students to play in accordion bands and smaller groups, competing in local accordion contests. He adapted and arranged classical music for his students, with many of his groups winning top awards.

John closed his studio in the 1980s but played in groups until 1999. He directed choirs at Saint Catherine's and Our Lady of Mount Carmel and established the Sons of Italy Denver Lodge No. 2075 singing group. Today, John and Gloria live in Arvada.[549]

di Benedetto

Angelo di Benedetto

Angelo di Benedetto was born in Patterson, New Jersey, in 1913. His parents, Simone and Margaret (D'Amelio) di Benedetto came to the United States in 1911 from the southern Italian region of Campania. Angelo's father worked at a grocery store and pool room and as a junk dealer to support his family.[550]

Angelo became interested in art at a young age, and in 1925, his drawings were published in a local newspaper. Although his parents supported his decision to pursue art, Angelo, who grew up in an industrial town that was predominantly Irish, endured teasing by many in his neighborhood who not only disliked Italians but questioned

Angelo's manhood as an artist, throwing rocks at him while he painted outside his home.[551]

In 1934, Angelo graduated from the Cooper Union College of New York with a degree in art and went on to attend the Boston Museum School of Fine Arts and Harvard University. After completing his studies, he moved to New York, hoping to launch his career. After several unsuccessful attempts with art galleries and dealers in New York, Angelo returned to New Jersey, where he gave private painting lessons. In 1938, Angelo was hired by the Royal Netherlands Steamship Company to design travel posters for the company. After traveling to Haiti, he returned to the United States, and in 1939, *Life* magazine published an article on him, launching his art career.

While serving in World War II, Angelo and his wife Lee, whom he married in 1942, were stationed at Buckley Air Force Base in Denver, where Angelo taught orientation classes to new recruits. After his discharge in 1946, the di Benedettos moved to Central City, where they bought and renovated the old Sauer-McShane Mercantile Company. In 1953, Lee and Angelo di Benedetto divorced, and Lee moved to Scottsdale, Arizona, with the couple's two daughters, Michelle and Mia. For Angelo, raised in the Roman Catholic tradition, the breakup of his marriage and distance from his children was a major shock. For the next ten years, he produced little art. During this period, he supported himself by giving art lessons to the locals in his art studio in Central City.[552]

Angelo slowly returned to his artwork, focusing on painting and sculpture, and working in his studio and on many public art projects. In 1971, in an effort to bring modern sculpture to Denver, Angelo's work was installed at Burns Park at Colorado Boulevard and East Alameda. A series of commissions followed, including Angelo's 1976 mural for the ceiling of the Colorado State Judicial Building in Denver. Angelo worked on the 3,000-square-foot mural,

Sketch of Justinian for the Colorado Judicial Building mural by Angelo di Benedetto, c. 1975. Gift Angelo di Benedetto Living Trust. 93.316.168

Justice Through the Ages, for eighteen months. The mural features sixty individuals who significantly contributed to the development of human rights and justice.[553] Other major works by di Benedetto include a mural and fresco at St. Michael's Chapel in his hometown, Patterson, New Jersey; an eighty-foot hammered copper wall at the Jewish Community Center in Denver; several metal sculptures for Colorado Fuel & Iron Steel in Pueblo; two sculptures for the city of Yonkers, New York; a sculpture for the city of Northglenn, Colorado; and a sculpture at the Ice Rink Plaza in Pueblo, Colorado.[554]

One of Colorado's truly accomplished artists who gained international fame, Angelo di Benedetto's work has appeared in *The New Yorker, Newsweek, Fortune, Holiday,* and *Life*. Additionally, his work has appeared in over one hundred galleries and museums including the Metropolitan Museum of Art in New York City and the National Gallery in Washington, D.C.[555] As an accomplished artist who also served as a consultant on public sculpture in over twenty states, Angelo became the first to receive the Governor's Award for contributions to the arts in Colorado in 1969.[556] Angelo di Benedetto died on April 26, 1992.

DiManna

Eugene "Geno" DiManna

Geno DiManna was born in 1930 to Louis and Mary DiManna. One of five children, he grew up poor in north Denver. While his mother stayed at home with the children, his father worked various jobs at the Sheet Iron and Wire Works Company, as a street cleaner in Denver, and as a custodian at the Denver Public Bath House.[557]

After graduating from Cathedral High School in 1949, Geno played catcher with the Chicago Cubs farm team in Visalia, California.[558] When an injury ended his baseball career, he returned to north Denver with his wife, Gloria, where they operated Pic's Corner Bar at Thirty-second and Umatilla Streets and Geno's Liquors at Thirty-second Avenue and Zuni Street while also raising their daughters, Pamela and Gayle.[559]

In 1971, Geno DiManna ran for Denver City Council in District 9, a seat previously occupied by Italian Americans Joe Ciancio Jr. and Ernest Marranzino Sr. Two of Geno

DiManna's opponents, Peter Garcia and Paul Sandoval, represented the growing Hispanic population in the district. Although Geno placed first in the May 1971 election, he faced a run-off with the second-place candidate, Peter Garcia. Geno DiManna won the run-off race with 4,339 votes to Garcia's 4,104 votes.

Almost immediately after Geno's election, Hispanic activists organized a recall petition that ultimately failed.[560] When residents later lobbied to change the name of Columbus Park to La Raza Park, Councilman DiManna opposed the measure, fueling animosity among Hispanics and Italian Americans. By 1972, activists circulated a petition for his recall. He faced more controversy when a patron who was forcefully removed from Pic's Corner filed a lawsuit against him. A month later, a hand grenade was tossed through a window at Pic's. A hero praised by Italians, Geno DiManna had become a villain to Chicanos. As one newspaper said, "Getting harmony from old-line Italians and aspiring young Chicanos is somewhat akin to getting Protestants and Catholics to kiss and make up in Northern Ireland."[561]

In 1975, Geno DiManna faced a recall election and won against Hispanic candidate Sal Carpio.[562] The two faced each other again in a regular election. This time, in another run-off, Carpio won.[563] Geno DiManna ended his political career but stayed active in the Italian American community until his death in 1984.

Sign, Geno DiManna, District 9 Councilman, 1971. Loan Fran (Coloroso) Daly. IL.2004.26.2

Fiore

John Rocco and Genevieve (D'Amato) Fiore

One of six children, Genevieve D'Amato was born in 1912 in Wyoming to Lorenzo and Anna (Carleo) D'Amato, Italian immigrants from the Salerno province. Her father came to America in 1903, but returned to Italy a few years later to fulfill his required military duty under Italian law.[564] In 1908, Lorenzo and Anna returned to America and settled in Pennsylvania, where Lorenzo worked in a steel mill. The family then moved to Wyoming, where Lorenzo worked as a miner and blacksmith before moving to Welby, Colorado, to farm.

In 1930, Genevieve met John Fiore at an Assumption parish dance.[565] The son of Rocco and Josephine (Arcieri/Archer) Fiore, John's father worked as a scissors sharpener while his mother took care of John and his siblings.[566] After John's father died in 1918, his mother married Rocco Malpiede, a vegetable peddler with whom she had three more children.[567] In 1933, John and Genevieve were married. They moved to north Denver, where John worked as a pressman for a publishing company while Genevieve cared for their three children: Hogan, Philip, and Roxanna.

In the mid-1940s, Genevieve began to promote and campaign for world peace, the result of two major events in her life: watching her father cry over the death of her nineteen-year-old brother in Italy during World War I and feelings of guilt because she had not tried to prevent World War II, a war in which three brothers, a brother-in-law, and many friends served—some who never returned and those who changed forever when they came home.[568] After working with pacifist Frederick Enholm and attending a conference of the newly formed United Nations Educational, Scientific and Cultural Organization (UNESCO), she co-founded the UNESCO Association of Colorado, the third UNESCO chapter in the world. A lifetime member, she served as president of the organization between 1947 and 1953.[569]

John and Genevieve Fiore, by James Baca, Denver Catholic Register, October 3, 1990. Courtesy Catholic Archdiocese of Denver. EX.ITAL.98

Genevieve's involvement in UNESCO led to work with other national and international programs, including the Peace Pole Project of the World Prayer Society—a project that inspires humankind to work toward harmony by erecting obelisks bearing messages of peace. The Peace Pole Project has spread to over 160 countries and succeeded in constructing over 100,000 poles; Genevieve Fiore led the Peace Pole project in Denver.[570] Genevieve was also involved in the Sister Cities program established in 1956 under President Eisenhower's administration. The aim of the organization, still active today, is to promote worldwide unity. Denver now has ten sister cities. Expressing her thoughts on peace and the Sister Cities program, Genevieve Fiore noted:

> I really believe in my heart that the Sister Cities sentiment, "together we can build a better world,"

is still very valid; and in this millennium we're going to reach a higher level of civilization. The world, and our government, should be solving our problems around the conference table.[571]

Genevieve's activism was lauded by the Dante Alighieri Society and *Denver Catholic Register*, and in 1975, the Italian government awarded her the title *Cavaliere*, an honor equivalent of knighthood, for her work with the Denver organization Il Circolo Italiano. In 1991, she was inducted into the Colorado Women's Hall of Fame.[572]

In 1975, John Fiore retired after more than fifty years in the printing business.[573] He died in 2000 at age ninety-three. Genevieve worked for peace until her death in 2002 at age ninety.[574]

Garramone

Amadeo "John" Garramone

Amadeo "John Maedio" or "John" Garramone was born in Denver on January 1, 1897, to Luigi and Maria Angelina Concetta (Losasso) Garramone. His father came from Potenza, Italy, in 1886 and worked in Denver as a produce peddler. His mother was also from Potenza and came to America with her parents in 1881.[575]

Catherine and John Garramone with son Lou, Denver, 1943. CIAPA Archive. Courtesy Lou and Bonnie Garramone. PCCLI5781

Luigi Garramone (father of John Garramone), Denver, c. 1916. CIAPA Archive. Courtesy Lou and Bonnie Garramone. PCCLI0861

In 1918, John married Catherine Sanfilippo at Our Lady of Mount Carmel Catholic Church. Catherine's parents, Salvatore and Nunzia (Cefalú) Sanfilippo, came to the United States from Palermo, Sicily, in 1893, settling in New York first. In 1907, after her mother died from blood poisoning, her father moved to Denver, where Catherine was sent to live at the Queen of Heaven Orphanage until after her father remarried.[576] John and Catherine had five children together: Angeline, Louis "Lou," Nancy, Estella, and Eugene "Gene."

John and his family first lived in a house they rented at 3744 Mariposa. In 1935, John's father Luigi died, leaving his house at 1230 West Thirty-eighth Avenue in north Denver to both John and John's brother Clyde. After purchasing Clyde's share of the property, John and his family moved into the home. A two-story structure, the house included a living room, dining room, kitchen, bedroom, and bathroom on the main floor and three bedrooms upstairs.[577] John worked as a mail clerk, a job he held for twenty-six years, and also at a local grocery store, Safeway, for eighteen years. Additionally, John and Catherine owned and operated the Navajo Cleaners and Tailors from 1938 to 1948.[578]

In 1952, John and Catherine opened a restaurant called the House of Luigi, which the couple built into their home on Thirty-eighth Avenue by remodeling the downstairs of the home to include a kitchen, dining area, and a small bar. A neighborhood Italian restaurant, the House of Luigi, named after John's father Luigi, served mostly pasta dishes, including lasagna on Sundays. The

John and Catherine Garramone's children, left to right: Eugene "Gene," Angelina, Estella, Nancy, and Louis "Lou" Garramone, 1950, Denver. CIAPA Archive. Courtesy Lou and Bonnie Garramone. PCCLI5295

restaurant was primarily run by Catherine, who planned the menu, purchased the food, did most of the cooking, kept the books, and supervised eight employees. In addition to serving meals, the restaurant also hosted wedding dinners and special events. When John and Catherine decided to retire, no one in the family took over the business and so the House of Luigi closed in 1959.[579]

John and Catherine Garramone were longtime members of Our Lady of Mount Carmel Church and were active in the Italian American community, belonging to several organizations, including the Knights of Columbus, Potenza Lodge, the Saint Anne's Society, the North Denver Civic Association, the North Denver Alliance, and the Northside Community Center. John Garramone died in Denver in 1972, followed by Catherine, who died in 1994.[580]

Angelina Lillian (Garramone) Volpe

Angelina Garramone, the oldest child of John and Catherine (Sanfilippo) Garramone, was born in Denver in 1919. In 1941, she married Arthur "Art" Volpe, born in Salida, Colorado.[581] They met when Angelina took sewing lessons from Art at a local tailor shop. Shortly after their wedding, Art was drafted into the United States Army, serving as a tailor while stationed at Fort Logan. In his absence, Angelina worked at the local ammunition plant.[582] Nearly four years later, Art returned to Denver, where Art and Angelina's son Michael "Mike" was born in 1946.

After World War II, Angelina and Art became partners in Navajo Cleaners with Angelina's parents, who purchased the business in 1938. The business expanded and moved to Thirty-sixth and Navajo with the Volpe family living in an apartment behind the shop. In 1948, Art and Angelina became sole owners of Navajo Cleaners, continuing to operate and expand the business by offering new services and products, including selling men's suits.

In the 1960s, with the advent of wash-and-wear and permanent press and the fact that many friends and customers were moving to the suburbs, Navajo Cleaners experienced a decline in business.[583] In 1966, Angelina was forced to get a job at a nursing home so that she and Art could have good medical insurance and other benefits. Art Volpe ran the business for another ten years until his health began to fail. Art and Angelina Volpe closed the business in the 1970s and a few years later Art died. Angelina Volpe still lives in Denver today.

Louis "Lou" Raymond Garramone

Lou Garramone was born in Denver in 1924 to John and Catherine (Sanfilippo) Garramone. After graduating from North High, he joined the United States Navy, and after a tour overseas, returned to Colorado, where under the G.I. Bill he enrolled in the teachers' college in Greeley.[584] He then went on to teach and coach in the Denver Public School system for forty years. In 1946, Lou married Bonnie Jean Lynch at Our Lady of Mount Carmel Catholic Church. Together Bonnie and Lou raised four daughters: Lynne, Jill, Kim, and Missy.[585]

As a third-generation Italian American in Colorado, exposed to new experiences, cultures, financial resources, and opportunities as a result of serving in World War II, Lou—unlike his sisters—reared his family outside of Little Italy. Wanting his children to attend good schools and have opportunities he never had, he adopted a new community when he moved to Englewood, Colorado. As a result, during the 1950s and 1960s, Lou and Bonnie did not continue many Italian customs. They visited Lou's family during the holidays but did not keep up the regular Sunday dinners, traditional feast days, or birthday parties. Bonnie, who was welcomed by Lou's family and enjoyed being with them, was not interested in Italian cooking, and like others from non-Italian families, felt intimidated and overwhelmed by Lou's very vocal and gregarious relatives.[586] This, combined with the fact that Lou and Bonnie were raising their family some distance away from the old neighborhood, resulted in their being disconnected from the Italian American community, like many others of their generation.

Lou and Bonnie Garramone on their wedding day, 1946. CIAPA Archive. Courtesy Lou and Bonnie Garramone. PCCLI5778

In later years, Lou and Bonnie Garramone reconnected with the Italian American community in Denver through social events, genealogical research, and organizations including Potenza Lodge. Like many others, they realized that something had been lost and that Italian traditions and culture were slipping away. They came to understand the tremendous value in belonging to the Italian American community and that active participation is necessary to ensure its survival.

Today, Bonnie and Lou live in Centennial, Colorado, and remain active in the Italian American community.

Nancy Lena "Lee" (Garramone) Walrath

Nancy Garramone, the third child born to John and Catherine (Sanfilippo) Garramone, was born in Denver in 1925. She grew up in north Denver and at age sixteen enrolled in beauty school at the Emily Griffith Opportunity School.[587] Two years later, she became the manager of the Snow White Beauty Salon at 3614 Navajo Street. In 1943, after three successful years in business, she purchased the business and building. Over the years, the business grew from two beauty operator stations to eight, as more women in Little Italy could afford the added expense of a hair appointment to their budget. With the addition of new stations, Nancy hired more beauty operators, including many Italian American women just out of beauty school.[588]

In 1942, Nancy married Edmund James Walrath, and in 1947, the couple moved into a home in back of the shop. Together Nancy and Edmund had three children: Nikki, Rikki, and Randy. In 1999, Nancy retired from the business and today lives in Wheat Ridge.[589]

Iacino

Frank Maria and Rose (Occhiato) Iacino

Frank Iacino was born in 1887 in the southern Italian town of Grimaldi. At the age of thirteen, he came to America, where he found work with the Denver & Rio Grande Railroad. Around 1905, Frank made his way to Colorado, where he married Rose Occhiato in 1906. Rose was born in Missouri to Italian immigrants who later settled in Pueblo, Colorado.[590]

In 1903, Frank's brother Marion joined him in Denver, followed by his parents Francesco and Maria Rosaria (Varone) Iacino and siblings Joseph "Joe," Moses "Mose," James, Rose, and Carmella three years later. In 1910, Frank established the Diamond A Market with his brothers Marion and Joseph. Located at 1501 Lawrence Street, the market carried groceries, meats, poultry, and imported and domestic goods, and sold lard by the pail.

Iacino family, back row, left to right: Mike, George, and Joe; front row, left to right: Al, Frank, Marie, and Rose, c. 1920. CIAPA Archive. Courtesy Joe and Frances Iacino and family. PCCLI1457

Change 1960–1989

Diamond A Market, behind the counter, left to right: Marion Iacino, George Iacino, John Hays, Isadore Saliman, Tony Ciddo, and Al Iacino, c. 1928. CIAPA Archive. Courtesy Joe and Frances Iacino and family. PCCLI1458

The Diamond A Market, 1501 Lawrence Street, by Rocky Mountain Photo, c. 1925. CIAPA Archive. Courtesy Joe and Frances Iacino and family. PCCLI2971

In addition to caring for their seven children (including Maria "Marie," born in 1911, and Albert "Al," born in 1916), Frank and Rose were active in their community. During the 1920s and 1930s, Frank sponsored semi-professional baseball teams that played at the old Merchants Park, including the Diamond A Baseball Team. Rose was a longtime member of the Venetian Sewing Club, a social group that worked on sewing projects but also held dress-up parties and picnics and supported community causes including collecting clothes to send to friends and families in Italy during World War II and helping with the needs of those at the Queen of Heaven Orphanage.[591] Frank Iacino died in Denver in 1969, followed by Rose, who died in 1988.

Diamond A Baseball Team at Thirty-seventh and Wyandot, Denver, 1922. Pictured in the photograph, back row, left to right: Ed Serafini, Howard Johnson, Mr. McGuire, Lefty Herstrom, Felix Serafini, Mr. Fentres, and Park Kinney; front row, left to right: Mr. Fentres, Mr. Lawlor, Jiggs Langton, Joe Iacino, Freddy Leonard, Jim Iacino, and Fritz Serafini. CIAPA Archive. Courtesy Joe and Frances Iacino and family. PCCLI1433

A Closer Look
The Seattle Fish Company

Moses "Mose" Iacino was born on December 13, 1902, in Grimaldi, Italy, and came with his family to Denver in 1906, where his brothers Frank and Marion were already established. While attending school, Mose Iacino also helped in his brothers' store, the Diamond A Market. Soon he was selling oysters in a corner of the family store. In 1918, when he was just sixteen, he opened the Seattle Fish Company in downtown Denver. The fish he sold, such as salmon and halibut, were packed in ice in railcars and sent from Seattle to Denver by railroad. The trip took a week and at stops along the way new ice was added to keep the fish cold. Mose Iacino sold his products from his store and also to restaurants and hotels in Denver.[592]

In 1935, Mose Iacino moved the retail store and the Seattle Fish Company warehouse to a larger building at 1537 Market Street, where it remained for nearly fifty years.

Change 1960–1989

The Seattle Fish Company, 1537 Market Street, c. 1970. CIAPA Archive. Courtesy Tom Noel. PCCLI0809

In 1982, when Edward Iacino, Mose's son, took over operations of the company, he moved the Seattle Fish Company to a new $5-million state-of-the-art facility near Stapleton International Airport.

After the death of Mose in 1995 and after over eighty-five years in business, the Seattle Fish Company remains in the Iacino family. One of the largest wholesale distributors of fresh and frozen seafood in the Rocky Mountain region, the company meets approximately 98 percent of Colorado's seafood needs.[593]

Joseph "Joe" Frank and Frances Cosmas (Bruno) Iacino

Joe Iacino was born in Denver in 1913 to Frank and Rose (Occhiato) Iacino. While still in school, he worked at his father's Diamond A Market and later for his uncle Mike Occhiato in Pueblo, who owned a soft drink business. In 1933, Joe married Frances Cosmas Bruno at Saint Catherine's Church. The daughter of Rafael "Ralph" and Lucille (Lombardi) Bruno, both Italian-born immigrants, Frances was born in Denver in 1914. Together Joe and Frances had two children: Lucille Rose "Dutchess" and Joseph Frank Jr.[594]

The same year he married Frances, Joe founded the Rocky Mountain Beverage Company, located at Sixteenth and Market in downtown Denver. Initially the company sold beer, later branching out into the soft drink market, distributing products to corner grocery stores and later to supermarkets in the Denver metropolitan and northern Colorado areas.[595]

As the business grew, Joe developed new ways to promote his products, and in 1977 he partnered with the Denver Broncos to promote the team as the "Orange Crush." Soon, Orange Crush fever exploded in Denver with people painting their cars and houses orange and stores carrying a variety of Orange Crush products including hats, belt buckles, and soda pop. So popular was the campaign that Governor Richard Lamm proclaimed October 30, 1977, "Orange Crush Day" in Colorado. Even after the Broncos lost in the Super Bowl, the team's nickname stuck and helped boost Joe's business, and in 1981, his company was the first ever to license a product—Orange Crush soda—with any team in the National Football League.[596] After fifty-four years in business, Joe Iacino retired and sold the Rocky Mountain Beverage Company in 1987.

In a 1999 letter of support for Joe Iacino's induction into the Colorado Sports Hall of Fame, Denver's Mayor

Frances and Joe Iacino, 1931. CIAPA Archive. Courtesy Joe and Frances Iacino and family. PCCLI1402

Employees and delivery trucks of the Rocky Mountain Beverage Company, 2915 Walnut Street, Denver, Colorado, c. 1940. Pictured in the photograph, near trucks, left to right: Mike Iacino, George Iacino, Vern Davis, Jim Reefe, Red Williams, Al Iacino, Nick Occhiato, Jake Barnholtz, and Joe Iacino; on the dock, left to right: John Zucca, unidentified man, Al Vera, Nick Tolve, and Pasquale Pietro. CIAPA Archive. Courtesy Joe and Frances Iacino and family. PCCLI1470

Wellington Webb commended "Joe Iacino whose commitment to our sports community has helped to catapult the City of Denver into the mega-sports town that it is today."[597]

Joe and Frances Iacino still live in Denver, where they continue to support Colorado's Italian American community through participation in events such as the Rocky Mountain Italian American Association Golf Tournament.

Mancinelli

Antonio "Tony" Mancinelli

The youngest of five sons born to Antonia (Brancato) and Raffaele Mancinelli, Antonio "Tony" Mancinelli was born in Potenza, Italy, in 1886. Growing up, he worked on his parents' fruit and nut orchard and grape vineyard. After the death of his father in 1905 and because of the poor living conditions in Italy, Tony and his mother left their homeland for America. They arrived in New York in 1907, where they settled near Tony's brothers. In 1912, Tony married Maria Gaetana LaTegana. Maria was also from the Basilicata region and came to the United States in 1912. While Tony worked as a tailor, Maria cared for the couple's children: Raffaele Frederick "Fred," Savino "Sam," and Helen.[598] Tragically, Maria contracted tuberculosis in 1921, and after being confined to a sanatorium for two years, died in 1923. After her death, doctors told Tony that the children had been exposed to tuberculosis, and recommended that they move to Colorado, where the clean air would give them a better chance of survival.[599]

Angelo Stone (left) and Tony Mancinelli wearing Potenza Lodge Sashes at the Saint Rocco Feast, c. 1953. CIAPA Archive. Courtesy Ralph F. and Rosemary Mancinelli. PCCLI1294

After settling in Denver near friends, Tony met Mary (DeBell) Marchese, whose husband, Rocco, died in 1918, leaving Mary the single parent of two children: Mike "Smokey" and Clyde.[600] After a brief courtship, Tony and Mary were married in 1925, and in 1935 their son Anthony "Butch" Mancinelli was born.

In Denver, Tony worked as a tailor until the Depression hit, and Tony returned to farming. He leased three acres of land around Thirty-eighth Avenue and Fox Street from the Burlington Railroad. He and Mary raised onions and radishes until around 1936, when Tony sold the lease to Mike Leprino Sr. Tony and Mary then opened the Pelican Club, a family restaurant in downtown Denver. Tony eventually returned to tailoring and retired in 1951.[601]

In addition to fishing, hunting, gathering mushrooms and dandelions, passing the time with friends, playing bocce, morra, and card games such as Tre-Sette (3-7), Tony was active in his community. He belonged to Potenza Lodge, Saint Michael's Lodge, the Eagles Lodge, and the Amalgamated Clothing Workers of America Union.[602] Tony Mancinelli died in Denver in 1966, followed by his wife Mary, who died in Denver in 1981.

Ralph Frederic Mancinelli Jr.

The son of Raffaele Fredrick Sr. and Catharine (Pisto) Mancinelli, Ralph Mancinelli Jr. was born in Denver in 1939. Growing up, he, his parents, and his sister Barbara lived in the basement of his grandparents' house—the home of Tony and Mary Mancinelli—on Thirty-ninth Avenue and Navajo. Ralph was also close to his mother's parents, Tony and Carmella (Sacco) Pisto, who lived at Thirty-third Avenue and Navajo Street in north Denver. According to Ralph, he spent the first sixteen years of his life walking or riding his bike those six blocks up and down Navajo Street, from one grandparents' house to another.[603]

Recalling his childhood, Ralph said:

> Looking back, my sister and I grew up at an unusual time. As small kids growing up during and after WWII, times were lean. The war effort was the number-one priority in the country from 1941–45. Everything was in short supply, ration stamps for almost everything. Even when the war ended it was almost a decade before we had anything. There were no toys for kids as we see toys today; everything that was made was produced for the war effort. We had board games, paper-cutouts, and wood toys. My best friend Donald "Duck" Ackerman and I made our own toys. Two empty cans with about a ten-foot string through the middle acted as telephones. We made wood slingshots and rubber-guns. Our best toy was a scooter we made from an old skate, a two-by-four board, and an orange crate. That lasted a long time.

Change 1960–1989

Life was the same for all of us. It was no different for Duck and I than it was for the kids across the street or down the block, we were all happy. I don't remember anyone ever locking their doors and windows in north Denver. That procedure came about when we moved to Perl-Mack in 1955. If we did lock the doors for some reason, the skeleton key we used, fit the doors at almost every house on the block. We all had chores to do like emptying the pan from under the icebox. The winter was a little different. Those big chunks of ice stayed out on the back lawn for a long time. My job was to put water in the humidifier along the coal furnace. My Uncle "Butch" (Anthony L. Mancinelli) who was four years older than me, had to shovel in the coal and I cleaned out the ashes. Everyone was very respectful to one another. We took pride in our family, our religion, our work ethics, our honesty and integrity. Business was done on a handshake. Your word was your bond.

Transportation for us was walking, taking the bus or streetcar. Duck and I always had odd jobs to make some money. We shoveled snow in the winter, sold brooms for a blind man and passed out posters for the Navajo Theater (known as the Bug). The only thing Duck and I received for passing out the posters was a free pass for the month that was advertised on the poster. The Navajo Theater only changed their movie once a week, so Duck and I saw every movie at least three times. Even when we had to pay it was only ten cents and there was penny candy next door at the Se Cheverell-Moore's Drugstore. We shared everything, and with the small change we made from the odd jobs, there was still enough to go around. We swam at Columbus Park in the summer, played basketball there in the fall and winter, and tennis almost year-round. Duck and I became altar boys and cub scouts; there was more than enough to do.

It seemed like every family had their own page in the ledger of the North Denver Department Store. If there were any heroes to the Italian people, it was Gus

Ralph F. and Rosemary Lee (Nuoci) Mancinelli, Denver, 1961. CIAPA Archive. Courtesy Ralph F. and Rosemary Mancinelli. PCCLI5776

and Bonnie Levine. Everyone charged at the store and paid when they could. Those two brothers were wonderful to all of us. It was the same with Bill and Dominic at the Lombardi Brothers grocery store where we traded.

We always had Sunday dinner at gram and gramp's at 1:00 P.M. We had spaghetti every Sunday just like every other Italian; you could smell the sauce cooking on every block. Visiting friends and family on Saturdays or Sunday was common practice. The old-timers dressed in suits on Sunday even when they went on picnics. We had closeness to our neighbors and friends.

...Duck and I, his sister Darlene, and my sister Barbara all started school at the old Mount Carmel grade school, all of us ended up graduating from the new high school at 36th and Zuni. As Father Tom said "The school was built for Italians, by Italians." We all stuck together, we were more like brothers and sisters than classmates. We never told on each other; we took the punishment rather than stool. Corporal punishment was the rule of the day. If you got in trouble at school you also got into trouble at home. The teachers pressed for obedience, study, and hard work. You were as obedient to your neighbor as you were to your own family.[604]

After graduating from Mount Carmel High School in 1957 and attending college, Ralph and his uncle Anthony L. "Butch" Mancinelli purchased the Fred and Butch Standard Service station from Ralph's father in 1960. Their auto repair business lasted until 1983, when Ralph sold his share to Butch. The two remained partners in business ventures until Butch's death in 1999.

In 1961, Ralph married Rosemary Lee Nuoci, born in Welby to Michael and Philomena (Persichette) Nuoci. Ralph served on the Wheat Ridge City Council from 1997 to 2003. Today Ralph and Rosemary are retired and live in Wheat Ridge.[605]

Leprino

Michael Leprino Sr.

Michael Leprino Sr. was born in Potenza in 1898. The son of Rocco and Concetta Leprino, he left Italy at the age of sixteen, traveling with his cousin, Mike Marchese.[606] In 1914,

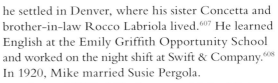

Mike Leprino Sr., on the day he wed Susie Pergola, November 7, 1920. CIAPA Archive. Courtesy Gerry Pergola. PCCLI3921

he settled in Denver, where his sister Concetta and brother-in-law Rocco Labriola lived.[607] He learned English at the Emily Griffith Opportunity School and worked on the night shift at Swift & Company.[608] In 1920, Mike married Susie Pergola.

Around 1925, Mike became a United States citizen and went to work as a laborer in the Denver brickyards for the Denver Pipe and Clay Company.[609] He also farmed a small piece of land around Thirty-eighth Avenue and Fox Street to support his family, which by 1930 included Sue and their children: Angelina, Louis, Marie, and Mike Jr. When the Depression hit and Mike could no longer afford the rent, the family moved to a little farm on Pecos Street. Their house had no electricity and no indoor toilets. Towards the end of the Depression, the family moved back to Thirty-ninth Avenue, where in 1937 Mike and Sue's fifth child, James "Jim," was born.[610]

Mike Sr. continued in the truck farming business until he was forced off the land to make way for the Valley Highway, near what is now the junction of I-70 and I-25. He then opened a small grocery store on the site of today's Leprino Foods. In 1950, Mike started making small batches of ricotta cheese for his daughter, Angelina, and her husband, Frank, who sold their raviolis locally under the label "Frangi's."[611] Although he had never made cheese before, a determined Mike Leprino hired the man who had worked with Angelina's previous cheese supplier. Soon, Frangi's moved from Angelina's home to the front of her father's grocery store, and Mike made cheese in the back.[612]

Leprino family, left to right: Marie, Mike Jr., Susie, Jim (in front of Susie), Lou, Mike Sr., and Angelina, Denver, 1944. CIAPA Archive. Courtesy Gerry Pergola. PCCLI3945

With the success of the ricotta, Mike began making *scamorze*, a smoky mozzarella sold in pear-shaped balls, which he sold to local grocery stores and businesses. Over twenty years, the company added more manufacturing plants and products. In 1956, Mike Leprino's son Jim entered the family business, and upon his father's death in 1972, Jim became chairman and chief executive officer of Leprino Foods, today the world's largest producer of mozzarella.[613]

A Closer Look
Leprino Foods and Frangi's

Mike Leprino's American dream came true, but only after decades of hard work. He came to the United States in 1914, worked tough jobs, and farmed to supplement his income during the Depression. In 1950, under the name Gina Marie, he started making batches of ricotta cheese for his daughter's budding ravioli business.[614] Those batches launched Leprino Foods, today the world's largest mozzarella producer.

Mike's son Jim joined the business in 1956. Jim added new cheese-making methods and new manufacturing plants that made more products, including whey, ice cream, and baked goods. In the 1970s, Leprino Foods expanded again to include food service. The company scaled back to its core product line in the 1990s.

Mike's daughter, Angelina (Leprino) Testa, also made good on a dream. Her raviolis, made with those first batches of ricotta, sold well in Denver restaurants. She made them by hand at home using her mother Sue's recipe.

Angelina and Frank Testa inside Frangi's, 1842 West Thirty-eighth Avenue, 1979. From The Denver Post, *October 3, 1979. Courtesy Angelina Testa. PCCLI3242*

But demand called for expansion, so she and her husband Frank moved into a store owned by her father. They called their enterprise Frangi's—a combination of "Frank" and "Angelina."[615]

By 1959, Frangi's was cranking out raviolis, gnocchi, noodles, macaroni, and other products from a building occupying half a block. Frank died in 1984, but Angelina continued with help from her daughter, Lynn.[616] Later, Frangi's moved to a new facility and made 100,000 raviolis a day.[617] In 1997, Angelina sold Frangi's after forty-seven years of success.[618]

Pergola

Gerardo "Jerry" and Angelina (Brancucci) Pergola

In 1899, Gerardo "Jerry" Pergola left his home in Potenza, Italy, and came to Colorado with the help of Michele Notary.[619] After saving enough money, he returned to

Change 1960–1989

Pergola family, left to right: Susie, Nick, Mike, Jerry, Angelina, and Nettie (in front of Angelina), Potenza, Italy, 1913. CIAPA Archive. Courtesy Gerry Pergola. PCCLI3920

Italy, where he married Angelina Brancucci in 1900. After a few years of farming a small piece of land that he owned, Jerry Pergola, no longer able to support his family, returned to America in 1905, leaving his pregnant wife Angelina and his daughter Susie behind in Italy.[620]

Jerry dug ditches and shoveled coal for the railroad, and in 1906, sent for his family. In 1913, homesick for her own family, Angelina talked her husband into going back to Italy. Jerry farmed again in Italy for a while but concluded that he could not earn a living there. He returned to the United States in 1914 and, just prior to World War I, sent for his wife and five children: Susie, Mike, Nettie, Nick, and Nancy.[621]

The Pergola family settled in Denver along Clear Creek, where Jerry leased about five acres of farmland, growing vegetables he then sold at the City Market at Colfax and Speer. Around 1919, the Pergola family, which had grown to include a sixth child, Lucille, born in 1918, moved to north Denver and settled in a home at 4025 Osage Street. In 1920, Jerry and Angelina's seventh child, a boy named Sammy, was born. Tragically, Angelina died three days after giving birth to Sammy; she was just thirty-six years old.[622]

Page from Jerry Pergola's alien registration, 1942. Loan Gerry Pergola. IL.2005.31.5

Jerry Pergola, now a single father of seven children, never remarried. His sister Theresa helped him care for the newborn, Sammy. Jerry continued to work on his farm until he was stricken with cancer. He moved in with his daughter Susie and her husband, Mike Leprino Sr., where he stayed until his death in 1943.[623]

Mike M. Pergola

Mike Pergola was born in Potenza in 1905 to Jerry and Angelina (Brancucci) Pergola. He left Italy with his mother and siblings in 1914, traveling by ship in steerage for fifteen days. He slept on a wooden bunk with a bed and pillow made of straw. When he and his siblings were seasick, his mother gave them a slice of raw onion soaked in wine to settle their stomachs.[624] Upon arriving in New York, Mike was very ill. Luckily, his sister Susie, age eleven, spoke enough English to move the family through customs at Ellis Island and across the country to Denver, where his father was already living.[625]

In 1920, when his mother died, Mike dropped out of school to help support his family. He earned money playing saxophone and violin, but his primary employment was with the Shwayder Trunk Manufacturing Company (later known as Samsonite). In time, other young Italians looked to him for assistance in getting jobs at the company.[626]

In 1930, Mike met Josephine Santamoro. The daughter of Italian immigrants, Josephine was born in Tennessee and moved to Denver to live with her sister after her parents died. She worked for the Great Western Sugar Company sewing bags. After their marriage, the couple lived in Mike's father's house. In 1939, the Pergolas moved to Wyandot Street, and in 1950, the Pergola family, including daughters Joanne and Geraldine "Gerry," moved into a home Mike designed and built.[627]

In 1968, Mike retired from Samsonite after forty-nine years. Active in the community, he was involved with the ITAMs Club (an Italian American businessmen's club), Sister Cities International, and Potenza Lodge.[628] Josephine Pergola died in 1984, followed by Mike Pergola, who died in 2000.

Mike and Josephine (Santamoro) Pergola, by Universal Studio, Inc., Denver, 1931. CIAPA Archive. Courtesy Gerry Pergola. PCCLI3936

Guglielmo "William" Lombardi

One of eight children, Guglielmo "William" Lombardi was born in 1899 in the southern Italian province of Campobasso.[629] In 1903, his father, Michele, left for America with William's grandfather Antonio and his uncle Raffaele Iannacito.[630] They settled in Louisville, Colorado, near relatives, and in 1904, William and his mother Carolina joined them. The family moved to north Denver after Carolina's brother was killed in the area coal mines.

In Denver, Michele found work with the railroad and at a tailor shop. In 1921, he opened the M. Lombardi Grocery & Market at 3801 Osage Street. The market offered customers a variety of products from Italian imported goods to washboards. According to William's daughter Phyllis, a former store employee:

> ...most everyone who traded there had credit. They either paid their bill weekly, or monthly, and some of the farmers from Welby or closer, paid in the fall when the crops were harvested and the stock slaughtered. The accounts were kept in a fire-proof metal file located next to the cash register. They were

M. Lombardi Grocery & Market with Michele Lombardi Sr. (right), Pete DiAnne (center), and William Lombardi (left), Denver, 1921. CIAPA Archive. Courtesy Phyllis (Lombardi) Greb. PCCLI0157

filed in alphabetical order, and each page was metal with 5 or 6 spring-loaded clips across for each account and 5 or 6 rows down. You wrote the name of the customer on the top line, brought the balance forward from the receipt of the last transaction, added groceries bought that day and totaled it. The receipts were made with a carbon copy, one for the store and one for the customer.[631]

In 1922, William Lombardi married Mary Tate. The couple had four children: Evelyn, Michael, Dorothy, and Phyllis. After his father's death in 1925, William, his sister Assunta, and his brothers Dominic and George took over the store. The store prospered despite changes in the business including competition from chain grocery stores in the 1940s and the exodus of Italians out of the community to suburbs further west in the 1950s and 1960s. In 1963, William Lombardi retired, and after over forty years in business, sold his share of the M. Lombardi Grocery & Market to his nephew Robert Monaco, who continued to operate the store with Dominic Lombardi despite changes in the community and struggles between Italians and Hispanics—including confrontations over the name of Columbus Park across the street. In 1972, a fight broke out at the park, and the Lombardi store was set on fire. Protestors challenged firefighters who were trying to put out the blaze. As a result of damage to both building and stock, and the fact that insurance only covered part of the expense, the M. Lombardi Grocery & Market closed in September 1972. William Lombardi died in Denver on May 24, 1964.

Advertisement, M. Lombardi Grocery & Market, Denver, 1938. CIAPA Archive. Courtesy Phyllis (Lombardi) Greb. PCCLI0555

Pomponio

Felice Pomponio

Felice (also known as Felix or Phillip) Pomponio was born in Potenza in 1872 and came to the United States in 1885 to

Change 1960–1989

Felice and Michelina Pomponio, in their yard at 4142 Osage, c. 1945. CIAPA Archive. Courtesy Al Donelson. PCCLI0163

join his older brother Nicholas. He and Nicholas worked for the Midland Railroad Company at De Beque, Colorado. Around 1890, Felice moved to Denver and worked as a peddler.[632]

In 1892, Felice married Michelina Meolfese at Sacred Heart Church. Michelina had come to America from Potenza when she was seventeen.[633] In 1893, Felice and Michelina's first child, Antoinette "Nettie" was born, followed by Catherine, Rocco "Roxie," Rose, Michael "Mike," Julia, Nick, Louis, and Frank. By 1900, the Pomponios were living in a house on Bell Street (now Osage) and Felice was working as the first assistant market master of the Denver City Market.

In 1915, Felice was appointed market master, a position he held until 1935, when his son Mike succeeded him. In 1943, Felice retired from the produce business.[634] Active in the Italian American community, he was a member of Mount Carmel Church, for which he served on the building committee in the early 1890s, and Potenza Lodge, of which he was a founding member.[635] Felice Pomponio died in Denver in 1953 at the age of eighty-one, followed by his wife, Michelina, who died in Denver in 1960 at age eighty-six.

Potenza Lodge and Hall (awning was the entrance for Pomponio's DX Café), c. 1945. CIAPA Archive. Courtesy Al Donelson. PCCLI2901

Michael "Mike" Pomponio

One of nine children born to Felice and Michelina Pomponio, Mike Pomponio was born in Denver in 1900. He graduated from North High in 1918 and married Henrietta Fallico. In 1919, their daughter Frances was born. The couple later divorced, and in 1935 Mike married Elsie Johnson.[636]

In 1930, Mike Pomponio was a Denver Health Board clerk. He became a city health officer and worked as a precinct committeeman. His political career took off when he was elected the Democratic captain of District 10 in 1933.[637] As captain, he controlled the Democratic vote for his district.

Business card, DX Café, c. 1945. CIAPA Archive. Courtesy Al Donelson. PCCLI2897

Although deeply involved in Denver politics for over thirty years, Mike held political office only once. Many believed that he preferred his behind-the-scenes role. Mike, whose district was 90 percent Democrat, was known for his ability to win votes. As former Colorado governor Stephen McNichols said in 1973, "anybody who was running for office knew that he had to talk to Mike because he could deliver his district like nobody else."[638]

Mike offered political candidates financial assistance by way of his business, the DX Café, named after District 10 (or District X). Opened around 1935 as a neighborhood tavern on West Thirty-eighth Avenue and Fox, it later moved to the basement of Potenza Lodge.[639] It was the site for many community events, including political rallies and fundraisers.

Mike also served as assistant market master of the Denver City Market between 1925 and 1938, a job previously held by his father. In 1946, he was market master of the Wazee Terminal and served three terms on the Denver City Zoning Board beginning in 1949.

In 1961, Mike sold DX Café, which in 1954 had moved to 1531 West Forty-eighth Avenue (on the corner of Forty-eighth Avenue and Pecos Street). He remained district captain until 1970.[640] He died in Denver in 1973.[641]

Mike Pomponio, c. 1930. CIAPA Archive. Courtesy Al Donelson. PCCLI2890

Natale

Gerald Albert Natale

One of four children, Gerald Albert Natale was born in 1917 in Denver to Giuseppe "Joseph" and Amelia "Clara" (Capolungo) Natale. Gerald's father came to the United States in 1903.[642] His mother was born in Denver in 1895 to Italian-born parents, Gerardo "Jerry" and Amelia (Sassana) Capolungo.[643] Gerald grew up in Little Italy. He played baseball and soccer, and he worked as a paperboy for the *Rocky Mountain News* and as a delivery boy for Se Cheverell-Moore Drugs. After high school he studied pharmacy at the Capitol College of Pharmacy in Denver.[644]

While working at a pharmacy at Thirty-second and Lowell Boulevard, he met Lucille Meehan, whom he married in 1941. After their marriage, Gerald and Lucille lived in a home at 2795 West Thirty-ninth Avenue, where they raised their five children: Marilyn, Jan, Jerry, Paul, and Roberta "Bobbie." In 1952, Gerald bought the Tejon Drug Company, a corner drugstore with tiled floors, dark wood walls, an old phone booth, and a soda fountain. He worked twelve-hour days, seven days a week, filling prescriptions for nearly fifty years. His wife and children often helped in the drugstore and made deliveries.[645]

Described by his family as a "simple man," Gerald enjoyed going to the horse races at Centennial Race Track and was known for his work ethic, honesty, and compassion. He once gave a robber half of a sandwich—along with the money from the store. His daughter Marilyn explained that the robber was shaky and

Gerald and Lucille Natale in front of Tejon Drug Company, c. 1990. CIAPA Archive. Courtesy Marilyn (Natale) Vecchiarelli. PCCLI4318

agitated, and her father thought the food might settle him down and avoid his hurting anyone.[646]

A member of the Colorado Pharmaceutical Association and the Denver Area Pharmacy Association, Gerald Natale was named Outstanding Italian American in 1988 by the *Denver Catholic Register*.[647] He died in 2005.

Scordo DePalma

Caterina (Noya) Scordo DePalma

Caterina (Noya) Scordo DePalma was born in Brindisi, Italy, to Maria (Marrone) and Ernesto Noya. Educated in Italy, she graduated with a teaching degree at the age of sixteen before meeting her future husband, an Italian American G.I. named Frank Scordo, in 1944.[648] Raised in Italy, Frank came to America with his mother at the age of eighteen. He returned to Italy during World War II where he was stationed in Bari and met Caterina's brother, who introduced the couple. After approaching Caterina's parents with his intention to marry their daughter, the match was made, and in 1946 Caterina and Frank were married in Italy. Shortly after their marriage, the couple left for the United States, settling for a short time in Denver before moving to New York, where their twin girls, Maria and Angela, were born in 1947.[649]

In 1955, the Scordos returned to Denver, where Frank worked as a barber, eventually owning several shops. After her daughters started school, Caterina began working for the Italian Consulate, eventually becoming the Italian vice consul, a position she held until 1969 when the consulate moved to Chicago.[650] Caterina then taught Italian at Loretto Heights College and for Il Circolo Italiano.[651]

In 1978, the Italian government appointed Caterina honorary vice consul for Italy in Colorado. For eighteen years, she handled the business and personal needs of Italians visiting and living in Colorado and Wyoming, and fostered Italian culture.[652] She worked with the People to People and Sister Cities organizations to establish Potenza as Denver's sister city. In the 1990s, she continued her consular work, welcoming Italian Prime Minister Romano Prodi to Denver for the G7 summit.[653]

After Frank's death in 1984 from cancer, Caterina married Mike DePalma in 1997. Mike was also born in

Bari, and came to the United States in 1943, settling in Denver, where his uncle, Sam Giglio, lived.⁶⁵⁴ Upon arrival in Denver, Mike worked first for his uncle in his grocery store, later opening his own grocery store, followed by three pizza stores and a liquor store. He also managed strip malls in Denver.⁶⁵⁵

In 1998, when Caterina retired, her daughter Maria (Scordo) Allen took the consular position. Today, Caterina Scordo DePalma lives in Golden with her husband and remains involved in Denver's Italian American community.

Tancredo

Tom Tancredo

Married to Jackie Tancredo since 1977, and the father of two children, Tom Tancredo describes himself as a "very emotional Italian kid."⁶⁵⁶ Born in Denver in 1945, to Italian American parents Gerald and Adeline Tancredo, he grew up in north Denver.⁶⁵⁷ While attending Holy Family High School he started working at Elitch Gardens, a job he kept for ten years. He worked as a grounds sweeper and park manager before leaving to attend college.⁶⁵⁸ In 1968, he graduated from the University of Northern Colorado with a B.A. in education and went on to teach at Drake Junior High in Jefferson County, Colorado.

In 1976, Tom Tancredo decided to run for a seat in the Colorado House of Representatives. A political newcomer, his campaign included a flyer that had his mother's spaghetti sauce recipe on one side and his "recipe" for better government on the other.⁶⁵⁹ Tancredo won the election and went on to serve six years in the Colorado State Legislature, as part of a tight-knit group of conservative Republicans who dominated Colorado House politics between 1977 and 1979.

In 1981, Tom Tancredo resigned from the Colorado legislature when he was appointed to serve as the Regional Representative of the United States Department of Education under the Reagan administration.⁶⁶⁰ In his position, a job he held for eight years, Tancredo was responsible for advancing the administration's educational goals and for overseeing the department's regionalized activities. Serving in that capacity, Tancredo became the center of controversy. Aside from his support for a school voucher program, he was criticized for sending out a mailing to private schools that referred to the United States as a "Christian nation."[661] His supporters countered that he was not a religious fundamentalist, but in fact a "fallen away Catholic" (now an "evangelical Presbyterian") who valued his private education and supported the idea of parents having a choice and the ability to choose among the best schools for their children.[662] Further, Tancredo responded to his critics by saying that he ran "a department of education, not a department of public education."[663]

Many Italian American politicians have followed in the political footsteps of their predecessors. Tancredo is not one of them; instead, his politics lay more to the conservative side. Though not necessarily liberal, Italian Americans have been historically stalwart Democrats. Denver's District 10, with its strong Italian American presence, was for many years predominantly Democratic.

After working in the education department under Reagan, Tancredo was reappointed by George H. W. Bush to the position. At the end of the Bush administration in 1992, Tancredo returned to Colorado as director of the Independence Institute, a libertarian, Golden-based think tank. In 1998, he ran for Colorado's representative from the sixth congressional district.[664] He has held the seat since 1998 and has become a high-profile, nationally recognized politician due in large part to his views against illegal immigration and his bid for the 2008 presidency.

CHAPTER 8

Renewal

1990–Today

▩ ▩ ▩ Today, more than 200,000 Coloradans claim Italian ancestry. Denver's Little Italy is gone as a neighborhood, but it lives on in people's hearts. Third-, fourth-, even fifth-generation Italians are drawing their family trees and tracing ethnic roots. For many, the ultimate step is a trip overseas to the region or town that holds family seeds. An event such as Denver's annual Columbus Day parade sparks a lively dialogue; Italians are looking at the celebration's meaning, and how it expresses "Italianness." Individuals wrestle with their identities as Italian Americans, or American Italians.

The most visible face of the Italian community is on menus and restaurant signs, wine labels, and specialized products. But it goes much deeper than that. Besides the delis and markets and restaurants, Denver is home to Italian American studios, agencies, shops, and entrepreneurial establishments. Some businesses have stayed popular—or notorious—since Little Italy's heyday, while others are springing from a trickle of young immigrants and degreed students. The church still plays a central role in the Italian American community, and *la famiglia,* the family, still centers everyday life.

Coloradans take part in forty Italian American organizations statewide.[665] Affiliations, long-standing and new, promote awareness, charity, spiritual growth, and education and scholarship for Italian American youth.

Italian Americans are in full stride, reviving and reshaping traditions that arrived with Colorado's early Italian immigrants. This rich heritage is being explored as today's Italian Americans identify with the values and traditions of the generations who came before them.

Opposite: Procession, Our Lady of Mount Carmel Feast Day celebration with Mount Carmel Men's Club members carrying the statue of Our Lady of Mount Carmel, from right to left: Mike Pomponio, Duke LaConte, and Ernie Paul Marranzino, by Michael "Spydr" Wren, Denver, July 2004. PCCLI5962

Aiello

Joseph "Joe" Michael Aiello

The son of Joseph Peter Aiello and Jeanne Marie (Scott) Aiello, Joe Aiello was born in Newburgh, New York, in 1953. His paternal grandfather, Peter, was born in Bagheria, Sicily, and came to the United States around 1903.[666] A cabinetmaker in Italy, Peter worked as a refinisher for Steinway Pianos in New York. Joe's paternal grandmother, Edith, was born in New York to Sicilian parents. Peter and Edith left Manhattan's Little Italy around 1930 and moved upstate.[667]

Joe's family moved to Colorado in 1965, where his father and his uncle Louis Aiello opened an interior design business. The family lived in the Cheesman Park area, and Joe attended St. John's School, Regis High School, and East High School.[668]

In 2003, Joe founded Colorado's Italian American community newspaper, *Andiamo!* Other projects he has spearheaded include the Order of Basilone, founded in 2003 to honor Italian American veterans; Colorado's Italian American Hall of Fame, founded in 2004 to recognize outstanding service in the Italian American community; the Rocky Mountain Italian American Chamber of Commerce, founded in 2004; and the Italian American Business Association of Greater Denver, founded in 2006.[669]

Joe also established the Primo Awards in 2005 to recognize the contributions of Italian Americans to the state of Colorado in areas including business, education, art, and music, and the preservation and promotion of Italian American culture and heritage. Each year, the Colorado Italian American community nominates and votes for the candidate of their choice. The winners then receive their Primo Awards at a community dinner and awards ceremony held annually in June.

Today, Joe Aiello lives in Littleton with his wife, Julie, and is active in helping to revitalize the Colorado Italian American community's traditions, culture, and history.

Joseph and Jeanne Aiello (parents of Joe Aiello), Wappinger Falls, New York, 1950. CIAPA Archive. Courtesy Joe Aiello. PCCLI5560

Alonzi

Louis "Lou" Alonzi

Lou Alonzi was born in 1924 in Denver.[670] His father, Loreto Alonzi, was born in Rome and came to America in 1912 at the age of seventeen, settling first in Chicago, where he found work with the railroad as a laborer.[671] Lou's mother Rosa was born in Ogden, Utah, in 1902, to Italian-born parents. By 1920, Lou's parents and brother Joseph, along with Rosa's brother Peter DiAnni, mother Jennie, stepfather Antonio Lombardi, and their five children had settled in Denver, and were all living together at 3641 Mariposa Street.[672]

Lou's interest in music began in his teens when his mother bought him his first horn. While still in high school, he began playing in local taverns and at the Saint Rocco feast day celebration and events at Our Lady of Mount Carmel Church. After graduating from North High in 1944, Lou formed his own band and was playing at clubs including the My-O-My Supper Club, the Starlight, and Club La Ronda.[673]

In 1947, Lou Alonzi married Dorothy Beall at Our Lady of Mount Carmel Church. Dorothy was not Italian and according to Lou, his parents never thought anything about it. Together Lou and Dorothy had four children: Karen, Louis, David, and Clifford.[674]

In addition to his professional career as a musician, Lou Alonzi also worked as an apprentice with the railroad, for the Brick Yard in Golden, and for Coors Ceramics, from which he retired after thirty-three years.[675]

In 1982, Lou Alzoni made his first trip to Rome to see his father's family. Today, he is still active in Denver's Italian American community and continues to entertain people with his music.[676]

Lou Alonzi and his Orchestra at the Club La Ronda, left to right: Earl Peters, Lou Alonzi, Herb Price, Homer Chambers, and Karl Leonard, Denver, c. 1960. CIAPA Archive. Courtesy Lou Alonzi. PCCLI2096A

Amato

Frank Carlo Amato

Carlo Amato's childhood memories include Sunday Mass, his grandmother's simmering spaghetti sauce, garlic-roasted peppers, grapes from the vineyard, and his grandfather's mandolin and entrepreneurial spirit.[677]

Carlo was born in Denver in 1948 to Frank J. and Myrtle Amato.[678] His paternal grandfather, Carlo, had come to the United States from Italy in 1921. When he settled in Denver a year later, Carlo's grandfather, a master cabinetmaker, opened a store at Thirty-sixth and Navajo in Denver, where he crafted decorative art in concrete.[679] In 1924, he married Lillian Lombardi, born in Colorado to Giovanna and Fiore Lombardi.[680]

In 1962, at age fourteen, Carlo started helping his grandfather and father with the family business. The first piece he worked on was a birdbath. After learning the statuary trade, he took over operations of Amato of Denver in 1976.[681] From his father and grandfather, Carlo learned not only a trade but a work ethic and the value of respect for customers. Today, Amato of Denver is still owned and operated by Carlo Amato, along with his wife Rhonda, and sons Chris and Anthony.[682] Located at 2501 Sixteenth Street since 1945, the company specializes in statuary and garden art.

Frank J. Amato (left) and Carlo Amato, inside Amato of Denver, by Dawn DeAno, 2005. CIAPA Archive. PCCLICPC0031

Carlo is active in Our Lady of Mount Carmel's Men's Club, the Sons of Italy Lodge No. 2702, and Fiori D'Italia. He has donated statuary to a variety of causes and volunteers his time to repair statues at local parishes. In recognition of his contributions to his community and benevolent services, Carlo received the 2005 Primo Award for Italian American of the Year.

Antonelli

Philip Dalla Antonelli

Philip D. Antonelli was born in Silverton, Colorado, in 1924 to Fidenzio "Phil" and Rena (Dalla, shortened from Dallavalle) Antonelli. His father was born in Fornace, Tyrol, in northern Italy, and settled in Silverton in 1913, where he worked as a millwright, blacksmith, and miner. His mother Rena, the daughter of Tyrol natives, was born in 1903 in Silverton, where her father ran several businesses, including a boardinghouse, saloon, bottling works, and a dairy.[683]

In 1942, Philip moved to Denver to attend Regis College. The following year he was drafted into the Army. During World War II, he served as a machine gunner, telephone and telegraph wireman, and battery clerk in the artillery division. After the war, Philip returned to his studies at Regis College, graduating in 1949 with a degree in business and economics. In 1951, Philip enrolled in the master's program at the University of Denver, studying school administration. While attending D.U., he taught and coached basketball at Regis High School.

In 1955, Philip graduated from the University of Denver and married Lois Madonna Buckley. Philip and Lois had four children: Therese, Philip II, Cecilia, and Mark. In 1956, Philip began working for Buckley Powder Company, selling dynamite. By 1970, he was the company's vice president. For the next fifteen years, Philip worked for seismic data companies and other explosive sales firms before retiring in 1985.

In 1985, Philip married his second wife Romana Rosa (Svaldi) Pier Heinbaugh in Denver. Romana was born in Trento, Italy, in 1933 to Clemente and Enrica (Mattivi) Svaldi. One of nine children, she came to the United States in 1950 and settled in Denver in 1964.

Back row, left to right: Jack Mattivi, John Fedel, and unidentified man; front row, left to right: Joe Cadrobi Mattivi with accordion and Phil Antonelli (Philip's father) with guitar, Silverton, Colorado, 1926. Gift Philip D. and Romana Antonelli. 2005.20.3

Renewal 1990–Today

Influential in reorganizing Denver's Columbus Day Parade in 1991, Philip and Romana today remain active in the Italian American community, including membership in The Tirolian Trentini di Colorado club, which Philip helped found in 1982, and served as president until 2004.

> **A CLOSER LOOK**
> *The Tirolian Trentini di Colorado*

In 1972, Denver's Italians from the northern Trentino Alto Adige or Trento-South Tyrol (Tirol) region began meeting socially. Ten years later, Philip D. Antonelli and others officially founded the Tirolian Trentini di Colorado.[684] The purpose of the organization is to recognize and acknowledge Italians who came from the Tyrol region in northern Italy and to promote and preserve their culture and traditions.[685] Before World War I, the Tyrol region belonged to the Austro-Hungarian Empire. After the war and the Treaty of St. Germain, it became part of Italy, and its residents are referred to as "Trentini."

Many Trentini share customs with other Alpine dwellers, including the Austrians and the Swiss. They eat sauerkraut with pasta, use butter instead of olive oil, and

Romana and Philip D. Antonelli in traditional Trentini costumes, dancing at Tirolian Trentini di Colorado event, 1987. CIAPA Archive. Courtesy Philip D. and Romana Antonelli. PCCLI3122

Judges evaluating polenta entries to determine the winners of the 1987 Polenta Fest and to crown the Polenta King and Queen. CIAPA Archive. Courtesy Philip D. and Romana Antonelli. PCCLI2628

eat polenta (a cornmeal cake and staple in northern Italy) with brown gravy instead of tomato sauce. The Trentini traditionally wear Alpine costumes such as the men's *lederhosen* (leather trousers in German) and *Alpini* hats.[686]

The Tirolian Trentini di Colorado keeps Trentino traditions alive through social potlucks, spaghetti dinners, dances, picnics, and the annual Polenta Fest. During the Polenta Fest, members wear traditional Austrian-Italian costumes, dance, and hold a contest to determine the best polenta. The winners are the festival's Polenta King and Queen.[687]

Broncucia

Michael "Mike" Frank Broncucia

Mike Broncucia was born in Denver in 1936 to John and Laura (Biamonte) Broncucia.[688] Mike's grandfather Joseph Broncucia immigrated to Denver from Potenza, Italy, in the early 1890s, and after marrying Josephine Petrillo, homesteaded land in Adams County at Seventieth and Broadway. Referred to as "Broncucia Village," Joseph and Josephine, along with their children, all eventually lived on the land. Today, Mike Broncucia owns and operates Mickey's Top Sirloin on the same property.[689]

Started in 1952, Mickey's includes a restaurant and bocce courts. The original Mickey's Top Sirloin was located in an old building on the corner of the property that once belonged to Mike's father.[690] There he installed grass bocce courts along the outside of the building. In 2005, Mike constructed a new building on his property that boasts two indoor bocce courts. The new place is as popular as ever, especially with Italian American clubs. The bocce courts are Mike's way of upholding Italian traditions. His granddaughter, Stacey Hamilton, is continuing the family legacy, and now handles all the scheduling for the courts, which are open to anyone who wants to use them.[691]

Left to right: Mike Broncucia, Louis Broncucia, and John Broncucia (Mike Broncucia's father), in leaf lettuce field on the Broncucia family farm, Adams County, 1930. CIAPA Archive. Courtesy Mike Broncucia. PCCLI5655

Carmosino

Albert "Al" Anthony and Mildred "Millie" Victoria (Yacovetta) Carmosino

Al Carmosino was born in Elwood City, Pennsylvania, in 1930. His parents, Olindo and Maria Lucia Carmosino, had come to America in the 1920s from Pagliarone, in southern Italy. In 1948, the Carmosinos moved to Denver. Al attended the University of Denver, where he earned his bachelor's degree in 1952 and his law degree in 1955. He soon opened his first law practice in the old Majestic Building at Sixteenth and Broadway. Fifty-two years later, Al is still in private practice as a lawyer.[692]

In 1957, Al met Mildred "Millie" Yacovetta at a cousin's wedding. They married in 1961. Millie was born in Denver in 1932 to Robert and Matilda (Mollicone) Yacovetta; her grandparents had come to Denver from southern Italy. Her paternal grandfather, Bernardino Yacovetta, worked as a laborer on the Moffat Tunnel rail line and Glenwood Canyon road, and he eventually bought a farm in Aurora. After high school, Millie went to work in the banking industry, from which she retired after thirty-two years.[693]

Millie and Al Carmosino, 1985. CIAPA Archive. Courtesy Al and Millie Carmosino. PCCLI5334

Today, Al and Millie Carmosino have raised over $1.5 million for charity, primarily through their work with the Rocky Mountain Italian Golf Association and Bocce Festival.[694] Established in 1977 by Al and others, the festival, now organized by Al, Millie, and the association's board, is run entirely by volunteers and without sponsors.[695] The two-day event includes a golf and bocce tournament, a banquet, and a picnic for the bocce players. The festival is also an occasion for Colorado's Italian Americans to reunite and enjoy camaraderie.

Caruso

Louise Pasqualina (Panzini) Caruso

Louise Panzini was born at home at 3604 Kalamath Street in Denver on Easter Sunday in 1920 to Anthony and Eliza (Barbato) Panzini. She was named after her grandmother Luisa (Trombetta) Panzini, who never left Italy, and for the date of her birth—Easter—*Pasqua* in Italian.[696] Louise's father, Anthony, was born in Calabria and arrived in Denver in 1909. In 1915, he married Eliza Barbato of Campobasso, Italy.[697] The youngest of three daughters, Eliza could not travel with her mother, Filomena, and sisters, Lucia and Christina, to the United States in 1902 due to illness. She stayed behind with family until 1905, when she made the passage alone at age nine with a message fastened to her clothing: "GOING TO DENVER, COLORADO." She arrived in Denver to learn that her father, Nicola, had died, her mother worked on a farm, and her two sisters lived in Mother Cabrini's Queen of Heaven Orphanage. Eliza joined her sisters at the orphanage for four years before moving in with her mother and stepfamily. Her sister Lucia married at age eighteen, and Christina became a Missionary Sister of the Sacred Heart.[698]

Louise and Tony Caruso, 1946. CIAPA Archive. Courtesy Tony and Louise Caruso. PCCLI0142

Eliza (Barbato) Panzini (Louise's mother, back row, far right), first Holy Communion, Queen of Heaven Orphanage, c. 1908. CIAPA Archive. Courtesy Tony and Louise Caruso. PCCLI0140

Renewal 1990–Today

In 1946, Louise Panzini married Anthony "Tony" Caruso at Our Lady of Mount Carmel; the church has been the bedrock of the couple's life ever since. Louise took part in the Saint Theresa's Club, the Altar and Rosary Society, processions, bazaars, and holiday dinners. Raising sons John and Gerard, she also worked at the Associated Tailor Shop and attended night courses at the Emily Griffith Opportunity School after graduating from North High. She has helped many in the Italian community obtain their U.S. citizenship.[699]

Iantorno/Yantorno

Frank Robert Yantorno

Frank Yantorno was born in Denver in 1934 to Francesco and Adelina (Calomino) Iantorno. In 1909, Frank's parents left Gesuiti, Italy, for America, where immigration officials in New York changed the family name to Yantorno. After a short stay in New York, they made their way to Denver. In 1960, Frank married Marilyn Jean Westdal at Holy Family Church. Together, Frank and Marilyn raised four children: Monica, Frank Jr., Dominique, and Anthony.[700]

A dentist by profession, Frank became interested in art during a family trip to Taos, New Mexico, in 1970. After watching an artist sculpt, he decided to try the process himself. He continued sculpting and eventually established a studio at his dental office, seeing patients three days a week and working in the studio three days a week.[701] He went on to study art at Creighton University, the University of Colorado, the University of Denver, and the Art Students League of Denver.

Now retired from his dental practice, Frank Yantorno focuses on his art full-time. He lives in Italy part of the year, and draws inspiration from Italian culture and daily life.[702] His works are exhibited throughout the country and are held in private collections. His pieces include a sculpture in Lakewood's civic center and a cross in Denver's Immaculate Heart of Mary Catholic Church.

Yantorno family, back row, left to right: Adelina, Charlie, Ray, and Eva; front row, left to right: Francesco, Trish, and Frank, c. 1955. CIAPA Archive. Courtesy Frank Yantorno. PCCLI4518

Rossi

Marguerite "Margaret" Helen (DiSalvo/DeSalvo) Rossi

Joseph DiSalvo left Pietrabbondante, Italy, for South America after being drafted in the Italian army. In 1894, he made his way to Denver, where he found work with the Zarlengo family. The Zarlengos, from the same area in Italy as Joseph, arranged for him to marry Beatrice Mucillo, also from Pietrabbondante, Italy, and twenty years his junior. Joseph and Beatrice moved to Denver and settled in the Bottoms. Joseph continued to work for the Zarlengo family in the summers, cutting trees by hand during the day, sleeping in a shack in Tolland at night, and seeing his family when he could. During the winter, he traveled by horse and buggy to Louisville to work in the coal mines during the week, returning to Denver on the weekends. In 1906, a flood destroyed the DiSalvo home and the family moved to Quivas Street in north Denver.[703]

Margaret (DiSalvo) Rossi, 1939. CIAPA Archive. Courtesy Margaret Rossi. PCCLI5352

The youngest of Joseph and Beatrice's six children, Margaret DiSalvo was born in 1914. When the Depression hit, she left North High and took a job on an assembly line, working six days a week at Bailey-Underhill. In 1944, she married Mario A. Rossi, a friend of her brothers. Born in Italy in 1886, Mario was the youngest of twelve children. Despite a relatively privileged life and education, Mario had trouble finding work, and he knew that his oldest brother would inherit the family estate, so he followed his other brothers to the United States. In Denver, he sold insurance and managed a restaurant. Margaret and Mario had three children together: Philip, Patricia, and Mary Ann.

Today, Margaret Rossi still lives in the DiSalvo family home on Quivas Street in north Denver. Her vivid memories of over ninety years include the big outdoor oven where her mother baked loaves of bread, her mother's home altar, the old arbor and grape vines in the backyard, her mother combing olive oil in her hair to make it softer, her father making wine during Prohibition, the garden where her family grew their vegetables, and the peddlers who rode through the neighborhood selling produce.

Rotola

Mary Ann (Gallo) Rotola

Mary Gallo was born in 1914 in her grandmother's house in north Denver. Her parents, Cesarino "Jess" and Margaret (Iannacito) Gallo, were both from Italy.[704] After attending Bryant-Webster School through the eighth grade, she sold handkerchiefs at the Daniels & Fisher department store, then worked at the Diamond A Market, owned by her cousins, the Iacinos.[705] Later, she worked at other department stores and made priests' garments for Montaldo's.

In 1934, Mary and Al Rotola married at Our Lady of Mount Carmel. They settled in north Denver, where they raised their children: Albert, Richard, and Mary Ann. Al ran a filling station and then partnered with his brother-in-law, Jimmy Capillupo, to buy his grandmother's beer joint: the Wazee Lounge.[706]

Mary Rotola is credited with introducing the Saint Joseph's Day Table to Our Lady of Mount Carmel in 1978. She discovered the ritual in St. Louis on a trip to see her son ordained as a priest.[707] According to tradition, a feast is laid in thanks for the miracle in which Saint Joseph answered the prayers of the hungry in Sicily during the Middle Ages. Everyone is invited to the table, particularly those in physical, spiritual, or financial need. Mary had recently been cured of colon cancer and offered the first "table" at her home in gratitude; the turnout was tremendous.[708] Subsequent tables have been held at the Mount Carmel parish hall. In recent years, nearly seven hundred people have come to the event. Parishioners and guests buy hundreds of loaves of Easter bread (with Easter eggs baked inside), and proceeds go to the needy.[709]

Al and Mary (Gallo) Rotola (Mary wears a dress and hat she designed and made), 1933. CIAPA Archive. Courtesy Mary Rotola. PCCLI4586

A Closer Look
Our Lady of Mount Carmel Organizations

Our Lady of Mount Carmel Church—Denver's Italian parish established in 1894—has been associated with more than twenty Italian societies and organizations. The Altar and Rosary Society and Men's Club are among the largest today.

Founded in 1918, the Mount Carmel Altar and Rosary Society began with separate English- and Italian-speaking branches. This division persisted into the 1940s, with both sections caring for the church altar, making vestments for priests, and working for the betterment of the parish.[710] No longer separate, the society counts about 150 members today. Many of its traditions survive, including the use of its banner at Mass and on feast day celebrations and running the cake booth and contributing a hope chest for the church's annual bazaar.[711]

Established in 1953, the Mount Carmel Men's Club (originally called the Father's Club) initially supported the parish schools. When the schools closed in 1968, the club turned its attention to church programs.[712]

Membership declined in the 1980s, but surged again after 2003 under the leadership of Ernest "Ernie" Marranzino Jr. He and others developed new programs and coaxed

Our Lady of Mount Carmel Altar and Rosary Society outside of Our Lady of Mount Carmel Church, c. 1950. CIAPA Archive. Courtesy Mary Pomarico. PCCLI5603

Renewal 1990–Today

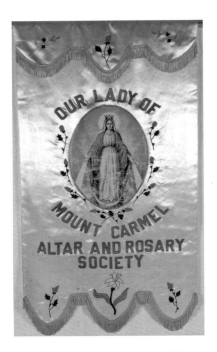

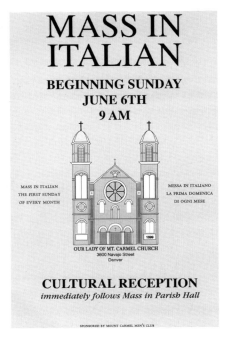

Banner, Our Lady of Mount Carmel Altar and Rosary Society, c. 1965. Gift Our Lady of Mount Carmel Church. 2003.109.1.A

Poster, Mass in Italian, 2003. Gift Mount Carmel Men's Club. 2004.79.1

former Mount Carmel Church-goers—many of them graduates of Mount Carmel High School—back to the parish. Today, the Men's Club supports the annual bazaar in celebration of the Feast Day of Our Lady of Mount Carmel and the parish golf and bocce tournament. The Men's Club is also involved in La Prima Domenica, a Mass celebrated in Italian on the first Sunday of every month.[713]

Marranzino

Michele "Michael" Antonio "Anthony" Marranzino Sr.

Michael Anthony Marranzino Sr. was born in Argentina in 1890 to Pasquale and Maria Giuseppa (Nigro) Marranzino. His parents had moved there from Avalino, Italy, around 1880. At age ten, Michael came with his family to the United States, settling in Denver to be near friends.[714]

In 1914, he married Grace Cavarra, and the couple moved into the Cavarra home at 3556 Osage Street in north

Denver.⁷¹⁵ The house became a center for the extended family, including Michael and Grace's four children: Joseph, Ernest, Pasquale, and Marie. Around 1925, Michael opened a grocery store in the lower level of the home. He spent much of his money on stock, but then gave away the groceries on extended credit. Unwilling to ask his customers for repayment, he closed the business when all the merchandise disappeared.⁷¹⁶

Michael's concern for others may have sabotaged his grocery store, but it advanced his career as a court interpreter and politician. He spoke Italian, Spanish, Portuguese, French, and English, and he translated court proceedings for the immigrant community—not just for Italians. He served two terms as District 9 city councilman, from 1939 to 1946.⁷¹⁷ His unabashed efforts on behalf of immigrants did not sit well with all; he received threats and was the target of a car explosion. Many believed the attack to be the work of the Ku Klux Klan.⁷¹⁸ Michael Anthony Marranzino died in 1946 at age fifty-six, before completing his second city council term.

Michael Anthony Marranzino Sr. family, left to right: Joseph, Michael, Ernest, Pasquale, Grace, and Marie, 1925. CIAPA Archive. Courtesy Michael Marranzino II. PCCLI0842

Swearing in Denver City Council with Michael Marranzino Sr. of District 9, third from right, 1943. CIAPA Archive. Courtesy Michael Marranzino II. PCCLI0841

Renewal 1990–Today

Ernest "Ernie" Marranzino Jr., president of the Mount Carmel Men's Club, inside Our Lady of Mount Carmel Church, by Dawn DeAno, 2006. CIAPA Archive. PCCLICPC0029

Ernest "Ernie" Pasquale Marranzino Jr.

Ernie Marranzino Jr. was born in Denver in 1950 to Ernest and Eleanor (Carlone) Marranzino.[719] A graduate of Regis College and a veteran of World War II, Ernie's father served on Denver's city council. Elected in 1947, he replaced his father Michael, who previously held the position.[720] He also ran a school for electronics and radio repair in the lower level of the family's north Denver home on Osage Street. He turned the school into an electronics repair shop, Marranzino Television.[721]

Ernie Jr. attended Mount Carmel High School until it closed in 1968. After graduating from North High, he married Annette Gallegos and went to work as a pipe fitter. In 1992, he became a Denver firefighter, a job he still holds. A leader in the Italian American community, he is involved with Our Lady of Mount Carmel Church and organizations including the Mount Carmel Men's Club, the Sons of Italy Denver Lodge No. 2075, and the Morra Society of Denver.[722]

Pasquale "Pocky" Leonardo Marranzino, Jr.

The grandson of Michael and Grace Marranzino and the son of Pasquale "Pocky" and Elsie (Risoli) Marranzino, Pocky Marranzino Jr. was born in Denver in 1948. His father, a veteran of World War II, worked for the *Rocky Mountain News* for thirty-three years and his mother was a dancer in the dance group the "DeGaetano Dancers."[723]

Pocky Jr. grew up on Denver's east side but spent much of his time on the north side with family and friends—graduating from Regis High School in 1966, followed by studies at Regis University. He landed his first job in the mailroom of an advertising agency. In the 1980s he joined Karsh & Hagan, a promising ad agency. After nearly twenty years, he bought the firm in 1996. Today, he is president of Karsh & Hagan Communications, Inc., which has seventy-five employees and offices in five states. The agency balances a diverse list of clients and accounts, including McDonald's Restaurants, the Denver Newspaper Agency, and the Colorado Lottery.[724]

Christmas card with Pasquale Marranzino Sr. at back left (holding Lisa), Elsie (back right) and Marilyn and Pasquale "Pocky" Marranzino Jr., c. 1952. CIAPA Archive. Courtesy Pocky Marranzino Jr. PCCLI5705

A Closer Look
Federal Fruit and Produce

In 1945, Joe Naimen bought Federal Fruit Incorporated, a small fruit and produce distributor operating out of the Denargo Market. A year later, he renamed the company Federal Fruit and Produce. By 1964, he was doing three million dollars' worth of business a year and employing twenty-one people full-time.[725]

Mike Martelli worked under Naimen for several years, but left in 1971. His father, Sal, worked there for thirty years and was the company's general manager until his death in 1978.[726] Mike renewed his connection to Federal Fruit and Produce in 1987 by teaming up with John Domenico and Stan Kouba to buy the company.[727]

Denver natives Martelli and Domenico are both sons of Italian American parents and have family connections to the farming and produce business. They ran the company's Denver division, while Chicagoan Stan Kouba moved to Colorado after the buyout and operated the Colorado Springs division.[728]

After ten successful years under Martelli and Domenico, the Denver division moved from Denargo Market to its present location at 1890 East Fifty-eighth Avenue in Denver. The 46,000-square-foot facility has 28,000 square feet of cooler space and six pressurized ripening rooms. The division is the largest produce wholesaler in Colorado and employs about eighty people.[729]

Laurita

Fred Michael "Mick" and Rosemary (Spano) Laurita

Fred Michael "Mick" Laurita was born in Denver in 1940 to Fred Arthur and Rose Carmela (Dardano) Laurita. His maternal grandfather, Saverio Dardano, was the first of the family to arrive in Colorado in 1900 from Sorbo San Basile, in southern Italy. He worked as a water boy on the Moffat Tunnel construction site and later grew lettuce, celery, and peppers on his south Denver farm.[730]

Married in 1938, Mick's parents owned a grocery store near their home at Forty-fourth and Sheridan. Mick's mother ran the store when his father served in World War II. After the war, Fred and Rose sold the store and bought a motel on West Colfax, where the whole family pitched in with the chores.[731]

Working on a farm in south Denver, Mick met Rosemary Ann Spano, the daughter of Vincent James and Louise (Garramone) Spano. Married in 1962, Mick and Rosemary moved to Georgetown in 1971.[732] They opened Laurita's Italian Restorante, which featured their families' recipes along with others from the couple's world travels. In 1980, they sold the restaurant and moved to the foothills near Evergreen, where they established Laurita's Mediterranean Market, a retail market and deli that carried imported goods.[733]

Mick and Rosemary soon launched a new business venture: Italco Food Products. A supplier of imported gourmet goods for the Rocky Mountain region, Italco sells products ranging from appetizers and coffee to spices and produce, and more than 400 kinds of cheese. Mick and Rosemary's sons Michael and Christopher now run the successful enterprise.[734]

Massaro

Gary Massaro

Gary Massaro was born in Pueblo in 1950 to Angelo Laurence and Alice Margaret (Okicich) Massaro. Gary's father was born in Coal Creek, Colorado, in 1915, the son of Italian Americans Antonio and Rose (Fabrizio) Massaro. Angelo worked on his parents' farm north of Pueblo and later as an engineer on the Denver & Rio Grande Western Railroad.[735]

In 1968, Gary Massaro graduated from Pueblo Central High School. In 1976, he completed his degree in political science from the University of Southern Colorado–Pueblo (today's Colorado State University–Pueblo). Throughout college, he worked in construction, as a railroad switchman, and as a boiler man. At age twenty-six, he left Pueblo to take a job with the *Delta County Independent*. For eleven years, he worked at newspapers on the Western Slope. His family, including his wife, Cathy, and three sons, lived in towns such as Hotchkiss and Grand Junction.[736] Today, Gary is a seasoned columnist for the *Rocky Mountain News*, and his insightful profiles of everyday people have a devoted following.

Gary Massaro inside the Rocky Mountain News *offices, by Dawn DeAno, 2006. CIAPA Archive. PCCLICPC0036*

Looking back, Gary Massaro has fond memories of Pueblo's Italian American life, including his mother's Sicilian tomato sauce, with a touch of sugar, he says, to counter the tartness of freshly farmed tomatoes. He recalls especially the Italian weddings: "the grand march, presided over by two 'ancient' women in black shoes and ankle-length dresses; candy-covered almonds flung at the bride and groom; and much laughter."[737]

A Closer Look
The Onofrio Piano Company

The Onofrio family is celebrating its 108th year in the piano business. It all began when Angelo Filippo Onofrio, a native of Rome, Italy, came to America in 1895.[738] After

Renewal 1990–Today

Joe Onofrio Music Company with Joseph Onofrio Jr. (second from left) and Joseph Onofrio Sr. (third from left), Denver, c. 1955. CIAPA Archive. Courtesy Vivian Onofrio. PCCLI2114

settling in Chicago with his three brothers, he went to work at the Lyon & Healy Piano Company.[739] In 1898, he moved to Denver with his wife Rosa and son Joseph and soon began selling pianos out of the back of his home in Denver. In 1900, he opened the Colorado Music Company in downtown Denver. After learning the art of piano making, Filippo's son Joseph joined him in the business. Father and son traveled across Colorado, Utah, Wyoming, and New Mexico, selling pianos by bicycle. They delivered their products by train and buckboard wagons.[740]

Hard times hit the Onofrios in the late 1920s. Filippo died in 1928. Joseph sustained the family business through the Great Depression by taking jobs with the city of Denver. Then, during World War II, the United States suspended piano manufacturing altogether.[741]

After the war, demand for pianos increased. Joseph opened a new store under a new name, Joseph Onofrio Music Company, on Broadway.[742] His son, Joe Jr., ran another at Seventh and Santa Fe. In 1952, father and son consolidated their locations into a single store near Denver's Civic Center. Eventually, the business occupied half a city block.

After the death of his father in 1962, Joe Jr. continued to run the family business from the same location until the city forced him to move in 1974 to make way for the new Colorado History Museum. The business relocated to 1332 South Broadway, where the Onofrio Piano Company continues today under the leadership of Joe Onofrio III, Filippo's great-grandson.[743]

Primavera

Dominic Peter Aquila "Dr. Peter Emily"

In 1900, Dominic Primavera left his home in Potenza, Italy, in search of a better life.[744] He settled first in Pennsylvania and then made his way to Colorado, where in 1904, he married Josephine Cioffi, born in Siena, Italy. In 1908, their daughter Olivia was born, one of sixteen children. The Primavera family lived for many years at 1834 West Thirty-sixth Avenue. Dominic supported his family by working in the foundry of the C. S. Cart Iron Works Company in downtown Denver. There, he poured hot iron into moulds to make train wheels. Later, Dominic and Josephine also opened the Primavera Creamery out of their home at Thirty-sixth and Shoshone.[745]

*Peter Emily, c. 1950.
CIAPA Archive.
Courtesy Dr. Peter Emily.
PCCLI2861*

In 1929, Dominic and Josephine Primavera arranged for a marriage for their daughter Olivia to Dominic Aquila. In 1932, Olivia and Dominic's son, Dominic Peter, known as Peter, was born. Shortly after, Dominic Aquila decided that he did not like America and returned to Italy. The family never heard from him again. Olivia and Peter moved in with Olivia's parents. During this time, Peter spent a great deal of time with his grandparents, who taught him much about living. He spoke only Italian with them and has many fond memories of his grandmother Josephine's small garden, neat backyard, and her praying every morning, afternoon, and night. Of his grandfather Dominic, he recalled that he made great wine and on every Sunday walked to the Alpine Inn for dinner, a shot of whiskey, and card games with his friends.

In 1935, Peter's mother Olivia married Allen Donald Emily. The Emily family then moved to 3050 Zuni Street and Dominic Peter Aquila became Clifford Emily, a name he kept until after he graduated from Dental School in 1959. He then changed his name back to Peter but kept the surname of Emily.

After attending Regis College and serving in the Korean War, Peter applied to the School of Dentistry at Creighton University under the G.I. Bill. In 1954, he married Marcella Schneider, and in 1955, started his studies at Creighton University in Nebraska. In 1955, Peter and Marcella's first child, a daughter named Gina, was born, followed by Joni, Anthony, and Joseph.

In 1959, Peter Emily went into private practice as a dentist. Later, he became interested in animal dentistry and began working with veterinarians and developing new techniques in the field. After completing his degrees in perintology and clinical veterinary, he became a specialist in animal oral surgery and has since achieved tremendous success in the field. In addition to winning numerous awards, he has authored three textbooks for veterinarians and founded the College of Veterinarian Dentistry, which awards the Peter Emily Award annually for outstanding contributions to animal dentistry.[746]

Today, Dr. Peter Emily continues to teach and lecture around the world; he lives in Colorado, where he works as the director of Animal Dentistry at Colorado State University and director of Exotic Animal Dentistry at the Denver Zoological Gardens.[747]

Spano

Phillip "Phil" John Spano

Phil Spano was born in Copeland Ranch, near Welby, Colorado, in 1927 to Giuseppe "Joe" and Giovanna "Jennie" (Vassallo) Spano, both natives of Palermo, Sicily.[748] Joe and Jennie came to the United States in the early 1920s after Joe's cousin Sam had established himself in Adams County. The Spanos, along with Joe's two brothers, soon bought their own land in Welby and went into truck farming.[749]

Joe and Jennie Spano had seven children: Tony, Rose, Carmella, Anna, Marietta, Lena, and Phil. The entire family worked on the farm, growing vegetables to sell at Denver's produce markets. Their son Phil started going with his father to the Denver City Market when he was around five. Eventually, Phil and left school to help on the family farm. The Spano family was particularly known for the specialty crop Pascal Celery, and from the 1930s through the 1950s their farms were the area's largest producers of the labor-intensive crop.[750]

In 1949, Phil married Ruth Mihelcich. After their marriage, Phil continued farming for several years. An entrepreneur at heart, he started a successful sand and gravel business and bought undeveloped property. By the early 1990s, he was president of four companies: Midwest Haulers, a trucking firm; Conservation Services, a non-hazardous industrial waste site; Green Valley, a real estate holding firm, and F & M Ranch in Wyoming. Today, Phil Spano enjoys giving back to the Italian American community and honoring his Italian heritage.[751]

Ruth and Phil Spano, 1992. CIAPA Archive. Courtesy Phil and Ruth Spano. PCCLI5675

Taddonio

Tony Michael Taddonio Jr.

Tony Taddonio Jr. was born in Denver in 1946 to Louise (Matzen) and Tony Taddonio Sr.[752] His grandfather, Michele, was born in Potenza, Italy, and came to the United States in 1901.[753] He worked as a peddler in Denver.[754] Tony's father and uncles Salvatore "Sam" and Rocco "Roxie" started a produce business around 1945 called Taddonio Brothers. They had one truck and sold potatoes out of their father's Jason Street garage in north Denver. Soon, they moved the business to the Denargo Market under the name of Mile High Fruit & Vegetable Company and sold produce to local restaurants and grocery stores.[755]

Tony Taddonio Sr., in front of display for Mile High Fruit & Vegetable Company, c. 1950. CIAPA Archive. Courtesy Tony Taddonio Jr. PCCLI5453

Renewal 1990–Today

In 1956, McDonald's opened its first restaurant in Denver, and the company needed a potato supplier. Mile High Fruit & Vegetable Company got the contract, and as McDonald's grew, so did the Taddonios' company. Mile High soon supplied McDonald's with ketchup, pickles, and baked goods.

In 1968, after graduating from Regis College, Tony Taddonio Jr. joined Mile High Fruit & Vegetable Company. As the founding brothers retired or died, Tony became the sole owner of the company, renaming it Mile High Frozen Foods in 1979. Today Tony runs the company with his wife, Pam, and daughters, Kristy and Toni. After fifty-one years, Mile High Frozen Foods is still the only supplier for McDonald's products in an eight-state region. The company also provides supplies to such clients as Boston Market, Chipotle, Red Robin, and Starbucks.[756]

Valente

Ray Valente

One of nine children, Ray Valente was born at home in 1924 to Jerry and Anna (DiAsenz) Valente.[757] His father came from Potenza, Italy, in 1893 and was employed by the railroad and Hungarian Flour Mill in addition to working on the family's north Denver farm. Ray's mother, also a native of Italy, came to the United States around 1900.[758]

Hungarian Flour Mill, with Joe Lewis (left) and Jerry Valente (Ray's father), Denver, c. 1930. CIAPA Archive. Courtesy Ray Valente. PCCLI2162

Ray Valente grew up on the family farm, attending Beechcourt and Columbian grade schools, Horace Mann Junior High, and North High. In 1943, he was drafted into the Army at age eighteen. He served in the trucking company division on Guadalcanal for twenty-seven months and was honorably discharged in 1946. Ray returned to Denver and worked at his brother's service station, where he met his future wife, Elaine Perri. Married in 1951 at Our Lady of Mount Carmel Church, Ray and Elaine have two sons.[759]

Elaine (Perri) and Ray Valente, c. 1950. CIAPA Archive. Courtesy Ray Valente. PCCLI5671

In 1964, Ray went into business with Pat Aiello (brother of Chubby Aiello), opening Jenny's Pizzeria on West Thirty-eighth Avenue. In 1971, after Pat retired, Ray renamed the restaurant Valente's.[760] It remains a popular restaurant today. For years, Elaine helped make the pastas and sauces while Ray's sister Viola supplied the meatballs that anchored the menu.[761] Viola died in 2006, and today the Valentes' sons, Ray Jr. and Mark, help run the business.

Ray Valente has been a generous contributor to charitable organizations and churches, and the community at large. In 1989, the *Denver Catholic Register* saluted Ray as an "outstanding member of the Italian American community,"

Chitarra pasta cutter with rolling pin used by Anna (DiAsenz) Valente, c. 1920. Gift Ray Valente. 2005.48.2.A-.B

noting his unselfish nature and charitable giving. Today Ray remains active in the Italian American community in Denver, including belonging to the Potenza Lodge, for which he often provides macaroni and fried peppers for fellow members at the monthly lodge meetings.

A Closer Look
Potenza Lodge

The Società Nativi di Potenza Basilicata, or Potenza Lodge, was incorporated on October 20, 1899. The mutual aid society offered English-language support, job search assistance, help locating reliable doctors and attorneys,

Renewal 1990–Today

Tony Mancinelli's San Rocco Society memoriam badge, c. 1930. Gift Ralph F. and Rosemary Mancinelli. 2004.112.2

and insurance to its members. Membership was limited to men from Potenza, Italy, or their descendants.[762] By 1901, the lodge had 200 members.[763]

When the San Rocco Society disbanded in 1926, Potenza Lodge assumed responsibility for the celebration of the feast day of Saint Rocco.[764] Since then, the lodge has organized the Saint Rocco bazaar, which includes food, music, games, and the traditional bidding for the honor of carrying the Saint Rocco statue in the annual procession.

Originally, lodge members met on Sundays at Coors Hall at Thirty-fourth and Navajo. In 1939, construction began on the Potenza Lodge Hall on West Thirty-eighth Avenue. Still used by the lodge, the building was completed in 1941 at a cost of $30,000.[765]

Today, Potenza Lodge is Denver's oldest Italian lodge, with a membership of around 250. Full membership is still restricted to male descendants of immigrants from Potenza, although women take part through a ladies' auxiliary.[766]

Potenza Lodge bazaar wheel, used by Potenza Lodge during bazaars in celebration of the feast day of Saint Rocco, c. 1985. Loan Potenza Lodge. IL.2004.25.1

Statue of Saint Rocco inside Our Lady of Mount Carmel, during the feast day celebration for Saint Rocco, by Barb Fenton, 2006. CIAPA Archive. PCCLI5672

Villano

Salvatore "Sal" Villano Jr.

Salvatore "Sal" Villano Jr. was born in 1938 to Salvatore Sr. and Olive (Harman) Villano. His paternal grandparents Raffaele "Ralph" and Josephina "Josephine" Villano were Italian immigrants who came to the United States in 1905 from Potenza, Italy.[767] An only son, Sal grew up in north Denver. "We were dirt poor," he says.[768] "My mother was actually my first boss. When I was eight years old she sent me door-to-door selling knitting and crocheting."[769] Sal attended Our Lady of Mount Carmel grade school and high school, where he drew recognition as a talented athlete. After graduating from Colorado State University with an education degree, he taught science and coached at Merrill Junior High. While teaching, he met and married his college sweetheart, Marilyn Mooney.[770]

Marilyn's father, Major General H. K. Mooney, convinced Sal to join the Air Force in 1966. After his officer training, Sal was commissioned as a second lieutenant. He was assigned to a student squadron in Biloxi, Mississippi, continuing his teaching career by preparing airmen for duty in Vietnam. Released from active duty in 1972, Sal completed his master's of science at George Washington University and joined the Colorado Air National Guard. He accepted an assignment at Buckley Air Force Base as a logistics officer and chief of maintenance.[771]

Brigadier General Sal Villano, after twenty-five years of service, retired from the Colorado Air National Guard in 1997. In 1998, he established the Forgotten Heroes Program, dedicated to the recognition of veterans from the wars in Korea and Vietnam.

Today, Sal Villano Jr. and his wife Marilyn live in Highlands Ranch, Colorado, and enjoy time spent with their five children: David, James, Edward, Susan, and Carol.[772]

Lieutenant Sal Villano Jr. getting his bars pinned on him by his wife Marilyn and his father-in-law, Major General H. K. Mooney, c. 1966. CIAPA Archive. Courtesy Sal Villano Jr. PCCLI4049

Appendix

Italian American Organizations in Colorado 2008

1. American Italian Cultural Club—Denver
2. Amici D'Italia—Denver
3. Amici Italiani (Queen of Peace)—Denver
4. Amici, University of Denver—Denver
5. Colorado Italian American Organization (CIAO)—Denver
6. Colorado Italian American Preservation Association (CIAPA)—Denver
7. Columbus Day Parade Committee—Denver
8. Dante Alighieri Society of Denver
9. Dante Alighieri Society of Pueblo
10. East Meets West Italian Club—Denver
11. Fiori D'Italia Club—Denver
12. Honorary Vice Consul of Italy (Maria E. Scordo Allen)—Denver
13. Italian Club of Trinidad
14. Il Circolo Italiano—Denver
15. Italian-American Business Association—Colorado
16. Italian Cultural Society, Inc.—Denver
17. Italians of America Cultural Society, North Denver
18. Italian Speaking Group—Denver
19. Knights of Columbus—Denver
20. La Famiglia Italiana—Pueblo
21. The Morra Society of Denver
22. Mother Cabrini Lodge No. 18—Denver
23. Società Nativi di Potenza Basilicata (Potenza Lodge)—Denver
24. Società Nativi di Potenza Basilicata (Potenza Lodge), Ladies' Auxiliary—Denver
25. Order of Basilone—Denver
26. Our Lady of Mount Carmel Church Men's Club—Denver
27. Our Lady of Mount Carmel Church Altar and Rosary Society—Denver
28. Order Sons of Italy, Grand Lodge
29. Order Sons of Italy, Lodge No. 2075—Denver
30. Order Sons of Italy, Lodge No. 2702 New Generation—Denver
31. Order Sons of Italy, Lodge No. 2738—Pueblo
32. Order Sons of Italy, Cabrini Lodge No. 2826—Pueblo
33. Order Sons of Italy, Lodge No. 139—Salida
34. Parliamo Italiano—Denver
35. Saint Anthony's Society—Denver
36. Saint Joseph Italian Lodge—Pueblo
37. Saint Michael's Society—Denver
38. Sister City Potenza Committee—Denver
39. Society of Italian Americans—Louisville
40. Tirolian Trentini di Colorado—Denver

Notes

Endnote Key
Colorado Historical Society
- Abbreviation CHS.

Book References - Five books provided a generous amount of information included in this research. They are:
- Dr. Giovanni Perilli, *Il Colorado e gl'Italiani nel Colorado/Colorado and the Italians in Colorado* (Denver, CO: Giovanni Perilli, 1922)
    - After first reference, will be cited as:
        - Perilli
- Marcello Gandolfo, *Gli Italiani nel Colorado, 1899–1900* (Denver, CO: Dover, 1900)
    - After first reference, will be cited as:
        - Gandolfo
- *Attività Italiane nella Intermountain Region* (Salt Lake City, UT: International Publishing Company, 1930)
    - After first reference, will be cited as:
        - *Attività*
- Our Lady of Mount Carmel, *Our Lady of Mount Carmel*, Denver, CO (So. Hackensack, NJ: Custombook, Inc., 1975)
    - After first reference, will be referred to as:
        - Mount Carmel History, 1975.
- Joanne West Dodds, *100th Anniversary Celebration: Pueblo, Colorado* (Pueblo, CO: My Friend, The Printer, Inc., in association with The Order Sons of Italy in America, Southern Colorado Lodge No. 2738, 2005.)
    - After first reference will be cited as:
        - Dodds

Census References
- Most U.S. Bureau of the Census records were accessed on the Ancestry.com website. All U.S. Bureau of the Census records will be abbreviated to USBC, date Federal Census, and location.

Newspaper References
- *Rocky Mountain News* (Denver, CO)
    - Will be cited as: *RMN*
- *The Denver Post* (Denver, CO)
    - Will be cited as: *DP*
- *The Denver Catholic Register* (Denver, CO)
    - Will be cited as: *DCR*

Colorado Italian American Preservation Association (CIAPA)
CIAPA Archive, Denver, CO
- The archive contains materials on families, businesses and traditions of Italians in Colorado, as well as oral histories, artifacts, photographs, ephemera, family memoirs, and genealogical data actively collected over a five-year period (2002–2007). The archive spans a timeline from approximately 1850 to the present. These files provide primary source research materials collected, archived, and stored by the Colorado Historical Society (CHS) staff and community volunteers. The archive is available for research purposes at the CHS, Stephen H. Hart Library (SHL), and the Colorado History Museum. The collection continues to grow.
- The CIAPA Archive files and oral histories served as primary reference material for the development of many of the family histories in this publication.
- If an endnote contains a citation for "CIAPA Archive," the citation source will always be the

Notes

- CIAPA Archive housed at the Colorado Historical Society's Stephen H. Hart Library, Denver, CO.
- Initial CIAPA Archive Citation Formats
  - Archive Files (project documentation forms, family genealogy, etc.)
    - Joann Zamboni CIAPA Archive File.
  - Oral Histories
    - Bonnie Garramone, CIAPA Archive OH with Julie Anderies, Ja 1, 88.
  - Interviews (the use of the term "interview" is included in an endnote citation to indicate that an interview—including telephone interviews or conversations where notes were taken but no recorded interview exists—occurred, however, no tape exists in the CIAPA Archive, only the notes from the interview)
    - Louis Albi, interview by Tom Noel, F 6 and 8, 1975. Peter Albi Family CIAPA Archive File.
  - Document Citations (unpublished papers, incomplete newspaper citations)
    - "Snow in the Rockies" (any known information about citation), CIAPA Archive NC, Joann Zamboni File.
- All subsequent CIAPA Archive references will be cited as:
  - Archive Files (project documentation forms, family genealogy, etc.)
    - Joann Zamboni CIAPA Archive File.
  - Oral Histories
    - Bonnie Garramone, CIAPA Archive OH by Julie Anderies, Ja 1, 88.
  - Document Citations (unpublished papers, incomplete newspaper citations)
    - "Snow in the ..."
  - Abbreviations for CIAPA document names:
    - Oral History: OH
    - Incomplete or unidentified newspaper clippings: NC
    - Unpublished Papers: UP

Chapter One

1. Margherita Marchione, *The Adventurous Life of Philip Mazzei* (Lanham, MD: University Press of America, 1995), 19.
2. Giovanni Perilli, *Il Colorado e gl'Italiani nel Colorado/Colorado and The Italians in Colorado* (Denver, CO: Giovanni Perilli, 1922), 25.
3. "Two Day Opening," *RMN*, S 7, 1881, p 4, c 2. Note: The author was unable to determine why the name Garbarino appears as Garbareno on the Union Depot Exchange Building and in the *RMN* article.
4. "Old Timer Dead," *Boulder Daily Camera* (Boulder, CO), N, 1904.
5. "Eagle Restaurant," *Daily Colorado Republican and Rocky Mountain Herald* (Denver, CO), N 9, 1861.
6. "Local and Miscellaneous," *Weekly Commonwealth and Republican* (Denver, CO), Vol. 4, No. 14, Ag 20, 1863.
7. "Star Restaurant," *RMN*, morning edition, D 29, 1872.
8. Correspondence between Marty Miles and Tom Noel, D 24, 1994, Louis Garbarino CIAPA Archive File.
9. John Louis Garbarino CIAPA Archive File.
10. Correspondence between Marty Miles and Tom Noel, D 24, 1994, Louis Garbarino CIAPA Archive File.
11. Gene Veronesi, *Italian-Americans and Their Communities of Cleveland* (Cleveland State University Library, print edition, 1977, scanned for web as e-book by Pacific Data 2003), http://web.ulib.scuohio.edu/italians/table.html (accessed 4/19/2006), e-book, 90.

Chapter Two

12. Vincenza Scarpaci, *The Portrait of Italians in America* (New York, NY: Charles Scribner's Sons, 1982), xiv.
13. "Marched Along Together 70 Years, But Only One Came Back This Time," *RMN*, O 28, 1933, p 1, 4 c 3.
14. Janet Goodwin CIAPA Archive File.
15. Perilli, 27.

16. "Grand Festival," *RMN*, O 14, 1873, 4.
17. Angelo Capelli CIAPA Archive File. Archive file contains a copy of the 1880 Arapahoe County Grantee Book showing Losasso land purchase witnessed by Capelli and a copy of the Vignola Marriage Certificate issued by Sacred Heart of Mary Church showing Capelli as witness.
18. "Mr. Angelo Capelli," *RMN*, F 20, 1881, p 8, c 1.
19. USBC, *1920 Federal Census,* Welby, Adams, Colorado.
20. Wilber Fiske Stone, *History of Colorado* (Chicago, IL: S.J. Clarke, 1918–19), 579.
21. Alice (Gacetta) Nichol CIAPA Archive File.
22. Ibid.
23. Perilli, 27 and 181.
24. Colorado Genealogical Society, *Colorado Families: A Territorial Heritage* (Denver, CO: Colorado Genealogical Society, 1982), 155-156.
25. Perilli, 37.
26. Marcello Gandolfo, *Gli Italiani nel Colorado*, 1899–1900 (Denver, CO: Dove, 1900), 45-46.
27. "Marched Along Together 50 Years: But Only One Came Back This Time," *RMN*, O 29, 1933.
28. Ralph F. Mancinelli CIAPA Archive File; Ralph F. Mancinelli, CIAPA Archive OH with Alisa Zahller, Jl 8, 2004.
29. Perilli, 28.
30. Mary (DiLuzio) DeBell CIAPA Archive File; Mary (DiLuzio) DeBell, CIAPA Archive OH with Clair Villano, Ja 26, 2004.
31. Ibid.
32. Ibid.
33. Clyde R. Archer CIAPA File; Clyde R. Archer, CIAPA Archive OH with Bonnie Garramone and Ralph Mancinelli, Mr 28, 2005.
34. Ibid.
35. Ibid.
36. Tony DeBell, *Autobiography* c. 1950, Ralph F. Mancinelli CIAPA Archive File.
37. Ibid.
38. Ibid.
39. Guerrieri Family CIAPA Archive File; Carol Tucker Andrix CIAPA Archive File. According to Carol Tucker Andrix, Vincent had a twin brother named Ralph who died in his teens (prior to 1880 when a family portrait was taken in Leadville that does not include Ralph, who would have been sixteen at the time). It is unknown if he remained in Italy or came to the United States with his brothers.
40. Perilli, 37.
41. "Vincent Guerrieri" obituary, *RMN*, D 6, 1949.
42. Office of Archeology and Historic Preservation, Site Files Guerrieri-DeCunto House, 5DV.147, S 10, 1979, CHS, Denver, CO.
43. Colorado Genealogical Society. *Colorado Families: A Territorial Heritage*, p 358-359.
44. John Edward McEahern, "A Short Family History" (Class paper for Professor Tom Noel, History 370, Denver, 1977), p 2, Siro Mangini CIAPA Archive File.
45. John Edward McEahern CIAPA Archive File.
46. Colorado Genealogical Society, *Colorado Families: A Territorial Heritage*, p 159.
47. Ibid., 359.
48. "Denver Maka Da Macaron: Only Macaroni Factory Between Kansas City and the Coast is Located Here Supplying Big Territory," *The Denver Times*, F 2, 1902, p 28, c 6.
49. Gandolfo, 48-51.
50. USBC, *1900 Federal Census,* Denver, Arapahoe, Colorado.
51. "Italian Residents of Denver Organize into Six Societies," *The Denver Times*, N 17, 1901, p 24.
52. Ibid.
53. Elizabeth (Ruote) Pelegrin CIAPA Archive File. This file contains Ruota family photographs and documents including the Potenza marriage record for Rocco and Arcangela dated Ag 7, 1887, which lists the age of the bride and groom, their occupation, and that they were illiterate.
54. USBC, *1900 Federal Census,* Denver, Arapahoe, Colorado.
55. *Denver City Directory, 1880–1889* (Corbett, Hoyt & Company: Denver, CO).

56. *Denver City Directory, 1890*, [database on-line]. (Provo, UT, USA: MyFamily.com, Inc., 2000).
57. Perilli, 33.
58. Ibid., 34.
59. Gandolfo, 54-57.
60. "Sons of Colorado: Joseph Turre Obituary," *The Trail Magazine*, Jl, 1909, No. 2, 21.
61. Office of Archeology and Historic Preservation, Site Files, J. Turre Building, 5DV.64, My 2, 1990, CHS, Denver, CO.
62. Angelo Vignola CIAPA Archive File. Contains research notes by Bonnie Garramone and Vignola land, citizenship, and marriage documents.
63. Obituary for Father Guida, *RMN*, My 25, 1919, p 11, c 5.
64. Thomas J. Noel, *Colorado Catholicism and the Archdiocese of Denver 1857–1989* (University Press of Colorado, 1989), 342.
65. Ibid.
66. Pasquale Vitullo CIAPA Archive File. Contains census records, newspaper articles and research notes by Bonnie Garramone.
67. Irene G. (Fallico) Falbo Fanning CIAPA Archive File. Irene G. (Fallico) Falbo Fanning, CIAPA Archive OH with Alisa Zahller, Jl 8, 2003.

Chapter Three

68. Ben Morreale and Robert Carola, *Italian Americans: The Immigrant Experience* (China: Hugh Lauter Levin Associates, Inc., Beaux Arts Editions, 2000), 51.
69. "Awaiting Millions," *RMN*, O 24, 1892.
70. "Broadway Theater," *The Denver Republican*, Ag 3, 1890, p 17, c 1-c.
71. Albino Abbiati Family CIAPA Archive File. File includes research paper by Julie Anderies, "Albino Abbiati: Cultural Pioneer in Denver" (University of Denver, N 23, 2004).
72. "Albino Abbiati, Denver Artist, Has Passed Away," *DP*, S 25, 1909, p 2.
73. Ralph Acierno CIAPA Archive File. Contains a copy of the 1881 Potenza marriage record for Angelo and Antonia Acierno.
74. Palma Rose Finney, *The Family Book: Ursetta, Veraldi, Piccoli, Acierno* (Baltimore, MD: Gateway Press, Inc., 1979), 111.
75. "Mrs. Antonia Acierno Obituary," *RMN*, M 24, 1935, p 6.
76. "Salvatore & Della Acierno – 1924," *Our Lady of Mount Carmel Church Bulletin*, F 19, 1995 (copy in Ralph Acierno CIAPA Archive File).
77. Ralph Acierno, CIAPA Archive OH with Bonnie Garramone and Frank Palmeri, Jl 8, 2004; Ralph Acierno CIAPA Archive File.
78. George Victor Mazzotti CIAPA Archive File; George Victor Mazzotti, CIAPA Archive OH with Alisa Zahller, Je 8, 2005.
79. "Northern Colorado's forgotten railroad," *Denver Post, Empire Magazine*, F 9, 1975, 32.
80. Albin Wagner, *Adams County: Crossroads of the West* (Denver, CO: Century Graphics, 1977), 36.
81. Albin Wagner, *Adams County, Colorado: A Centennial History 1902–2002* (Virginia Beach, VA: Donning, 2002), 118.
82. Our Lady of the Assumption, *Our Lady of the Assumption 1912–1987* (Denver, CO: Montano Brothers Printing, 1987), 9. A copy of this book along with other information on the history of Welby and Assumption parish are included in the Colorado Historical Society's Stephen H. Hart Library manuscript collection, MSS 3015.
83. Rocco and Violet (Acierno) Astuno CIAPA Archive File.
84. Rocco and Violet (Acierno) Astuno, CIAPA Archive OH with Bonnie Garramone, Ja 31, 2006.
85. "Great Host of Sorrowing Friends at Funeral of Camillo Aiello," *The Trinidad Chronicle*, My 10, 1920.
86. Claudia Carbone Family CIAPA Archive File.
87. Claudia Carbone, "Myth or Murder: The Mystery Surrounding the Death of Trinidad's Camillo Aiello," *Andiamo!*, My/Je 2006, 10, 11.
88. Claudia Carbone, "Carbone Wine," *Andiamo!*, Mr/Ap 2006, 16.
89. "Anthony Carbone Dies at Hospital," *DP*, Je 12, 1930, 20. Claudia Carbone CIAPA Archive File.
90. *Attività Italiane nella Intermountain Region* (Salt Lake City, UT: International Publishing Company, 1930), 207.

91. *Souvenir Edition of A. Carbone & Company,* A. Carbone & Company, 1942. Claudia Carbone CIAPA Archive File.
92. "Drug Firm Buys Carbone & Company Liquor Business for $2,000,000," *RMN,* Ja 28, 1953.
93. Gandolfo, 37-40.
94. Louis Albi, interview by Tom Noel, F 6 and 8, 1975. Peter Albi Family CIAPA Archive File.
95. "Peter Albi, First Italian 'Consul' in Denver, Succumbs," *DP,* My 5, 1936.
96. Ibid.
97. "I Will Lay Me Down in Peace," *RMN,* O 24, 1952, p 75.
98. Perilli, 47.
99. The Colorado Press Association, Inc., *Who's Who in Colorado* (Boulder, CO: University of Colorado, 1938), 201.
100. "Italy Honors Dr. Rudolph Albi," *RMN,* O 23, 1949, 34.
101. Dr. Rudolph Albi CIAPA Archive File; Dr. Rudolph L. deLuise CIAPA Archive File.
102. Charles "Chuck" H. Albi CIAPA Archive File.
103. Charles H. Albi, Charles Abli family history, Mr 1, 2005, p 2, Charles "Chuck" H. Albi CIAPA Archive File.
104. Ralph Albi CIAPA Archive File; Charles "Chuck" H. Albi CIAPA Archive File.
105. Joseph R. "Joe" Albi, "The Life of Ralph Albi," n.d. Ralph Albi CIAPA Archive File.
106. Frank J. Albi, "Frank Samuel Albi: Mr 13, 1899–D 25, 1992," n.d. Frank Albi CIAPA Archive File.
107. Charles "Chuck" H. Albi CIAPA Archive File. Contains biographical information on Salvatore "Sam" Natale Albi provided by Charles Albi.
108. "Coal Making A Comeback," *DP,* My 21, 1973, 37.
109. Michael B. Albi CIAPA Archive File. Archive file contains biographical information on Michael Albi submitted by Roberta Albi and Charles Albi.
110. Ann Chiolero, "Peter Chiolero Family Biography, 1851–1917," (Brief family history written for the Colorado Historical Society, Ap 20, 2006). Ann Chiolero CIAPA Archive file.
111. "Frank Damascio" obituary, *Evening Picketwire,* My 31, 1922, 4.
112. Sebastian J. Sinisi, "North Denver's Unwavering Italians," *The Sunday Denver Post, Contemporary Magazine,* My 16, 1982, 10-15.
113. Sebastian J. Sinisi, "Old Damascio House Visually Impressive," *DP,* M 15, 1980, 33-35.
114. Perilli, 49.
115. Frank Damascio and Mary Louise (Damascio) Keating CIAPA Archive Files.
116. Perilli, 47 and 48.
117. "They Came a Long Way, Baby: Italians in Denver," *DCR,* O 11, 1978, 8A and 10A.
118. Damascio Family History, Mary Lou (Damascio) Keating, n.d. Mary Lou (Damascio) Keating CIAPA Archive File.
119. Frank J. Francone, *The Carlo Francone-Caterina Alberti Families of San Benigno Canavese, Piemonte, Italy ancestors and Descendants 1645–1997* (Colorado: Frank J. Francone, 1997), Chapter 1, 17.
120. Ibid., Chapter 1, 19 and 21.
121. Ibid., Chapter 3 and 5.
122. Ibid., Chapter 3 and 7.
123. Frank J. Francone, *The Plume on Their Cappello* (Colorado: Frank J. Francone, 2006), 47-49; Frank J. Francone CIAPA Archive File.
124. Francone, *The Plume on Their Cappello,* 1.
125. Ibid., 4.
126. Ibid., 12.
127. *Statuto-Regolamento della Società Bersaglieri di Savoia in Silver Plume, Colo.* (Chicago, IL: Società Bersaglieri di Savoia in Silver Plume, CO, 1889), 11-12. George Rowe Museum, Silver Plume, CO, collection catalog no. A 890123A-C.
128. Perilli, 27.
129. Ibid., 38.
130. "Ag L. Mattei" obituary, *RMN,* F 7, 1960, 51.
131. Horan Burial Record, Denver, CO, "Frank Morrato" Mr 17, 1937.

132. "Do Honor to Whom, Honor is Due," *America*, O, 1923, 15.
133. USBC, *1900 Federal Census,* Denver, Arapahoe, Colorado.
134. "Do Honor to Whom, Honor is Due," *America*, O, 1923, 15.
135. "Morrato Block," *America*, Mr 1924, 17.
136. "Death Takes Pioneer," *DP*, Mr 17, 1937.
137. "Michael Notary" obituary, *RMN*, Je 20, 1935, 5A.
138. Sacred Heart Catholic Church Marriage Register, Vol. 1, 1879–1892. Michele Notary CIAPA Archive File.
139. USBC, *1900 Federal Census,* Denver, Arapahoe, Colorado.
140. Our Lady of Mount Carmel, *Our Lady of Mount Carmel Denver, Colorado* (So. Hackensack, NJ: Custombook, Inc. 1975), 17.
141. Perilli, 80.
142. "Mrs. Rosie Notary, Long Time Resident of Denver, is Dead," *RMN*, N 4, 1911, 3.
143. "Residents of Denver Organized into Six Italian Societies," *The Denver Times*, N 17, 1901, 24.
144. *Mount Carmel History,* 1975, 54.
145. Harold Benoit (grandson of Antonio Pavoni), interview with Julie Anderies, Ja 25, 2006.
146. "Anthony [Antonio] Pavoni" obituary, *RMN*, D 22, 1939, 6.
147. "Anthony [Antonio] Pavoni, 73, 50 Years in Denver Dies From Illness," obituary, *DP*, D 22, 1939, 7.
148. Antonio Pavoni CIAPA Archive File.

Chapter Four

149. Michael G. Buccino CIAPA Archive File.
150. Angelina Buccino, CIAPA Archive OH with Frank Palmeri, Je 8, 2005.
151. Michael G. Buccino, "The Artistic Ability of the Michael Buccino Family" Ja 3, 2006, p 1. Michael G. Buccino CIAPA Archive File.
152. Ralph Long CIAPA Archive File.
153. USBC, *1910 and 1920 Federal Census,* Denver, Colorado; *1920 Federal Census,* Denver, Colorado.
154. Perilli, 35.
155. Ibid., 29.
156. Ancestry.com, U.S. Military Records, *United States World War I Draft Registration Card A*, Je 5, 1917 [database on-line]. Provo, UT, USA: MyFamily.com, Inc., 2005.
157. USBC, *1910 Federal Census,* Precinct 6, Denver, Colorado.
158. Perilli, 47.
159. Research notes Alisa Zahller, Clair Villano and Adrianne Christine Trunk. Nick Cavarra CIAPA Archive File.
160. *Mount Carmel History,* 1975, 9.
161. Esther (Colacito) Head, Family History, O 17, 2006, p 1 and 2. Esther (Colacito) Head CIAPA Archive File.
162. USBC, *1920 Federal Census,* Denver, Colorado; USBC, *1930 Federal Census,* Denver, Colorado.
163. USBC, *1930 Federal Census,* Denver, Colorado.
164. Ibid.
165. Denver Metro Amateur Softball Association Hall of Fame Program, 1984, p 12; Lucille (Appugliese) Colacito CIAPA Archive File.
166. Bud Wells, "Lou Colacito 'caught' scout's eye," *RMN,* Ag 8, 1996, 11S.
167. Research notes Alisa Zahller and Nicole Makinster; Lucille (Appugliese) Colacito CIAPA Archive File.
168. USBC, *1910 Federal Census,* Precinct 3, Denver, Colorado.
169. George DeRose, "Denver and Italian Immigrants," (Public History Course Paper, Denver, Ag 7, 1987), p 2. CHS, SHL.
170. Dick DeRose CIAPA Archive File; Dick DeRose, CIAPA Archive OH with Alisa Zahller, Ja 10, 2006.
171. Dan Fante CIAPA Archive File; research notes Claudia Carbone and Alisa Zahller, Dan Fante CIAPA Archive File.
172. John Fante, *Wait Until Spring, Bandini* (Black Sparrow Press, Santa Rosa: CA, 2001), biographical sketch page, 269.

173. David McQuay, "John Fante finally famous," *DP*, Jl 18, 1989.
174. Ibid.
175. Marie (Ferrero) Cosimi CIAPA Archive File.
176. Marie (Ferrero) Cosimi, CIAPA Archive OH with Alisa Zahller, My 4, 2004.
177. USBC, *1920 Federal Census*, Welby, Adams, Colorado.
178. Lawrence Lotito, "Rocco Lotito Family History: Ap 3, 1887–Ap 14, 1967" (family history, 1995); Lawrence Lotito CIAPA Archive File; Lucille (Lotito) Pesce CIAPA Archive file.
179. Ellen Aiken, "A Place Called Arvada" (Booklet of the Arvada Historical Society), n.d.
180. Lucille (Lotito) Pesce CIAPA Archive File.
181. Elana Ashanti Jefferson, "The Immigrants, The Mancinellis, 1906," *DP*, Je 16, 2002, 4L.
182. "Her colorful life is a lesson in history," *DCR*, O 4, 1989, 21 and 25.
183. USBC, *1920 Federal Census*, West New Castle, Garfield, CO.
184. "Italian market calls it quits," *La Gazzetta Italiana* (Denver, CO), Vol. 1, No. 3, O/N, 1993, 1 and 6.
185. Gary Massaro, "Owner of Italian deli hanging up his cleaver," *RMN*, S 17, 1993, 4A.
186. Molly Sweeney, "Family Market Endures Change," *Denver Magazine* (Denver, CO), Ag, 1989, S-4, S-5.
187. Frances Melrose, "Catching up with a Golden Gloves legend," *RMN*, Jl 4, 1999.
188. Albert "Ice" and Marie Mancinelli, CIAPA Archive OH with Alisa Zahller, N 18, 2003.
189. Albert "Ice" and Marie Mancinelli CIAPA Archive File.
190. Frank Mancini CIAPA Archive File.
191. "Frank Mancini Sr. working man's hero," *DRC* (Denver, CO), 22.
192. Aldo Notarianni CIAPA Archive File.
193. Rosemary Donofrio Canino Ricci, "Genealogy of Rosina Mastroianni" (Family history, before 1950), Rosalyn A. (Mastroianni) Hirsch CIAPA Archive File.
194. Rosalyn A. (Mastroianni) Hirsch CIAPA Archive File.
195. Umberto Morganti's passport, 1907. Morganti Family CIAPA Archive File.
196. Noemi's Italian Republic Passport and Italian Passport give her maiden name, Rossetti. Morganti Family CIAPA Archive File.
197. "Victor Morganti" obituary, *DP*, Ag 6, 1958, 34; "Manlio Rossetti" obituary, *RMN*, 1952; "Sister of Denverite is dead in London," Morganti CIAPA Archive File.
198. "Denver Immigrants Recall Time on Ellis Island," *RMN*, O 7, 1956, 76.
199. Ibid.
200. "Famed Photographer Dies at 82," *RMN*, Mr 21, 1965, 47.
201. Copies of Italian newspapers published and edited by Umberto and Cesare Morganti. Morganti CIAPA Archive File.
202. Lois Cress, "The Gallant Morgantis: 60 Happy Years Together," *DP*, Ja 15, 1961, 4D.
203. Hafen, *Colorado and Its People* (Denver, CO: 1948), Vol. 4, 410.
204. "Morgantis Celebrate 50 Years of Marriage," *RMN*, Ja 14, 1951, 22.
205. "Umberto Morganti" obituary, *DP*, Mr 21, 1965, 72; Pasquale Marranzino, "Stirring Sad, Lovely Memories," *RMN*, Ja 1, 1968, 47.
206. "Cesare Morganti Photographer, dies," *RMN*, Je 4, 1983, 118.
207. "Cesare E. Morganti" Obituary, *DP*, Je 4, 1983, 6E.
208. Luanne Johansen, "Historical find called a 'gold mine'," *Greeley Tribune* (Greeley, CO), Ag 9, 1979, A-2.
209. Debbie (Spaulding) Fugate and Sandra (Morganti) Spaulding CIAPA Archive File; Dave Lubbers CIAPA Archive File.
210. "Sunsets and Sunrises: Morganti exhibition begins Monday at GNB," NC, 1976. Morganti Family CIAPA Archive File.
211. Gerrie Grabow, "Umberto Morganti Continues to Captivate Hearts of S.F. Seniors After 21 Years," NC, 1976. Morganti Family CIAPA Archive File.
212. Perilli, 14.
213. Angelo Noce CIAPA Archive File.
214. Barbara Browne, "2 Italians Left Deep Imprint on Denver," *RMN*, O, 22, 1957, 32.

215. Perilli, 15; Angelo Noce, *Columbus Day in Colorado* (Denver, CO: Angelo Noce).
216. Doug Nassif, "Angelo Noce: Columbus Day founder," *Twin Circle* (location unknown), O 18, 1974, 1.
217. Angelo Noce: 1905–1920 Manuscript Collection MSS 2511, CHS, SHL, 97003885.
218. "Funeral for Angelo Noce, Italian Printer, To be Held in California," *RMN*, Ja 6, 1922, 4.
219. "Largest Individual Shareholder Dies," *News Lines, Public Service Company*, Vol. 6, No. 19, (Denver, CO), N 8, 1979, 1.
220. Mildred (Pastore) LaConte and Corrine (LaConte) Bush CIAPA Archive File.
221. *Mount Carmel History*, 1975.
222. John Pollice CIAPA Archive File.
223. "Musician, 72, Feted Here By Usaly's," *DP*, N 10, 1948, 25.
224. Ralph Paul Santangelo, CIAPA Archive OH with Bonnie Garramone, F 1, 2006.
225. Perilli, 31.
226. Chamberlain, "The last of North Denver's vegetable peddlers," *Denver Post Empire Magazine* (Denver, CO), D 17, 1978, 20.
227. Ralph Santangelo and Al Santangelo CIAPA Archive File.
228. Jack Phinney, "Grocers Long on Years, Big on Variety," *DP*, O 2, 1976, 23.
229. Vallero Mercantile Catalog 2004–2005, Denver, CO. Vallero Mercantile CIAPA Archive Files.
230. Michael C. and Clair Villano CIAPA Archive File. Contains Paul J. Villano and the Michael C. Villano family histories.
231. Paul Joseph Villano Sr., interview by Michael C. Villano Jr., 1975; Clair Villano (research paper in Sociology Urban Studies class, University of Colorado at Denver, 1975). Paul Joseph Villano CIAPA Archive File.
232. Michael C. Villano, CIAPA Archive OH with Clair E. Villano, Mr 31, 2005.
233. *Attività*, 209.
234. USBC, *1910 Federal Census*, Pueblo, Colorado, Ward 7.
235. Dodds, 33.
236. John Morton, publisher, *2nd Annual Grand Reunion of States and Countries* (Pueblo, CO: Opera House Block, 1898).
237. Gandolfo, 139.
238. USBC, *1910 Federal Census*, Pueblo, Colorado, Ward 6.
239. Pauline Annette DiSipio CIAPA Archive File.
240. Dodds, 41.
241. *Attività*, 215.
242. Ibid., 214.
243. John Panepinto CIAPA Archive File.
244. Dodds, 42.
245. Ralph C. Taylor, "At 100, Occhiato Looks Back on Accomplishments," *Pueblo Star-Journal*, (CO), S 17, 1978.
246. Ibid., 43.
247. *Attività*, 229.
248. Rose Marie Occhiato. Rose Occhiato CIAPA Archive OH with Claire Marie (Mauro) TeBockhorst, Mr 2, 2006.
249. John Panepinto CIAPA Archive File.
250. USBC, *1930 Federal Census*, Pueblo, Colorado.
251. Dodds, 45.
252. Ibid.
253. Richard Bonacquista (At some point after settling in America, some of the descendants of Margaret and Ambrogio Bonacquisti changed the spelling of their last name to Bonacquista), CIAPA Archive OH with Alisa Zahller and Yvonne Tricarico, Ja 26, 2006.
254. Ibid., 4.
255. Richard Bonacquista CIAPA Archive File.
256. Veronica (Marta) Goodrich CIAPA Archive File.

257. Veronica (Marta) Goodrich, "Marta Family," 9/15/2006, from 101 Trinidad Area Family Histories, collected by Allen Bachoroski, *Tales Along the Highway of Legends*. "Trinidad Colorado: An Historic Old West Victorian Town" on the Santa Fe Trail website: http://www.trinidadcocom/101Families/Families/Marta.asp.

258. Veronica (Marta) Goodrich CIAPA Archive File.

259. Loretta Bonino Rawlins and Veronica (Marta) Goodrich, "Bonino Family," 10/16/2006, from 101 Trinidad Area Family Histories, collected by Allen Bachoroski, *Tales Along the Highway of Legends*. "Trinidad Colorado: An Historic Old West Victorian Town" on the Santa Fe Trail website: http://www.trinidadcocom/101Families/Families/Bonino.asp.

260. Angela Ann Cesario, "Cesario/Vallone Family History For Italians in Colorado" Angela Ann Cesario CIAPA Archive File. Contains the Al and Mary (Vallone) Cesario, Angela Ann Cesario, and Francesco and Angela (Marretta) Vallone family histories.

261. Colorado Genealogical Society, *Colorado Marriages 1858–1939 CD: Index of Denver Public Library*, Denver CO: Colorado Genealogical Society, 2004. p 12, 519.

262. Jocelyn Cessar, "First Church of the Nazarene unveils new sign," *The Chronicle-News* (Trinidad, CO), Ap 25, 2006, 4.

263. Angela Ann Cesario, "Going from Trinidad to Berkeley," Je 30, 2006, Angela Ann Cesario CIAPA Archive File.

264. "Francesco Vallone Dies Wednesday at Pueblo," Angela Ann Cesario CIAPA Archive File.

265. Tom Cimino, "Dominico and Mary Cimino, Century Family," 11/8/2006, *Tales Along the Highway of Legends*…

266. Jay Cimino CIAPA Archive File. This file includes research by Colleen M. O'Dwyer and Alisa Zahller and correspondence between Jay Cimino and Mary Ann (Cimino) Johnson and Alisa Zahller.

267. Michelle Narron, "Jay Cimino," (Biography for Phil Long Dealerships, 2005). Jay Cimino CIAPA Archive File.

268. *Attività*, 228.

269. Eugene Maio and Silvia (Maio) Lackey CIAPA Archive Files.

270. Dr. Eugene A. Maio, "Giuseppe Maio," 6/22/06, *Tales Along the Highway of Legends*…

271. Copies of *Corriere di Trinidad* are available on microfilm at SHL at CHS.

272. "Giuseppe G. Maio" obituary, *The Morning Light* (Trinidad, CO), S 19, 1941.

273. Charles Latuda (son of Frank Latuda), telephone interview with Alisa Zahller, N 13, 1906. Charles Latuda CIAPA Archive File.

274. Vincenza Scarpaci, e-mail message to author, Ja 20, 2007. Charles Latuda, CIAPA Archive File.

275. Charles Latuda CIAPA Archive File.

276. *Attività*, 216.

277. Mary Bernarda Scavotto CIAPA Archive File. File includes research notes by Paula Manini.

278. Pat Donachy, "Recent trend toward midwifery nothing new to Mrs. Mendine," *Pueblo, Chieftan* (Pueblo, CO), My 10, 1980.

279. USBC, *1920 Federal Census*, Seattle, King, Washington.

Chapter Five

280. Chubby Aiello CIAPA Archive OH transcript with Kim Kendrick and Lisa D. Olken for PBS, 1999.

281. USBC, *1910 Federal Census*, Denver, Colorado; USBC, *1920 Federal Census*, Denver, Colorado.

282. *The Mount Carmel Eagle*, (Denver, CO), "Meet Mrs. Canino," F/Mr 1968.

283. John Polly, "White Wings," *RMN*, Ja 29, 1939.

284. Clair Villano to Alisa Zahller, Ja 20, 2007, Frank Canino CIAPA Archive File.

285. Rose (Canino) Villano CIAPA Archive File.

286. USBC, *1920 Federal Census*, Sharpsburg, Allegheny, Pennsylvania.

287. Patricia Callahan, "Building Generations: Northside a haven for immigrants," *DP*, Ag 10, 1997, 2.

288. Anthony "Tony" J. Canino, CIAPA Archive OH with Frank Palmeri, Je 10, 2003.

289. Tony Canino CIAPA Archive File.

290. Thomas Jacob Noel, *Mile High City* (Denver, CO: Hirschfeld Press, 1997), 492.

291. Roger Fillion, "Canino Sausage turns 80: Couple's Old World recipe still popular in a new age," *RMN*, 3C.

292. Sonia Weiss, *Denver Metro 2000: A Millennium Celebration* (Carlsbad, CA: Heritage Media Corporation, 2000), 259.
293. Diana Payne CIAPA Archive File.
294. Colorado Genealogical Society, *Colorado Marriages 1858–1939 CD: Index* (Denver, CO: Denver Public Library, 2004), 3,073.
295. USBC, *1910 Federal Census*, Precinct 10, Denver, Colorado; USBC, *1930 Federal Census*, Denver, Colorado.
296. Linda Castrone, "Clyde Canino: Grandfather's determination set Canino standard," *DP*, N 21, 2003.
297. Ibid.
298. Clyde G. Canino CIAPA Archive File.
299. Bonnie Schuldt, "Cerrone's 'Little Italy' Grocery Store Holds Out," *DP*, O 7, 1981, 4.
300. Daniel Shosky, "A Short History of A.T. Cerrone's Market: From Italian Market to Milongas," *Andiamo!* (Denver, CO), Mr/A 2005, 21.
301. USBC, *1930 Federal Census*, Denver, Colorado.
302. Mildred Cerrone CIAPA Archive File; Mildred Cerrone, CIAPA Archive OH with Alisa Zahller, O 1, 2003.
303. KUSA Channel 9 News staff, "Carl Akers visits North Denver....." Script of 3-part news series, (Denver, CO, 1981). Cerrone's Market CIAPA Archive File.
304. "Cerrone's Grocery," *DCR*, O 9, 1984, 15.
305. Janet E. Worrall, "The Impact of the Ku Klux Klan and Prohibition on Denver's Little Italy," *Journal of the West*, Vol. 43, No. 4 (Fall 2004), 32–40.
306. Inez Allan, "Little Women of 'Little Italy' Eagerly Flock to Neighborhood House for Lessons in Sewing," *The Denver Times* (Denver, CO), O 30, 1909.
307. Louise DeBell CIAPA Archive File.
308. Antoinette (Martelli) Massimino, "Fruit Peddler Antonio Carabetta," D 19, 2006, Antoinette (Martelli) Massimino CIAPA Archive File.
309. Antoinette (Martelli) Massimino biographical sketch Sadie (Carabetta) and Frank Martelli, Antoinette (Martelli) Massimino CIAPA Archive File.
310. "Detective is Held for Murder of Corbetta Killed in Raid," *DP*, Je 11, 1919.
311. Some of Antonio and Antonia Carabetta's descendants went by the last name of Corbetta. By 1917, Jerry Carabetta had changed his name to Corbetta as evidenced by his 1917–18 World War I draft registration from on which he signed his name Jerry Corbetta. This would explain why newspaper accounts at the time of his death spell his last name Corbetta. Also, the newspapers list the business name Corbetta Bros. and Guida, indicating that other relatives also changed their names. Interestingly, Jerry's grave marker reads "Jerry Carabetta." It is likely that Jerry's parents Antonio and Antonia Carabetta selected and paid for the marker, which would explain the use of Carabetta on it.
312. "Detective is Held for Murder of Corbetta Killed in Raid," *DP*, Je 11, 1919.
313. Janet E. Worrall, "The Impact of the Ku Klux Klan and Prohibition on Denver's Little Italy," *Journal of the West*, Vol. 43, No. 4 (Fall 2004), 34.
314. *DP*, Je 10, 1919.
315. "2,000 Marching Italians Urge Vengeance for Jerry Corbetta," *DP*, Je 12, 1919.
316. "Jury Exonerates Klein, Corbetta's Friends Roused," *DP*, Je 13, 1919.
317. Anthony "Tony" Corbetta CIAPA Archive File. Includes research by Alisa Zahller, Bonnie Garramone, Janet Worrall, and Nicole Makinster.
318. Anthony F. Corbetta and Alice Piro, Anthony "Tony" Corbetta CIAPA Archive interview by Janet Worrall, Mr 4, 1995.
319. Ibid.
320. Frances (Carpenter) Sawyer CIAPA Archive File.
321. USBC, *1920 Federal Census*, Chicago Ward 19, Cook (Chicago), Illinois.
322. "Sam A. Carpenter" obituary, *RMN*, 1969.
323. "Recalls Mining Coal Here for 52 cents a Ton," *Louisville Times* (Louisville, CO) Ag 1, 1968, 3. (Reprinted from the Colorado *Trumpet*)
324. "Former Union, Demo Leader Recalls How He Helped Fenolia Get PM Job," NC, Sam and Emma Carpenter CIAPA Archive File.

325. "Recalls Mining Coal Here for 52 cents a Ton," *Louisville Times* (Louisville, CO) Ag 1, 1968, 3. (Reprinted from the Colorado *Trumpet*)

326. "Bailiff Named by Finesilver," NC, Sam and Emma Carpenter CIAPA Archive File.

327. Sam and Emma Carpenter CIAPA Archive File.

328. Fran Sawyer, e-mail message to author, S 4, 2006. Frances (Carpenter) Sawyer CIAPA Archive File.

329. Ibid.

330. Mark DiVecchio, website creator, *"Propsero Pio Frazzini and Family Genealogy Page,"* http://www.silogic.com/genealogy/Prospero_Frazzini.html, 11/24/2006, p 1.

331. Perilli, 50; "A Frazzini Dies After Operation," *DP*, F 25, 1912 (article notes Antonio died of appendicitis).

332. See Denver City Directory and Census listings from the DiVecchio website listed above. Copy of listings in the Prospero Frazzini CIAPA Archive File note the different business ventures the Frazzini family was involved in.

333. Perilli, 50.

334. Cesare Frazzini obituary, posted on the DiVecchio website under "Brother Cesare Frazzini." Copy of obituary in the Prospero Frazzini CIAPA Archive File.

335. "Police Throw Out Dragnet As Bank Head Disappears," *RMN*, Ja 30, 1925.

336. *Mount Carmel History*, 56.

337. "Thomas Nicoletti, Long-Time Denver Businessman, Dies," *DP*, D 5, 1929.

338. Juliet "Julie" (Nicoletti-Schray) Jiracek CIAPA Archive File. Includes the Joseph Nicoletti, Raffaele Riley and Marietta (Guida) Mauro family histories.

339. "Alleged Bootlegger and Whisky Seized," and "Visitor Fine $100 for Totin' Hootch But Gets $75 Back," NC, Juliet "Julie" (Nicoletti-Schray) Jiracek Archive File.

340. Juliet Jiracek, e-mail message to author, Ag 6, 2004, Juliet Jiracek CIAPA Archive File.

341. *Attività*, 225.

342. Aldo Notarianni CIAPA Archive File.

343. Aldo Notarianni, CIAPA Archive OH with Frank Palmeri, D 10, 2003; CIAPA Archive interview by Alisa Zahller, My 11, 2004.

344. USBC, *1920 Federal Census*, Denver, Colorado.

345. Patricia Callahan, "Building the Generations: Northside a haven for immigrants," *DP*, Ag 10, 1997, 1.

346. Ibid.

347. USBC, *1910 Federal Census*, Denver, Colorado.

348. Louis Zimmerman CIAPA Archive File.

349. Elaine (Zimmerman) Ciccone, CIAPA Archive OH with Frank Palmeri, Ag 8, 2004.

350. USBC, *1920 Federal Census*, Denver, Colorado.

351. Gus Levine, CIAPA Archive OH with Frank Palmeri, Ja 22, 2004.

352. Frank Palmeri, e-mail message to author, Ja 25, 2007. Edward K. Moore CIAPA Archive File.

353. Ibid.

354. "Elderly Woman in Denver Killed by Shock of Robbery," NC, Richard Rose CIAPA Archive File.

355. Richard Rose CIAPA Archive File.

356. D. R. Miller, "The Homicide of Officer Richie Rose (as I recall it)," *Code 109* (Publication of Denver Police Union Local 109, Denver CO), Vol. 10, No. 26, Ag 1981, 13-18. Richie Rose CIAPA Archive File.

357. Fran Sawyer for Richard Rose, e-mail message to author, D 17, 2006. Richie Rose CIAPA Archive File.

358. Stefania Massari, *English Guide for the Museo Nazionale Delle Arti e Tradizioni Popolair* (Roma, Italia: Museo Nazionale Delle Arti e Tradizioni Popolair Grafica, 2001), 166-171.

359. USBC, *1900 Federal Census*, Arapahoe County, Denver, Colorado.

360. Luigi Smaldone CIAPA Archive File.

361. According to the Denver City Directory for 1890, published by Ballenger and Richards, Luigi worked for the F. Mazza & Company as a laborer.

362. "Insane from Grief," *Il Roma* (Denver, CO), My 13, 1893.
363. Horan Mortuary Burial Records, Gaetano Smaldone, O 17, 1917. DPL, Western History/Genealogy Department.
364. USBC, *1930 Federal Census*, Denver, Colorado.
365. "The Funeral of Luigi Smaldone," *Il Roma* (Denver, CO), My 13, 1893.
366. "Married Half A Century," NC, Luigi Smaldone CIAPA Archive File.
367. Alisa Zahller, e-mail message to Luigi Smaldone and Pat Taylor, My 29, 2007. E-mail included revisions to text about Luigi's father Fiore and Fiore's work in Denver. Luigi Smaldone CIAPA Archive File.
368. Ibid.
369. USBC, *1900 Federal Census*, Arapahoe County, Denver, Colorado.
370. "'Wonderful Mother' Mrs. Smaldone Dies," *DP*, My 2, 1962, 3.
371. Eugene Smaldone CIAPA Archive File.
372. USBC, *1910 Federal Census*, Precinct 6, Denver, Colorado; *1920 Federal Census*, Denver, Colorado.
373. Eugene "Gene" C. Smaldone, CIAPA Archive OH with Bonnie Garramone (Alisa Zahller present), Ja 17, 2007.
374. Alisa Zahller, letter to Gene Smaldone, My 29, 2007. After several telephone calls and a meeting on My 9, 2007 revisions were made to the family history with new information including Clyde and Gene going to jail on behalf of their parents (this according to Clyde's son Gene).
375. Eugene "Gene" C. Smaldone, CIAPA Archive OH with Bonnie Garramone (Alisa Zahller present), Ja 17, 2007.
376. Charles "Chuck" Smaldone, telephone interview with Bonnie Garramone, Ja 17, 2007. Charles "Chuck" Smaldone CIAPA Archive File.
377. Claudia "CJ" (Smaldone) Foxx and Paul Smaldone CIAPA Archive Files.
378. Claudia "CJ" (Smaldone) Foxx, CIAPA Archive OH with Bonnie Garramone, F 27, 2007.
379. CJ Foxx, e-mail to the author, My 14, 2007, Claudia "CJ" (Smaldone) Foxx CIAPA Archive File.
380. William Gallo, "The twilight time of 'Checkers' Smaldone," *RMN*, O 31, 1982.
381. Dick Kreck, "Brother Hoods," *DP*, N 5, 2007.
382. Smaldone Brothers CIAPA Archive File.
383. Denver District Attorney's Office Organized Crime Unit, "Arrest Statistics and Activities of the Organized Crime Unit, Jl 1, 1969 to Jl 1, 1970" and the Denver Police Department, *Intelligence Bulletin*, Vol. 3, No. 2, Denver, CO, Ap 20, 1966.
384. Isabel (Veraldi) Vecchiarelli and Catherine (Veraldi) Hebert, CIAPA Archive OH with Frank Palmeri, Ap 7, 2007.
385. *Attività*, 236.
386. "Honor Veraldi For Leadership In Civic Works," NC, copy of article in the CHS, Eugene Veraldi Family CIAPA Archive File, Denver, CO.
387. "They Came A Long Way," *DCR,* O 11, 1978, 10A.

Chapter Six
388. Frank Busnardo, "Busnardo/Ferrero Family Reunion 1998" (Family History written for 1998 family reunion). Frank Busnardo CIAPA Archive File.
389. "Bravo, bravissimo, Busnardo!" *DCR,* O 5, 1994, 13.
390. Ibid.
391. Luciano Busnardo, CIAPA Archive OH with Bonnie Garramone, My 5, 2005.
392. "Welcoming Italians to Denver," *DCR,* O 7, 1987, 1.
393. George V. Kelly with Harry Farrar, *Garden of Hope: Laradon Hall* (Boulder, CO: Pruett Publishing Company, 1980), 2-6.
394. "Joe rolled up his sleeves," *DP,* Jl 30, 1986.
395. Vincent J. Taglialavore CIAPA Archive File.
396. Vincent J. Taglialavore, CIAPA Archive OH with Bonnie Garramone, F 1, 2005.
397. U.S. Military Records, *World War I Draft Registration Cards, 1917–1918*, Denver City, CO, Michael (Michele is Michael in Italian) Calabrese, Je 5, 1917, Ancestry.com, on-line database.
398. Mike Calabrese was not related to Joe Calabrese or Margaret (Calabrese) Taglialavore.

399. Fran (Coloroso) Daly, e-mail to the author, Ja 15, 2007 with attached history of Mariano Michele Calabrese; Michael M. Calabrese CIAPA Archive File.
400. USBC, *1910 Federal Census*, Precinct 3, Denver, Colorado.
401. Michael M. Calabrese CIAPA Archive File.
402. *Mount Carmel History*, 1975, 56-57.
403. Saint Michael's Society CIAPA Archive File.
404. Joe Carpinello, CIAPA Archive interview by Bonnie Garramone, Ap, 2004.
405. USBC, *1910 Federal Census*, Denver, Colorado.
406. Bonnie Garramone, e-mail to the author, Ag 27, 2007. Joe Carpinello CIAPA Archive File.
407. Joe Carpinello, CIAPA Archive OH with Bonnie Garramone, Ap, 2004.
408. Joe Carpinello CIAPA Archive File.
409. Keith Chamberlain, "Europe to the Northside: The Birth of North Denver's Little Italy," *North Denver Tribune* (Denver, CO), Jl 7, 2005, 19.
410. Marilyn (Ciacco) Actor CIAPA Archive File.
411. USBC, *1920 Federal Census*, Denver, Colorado.
412. United States of America, *Declaration of Intent*, Ja 21, 1952.
413. Marilyn (Ciacco) Actor CIAPA Archive File.
414. Fran (Coloroso) Daly, letter to the author, O 31, 2005 with Dominic Anthony Coloroso biographical sketch by Fran Daly; Fran (Coloroso) Daly CIAPA Archive file.
415. Paul A. Distefano CIAPA Archive File.
416. Paul Distefano, CIAPA Archive interview by Bonnie Garramone, Ap, 2004.
417. Kate Ferretti, OH with Nancy Whistler, Ag 5, 1975, 1, SHL, CHS, Denver, CO.
418. Frances Melrose, "Denver milliner created top fashions," *RMN*, My 1, 1977, 8.
419. Ferretti, OH, 8.
420. Eva Hodges, "Milliner Kate Ferretti Tries Boutique," *DP*, Mr 24, 1970, Section E.
421. Melrose, 8.
422. Gretchen (no last name noted), "Milliner Ferretti Marks Her Fiftieth Year," *DP*, 1954. Kate Ferretti CIAPA Archive File.
423. Melrose, 71.
424. Alice (Gaccetta) Nichol CIAPA Archive File, "Project documentation form page 8"; Con and Laura Molinaro CIAPA Archive interview by Robin O'Dorisio, My 30, 2005, transcript p 1.
425. Steve and Robin O'Dorisio e-mail to the author, O 25, 2006. Robin O'Dorisio CIAPA Archive File. This file also includes family trees for the Gaccetta, Molinaro, and LoSasso families. The LoSasso family tree notes that Rose LoSasso was the daughter of Gaetano LoSasso. Gaetano was the brother of Genero, Gerardo, and Angelo Losasso and the half brother of Michael and Gaetano Losasso. In historical documents related to these brothers and their descendants, the name Losasso is sometimes spelled LoSasso, Lassaso, or LaSasso. The variation in spelling found in the documents is also found in families with some members using Losasso while others used LoSasso, Lassaso, or LaSasso.
426. Ibid.
427. Tillie Fong, "Angelo Gaccetta, Denargo Market Founder," *RMN*, Jl 23, 1992, 143.
428. Con and Laura Molinaro CIAPA Archive interview by Robin O'Dorisio, My 30, 2005, transcript p 28.
429. Ibid.
430. Con and Laura Molinaro CIAPA Archive File.
431. Rocco and Shirley (Losasso) Gioso, CIAPA Archive OH with Alisa Zahller, F 9, 2004.
432. Rocco and Shirley (Losasso) Gioso CIAPA Archive File.
433. Ibid.
434. Lisa Benoit, "'97 Italian American honoree a model of community service," *DCR*, O 2, 1996, 13.
435. Edward "Eddie" and Theresa (Allegretto) Iannacito CIAPA Archive File.
436. Gary Massaro, "Veteran 'trying to forget' Pearl Harbor," *RMN*, D 7, 2004.
437. Edward "Eddie" and Theresa (Allegretto) Iannacito, CIAPA Archive OH with Frank Palmeri, Ja 29, 2005.
438. Louise Maria Losasso, letter to Kristen, Mr 10, 1991. John Losasso CIAPA Archive File.
439. John Losasso CIAPA Archive File.

440. Stuart Steers, "John Losasso's Italian roots go deep into Denver's history," *Westword* (Denver, CO), O 10, 2002, 30.
441. Allan Temko, "An Empire's Market Place," *Rocky Mountain News Empire Magazine* (Denver, CO), Ag 15, 1948, 2.
442. Cindy Parmenter, "Early Morning at the Market," *DP*, Je 22, 1969, seventeen comments on the floods at the City Market. Quotation from Temko, 2.
443. "Welby Growers Incorporate Market Group," *RMN*, D 15, 1939.
444. *The Denver Food Terminal Market: Denargo*, a booklet promoting the new Denargo market, published by the Union Pacific Railroad, c. 1939.
445. "Address by J. L. Haugh, Vice President, Union Pacific Railroad Company, At Banquet Given by The Grower's Public Market Association to the Retail Grocers, Fruit and Produce Industry," Ap 11, 1939, 4.
446. Keith Chamberlain, "Denargo Market/Farmers built Denargo Market with no financing from the city," *North Denver Tribune* (Denver, CO), O 2, 2003, 22.
447. *The Denver Food Terminal Market: Denargo*, a booklet promoting the new Denargo market, published by the Union Pacific Railroad, c. 1939.
448. Daniel Shosky, "The Rise and Demise of the Denargo Market," *Andiamo!* (Denver, CO), My/Je 2005, 21.
449. Beverly (DeFrange) Christine CIAPA Archive File. Giuseppi (spelling according to Malpiede relatives) and Gerarda Malpiede were Beverly (DeFrange) Christine's great-grandparents.
450. "John Malpiede began display on $200 budget: Founder of Denver Christmas lighting dies" obituary, NC, see CHS, Mary Malpiede CIAPA Archive File for copy.
451. "Famous Christmas Lights Design of John Malpiede," *The Mount Carmel Eagle* (Denver, CO), Vol. 2, No. 2, D 15, 1955.
452. Frances Melrose, "Denver Christmas extravaganza was conceived by electrical wizard," *Rocky Mountain News Sunday Magazine* (Denver, CO), NC. John Malpiede CIAPA Archive File.
453. "Millennium Celebration: Holiday Lighting History," e-article, http://www.denvergov.org/Party/template31683.asp?cview=2, N 30, 2004.
454. Doris Kennedy, "Boy inspired City and County Building Lights," *Denver Post Online* (Denver, CO), Mr 22, 1998.
455. Mario Mapelli Jr. and Maria (Mapelli) Johnson, CIAPA Archive OH with Alisa Zahller, N 26, 2004. During this oral history, Mario and Maria indicate that there were thirteen children born to their Mapelli grandparents, including Joseph, Guido, George, Herman, Rudolph, Assunta, and Mario who came to America, and five siblings that stayed in Italy. There is no information given by Mario and Maria about the thirteenth child and the author was unable to find the name or what happened to the thirteenth child mentioned. It is possible that the child died in infancy.
456. Ibid.
457. "Mapelli Brothers go back a long way," *Restaurant News of the Rockies* (Denver, CO), S 1991, 7.
458. *Attività*, 222.
459. Ibid.
460. "Joseph Mapelli Dies After Brief Illness in Home," *News* (Denver, CO), My 24, 1935.
461. Mario Mapelli and Maria (Mapelli) Johnson, CIAPA Archive OH with Alisa Zahller, N 26, 2004.
462. Tecla (Guadagni) Smith CIAPA Archive File.
463. Rudy Mapelli and Pat Lauterbach CIAPA Archive Files.
464. Frank Palmeri, "The Palmeri Family From Calabria and Abruzzi to Denver," S, 2006, Frank Palmeri CIAPA Archive File.
465. Frank and Rosemary (LaBriola) Palmeri, CIAPA Archive OH with Janet E. Worrall, Ap 7, 1995.
466. Frank and Rosemary Palmeri CIAPA Archive File.
467. Frank Palmeri CIAPA Archive File, e-mail to the author, Ja 25, 2007.
468. "The man behind the microphone," *DCR*, O 7, 1987, 32.
469. Nick Pertito, *"I Just Happened to Be There..." Making Music with the Stars* (USA: Xlibris Corporation, 2004) 19-22.
470. Ibid., 17, 58 and 72
471. Nick Perito CIAPA Archive File.

472. Angelo and Frances (Schiola) Pastore CIAPA Archive File.
473. Frances and Angelo Pastore, CIAPA Archive OH with Alisa Zahller, M 2, 2005.
474. Ibid.
475. USBC, *1930 Federal Census*, Denver, Colorado. Sabatino is listed as Sam and Serafina as Mary.
476. Fred Sabell CIAPA Archive File.
477. Fred Sabell, CIAPA Archive OH with Alisa Zahller, Ja 11, 2005.
478. Ibid.
479. Ahnna Rose (Spano) Klug, "A Family History: Spano-Calabrese" (Family History, 2005). Ahnna Rose (Spano) Klug CIAPA Archive File, contains Samuel "Sam" Joseph Spano family history.
480. Lawrence Lotito, "Arvada Pascal Celery," UP, Lawrence Lotito CIAPA Archive File.
481. Lawrence Lotito, "Growing Pascal Celery in Arvada," *Historically Jeffco* (Jefferson County, CO), Vol. 11, Issue 19, 1998, 20.
482. Ahnna Rose (Spano) Klug CIAPA Archive File.
483. John Vecchiarelli CIAPA Archive File.
484. John Vecchiarelli, CIAPA Archive OH with Alisa Zahller, Ag 26, 2004.
485. Freddie Steinmark, *I Play to Win* (Boston, MA: Little, Brown and Company, 1971), 155-160.
486. Olga (Zarlengo) O'Dorisio CIAPA Archive File.
487. USBC, *1930 Federal Census*, Pueblo, Colorado.
488. Virginia Culver, "Spirited Olga O'Dorisio cared for everyone," *DP*, Je 18, 2004, 7C.
489. Steven J. O'Dorisio, letter to Nancy McLeod Carter, n.d. Olga (Zarlengo) O'Dorisio CIAPA Archive File.
490. Al Nakkula, "Zarlengos Leave Rich Heritage," *RMN*, Ag 24, 1969. This article notes that Giochino (spelled Giaocchino in the article) or Jack was also known as George. According to the Zarlengo family, (See Dante "Pinn" Zarlengo CIAPA Archive File) Giochino was "Jack."
491. Ibid.
492. USBC, *1930 Federal Census*, Denver, Colorado.
493. Vince Zarlengo CIAPA Archive File.

Chapter Seven
494. Anthony "Tony" Brunetti, CIAPA Archive OH with Bonnie Garramone, Ja 10, 2007.
495. "Mother of Ten Dies Here. Mrs. R. P. La Guardia, Long-time Resident of Denver, is Dead." *DP*, Mr 15, 1937.
496. James Hansen, "Tony Isn't Bitter About Being Shot," *RMN*, Je 9, 1961.
497. Luke Frost, "Innocent Bystander," *Front Page Detective*, Vol. 25, No. 8 (Dunellen, NJ: Dell Publishing Company, D, 1961): 21-25, 73-77.
498. Anthony "Tony" Brunetti, CIAPA Archive OH with Bonnie Garramone, Ja 10, 2007.
499. "Origins of Morra," http://www.usuarios.com/ib306535/morra/teruel/origen_eng.html, 1/25/06. Morra CIAPA Archive File.
500. George Lane, "Morra players join for love of the game," *DP*, n.d., Morra CIAPA Archive File.
501. "An American and a Democrat," *DCR*, O 5, 1988, 12.
502. Ibid.
503. "Ernest C. and Louise Capillupo," *Centennial Year, Weekly Bulletin*, Our Lady of Mount Carmel Church, Je 12, 1994. Ernie Capillupo CIAPA Archive File.
504. Ibid.
505. "An American and a Democrat," *DCR*, O 5, 1988, 18.
506. "Restaurant owner Capillupo dies," *DP*, Ap 26, 1994.
507. Carol Kreck, "Super Sausage Takes Time…but It's Worth It," *DP*, Ag 6, 1980, 12AA.
508. Tillie Fong, "Denver's Italian-Americans honor popular Rev. Carbone," *RMN*, O 13, 1987.
509. USBC, *1920 Federal Census*, Denver, Colorado.
510. "Meet Mrs. Carbone," *Mount Carmel Messenger*, S, 1967, 3.
511. "Father Carbone, his Italian roots run deep in the soul," *DCR*, O 7, 1987, 13.
512. "'I've come very far in life,' says pastor," *DCR*, O 3, 1984, 18.
513. "Mount Carmel Church sees ethnic changes," *DCR*, O 8, 1986.
514. Fong, "Denver's Italian-Americans…"
515. Father Joseph Carbone CIAPA Archive File.

516. Mother Frances Xavier Cabrini CIAPA Archive File.
517. "Italian School of Mount Carmel is Open," *Denver Times Monday Evening* (Denver, CO), N 17, 1902.
518. Mother Cabrini Shrine, *A Lasting Treasure* (Golden, CO: Mother Cabrini Shrine, n.d.), 19.
519. Ibid., 6.
520. Ibid., 7.
521. Margaret Malsm, "Former residents recall life at the Queen of Heaven Orphanage," *North Denver Tribune* (Denver, CO), Ap 6, 2005, 2.
522. *Mount Carmel History*, 1975, 42-44.
523. Alice Dempsey, "St. Cabrini: An American saint in our own time," *Bear Creek Sentinel* (Denver, CO), My 6, 2002, 16; Mother Ignatius Miceli, M.S.C., "Many miraculous things," *DCR*, O 3, 1990, 24.
524. *Mutual Benefit Society of St. Frances Xavier Cabrini Booklet*, (Denver, CO: Allied Printing, 1923), CHS Material Culture Collection.
525. USBC, *1910 Federal Census*, Denver, Colorado.
526. Joe Jr. and Rose Ciancio, CIAPA Archive OH with Alisa Zahller, Ap 14, 2005; U.S. Customs Service, *New York Passenger List 1900*.
527. Cindy Parmenter, "Politics passion of Colo. Delegate," *DP*, Ag 2, 1984, 8F.
528. Don Ciancio CIAPA Archive File.
529. "From Royalty To Underdogs, His Giving Has No Bounds, *DCR*, O 6, 1982, 33.
530. Sally Wagner, "Mr. and Mrs. Adams County," *Dispatch Sentinel*, (Denver, CO), Ja 8, 1976, 11.
531. Ibid.
532. Don Ciancio and guest Betty Reale Combs, CIAPA Archive OH with Bonnie Garramone, Mr 3, 2006.
533. Jesse Tinsley, "Dem Leader in Adams sees influence waning," *RMN*, Ap 12, 1987, 10.
534. Leroy Williams Jr., "Dem leader Frank Ciancio dies at 85," *RMN*, My 3, 1988, 10.
535. Wagner, 12.
536. Joe Jr. and Rose Ciancio, CIAPA Archive OH with Alisa Zahller, Ap 14, 2005.
537. Nello Cassi, "Joe Ciancio Jr. the Quiet, Athletic Type," *DP*, NC, Joe Ciancio CIAPA Archive File.
538. Frances Melrose, "Joe Ciancio thrives on parks management, *RMN*, Je 5, 1977, 8, 42.
539. Don Cardenas, "Chicano viewpoint: Tensions still exist in La Raza Park," *RMN*, Ag 6, 1972, 4.
540. Ibid.; "Chicanos fight as Ciancio tries to expel Bones," *El Gallo*, Vol. 4, No. 3, Ap, 1972, 1.
541. Joe Ciancio Jr. CIAPA Archive File.
542. Lillian Covillo CIAPA Archive File.
543. Lillian Covillo, CIAPA Archive OH with Tonia Williams and Joann Zamboni, Mr 22, 2005.
544. "The Grand Dames of Colorado Ballet," *Colorado Ballet, 40th Anniversary Season*, program, 2000-2001 season.
545. Beverly (DeFrange) Christine, e-mail to the author, Ja 14, 2007, Beverly (DeFrange) Christine CIAPA Archive File.
546. USBC, *1920 Federal Census*, Krebs, Pittsburg, Oklahoma.
547. Beverly (DeFrange) Christine, e-mail to the author, Ja 14, 2007, Beverly (DeFrange) Christine, CIAPA Archive File.
548. Ibid.
549. Ibid.
550. Angelo di Benedetto, OH with Liston E. Leyendecker, Je 16, 1976, CHS, SHL, Denver, CO.
551. Olga Curtis, "Angelo: Portrait of a fighting artist," *DP*, Ap 16, 1972.
552. Ibid.
553. Marjorie Barrett, "Depicting justice a 'labor of love' for artist, *RMN*, Ja 16, 1992, 78.
554. Natalie Soto, "Artist Angelo di Benedetto dies," *RMN*, Ap 27, 1992, 144.
555. Marcia Ward, "Into the Light," *Revue*, UP, Angelo di Benedetto CIAPA Archive File.
556. Curtis.
557. Eugene "Geno" DiManna CIAPA Archive File.
558. "Gene DiManna Signs With Cubs' Visalia Team," UP, Eugene "Geno" DiManna CIAPA Archive File.

559. Gloria DiManna telephone interview with Derek Holmgren, Ag 2006, Eugene "Geno" DiManna CIAPA Archive File.
560. Cecil Jones and Jeff Rosen, "Controversy swirls around DiManna, *RMN*, Jl 16, 1972, 5.
561. Ibid.
562. Suzanne Weiss, "DiManna survives recall," *RMN*, F 19, 1975.
563. "Carpio wins, gets chance to turn talk into action," *RMN*, Je 18, 1975, 6 and 17.
564. USBC, *1930 Federal Census*, Denver, CO; Genevieve Fiore, CIAPA Archive OH with Janet Worrall, Ap 29, 1995.
565. Genevieve N. D'Amato Fiore, interview with Sandy Vinnik and Fran Walloch, My 2000, p 1, Genevieve and John Fiore CIAPA Archive File.
566. John Fiore with wife, Genevieve Fiore present, CIAPA Archive OH with Janet Worrall, Jl 12, 1995, p 2.
567. John Fiore with wife, Genevieve Fiore present, CIAPA Archive OH with Janet Worrall, Jl 12, 1995, p 1.
568. Colleen Smith Mason, "A true bella donna Genevieve Fiore," *DCR*, O 3, 1990, 15-17.
569. Jeanne Varnell, *Women of Consequence: The Colorado Women's Hall of Fame* (Boulder, CO: Johnson Books, 1999), 159-1964.
570. Ibid.
571. Genevieve N. D'Amato Fiore, Genevieve and John Fiore CIAPA Archive OH with Sandy Vinnik and Fran Walloch, My 2000, p 7.
572. Gary Massaro, "A life devoted to peace and understanding," *RMN*, Mr 19, 2002.
573. "John Rocco Fiore" obituary dated 2000, UP, Genevieve and John Fiore CIAPA Archive File.
574. Laura Kilborn, "Devotion to peace changed lives," *DP*, Mr 18, 2002.
575. Bonnie and Lou Garramone CIAPA Archive File.
576. Ange Volpe Family History, Angelina "Ange" (Garramone) Volpe CIAPA Archive.
577. House of Luigi CIAPA Archive File.
578. "Everybody's idea of perfect grandmother," *DCR*, O 7, 1987, 30.
579. House of Luigi CIAPA Archive File.
580. "John M. Garramone" obituary, *RMN*, D 18, 1972, 115; "Catherine Garramone" obituary *DP*, N 1, 1994, 5B.
581. Angelina (Garramone) Volpe CIAPA Archive File.
582. Angelina "Ange" (Garramone) Volpe, CIAPA Archive OH with Alisa Zahller and guest Bonnie Garramone, Mr 23, 2004.
583. "Lifetime Principles," Ange Volpe, Ja 1, 1995, *Grand View AARP 1987*, Angelina (Garramone) Volpe CIAPA Archive.
584. "35 Years at West High: Lou Garramone Finally Retires," *Denver Herald-Dispatch* (Denver, CO), Je 22, 1989.
585. Bonnie and Lou Garramone CIAPA Archive File.
586. Bonnie Garramone, e-mail to the author, F 26, 2007, Bonnie and Lou Garramone CIAPA Archive File.
587. "Woman Runs Own Beauty Salon At 24—Thanks to Emily Griffith," *RMN*, D 5, 1949, 11.
588. Nancy (Garramone) Walrath CIAPA Archive OH with Bonnie Garramone, Ag 2, 2004.
589. Nancy (Garramone) Walrath CIAPA Archive File.
590. Joe and Frances (Bruno) Iacino with Dutchess and Kirk Scheitler present, CIAPA Archive OH with Alisa Zahller, O 21, 2003.
591. Joe and Frances (Bruno) Iacino CIAPA Archive File.
592. Seattle Fish Company, "Company History," F 12, 2007, http://www.seattlefish.com/index.php5?pageName=aboutUs, Seattle Fish Company CIAPA Archive.
593. Derek Figueroa, "Denver's Seattle Fish Company Takes Advantage of Astra Distribution Solutions," F 12, 2007, http://www.astrainfo.com/news/SEATTLE.html, Seattle Fish Company CIAPA Archive.
594. Joe and Frances (Bruno) Iacino CIAPA Archive File.
595. "Bottling company head loves the Orange Crush," *DCR*, O 8, 1986, 16.
596. "Take Advantage of the National Exposure, Set Up Your Superbowl Promotion Today!" UP, Joe and Frances (Bruno) Iacino CIAPA Archive File.

Notes

597. Wellington E. Webb, Mayor to, Sports Hall of Fame (concerning nomination of Joe Iacino for membership into the Colorado Sports Hall of Fame), O 1, 1999, Joe and Frances (Bruno) Iacino CIAPA Archive File.

598. Ralph F. Mancinelli, "Mancinelli Family History" (Family genealogy, n.d.), Ralph and Rosemary Mancinelli CIAPA Archive File.

599. Helen (Mancinelli) Eichler, CIAPA Archive OH with Ralph F. Mancinelli, Mr 19, 2007.

600. Michael "Smokey" A. Marchese, CIAPA Archive OH with Ralph F. Mancinelli, O 22, 2004.

601. Ralph F. Mancinelli, "Mancinelli Family History" (Family genealogy, n.d.), Ralph F. and Rosemary (Nuoci) Mancinelli CIAPA Archive File.

602. Ibid.

603. Ralph F. Mancinelli, "Autobiography by Ralph F. Mancinelli, Jr." (Autobiography for CIAPA Archive, Ag 2006), Ralph F. and Rosemary (Nuoci) Mancinelli CIAPA Archive File.

604. Ibid.

605. Ralph F. and Rosemary (Nuoci) Mancinelli CIAPA Archive File.

606. Geraldine Pergola, "Family History," *Bella Vita, Favorite Family Recipes* (Cookbook published for the Pergola Family Reunion 2004), Geraldine "Gerry" Pergola CIAPA Archive File.

607. USBC, *1920 Federal Census*, Denver, Colorado.

608. U.S. Military Records, *World War I Draft Registration Card, 1917–1918*, Denver, Colorado. Mike Leprino spells his name on the card Michele Leprini and signs it Michele Leprino. He lists his nearest relative Concetta Labriola (his sister).

609. USBC, *1930 Federal Census*, Denver, Colorado.

610. Angelina Testa, CIAPA Archive OH with Janet E. Worrall, N 21, 1998.

611. Jeffrey Leib, "Denver's Big Cheese," *DP Magazine*, Ap 16, 1995, 10-13.

612. Ibid.

613. Margaret Malsam, "Leprino's tops the success stories of Denver's 'Little Italy'," *North Denver Tribune*, Je 16-Jl 5, 2005 ed, 8.

614. Geraldine "Gerry" Pergola CIAPA Archive File.

615. Carol Kreck, "Frangi's: 'Special Treat' to Career," *DP*, O 3, 1979, 22AA.

616. "Mom and daughter create Italian food," *DCR*, O 7, 1987, 29.

617. "Quality carves niche for Frangi's foods," *DP*, Mr 11, 1997, 5C.

618. Ange Testa, "Sociological Autobiography of Ange Testa," UP, Ange and Frank Testa CIAPA Archive File.

619. New York Passenger List, Ship Manifest, *Trojan Prince*, 1899, Mike Pergola CIAPA Archive File.

620. Janet E. Worrall, "Labor, Gender, and Generational Change in a Western City," *The Western Historical Quarterly* 4 (Winter 2001), 437.

621. Mike and Geraldine Pergola, CIAPA Archive OH with Janet E. Worrall.

622. Ibid.

623. Geraldine "Gerry" Pergola CIAPA Archive File.

624. Geraldine Pergola, "Coming To America," *Bella Vita, Favorite Family Recipes* (Cookbook published for the Pergola Family Reunion 2004), Geraldine "Gerry" Pergola CIAPA Archive File.

625. Ibid.

626. Mike and Geraldine Pergola, CIAPA Archive OH with Janet E. Worrall.

627. Ibid.

628. Geraldine "Gerry" Pergola CIAPA Archive File.

629. Phyllis (Lombardi) Greb CIAPA Archive File; Phyllis (Lombardi) Greb CIAPA OH with Alisa Zahller, N 12, 2003.

630. USBC, *1930 Federal Census*, Denver, Colorado.

631. Phyllis (Lombardi) Greb, "The M. Lombardi Grocery & Market" (History for CIAPA, Ag 21, 2006), Phyllis (Lombardi) Greb CIAPA Archive File.

632. "Felice Pomponio, 81, Politician's Dad, Dies," *Post*, Mr 1, 1953.

633. "Mrs. Pomponio Mother of Denver Politian Dies," UP, Al and Mary Ann Donelson CIAPA Archive File.

634. "Denver Couple, Wed 57 Years, to Celebrate," *RMN*, Ja 22, 1949, 30.

635. "Felice Pomponio, 81…"

636. Al Donelson, e-mail to Derek Holmgren, Ag 9, 2006, Al and Mary Ann Donelson CIAPA Archive File.
637. Frank Jefferies, "Councilman May be Named," *DP*, NC, Al and Mary Ann Donelson CIAPA Archive.
638. Ken Pearce, "Pomponio Showed No Desire To Run for Political Office," *DP*, Ja 9, 1973, 3.
639. Ibid.
640. "Mike Pomponio Dead," *DP*, Ja 8, 1973, 2.
641. "Mike Pomponio dies at age 72," *RMN*, Ja 8, 1973, 5.
642. USBC, *1920 Federal Census*, Denver, Colorado.
643. Marilyn (Natale) Vecchiarelli CIAPA Archive File.
644. "He's one of the Lord's noblemen," *DCR*, O 5, 1988, 9.
645. Ibid.
646. Virginia Culver, "Druggist dispensed goodwill, good tips," *DP*, Ja 4, 2006.
647. "Denver druggist receives '88 Columbus Day award," UP, Marilyn (Natale) Vecchiarelli CIAPA Archive File.
648. "'Immigrants Suffered Blood, Sweat, Tears' Italian Americans Love Both Countries," *DCR*, O 5, 1988, 14.
649. Caterina (Noya) Scordo DePalma and Maria (Scordo) Allen CIAPA Archive Files.
650. Maria (Scordo) Allen CIAPA Archive File.
651. "Caterina Scordo Appointed Honorary Italy Vice-Consul," *DP*, Jl 2, 1978, 53.
652. "The honorary consul," *DCR*, O 7, 1987, 26.
653. *Denver Post* article, full, NC, Je 23, 1997, Caterina (Noya) Scordo DePalma CIAPA Archive File.
654. Sam Giglio CIAPA Archive File.
655. Mike DePalma CIAPA Archive File.
656. Cindy Parmenter, "Tancredo's fundamentalist views imperil education job," *DP*, S 1, 1985, 6C.
657. Associated Press, "Mother of Colo. Congressman dies," *The Daily Camera* (Boulder, CO), Ja 29, 2006.
658. "An educator and a risk-taker," *DCR*, O 5, 1998, 13 and 19.
659. Derek Holmgen, "Tancredo family history" (Biographical Sketch for CIAPA, 2006), Tancredo CIAPA Archive File.
660. "Rep. Tom Tancredo's Resignation from Colo. Assembly Final," *DP*, O 16, 1981, 7B.
661. A. Ryan Covarrubias, "Tancredo knows the ropes after 8 years in position," *RMN*, Ag 21, 1989.
662. Cindy Parmenter, "Tancredo's fundamentalist views…"
663. Ibid.
664. Tom Tancredo website, http://tancredo.house.gov/about_tom.html, S 3, 2007.

Chapter Eight
665. See Appendix for complete listing of Italian American organizations in Colorado.
666. Joe Aiello CIAPA Archive File.
667. Joe Aiello, CIAPA Archive OH with Bonnie Garramone, D 6, 2006.
668. Ibid.
669. Joe Aiello CIAPA Archive File.
670. Louis "Lou" Alonzi CIAPA Archive File.
671. USBC, *1910 Federal Census*, Chicago Ward 17, Cook, Illinois.
672. USBC, *1920 Federal Census*, Denver, Colorado.
673. Louis Alonzi, CIAPA Archive OH with Clair Villano, O 6, 2004.
674. Louis "Lou" Alonzi CIAPA Archive File.
675. Louis Alonzi, CIAPA Archive OH with Clair Villano.
676. Ibid.
677. Colleen Smith Mason, "Carlo Amato left his mark in Colorado in concrete," *DCR*, O 3, 1990, 22.
678. Carlo Amato CIAPA Archive File; Carlo Amato, CIAPA Archive OH with Frank Palmeri, O 7, 2005.
679. "Amato of Denver," http://www.amato-of-denver.com/, Je 18, 2003.
680. Frank Amato CIAPA Archive File.
681. Colleen Smith Mason, "Carlo Amato left his…"

682. Joseph Aiello, Four Generations, the Amato family of Denver, *Andiamo!* (Denver, CO), Jl/Ag, 2005, 4. This article also notes that Carlo and Rhonda have a daughter named Brianna.
683. Philip and Romana (Svaldi) Antonelli CIAPA Archive File.
684. "Tirolian Club-To the north," *DCR*, O 7, 1987, 24.
685. Tirolian Trentini di Colorado CIAPA Archive File.
686. "Tirolian Italians are unique breed," *DCR*, O 9, 1985, 20.
687. "Italian American organizations promote awareness of tradition," *DCR*, O 2, 1996, 17.
688. Mike Broncucia CIAPA Archive File.
689. Mike Broncucia, CIAPA Archive OH with Bonnie Garramone, Mr 12, 2007.
690. Ibid.
691. Gary Massaro, "Restaurant's land evolves with career," *RMN*, Jl 1, 2005, 26A.
692. Albert "Al" Anthony Carmosino, CIAPA Archive OH with Bonnie Garramone, Jl 21, 2006.
693. Mildred "Millie" (Yacovetta) Carmosino, CIAPA Archive OH with Bonnie Garramone, Je 9, 2006.
694. Al and Millie Carmosino CIAPA Archive File.
695. Dave Nelson, "First Italian Open to boast meatballs, golf balls," *RMN*, Je 3, 1977.
696. Louise (Panzini) Caruso, CIAPA Archive OH with Barb Fenton, Jl 21, 2003.
697. Louise (Panzini) Caruso CIAPA Archive File.
698. Louise Caruso, "Mother Cabrini, Saint of Immigrants," Louise (Panzini) Caruso CIAPA Archive File.
699. Cyns Nelson research notes; Louise (Panzini) Caruso CIAPA Archive File; Louise (Panzini) Caruso, CIAPA Archive OH with Barb Fenton, Jl 21, 2003.
700. Frank Yantorno CIAPA Archive File.
701. Alan Iannacito, e-mail to the author, Ag 31, 2005, Frank Yantorno CIAPA Archive File. E-mail from Alan Iannacito includes summary of his interview with Frank Yantorno.
702. "The Muse of Sculpture," *Ambassador*, No. 56, (Summer 2003), 25-27.
703. Margaret Helen (DiSalvo) Rossi with son Philip J. Rossi, CIAPA OH with Bonnie Garramone and Alisa Zahller, D 29, 2003; Margaret Rossi CIAPA Archive File. Note: Sometimes DiSalvo is spelled DeSalvo in family records and documents.
704. Mary (Gallo) Rotola CIAPA Archive File.
705. Mary (Gallo) Rotola, CIAPA Archive OH with Bonnie Garramone and Alisa Zahller, S 19, 2005.
706. Ibid.
707. Hsiao-Ching Chou, "The Other Saint Italians also celebrate a feast day in March," *DP*, Mr 17, 1999.
708. Mary (Gallo) Rotola, CIAPA Archive OH with Bonnie Garramone and Alisa Zahller, S 19, 2005.
709. Saint Joseph's Table CIAPA Archive File.
710. *Mount Carmel History*, 1975, 57.
711. Mount Carmel Societies CIAPA Archive File.
712. *Mount Carmel History*, 1975, 59.
713. Mount Carmel Men's Club CIAPA Archive File.
714. Michael Anthony Marranzino II, CIAPA Archive OH with Frank Palmeri, Je 17, 2004.
715. Grace Marranzino, "Story of an Immigrant," *Colorado Old Times*, My, 1976, 12.
716. Michael Anthony Marranzino II, CIAPA Archive OH with Frank Palmeri, Je 17, 2004.
717. "City Councilman Marranzino Dies," *NC*, Michael Anthony Marranzino II, CIAPA Archive File.
718. Michael Anthony Marranzino II, CIAPA Archive OH with Frank Palmeri, Je 17, 2004.
719. Ernie P. Marranzino Jr., CIAPA Archive File.
720. "Gallery of Fame MTC," *The Mount Carmel Eagle* (Denver, CO), Vol. 5, No. 1, O 22, 1953.
721. Ernest "Ernie" P. Marranzino, CIAPA Archive OH with Bonnie Garramone, N 27, 2006.
722. Ibid.
723. Pocky Marranzino CIAPA Archive File; Pocky Marranzino, CIAPA Archive OH with Bonnie Garramone, Mr 15, 2007.
724. Joseph Aiello, "Pasquale "Pocky" Marrannzino," *Andiamo!*, Mr/Ap, 2006, 16-17.
725. Alan J. Stewart, "Largest Empire Produce Wholesaler Completing Expansion," *DP*, S 27, 1964, 34.
726. Mike Martelli CIAPA Archive File.
727. Joseph Aiello, "Federal Fruit & Produce," *Andiamo!*, My/Je, 2005, 6.

728. John Domenico CIAPA Archive File; Mike Martelli and John Domenico, CIAPA Archive OH with Bonnie Garramone, F 12, 2007.
729. Brad Addington, "Market hits Rocky Mountain High," *The Packer*, (Lincolnshire, IL), 1997.
730. Fred "Mick" and Rosemary Laurita, CIAPA Archive OH with Bonnie Garramone and Alisa Zahller, Ag 24, 2006.
731. Ibid.
732. Mick and Rosemary Laurita CIAPA Archive File.
733. Pat Hanna, "A slice of Mediterranean food," *RMN*, Jl 2, 1980.
734. Mick and Rosemary Laurita CIAPA Archive File.
735. Gary Massaro, e-mail to the author, Jl 14, 2005, Gary Massaro CIAPA Archive File.
736. Gary Massaro, e-mail to the author, D 15, 2006, Gary Massaro CIAPA Archive File.
737. Gary Massaro, e-mail to the author, Jl 14, 2005, Gary Massaro CIAPA Archive File.
738. USBC, *1910 Federal Census*, Denver, Colorado.
739. "Pioneer spirit…Hard work…Honest dealing…," http://www.onofriopiano.com/Onofrio_Piano_History.htm, N 2, 2004.
740. "100 Years of Making Beautiful Music in Colorado," *DP*, D 31, 1999, 17E.
741. Joe Onofrio, e-mail to the author, Ap 5, 2007, Vivian Onofrio CIAPA Archive File.
742. "Onofrio Music Store Slates Grand Opening," *RMN*, Ap 29, 1956, 38.
743. Vivian Onofrio CIAPA Archive File.
744. USBC, *1910 Federal Census*, Denver, Colorado.
745. Dr. Peter Emily, CIAPA Archive OH with Clair Villano, Mr 13, 2005; Peter Emily CIAPA Archive File.
746. Mike McPhee, "In veterinary dentistry, Pete Emily wears crown," *DP*, UP, Peter Emily CIAPA Archive File.
747. "Participants from Five Countries Experienced the 'Fascination of Implant Dentistry' At Lake Starnberg/Munich Region," UP, Peter Emily CIAPA Archive File.
748. Phil Spano CIAPA Archive File.
749. Colleen Smith Mason, "Saluting Italian Americans, *DCR*, O 7, 1992, 13."
750. Phil Spano and his sister Rose (Spano) LaRusso, CIAPA OH with Bonnie Garramone, Mr 13, 2007.
751. Ibid.
752. Tony Taddonio CIAPA Archive File.
753. USBC, *1930 Federal Census*, Denver, Colorado.
754. U.S. Military Records, *World War I Draft Registration Cards, 1917–1918,* Michele Taddonio, Denver, Colorado.
755. Tony Michael Taddonio, CIAPA Archive OH with Bonnie Garramone, F 1, 2007; Tony Taddonio CIAPA Archive File.
756. "Mile Hi Companies," (Company History and Operations), Tony Taddonio CIAPA Archive File.
757. Ray Valente CIAPA Archive File.
758. USBC, *1920 Federal Census*, Denver, Colorado.
759. Ray Valente, CIAPA Archive OH with Alisa Zahller, Je 19, 2003.
760. "'A man for others'," *DCR*, O 4, 1989, 15.
761. "Valente's," UP, Ray Valente CIAPA Archive File.
762. Clair Villano, "The Potenza Lodge and the Saint Rocco Feast" (Research paper, Ap 2, 1974).
763. "Italian Residents of Denver Organized into Six Societies," *The Denver Times*, N 17, 1901, 24.
764. *Mount Carmel History*, 1975, 56.
765. "Founding," (History of the Potenza Lodge), Società Nativi di Potenza Basilicata CIAPA Archive File.
766. Potenza Lodge CIAPA Archive File.
767. Salvatore "Sal" Villano Jr. CIAPA Archive OH with Frank Palmeri, S 28, 2005.
768. Joseph Aiello, "General Sal Villano," *Andiamo!*, N/D, 2005, 14.
769. Ibid.
770. Salvatore "Sal" Villano Jr. CIAPA Archive OH with Frank Palmeri, S 28, 2005.
771. Joseph Aiello, "General Sal Villano…."
772. Salvatore "Sal" Villano Jr. CIAPA Archive File.

Bibliography

Abbott, Carl, Stephen J. Leonard, and David McComb. *Colorado: A History of the Centennial State*, revised edition. Niwot, CO: University Press of Colorado, 1982.

American Italian Historical Association (AIHA). *AIHA Proceedings: out-of-print volumes scanned onto CD*. Chicago Heights, IL: AIHA, June 2005. CD-ROM.

Anonymous. *Attività Italiane nella Intermountain Region*. Salt Lake City, UT: International Publishing Company, 1930.

Bolognani, Bonifacio. *Il Pane Della Miniera: Speranze, sacrifice e morte di emigrati trentini in terra d'America (Bread From Underground: Hope, suffering and death of Trentino people on American Soil)*. Trento, Italy: Edizioni Bernardo Clesio, 1988.

Brown, Robert L. *Saloons of the American West*. Silverton, CO: Sundance Books, 1978.

Caporale, Rocco, ed. *The Italian Americans through the Generations* (Proceedings of the 11th Annual Conference of the AIHA, St. John's University, NY, 1982). Staten Island, New York: AIHA, 1986.

Colorado Italian American Preservation Association (CIAPA) Archive. Colorado Historical Society. Stephen H. Hart Library and Colorado History Museum, Denver, CO.

Cole, Trafford R. *Italian Genealogical Records: How to Use Italian Civil, Ecclesiastical & Other Records in Family History Research*. Salt Lake City, UT: Ancestry Incorporated, 1995.

Conlin, Joseph. *Bacon, Beans, and Galantines: Foodways on the Western Mining Frontier*. Reno, NV: University of Nevada Press, 1980.

DeRose, Christine A. "Inside Little Italy: Italian Immigrants in Denver." *The Colorado Magazine*, Vol. 54, No. 3 (Summer 1977), 277-293.

DiSipio, Pauline Annette. *Echoes of Elm Street*. Pueblo, CO: Pauline Annette DiSipio, 1996.

———. *The Old Neighborhood: Elm Street—An Italian Heritage*. Pueblo, CO: Pauline Annette DiSipio, 2001.

DiStasi, Lawrence, ed. *Una Storia Segreta: The Secret History of Italian American Evacuation and Internment during World War II*. Berkley, CA: Heyday Books, 2001.

Dodds, Joanne West. *100th Anniversary Celebration: Pueblo, Colorado*. Pueblo, CO: My Friend, The Printer, Inc., in association with The Order Sons of Italy in America, Southern Colorado Lodge No. 2738, 2005.

Dorsett, Lyle W. *The Queen City: A History of Denver*. Boulder, CO: Pruett Publishing Company, 1977.

Ellis, Richard N., and Duane A. Smith. *Colorado: A History in Photographs*, revised edition. Boulder, CO: University Press of Colorado, 2005.

Formichi, Gianluca. *Risorgimento 1799–1861*. Firenze, Italia: Giunti Gruppo Editoriale, in cooperation with the Museo del Risorgimento, Milano, 2003.

Francone, Frank J. *The Plume on Their Cappello*. Lakewood, CO: Frank Francone, 2006.

Gandolfo, Marcello. *Gli Italiani Nel Colorado 1899–1900*. Denver, CO: Dove, 1900.

Ginex, Giovanna. *L'Italia liberale 1870–1900*. Roma, Italia: Editori Riuniti, 1998.

Goodstein, Phil. *Denver Streets*. Denver, CO: New Social Publications, 1994.

Hill, Alice Polk. *Colorado Pioneers in Picture and Story*. Denver, CO: Brock-Haffner Press, 1915.

Juliani, Richard N., ed. *The Family and Community Life of Italian Americans* (Proceedings of the 13th Annual Conference of the AIHA, Chicago, IL, 1980.) Staten Island, NY: AIHA, 1983.

——— , and Philip V. Cannistraro, eds. *Italian Americans: The Search for a Usable Past* (Proceedings of the 19th Annual Conference of the AIHA, Philadelphia, PA, 1986). Staten Island, NY: AIHA, 1989.

——— , and Sandra P. Juliani, eds. *New Explorations in Italian American Studies* (Proceedings of the 25th Annual Conference of the AIHA, Washington, D.C., 1986). Staten Island, NY: AIHA, 1994.

Krase, Jerome, and William Egelman, eds. *The Melting Pot and Beyond: Italian Americans in the year 2000* (Proceedings of the 28th Annual Conference of the AIHA, Providence, Rhode Island, 1986). Staten Island, NY: AIHA, 1987.

Landry, Harral E., ed. *To See the Past More Clearly: The Enrichment of the Italian Heritage, 1890-1990* (Proceedings of the 23rd Annual Conference of the AIHA, New Orleans, LA, 1990). Austin, TX: Nortex Press for the AIHA, 1994.

Leonard, Stephen J. and Thomas J. Noel. *Denver: Mining Camp to Metropolis*. Niwot, CO: University Press of Colorado, 1990.

Levi, Carlo. *Christ Stopped at Eboli: The Story of a Year.* New York: Farrar, Straus and Company, 9th printing, 1976.

Manoguerra, Paul A. *Classic Ground: Mid-Nineteenth-Century American Painting and the Italian Encounter.* Athens, GA: Georgia Museum of Art, University of Georgia. 2004. Published in conjunction with the exhibition "Classic Ground: Mid-Nineteenth-Century American Painting and the Italian Encounter" shown at the Georgia Museum of Art.

Massari, Stefania. *English Guide for the Museo Nazionale Delle Arti e Tradizioni Popolair.* Roma, Italia: Museo Nazionale Delle Arti e Tradizioni Popolair Grafica, 2001.

Morreale, Ben, and Robert Carola. *Italian Americans: The Immigrant Experience.* Hugh Lauter Levin Associates, Inc., Beaux Arts Editions, China: 2000.

Noel, Thomas J. "The Immigrant Saloon in Denver." *The Colorado Magazine* Vol. 54, No. 3 (Summer 1977), 201-219.

Office of Archeology and Historic Preservation. Site Files, Garbarino Family. Colorado Historical Society, Denver, CO.

Our Lady of Mount Carmel: Denver, Colorado. New Jersey: Custombook, Inc. for Our Lady of Mount Carmel Parish, 1975.

Pattem, Silvia. *Boulder: Evolution of a City.* Niwot, CO: University Press of Colorado, 1994.

Perilli, Dr. Giovanni. *Il Colorado e gl'Italiani nel Colorado/Colorado and The Italians in Colorado.* Denver, CO: Giovanni Perilli, 1922.

Rolle, Andrew. *The American Italians: Their History and Culture.* Belmont, CA: Wadsworth Publishing Company, Inc., 1972.

———. *The Italian Americans: Troubled Roots.* Norman, OK: University of Oklahoma Press, 1984. Originally published in New York: The Free Press, 1980.

———. *Westward the Immigrants: Italian Adventurers and Colonists in an Expanding America.* Niwot, CO: University Press of Colorado, 1999. Originally published as *The Immigrant Upraised* by University of Oklahoma Press in 1968.

Scarpaci, Vincenza. *A Portrait of the Italians in America.* New York: Charles Scribner's Sons, 1982.

Smiley, Jerome C., ed. *History of Denver 1901: With Outlines of the Earlier History of the Rocky Mountain Country.* Denver, CO: Old Americana Publishing Company, reprinted 1978.

Spinetti, Gaetone Silvano, ed. *Italy Today*. Roma, Italia: Documentation Center of the Presidency of the Council of Ministers, 1955.

Taylor, David A., and John Alexander Williams, eds. *Old Ties, New Attachments: Italian-American Folklife in the West*. Washington, DC: American Folklife Center, 1992.

The Colorado Genealogical Society, Inc. *Colorado Families: A Territorial Heritage*. Denver, Colorado: The Colorado Genealogical Society, Inc., 1981.

The Italians of New York: Five Centuries of Struggle and Achievement. Edited by Philip V. Cannistraro. New York: The New York Historical Society in association with The John D. Calandra Italian American Institute, 1999. Published in conjunction with the exhibition "The Italians of New York: Five Centuries of Struggle and Achievement" shown at the New York Historical Society.

Triani, Rocco. *Potenza e il suo Dialtetto*. Potenza, Italy: Zarafone & Di Bello, 1990.

Vecoli, Rudolph, ed. *Italian Immigrants in Rural and Small Town America* (Essays from the 14th Annual Conference of the AIHA, St. Paul, Minnesota, 1981). Staten Island, NY: AIHA, 1987.

Watkins, T. H. *Gold and Silver in the West: The Illustrated History of an American Dream*. Palo Alto, CA: American West Publishing Company, 1971.

West, Elliott. *The Saloon on the Rocky Mountain Mining Frontier*. Lincoln, NE: University of Nebraska Press, 1979.

Wiberg, Ruth Eloise. *Rediscovering Northwest Denver: Its History, Its People, Its Landmarks*. 2nd ed. Niwot, Colorado: University Press of Colorado, 1995.

Wilkins, Travis E. (Tiv), comp. *Colorado Railroads: Chronological Development*. Boulder, Co: Pruett Publishing Company, 1974.

Worrall, Janet E. "Labor, Gender, and Generations Change in a Western City." *The Western Historical Quarterly* 4 (Winter 2001), 437-467.

———, Carol Bonomo Albright, and Elvira G. Di Fabio, eds. *Italian Immigrants Go West: The Impact of Locale on Ethnicity* (Proceedings of the 34th Annual Conference AIHA, Las Vegas, Nevada, 2001). Cambridge, MA: AIHA, 2003.

Index

Note to the reader: The index that follows is a general index based on businesses, organizations, general subjects, places, and family names. Individuals sharing the same last name are grouped together by surname for organizational purposes and may or may not be related. For details regarding the relationship of individuals, please see the text reference.

A
A. Carbone & Company, 62, 63–4, 293
A. Fabrizio Saloon, 30
Abbiati, 54, 55, 292
Abruzzi, Italy, 12, 36, 53, 75, 93, 106, 113, 150, 188, 199, 201, 302
Academy Saloon, 179
Acierno, 55–8, 60, 292
Acams County, Colorado, 30, 60, 98, 190, 208, 224, 225, 267, 282, 292
Adams, John, 18
Aducci, 191
Agnone, Italy, 93, 205
agriculture, 10, 17, 54, 78
Aiello, 7, 61–2, 142–3, 153, 262, 285, 292, 297, 309
Albanese, 30
Albi, 61–2, 64–74, 290, 292–3
Albi Brothers Coal Company, 68, 73
Albi Mercantile Company, 65
Albrighton, 7
Aliberti, 77
Alishio, 139
Allegretto, 194
Alpine Inn, 182–3, 188, 281
Amalgamated Clothing Workers of America Union, 245
Amato, 264, 308
Amato of Denver, 264
American Beauty Bakery, 144, 145
American Beauty Macaroni, 63
American Fruit and Produce, 195
American House, 32
American Indians, 16, 112, 215
American Manganese Steel Company, 51, 218
American Protective Association, 87
Amici of the University of Denver, 181
Ammons, Elias, 130
Ancient Order of Foresters, 183, 190
Anti-Saloon League (ASL), 152
Antonelli, 7, 210, 265–6
Antonucci, 226
Appugliese/Appuglise, 94
Apulia, Italy, 12, 53
Aquila, 281–2
Aquino, 168
Archer, 27, 36–40, 234, 291
Archiere, 30
Arcieri, 27, 37, 234
Argentina; Italians living in, 25, 95, 274
Argonaut Hotel, 175
Arris, 23, 212
Arvada, Colorado, 37, 99, 100, 171, 197, 207, 208, 210, 230, 295, 302
Associated Tailor Shop, 270

Assumption Church, 31, 35, 59, 60, 97, 116, 190, 192, 224, 234, 292
Astuno, 60, 61, 292
Auraria, 15, 90

B
Bailey-Underhill Company, 89, 105, 271
Baily Manufacturing Company, 51
Baldi, 187
Bambino's, 147
Barbato, 269
Barbogalata, 85
Bari, Italy, 31, 257–8
Barnes Business School, 106
Barra, 26, 28, 33–4, 46, 74, 316
Bartolomeo, 80
baseball, 40, 73, 94, 150, 177, 187, 188, 192, 202, 232, 240–1, 256
Basilicata, Italy, 12, 53, 83, 244, 285, 288, 309
Battaglia, 122, 209
Begole, George, 77
Belshe, 20
Benallo, 169–70
Benedetto, 204
Bernard's Restaurant, 210
Bersaglieri Society in Denver (Bersaglieri Principe di Napoli), 44, 90
Bersaglieri Society in Silver Plume (Società Bersaglieri di Savoia), 80, 293
Bessemer, 121
Biamonte, 192, 267
Biancullo, 33
Billings, George, 20
Black Hawk, Colorado, 25
Blasi, 172, 203–4
boardinghouse, 30, 75, 97, 155, 265
bocce, 39, 102, 179, 245, 267, 268, 274
Bonacquisti, 129
Bonino, 131–2, 297
Bonvicini, 202–3
bootlegging, 141, 151–3, 160, 171, 173
Bortolini, 61, 65
Bottoms, 56–7, 88, 90, 114, 119, 149, 184, 271
Boulder, Colorado, 20, 21, 22, 68, 95, 134, 154, 183, 290, 300, 305, 307, 311, 312, 313
Bowman Biscuit Company, 58
Brancucci, 249–51
bread ovens, 88, 119, 141, 147, 185, 205, 271
Breckenridge, Colorado, 122
Brichetto/Brichett, 26
Brick Yard, 263
Briola, 229–30
Broadway Theater, 55, 65
Broncucia, 267
Brown, Molly, 189
Brown Palace Hotel, 55, 75, 147

Brownville, Colorado, 77–9
Bruno, 224, 242–3, 305
Brumidi, Constantino, 18
Brunetti, 184, 216–7, 303
Bryant-Webster School, 272
Buccino, 88–90, 294
Buckley Air Field, 231, 287
Buckley Powder Company, 265
Busnardo, 178–9, 300

C
Cabrini. *See* Mother Frances Xavier Cabrini
Calabrese, 7, 12, 180–184, 188, 206, 300, 302
Calabria, Italy, 12, 31, 49, 53, 58, 61, 64, 121, 132, 137, 143–5, 159, 186, 201, 218, 269, 301
California Gulch, Colorado, 23
California Typographical Union, 110
Calomino, 270
Camelleri, 21
Campania, Italy, 12, 48, 53, 121, 181, 230
Campobasso, Italy, 115, 155, 158, 193, 212, 252, 269
Canacari, 51
Canino, 143–7, 165, 218, 223, 295, 297–8
Canino's Casino, 146
Canino's Pizzeria, 146
Canino's Restaurant, 147
Canino's Sausage Company, 144–5
Capaldi, 76
Capelli, 28–30, 43, 48, 291
Capitale, La, 107
Capitol College of Pharmacy, 256
Capoferro, 30–1
Capolungo, 90–1, 95–6, 256
Carabetta, 107, 149–52, 298
Carbone, 7, 58, 61–4, 184, 219–20, 292–4, 303
Carbone's Italian Bakery, 58
Carbone Wines, 63
Carle, 23
Carlino, 157
Carlone, 276
Carmosino, 268
Carpanzano, 153–4
Carpenter, 4, 131, 153–6, 298–9
Carpinello, 4, 184–5, 188, 301
Carpio, 233, 305
Carpita, 135
Caruso, 269–70
Casagranda, 7
Cascade Laundry and Dry Cleaning Company, 70
Casino Theater, 141
Cathedral High School, 232
Catholic Art Services Bureau, 89
Catholic Church, 25, 90, 121

Cavaliere, 65, 137, 157, 235
Cavaliere Officiale, 157
Cavarra, 92–3, 105, 274, 294
Cefalú Bakery, 181
Cefalú, 236
Cella, 32, 46
Central City, Colorado, 23, 46, 68, 110, 116, 120, 231
Central Fruit House, 181
Central Pacific Railroad, 15
Cerrone, 147–8, 298
Cerrone's Market, 147–8, 298
Cesario, 132–5, 297
Cesario Bakery, 133–4
Chatfield Dam, 184
Checkers Night Club, 102, 170
Cheesman Dam, 84–5
Cheeseman Park, 262
Cheeseman Reservoir, 85
Chiariglione, 122
Chicago, Burlington, and Quincy Railroad, 182, 201
Chiolero, 28, 74–5, 162, 293
Christopher Columbus Hall, 43
Ciacco, 186, 301
Ciancio, 146, 175, 224–7, 232, 304
Ciancio Brothers grocery, 224–7
Ciancio's Famous Dinners, 225
Ciddo, 240
Cimino, 135–6, 297
City Market (Denver), 56, 60, 195–7, 204, 225, 250, 254–5, 283
Civil War, 15, 46
Civilian Conservation Corps (CCC), 225
Climax Molybdenum Mine, 68
Club Italo Americano Politico Indipendente, 44
Club La Ronda, 263
Clyde's Pub, 93
coal, 37, 53, 69, 70, 73, 75, 87, 94, 98, 104, 121, 123, 128, 129, 131, 133, 135, 139, 144, 153–4, 157, 163, 201, 205, 212, 218, 224, 246, 250, 252, 271, 293, 298
Coal Creek, Colorado, 279
Colacito, 93–4, 186, 294
Colarosa, 186
colonies; Italian in Colorado, 88
Colorado Air National Guard, 287
Colorado Ballet, 229
Colorado Concert Ballet. *See* Colorado Ballet
Colorado Fuel & Iron Company (CF&I), 62, 121, 123–4, 127, 131, 136, 153, 232
Colorado Historical Society (CHS), 6, 7, 9, 10, 11, 298
Colorado Italian American Preservation Association (CIAPA), 6, 10, 11, 262, 289
Colorado Music Company, 280
Colorado Saddlery Company, 98
Colorado School of Mines, 67, 70, 153
Colorado Springs, Colorado, 134, 136, 183
Colorado State Capitol, 84, 188, 199
Colorado State College of Education. *See* University of Northern Colorado
Colorado State Fair, 127
Colorado State University (CSU), 279, 287
Colorado Teachers College. *See* University of Northern Colorado
Colorado Wine and Liquor Company, 41

Colorado Women's Hall of Fame, 235, 305
Coloroso, 7, 182–3, 186–7, 233, 300, 301
Columbian Elementary, 211, 285
Columbian Federation, 125
Columbus Day, 28, 112, 113, 122, 261, 266, 296
Columbus Park, 175, 215, 226–7, 233, 246, 253
Columbus Park Inn, 217
Cominello, 185–6, 202
Comito, 184
Como, Colorado, 155
Conservation Services, 283
Coors, Adolph, 43
Coors Ceramics, 263
Coors Hall, 184, 286
Coors Porcelain, 194
Coors Tavern, 217
Corbetta, 149–53, 298
Cosenza, Italy, 64, 125, 186, 224
Cosimi, 59, 97
Country Gentleman Market, 39
Covillo, 94, 228–9, 304
Covillo-Parker School of Dance, 228
Creighton University, 270, 282
crime, 141, 152, 161, 162, 173, 300
C. S. Cart Iron Works Company, 281
Cuneo, 32, 46, 107
Cunio, 32, 46, 75
Curcio, 187

D
D'Alfeo, 206
D'Amato, 232
Daily Colorado Tribune, 20
Dalla, 265
Damascio, 75–7, 92, 147, 175, 223, 293
Daniels & Fisher, 272
Dante Alighieri Club Society, 77, 181, 235
Dardano, 278
Daughters of the American Revolution, 22, 149
Dawson Produce, 117
DeAndrea, 57
DeAno, 7, 36, 39, 58, 59, 98, 102, 147, 179, 264, 276, 279
DeBell, 34–41, 59, 207, 244–5, 291
DeCunto, 26, 33–4, 42, 291
DeFrange, 198–9, 229–30, 302, 304
DeFrange Accordion Studio, 230
DeJones Restaurant, 217
Delagua mines, 69, 129
Delmonico, 7
Democratic Party, 120, 154, 180, 187, 193, 218, 225–6, 232–3, 254–5
Denargo Market, 50, 60, 103, 169, 190, 195–7, 209, 225, 277, 278, 283
Denver, Colorado, 8–11, 13, 15, 17, 19, 20–3, 25–6, 28–30, 32–51, 53, 55–66, 68–73, 75–85, 87–95, 97–108, 110–23, 126, 135–7, 141–50, 152–75, 177, 179–90, 192–96, 198–207, 210–13, 215–25, 227–37, 234–244, 248–59, 261–313
Denver & Rio Grande Railroad, 100, 123, 126, 162, 239
Denver & Rio Grande Western Railroad, 279
Denver Art Institute Academy, 89
Denver Bootleg Squad, 150
Denver Broncos, 243, 315

Denver Catholic Register, 89, 235, 257, 285, 289
Denver City and County Building, 199
Denver Civic Center, 180, 198–9
Denver Coal & Timber, 162
Denver Dry Goods Company, 189, 210
Denver Gas & Electric Company (Public Service), 50, 186
Denver General Hospital, 66
Denver Grand Opera Company, 228
Denver, James W., 17
Denver, Laramie & Northwestern Railroad, 59
Denver Mint, 188
Denver Municipal Band, 116
Denver Musicians Union, 230
Denver Pacific Railroad, 17, 48, 56
Denver Pipe and Clay Company, 248
Denver Post, 66, 113, 180, 189, 211, 289, 292–3, 296, 302, 307
Denver Public Bath House, 232
Denver Public Schools, 91, 149, 181
Denver Republican, 126, 292
Denver Times, 69, 72, 107, 221, 291, 294, 298, 303, 309
DePalma, 257–8
Depression, 72, 73, 79, 89, 102, 105, 108, 118, 121, 127, 132, 141, 165, 190, 244, 248–9, 271, 280
DeRose, 94, 95, 146, 206, 294, 310
Diamond A Market, 119, 239–42, 272
DiAnnie, 191, 252, 263
DiAsenz, 284–5
di Benedetto, 230–2
DiBello, 34–5, 37, 39
DiCroce, 187
DiGiacomo, 27, 83, 154–5
Di Iorio, 201
DiLorenzo, 226
DiLuzio/DeLuzio, 35–6, 207
DiManna, 57, 93, 232–3, 304
Disabled American Veterans, 217
DiSalvo, 271
DiSciose, 81–2
discrimination, 71, 73, 78, 87, 91, 112, 141, 142, 147, 148, 151–2, 154, 224, 230
DiSipio, 123–4, 296, 310
DiStefano/Distefano, 26, 36, 182, 184, 187–8, 301
DiTirro, 51
Domenico, 277–8, 308
Douglas County, 84
Drake Junior High, 258
DX Café, 254–5

E
Eafanti, 7
Eddie Santangelo Combo, 230
Edgewater, Colorado, 97
Elitch Gardens, 186, 193–4, 258
Elitch's Summer Theater, 108
Ellis Island, 8, 106, 107, 135, 145, 205, 251
Elyria, Colorado, 224–6
Emily, 281–2
Emily Griffith Opportunity School, 72, 89, 108, 178, 180, 239, 248, 270
Empire, Colorado, 25
Ernie and Paul's Market, 120
Ernie's Supper Club, 218

Index

F

F. Mazza & Company, 43–4, 169
Fabrizio, 212, 279
Fairplay, Colorado, 25
Falbo, 50–1, 217, 292
Fallico, 49–51, 177, 184, 255, 292
Fallico Gas Station, 51
F & M Ranch, 283
Fante, 95–6, 294–5
Feast of the Seven Fishes (Christmas Eve meal), 58, 204
Federal Fruit and Produce, 277–8
Ferrero, 96–7, 178, 295
Ferretti, 188–90, 301
Festival of Italy 1955 (Denver), 177
Feuerstein, Henry, 21
Ficco, 41, 184
Figliolino, 91, 105, 170, 194
Fiore, 169–70, 233–5, 304–5
Fiorella Jewelers, 186
Fiori D'Italia, 264
Firestone, Colorado, 97–8, 157
First Church of the Nazarene (Trinidad), 133, 297
Florence, A. F., 23
Florence, Colorado, 94
Florence, Italy, 18, 106
Ford, Barney, 21
Foresters. *See* Ancient Order of Foresters
Fort Lewis Junior College, 205
Francone, 7, 77–8, 293, 311
Frangi's, 248–9, 306
Frank Leslie's Illustrated Newspaper, 18
Franklin School, 71
Fratellanza Italiana, 47
fraternal lodges, 13
Fraternal Order of Railroad Workers, 183
Frazzini, 44, 145, 157–8, 200, 299
Frederick, Colorado, 157, 212
Frusta, La, 107

G

Gaccetta, 31, 190–2, 301
Gaetano's, 40, 47, 170, 172–3
Gagliardi, 133, 136
Gallo, 272
Garbarino, 13, 18–22, 290, 312
Garcia, 233
Garden Association. *See* Vegetable Producers Cooperative Association
Gargaro, 184
Garibaldi, 162
Garibaldi Society, 112
Garramone, 7, 29, 82–3, 204, 235–9, 278, 290–2, 296, 298, 300–1, 303–5, 309
Gato, 31, 190
Geno's Liquors, 232
Genoa, Italy, 28, 42, 110
Georgetown, Colorado, 15, 20, 23, 25, 75, 78, 97, 278
Gerardi, 7
Giglio, 258
Gina Marie. *See* Frangi's and Leprino Foods
Gioso, 192–3, 301
Globeville, Colorado, 119, 205, 212
Gloria Briola and Her Sweethearts of Rhythm, 230

Gobatti, 125
Gobatti Manufacturing Company, 125
Goldberg Brothers Hardware Company, 106
Golden, Colorado, 19, 20, 212, 258–9, 263, 303
Golden Eagle Department Store, 171, 189
Gonzales, 209
Granata/Granato, 125, 143
Granby, Colorado, 207
Grand Junction, Colorado, 153
Great Migration, 53–4
Greeley, Colorado, 97, 109, 185, 188, 238, 295
Green Valley, 283
Grimaldi, Italy, 64–5, 67, 69, 74, 137, 162, 239, 241
Growers Public Market Association, 196
Grozer, 23
Gubitosi, Father, 221
Guerrieri, 26, 41–2, 291
Guida, 149–50, 160, 162
Guida & Mauro Saloon, 162
Guido, 153

H

Hanel, 177
Harriman, Averill, 225
Hershon and Fiorella Company, 186
Highland House, 28–9
Hinkydink, 179
Hollywood Auto Polish Company, 146
Holy Family Church, 270
Holy Family High School, 192, 205, 210, 258
Holy Trinity Church, 131, 135
Holy Trinity School, 134, 136
Home Dairy Restaurant, 69, 81
Homestead Act (1862), 15–6
Horace Mann Junior High School, 51, 285
House of Luigi, 236–7
Hungarian Flour Mill, 284

I

Iacino, 7, 119, 175, 239–44, 305–6
Iannacito, 146, 153–4, 193, 252, 272, 301
Iantorno, 270
IBM, 134
Ideal Bakery, 181
Il Circolo Italiano, 62, 235, 257
Il Circolo Filodrammatico Italo-Americano, 76–7
Immaculate Conception (Cathedral), 76, 84, 147
Immaculate Heart of Mary Church, 270
Immigration Act (1864), 15
Immigration Act (1924), 148
Inglese/English, 102
International Fuel Corporation, 158
International State Bank, 61
internment; during World War II, 177
Italco Food Products, 278
Italian American Bank, 157
Italian-American Civic League, 109
Italian-American Professional & Businessmen's Club, 175
Italian Colony Catholic Chapel Association, 44
Italian Consul, 65, 137, 293
Italian Consulate, 137, 257
Italian Draft Law (1871), 25, 55, 127, 233

Italian Fair 1889 (Denver), 46
Italian Independent Political Club, 79
Italian Ladies Committee, 46
Italian Mission, 138
Italian Presbyterian Church, 133
Italian Vice Consul, 29, 48, 257, 307
Italian Vice Consul, Honorary, 257–8, 288
Italian Village, 142
Italy America Society, 77
ITAMs Club, 251

J

Jachetta, 120
Jacovetta, 200
Jefferson County, Colorado, 29, 45, 258
Jefferson, Thomas, 18, 23
Jenny's Pizzeria, 285
Jess Hunter Ford, 136
Jewel Tea, 133
Johnson, Edward C., 225
Johnson & Loud Hardware, 106

K

K. Levine Dry Goods, 164, 166
Kansas Pacific Railroad, 17, 48, 56
Kansas Territory, 23
Karsh & Hagan Communications, 277
KDZA, 124
Kendall's Bakery, 133
KLZ, 203
Knights of Columbus, 97, 190, 230, 237
Korean War, 39, 70, 179, 205, 282, 287
Kouba, 277–8
Ku Klux Klan, 71, 73, 108, 141, 148, 152, 275

L

L. Barra and F. Guerrieri Cigar Company, 26, 28, 33
Labriola, 201, 248
LaCivita, 113
LaConte, 113–4, 261, 296
Lafayette Union Hall, 154
Laguardia/LaGuardia, 185, 192, 216
Lakeside Amusement Park, 141
Lamm, Richard, 243
Lammer's Bottling Works, 43
Lansley, 113
La Prima Domenica, 84, 115, 274
Laradon Hall, 180
LaRusso, 191
LaSala, 34
Las Animas County, Colorado, 61, 87, 128, 132, 135, 153
Latuda (Lattuda), 138–9, 297
Laurenti, 145
Laurita, 216, 278, 309
Laurita's Mediterranean Market, 278
Leadville, Colorado, 23, 25–6, 31, 33, 41, 46, 68, 94, 190, 206, 291
Lepore, Father Felice Mariano, 83, 104, 114, 221
Leprino, 245, 247–9, 251, 306
Leprino Foods, 248–9
Lester, 131
Levine, Bonnie, 247
Levine, Gus, 246, 299
Levine, Kadish, 164, 166

Liberty Fuel Company, 139
Libonati, 103, 163
Ligrani, 177
Ligury, Italy, 12
Lincoln, Abraham, 15
Little Casino, 75
Little Italy, Denver, 13, 88–90, 95, 102–3, 115–6, 120, 141, 147–8, 153, 164, 170, 174, 177, 193, 201, 215, 227, 239, 256, 261
Little Sisters of the Poor, 28
Locono, 80
Lombardi, 7, 37, 184, 200, 242, 252–3, 263–4, 306
Lombardi Brothers grocery. *See* M. Lombardi Grocery & Market
Lombardi's Roman Gardens, 217
Lombardy, Italy, 12, 138, 188, 220
Long, 167, 187. *See also* Capolungo
Longo, 184
Loretto Heights College, 257
Losasso (including LoSasso, LaSasso and Lasasso), 28, 47–8, 94, 190–5, 235, 291, 301–2
Losasso Greenhouse. *See* R. L. Losasso & Sons Greenhouse
Lotito, 98–100, 116, 227, 295, 302
Lotito Greenhouses, 99
Louisville, Colorado, 11, 30, 80, 153–4, 212, 252, 271, 288, 298
Lowry Air Force Base, 68, 205
Luchetta, 132, 187, 216
Lucy (Lucey), Dr. Daniel, 144, 165
Ludlow, Colorado, 104, 124, 129–31
Ludlow Massacre, 124, 129, 131, 132

M

M. Lombardi Grocery & Market, 37, 252–3, 247
M. Occhiato Mercantile, 127
Machebeuf, Bishop, 48
Madison, James, 18
magic and healing, 139, 167–8
Maio, 137–8, 297
Malnati, 188–9
Malpiede, 180, 198–9, 229, 234, 302
Mancinelli, 7, 35, 51, 100–3, 115, 183, 244–7, 286, 291, 295, 305–6
Mancini, 103–4, 163
Mangini, 30, 42–4, 291
Mangini's Place, 42–3
Mangone, 184
Manual High School, 74
Mapelli, 107, 144, 199–201, 302
Mapelli Brothers Grocery Company, 200
Mapleton Public Schools, 31, 193
Maracci, 118
Marchese, 244, 247, 306
Mariano, 116
Marino, 55
Marra, 181–2
Marranzino, 77, 175, 184, 232, 261, 273–7, 308–9
Marta, 130–2, 296–7
Marta Bakery, 131
Martelli, 149–51, 277–8, 298
Martino's Terrazzo Company, 179
Masciotra, 55
Massari, 122, 299, 312

Massaro, 279, 295, 301, 309
Mastroianni, 7, 91, 105–6, 158, 194, 295
Mattei, 80–1, 293
Mattivi, 265
Matz, Bishop, 221
Mauro, 7, 150, 159–63, 296, 299
Mautino, 7
Mazza, 43–4, 51, 169, 186, 299
Mazzei, 159
Mazzei, Philip, 18, 290
Mazzotti, 56, 58–60, 191, 292
McDermott, 7
MCI, 134
McNichols, Bill, 218
McNichols, Stephen, 255
Meolfese, 152, 254
Metropole, 65
Metropolitan Restaurant, 81
Mexican International Railroad Company, 61
Mickey's Top Sirloin, 267
Micky Manor Restaurant and Tavern, 187
Midland Railroad Company, 254
Midwest Haulers, 283
midwife, 66, 139
Mile High Frozen Foods, 284
Mile High Fruit & Vegetable, 283–4
Milne Granite Yard, 85
Mining Exchange Building, 75
Missionary Sisters of the Sacred Heart, 221–3
Moauro, 213
Moffat Tunnel, 200, 212, 268, 278
Molinaro, 191–2
Molise, Italy, 12, 53
Mollicone, 268
Monarch Accordion Studio, 230
Monroe, James, 18
Montezuma, Colorado, 178
Montgomery Ward & Company, 89
Montrose, Colorado, 78, 80
Moore, Edward "Eddie," 164, 167, 299
Morgan County, Colorado, 77
Morganti, 92, 106–110, 146, 157, 295
Morganti Studio, 108–110
Morning Light, 138, 297
Morra Society of Denver, 217, 276
Morrato, 81–2, 175, 293–4
Mortellaro, 180–1
Mosciaro, 65
Mosconi, Luigi, 44, 46, 65
Mother Cabrini Lodge, 223, 304
Mother Cabrini Shrine, 223, 304
Mother Frances Xavier Cabrini, 51, 82, 98, 220, 269, 288
Mother's Home Bakery, 181
Mount Carmel Altar and Rosary Society, 84, 270, 273–4, 288
Mount Carmel Church (Denver), 46, 51, 57, 76, 83, 84, 88–90, 93, 99, 101, 104, 113–6, 142, 145, 158, 163, 171, 174, 181–3, 186, 187, 193, 198, 201–2, 206, 215–7, 219–20, 222–3, 236–8, 247, 254, 263–4, 270, 272–4, 276, 285, 287, 289, 292, 294, 296, 299, 301–3, 312
Mount Carmel Church (Pueblo), 122, 124
Mount Carmel Church (Trinidad), 128, 129
Mount Carmel Grade School, 215, 223, 247, 287

Mount Carmel High School (Denver), 172, 215, 223, 247, 274, 276, 287
Mount Carmel Men's Club, 264, 273–4, 276, 288
Mount Carmel School (Denver), 222–3
Mount Carmel Society (Denver), 83–4, 114
Mucillo, 271
Muro, 169–70, 184
music (musicians), 13, 22–3, 32–3, 40–1 82, 95, 115–6, 124–5, 181, 201–3, 221, 230, 262–3, 280, 286, 302, 309
Mussolini, Benito, 142, 177
Mutual Benefit Society of Frances Xavier Cabrini. *See* Mother Cabrini Lodge
Muzzelo, 226
My-O-My Supper Club, 263

N

Naimen, Joe, 277
Naples, Italy, 26, 27, 33, 62, 66, 93, 94, 167, 194, 206, 216
Napoleon, 16
Nardillo, 184
Natale, 72, 167, 256–7, 293, 306
National Catholic Register, 89
Navajo Cleaners and Tailors, 236–7
Navajo Meat Market, 144
Navajo Theater, 153, 163, 246, 260
Nazione, La, 82, 104
Neff Brewery, 43
Neighborhood House, 149
Nevins Candy Company, 207
New Mexico, 43, 124, 136, 138–9, 270, 280
Newspapers, English Language:
  America, 163
  Andiamo!, 262
  Colorado, 104
  Colorado Leader, 104
  Daily Colorado Tribune, 20
  Delta County Independent, 279
  Denver Catholic Register, 89, 235, 257, 285, 289, 298, 300–7, 309
  Denver Post, 66, 113, 180, 189, 211, 289, 292–3, 296, 302, 307
  Denver Republican, 126, 292
  Denver Times, 69, 72, 107, 221, 291, 294, 298, 303, 309
  Frank Leslie's Illustrated Newspaper, 18
  Morning Light, 138
  Rocky Mountain News, 19, 33, 45, 47, 49, 69, 70, 72, 73, 88, 106, 107, 190, 256, 277, 279, 289, 301, 302
  Silver Standard, 79, 80
Newspapers, Italian Language:
  Capitale, La, 107
  Corriere di Trinidad, Il, 137, 138
  Frusta, La, 107
  L'Unione, 122
  Nazione, La, 82, 104, 114
  Reclame, 137
  Risveglio, Il, 104, 163
  Roma, Il, 64, 299, 300
  Stella, La, 110–1
  Trumpet, 108
Nicoletti, 7, 159–63, 299
Nicoletti Bros. saloon, 159–60
Nigro, 154, 274

Index

Noce, 110–12, 295–6, 303
North Denver Alliance, 237
North Denver Civic Association, 237
North Denver Department Store, 246.
    See also K. Levine Dry Goods
North Denver Liquor House, 82
North Denver Mercantile Company, 76, 147
North High School, 51, 62, 153, 171,
    185–6, 188, 193, 201, 203, 211, 255, 263,
    270–1, 285
Northside Community Center, 187, 206,
    210, 226, 237
NotarFrancesco, 82
Notarianni, 81, 103–4, 163–4, 295, 299
Notary, 81–3, 221–2, 249, 294
Nuoci, 246–7, 306

O

O'Dorisio, 7, 190–1, 211, 301, 303
Occhiato, 126–7, 239, 242–3, 296
Odisio, 108
Onofrio, 80–1, 279–81, 295, 309
Onofrio Piano Company, 279–81, 309
opera, 23, 55, 228
Orange Crush, 243
Orchard, Colorado, 77–8, 201, 244
Order of Basilone, 262, 288
Orlando, 209
OSIA. *See* Sons of Italy
Ottanto, 23
Our Lady of Assumption Church. *See*
    Assumption Church
Our Lady of Mount Carmel Church. *See*
    Mount Carmel Church (Denver)
oyster house, 46
oysters, 21, 241

P

P. Albi & Company, 64
P. Mancinelli & Sons Grocery and Market,
    101–2
Pacific Railroad Bill (1862), 15
Pagliano, 143, 144, 210
Pagliarone, Italy, 154, 268
Palermo, 191
Palese, 69, 100
Palladino, 77, 147, 175
Palmeri, 7, 89, 201–2, 292, 294, 297,
    299–302, 309
Palmesano, 198
Panepinto, 122, 125, 127–8, 296
Pantanella, Father, 221
Panzini, 269
Pascal Celery, 38, 45, 60, 153, 207–8, 283
Passanante, 124
Pastore, 113–4, 203–4, 296, 303
Patsy's Inn, 142–3, 217
Pavoni, 84–5, 294
Peace Pole Project, 234
Pearl Harbor, 193–4
peddlers, 53, 56–7, 91, 95, 99, 113, 114, 117,
    119, 126, 132, 149–50, 169–70, 180, 184,
    193–5, 204, 224, 234, 254, 271, 283, 296
Pedotto, 147–8
Pelican Club, 245
Peña, Federico, 218
People's Restaurant and Saloon, 21

Pergola, 7, 248–51, 306
Perito, 202–3, 302
Perri/Perry, 202, 224, 226, 285
Persichette, 247
Persichetti, 208
Perucca, 104
Pesce, 100, 295
Phil Long Ford, 136
Piccolo's, 147
Pic's Corner Bar, 232–3
Piedmont, Italy, 12, 74, 77, 96, 130–1, 178
Pietro, 243
Pigotti, 62
Pikes Peak Gold Rush, 15
Pint, Charles M., 121
Piscitella, 228
Pisto, 245
Pizzichino, 184
Polenta Fest, 266–7
Pollice, 115–6, 296
Pomarico, 83, 273
Pomponio, 120, 152, 253–5, 261, 306–7
Pontarelli, 177
Post Studio, 4, 92–3
Potenza, Italy, 34, 37, 39, 45, 47, 54–6, 58,
    82–3, 88–90, 95, 98–100, 105, 116–8,
    126, 145, 149, 168–70, 184–5, 192–3,
    202, 204, 216, 235, 237–8, 244–5, 247,
    249–51, 253–5, 257, 267, 281, 283–8,
    291–2, 309
Potenza Lodge, 39, 120, 121, 193, 238, 244–5,
    251, 254–5, 285–6
Primavera, 281
Primavera Creamery, 281
Primo Awards, 262, 264
Prohibition, 62–3, 121, 127, 141, 151–2, 160,
    162, 173–4, 225, 271, 298
Protective and Benevolent Society, 125
Public School Cottage, 149
Public Service Company. *See* Denver Gas &
    Electric Company
Pueblo, Colorado, 4, 11, 13, 53, 55, 79, 87,
    121–8, 136, 153, 205, 211, 228, 232, 239,
    242, 279, 288–9, 296–7, 303, 310, 311
Pueblo Ladies Fidelity Lodge, 128
Pullman Company, 154

Q

Queen of Heaven Orphanage, 46, 49, 51,
    222–3, 236, 240, 269

R

R. L. Losasso & Sons Greenhouse, 193
R. Mapelli Music Company, 201
railroads, 10, 15, 17, 25, 48, 53, 54, 121, 147,
    192, 212, 313
Rainbow dancehall, 141
Rankin School, 36, 190
Reale, 224, 304
Regis College, 39, 121, 265, 276, 282, 284
Regis High School, 38, 95, 218, 262, 265, 277
Rende, 174–5, 225
Republican Party, 258–9
Riccardi, 184
Rio Grande Railroad, 184, 206
Risoli, 177, 277
Risveglio, Il, 104, 163

Rockefeller Sr., John D., 124
Rocky Mountain Accordion Society, 116, 230
Rocky Mountain Beverage Company, 242–3
Rocky Mountain Italian Golf Association
    and Bocce Festival, 39, 244, 268
Rocky Mountain News, 19, 33, 45, 47, 49, 69,
    70, 72, 73, 88, 106, 107, 190, 256, 277,
    279, 289, 301, 302
Roma, Il, 64, 299, 300
Rome, Italy, 11, 16, 54, 66, 97, 220, 263, 279
Roosevelt, Franklin D., 112
Roosevelt, Teddy, 85
Rose, 167, 226, 290, 299
Rossi, 201, 271
Rotola, 272, 308
Rough Riders, 206, 210
Ruote (Ruoti/Ruota), 45, 291
Ruoti, 45, 99
Russomano, 184

S

Sabell (Sabelli), 50, 205–6, 302
Sabon, 187
Saccamano, 191
Sacco, 245
Sacred Heart Church, 65, 88, 149, 254
Saint Anne's Society, 237
Saint Anthony Hospital, 66
Saint Anthony's Society (Saint Anthony of
    Padua Society), 93, 157–8
Saint Catherine's Church, 211, 230
Saint Clara's Orphanage, 50
Saint Dominic's Church, 194
Saint Joseph's Day Table, 84, 272
Saint Michael's Chapel, 232
Saint Michael's Society (Saint Michael's
    Lodge), 183–4, 245, 288, 301
Saint Patrick's Church, 114, 162
Saint Patrick's School, 207
Saint Philomena's School, 228
Saint Rocco Chapel, 222
Saint Theresa's Club, 270
Sally Ann Creamery, 60, 116
Salmonase, 40
saloon, 13, 20–3, 26, 28–30, 33, 43, 46–7, 57,
    61–2, 64, 75, 77, 79, 82, 97, 120, 152, 157,
    159, 162, 179, 182, 265, 310, 312, 313
Samsonite Corporation, 89, 220, 251
Sandoval, 233
Sanfilippo, 236–9
San Michele Arcangelo Società (Saint
    Michael's Society), 183–4, 288, 301
San Rocco Chapel (Saint Rocco Chapel),
    76, 222
San Rocco Society, 44, 286
Santamoro, 251
Santangelo, 116–7, 145, 230, 296
Santangelo Produce Company, 117
Santarelli, 184–5
Save-A-Nickel, 39
Sbarbaro, 45–6
Sbarbaro & Company Oyster House, 46
Scavotto, 139, 297
Schiola, 203–4, 303
Schiola's Grocery & Market, 204
Schlitz Brewing Company, 29
Scordo, 257–8, 288

Se Cheverell-Moore Drugstore, 153, 164, 167, 246, 256
Seattle Fish Company, 241–2
Serafini, 42, 241
Sferra, 6
Shane Furnace Company, 146
Sheet Iron and Wire Works Company, 232
Sherman Silver Purchase Act (1893), 79
Shwayder Trunk Manufacturing Company. *See* Samsonite Corporation
Sicily, Italy, 12, 53, 84, 121, 127, 134–5, 139, 180, 206, 236, 262, 272, 279, 282
Sileo, 98
Silt, Colorado, 100
Silver Plume, Colorado, 11, 77–80, 84, 96–7, 117, 178, 212, 293
Silver Standard, 79, 80
Silverton, Colorado, 265
Sister Cities Program, 234, 251, 257
Smaldone, 168–74, 299–300
Snow White Beauty Salon, 239
social organizations, 13
Società Bersaglieri di Savoia. *See* Bersaglieri Society in Silver Plume
Società Cristoforo Columbo, 121, 127
Società di M. S. Vittorio Emanuele III, 127
Società di Madonna del Monte Carmelo, 127
Società Fedeltà Italiana, 121, 127
Società Nativi di Potenza Basilicata. *See* Potenza Lodge
Società Protettiva e Beneficenza di Pueblo, 121, 125
Solomanetti, Reverend, 133
Sons of Italy, 179, 202, 218, 228, 230, 264, 276
Sons of Italy, Grand Lodge of Colorado, 227
Sopris, 128, 135
South America; Italians living in, 15, 18, 25, 271
South Platte Granite Company, 85
Spano, 206–10, 278, 282–3, 302, 309
Spero, 188
Stapleton, Ben, 199, 224, 242
Starlight, 263
State Fruit and Vegetable Company, 195
Stella, La, 110–1
stereotypes; of Italians, 88, 148, 152, 161–2, 328
Sterling, Colorado, 11, 78, 80, 178
Stevenson, Adlai, 225
Stone, 244
Summer Fun Day Camp, 171
summer kitchen, 205
Sunset Billiard Parlor, 146
Sunshine Bakery, 180
Sunshine Laundry and Dry Cleaners, 160–1, 179, 192
Svaldi, 265–6
Swift & Company, 73, 248

T

Tabor, Elizabeth "Baby Doe," 48
Tabor Opera House (Leadville), 23
Tabor Grand Opera, 55
Taddonio, 44, 119, 283–4, 309
Taddonio Brothers, 283–4
Taglialavore, 7, 180–1, 300
Tancredo, 258–9, 307
Tejon Bar & Café, 170
Tejon Drug Company, 256
Tejon Street Café, 170

Testa, 249, 306
The Bug Theater. *See* Navajo Theater
Tico's, 147
Tirolian Trentini di Colorado, 256–7
Tolland, Colorado, 212, 271
Tolve, 142, 149, 167–8, 184, 243
Torino (Torin), Italy, 65–6, 96–7, 130–1, 178
Track Inn, 154
Trento, Italy, 12, 265, 310
Tricarico, 7, 39
Trinidad, Colorado, 11, 13, 21, 53, 61–2, 75, 79, 87, 128–9, 131–9, 142, 192, 288, 292, 296–7
Trinidad State Junior College, 136
Tritch Hardware Company, 106
Trocadero ballroom, 141
Trollo, 48
truck farming, 60, 99, 126, 177, 207–8, 215, 248, 282
Trumpet, 108
Turre, 26, 30, 44, 46–7, 292

U

Union Pacific Railroad, 17, 119, 150, 180, 196, 220, 225
Union Station, 28, 49, 56–7, 72, 94, 118
Unione e Fratellanza Italiana, 44
unions; trade and labor, 62, 104, 110, 127, 130–1, 152, 154, 179, 192, 230, 245
United Mine Workers of America (UMW), 130, 132, 154
United Nations Educational, Scientific, and Cultural Organization (UNESCO), 234
United States, 4, 8–9, 15–6, 18, 23, 45, 53–4, 67, 70, 72, 74, 77, 84, 87–9, 92–3, 97, 117, 122–3, 125–7, 129–30, 135–6, 142–3, 145, 159, 161–2, 165, 174, 177, 179, 188, 191, 194, 197, 199, 200–1, 206, 212, 216, 218–9, 228, 230–1, 236–8, 244, 248–9, 253, 257–9, 262, 264–5, 269, 271, 274, 280, 282–4, 287, 294
University of Colorado, 21–2, 74, 95, 134
University of Denver (Denver University), 41, 71, 108, 119, 136, 165, 171, 181, 203, 206, 210, 218, 228, 265, 268, 277
University of Northern Colorado (UNC), 97, 185, 188, 192, 238, 258
University of Southern Colorado–Pueblo, 279
Ursetta, 143
Usaly Club, 116

V

Valente, 284–5, 309
Vallero, 30, 117–8, 296
Vallero Mercantile, 120–1
Valley Highway (Interstate 25), 177, 248
Vallone, 133–5, 297
Varello, 96
Varone, 239
Vassalo, 282
Vecchiarelli, 93, 112, 174–5, 186–7, 210–1, 256, 300, 302–3, 306
Vegetable Growers Association, 60
Vegetable Producers Cooperative Association, 190
Veltri, 73
Venetian Sewing Club, 240
Venice, Italy, 55, 84, 179

Veraldi, 77, 112, 174–5, 292, 300
Veterans of Foreign Wars (VFW), 193, 217
Veto. *See* Vitullo
Victor-American Fuel Company, 69
Victor Emmanuel III, 65, 137
Vignola, 28, 47–8, 105, 118, 291–2
Villa de Paris, 189
Villani, 118
Villano, 7, 44, 88–9, 105, 118–21, 143, 223, 287, 291, 294, 296–7, 309
Vinnola. *See* Vignola
Visiting Nurses Association, 149
Vittorio Emanuele II, 15
Vitullo (Veto), 49–51, 64, 184, 292
Volpe, 237, 305

W

Walrath, 239, 305
Walsenburg, Colorado, 87, 133–4, 138
Walter's Brewery, 132
Washington, George, 18
Wazee Terminal produce market, 64, 255
Webb, Wellington, 218, 244, 305
Welby, Colorado, 30–1, 35–6, 58–60, 96–7, 116, 174, 190–2, 206–7, 220, 224–5, 228, 233, 247, 252, 282, 291–2, 295, 301
Welby Mercantile Company, 224
Weld County, Colorado, 68
Weldona, Colorado, 78–9
Wellington, Colorado, 155
Western Distributing Company, 200
Western Music and Radio, 201
Western Union Macaroni Factory, 63
Wheat Ridge, Colorado, 58, 99, 120, 193, 197, 201, 207–9, 239, 247
White Wings, 143, 297
Williams, 7
Windsor Turkish Baths, 162
Wolf, 7
Women's Christian Temperance Union (WCTU), 152
Works Progress Administration (WPA), 132, 184, 190, 225
World War I, 8, 129, 144, 159, 161, 190, 201, 218, 234, 250, 266, 294, 300, 306, 309
World War II, 13, 41, 51, 89, 94, 99, 103, 119, 133, 142, 154, 166–7, 172, 177–9, 185–6, 188–9, 193, 195, 201, 203, 208, 218, 226, 231, 234, 237–8, 240, 244, 245, 257, 265, 276–8, 280, 310
Wyman Elementary School, 67
Wyoming, 17, 124, 144, 181, 188, 201, 218, 233, 257, 280, 283

X–Y

Yacovetta, 153, 166, 268
Yantorno, 7, 270

Z

Zamboni, 7
Zang, Adolph, 43
Zarlengo, 49–50, 211–3, 271, 303
Zarlengo Brothers Contracting Company, 212
Ziccardi, Father Felix S., 128
Zimmerman, 164–6, 299
Zucca, 243

About the Author

Alisa Zahller is the associate curator of Decorative and Fine Arts at the Colorado Historical Society. In 2007, she curated the *Italians of Denver* exhibit at the Colorado History Museum. A fifth-generation Italian American in Colorado, she holds a B.A. in art history and photography from the University of Northern Colorado and an M.A. in art history and museum studies from the University of Denver.

Dear Eleanor and Bill,
Memories are a beautiful thing.
I hope you enjoy those within.
Sincerely, Alisa Zah